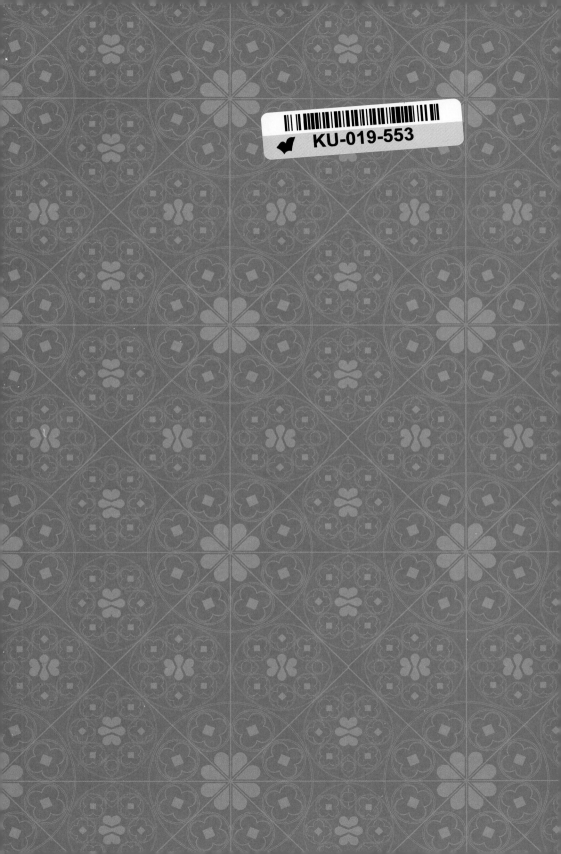

'Brings us into a complex, compelling world, suffused with intrigue, betrayal, love and heartbreak, centred around the fascinating figure of Lettice Knollys. She is well deserving of such a biography.'

History Today

Praise for *Crown of Blood: The Deadly Inheritance of Lady Jane Grey*

'Nicola Tallis … one of our great popular historians … History as it should be written: vivid, colourful, pacy and evocative, but – above all – authentic and based on sound and innovative research.'

Alison Weir

'A wonderful investigation … enlightening and gripping, full of superb research and beautifully written.'

Kate Williams

'A stunning debut.'   'Poignant.'

Spectator   *The New York Times*

'Stunning.'

BBC History Magazine

ABOUT THE AUTHOR

DR. NICOLA TALLIS is a British historian and researcher. Her two previous books, *Crown of Blood: The Deadly Inheritance of Lady Jane Grey* and *Elizabeth's Rival: The Tumultuous Tale of Lettice Knollys, Countess of Leicester*, were published to wide praise. She has previously lectured at the University of Winchester and worked with Historic Royal Palaces and the National Trust.

UNCROWNED QUEEN

The Fateful Life of
MARGARET BEAUFORT
Tudor Matriarch

NICOLA TALLIS

Michael O'Mara Books Limited

First published in Great Britain in 2019 by
Michael O'Mara Books Limited
9 Lion Yard
Tremadoc Road
London SW4 7NQ

A CIP catalogue record for this book is available from the British Library.

Papers used by Michael O'Mara Books Limited are natural, recyclable products
made from wood grown in sustainable forests. The manufacturing processes
conform to the environmental regulations of the country of origin.

ISBN: 978-1-78243-992-9 in hardback print format
ISBN: 978-1-78929-171-1 in trade paperback format
ISBN: 978-1-78929-148-3 in ebook format

2 3 4 5 6 7 8 9 10

Cover design by Estuary English
Typeset by Claire Cater

Printed and bound by CPI Group (UK) Ltd, Croydon, CR0 4YY

www.mombooks.com

In the hope that they would be proud, this book is dedicated to the memory of my dearly loved grandparents, to whom – like Margaret – family meant everything.

Richard and Sylvia Howard

Brinley and Joyce Tallis

CONTENTS

LIST OF ILLUSTRATIONS

Page 1: Calendar page for June from the 'Beaufort / Beauchamp Book of Hours' / Royal 2 A. XVIII, f.30v / British Library, London, UK (© British Library Board. All Rights Reserved / Bridgeman Images).

Page 2 (above left): John of Gaunt, Duke of Lancaster, attributed to Lucas Cornelisz (1495-1552); one of a series of portraits of Constables of Queensborough Castle in Kent, commissioned by Sir Thomas Cheney, Constable of Queensborough 1511-59 (Private Collection / Bridgeman Images).

Page 2 (below left): The East window of All Saints' Church, Landbeach, Cambridgeshire, UK (© Nicola Tallis).

Page 2 (below right): The tomb of John Beaufort, 1st Duke of Somerset and his wife, Margaret, in the minster church of St Cuthburga, Wimborne Minster, Dorset, UK (© Nicola Tallis).

Page 3: Margaret of Anjou, seated with her husband King Henry VI, illustration from the 'Shrewsbury Talbot Book of Romances', c. 1445, French School (15th century) / Royal 15 E. VI, f.2v / British Library, London, UK (© British Library Board. All Rights Reserved / Bridgeman Images).

Page 4 (above): Engraving of Lamphey Palace, Pembrokeshire, from 'Wales Illustrated, in a series of views, &c.' by Henry Gastineau, Jones & Co., London, 1830 (National Library of Wales).

Page 4 (right): Brass rubbing of the tomb of Edmund Tudor, St. David's Cathedral, Pembrokeshire, Wales (The Picture Art Collection / Alamy).

Page 5 (above): Aerial view of Pembroke Castle, Wales (Alexey Fedorenko / Shutterstock).

Page 5 (left): King Edward IV by Unknown English Artist, c. 1540 (National Portrait Gallery, London, UK / Art Collection 3 / Alamy).

Page 6 (above): Raglan Castle, Monmouthshire, Wales (© Nicola Tallis).

Page 6 (left): Elizabeth Wydeville, c. 1513-30, British School (16th century) (Royal Collection Trust © Her Majesty Queen Elizabeth II, 2019 / Bridgeman Images).

Page 7 (left): Richard III, c. 1504-20, British School (16th century) (Royal Collection Trust © Her Majesty Queen Elizabeth II, 2019 / Bridgeman Images).

Page 7 (right): 'The Two Princes Edward and Richard in the Tower, 1483', by Sir John Everett Millais, 1878 (Royal Holloway, University of London / Bridgeman Images).

Page 8 (left): Elizabeth of York, British School (16th century) (Royal Collection Trust © Her Majesty Queen Elizabeth II, 2019 / Bridgeman Images).

Page 8 (right): St Mary The Church of Our Lady, Merevale, Warwickshire, UK, originally part of Merevale Abbey (© Nicola Tallis).

Page 9: Rowland Lockey, *Lady Margaret Beaufort (1443-1509) at Prayer, Countess of Richmond and Derby, Mother of King Henry VII and Foundress of the College, c.* 1598 (by permission of the Master and Fellows of St John's College, Cambridge, UK).

Page 10: Portrait of young Henry Tudor by Unknown Artist (Fondation Calvet, Avignon, France).

Page 11 (left): Portcullis ensign above King's College Chapel, Cambridge, UK (© Nicola Tallis).

Page 11 (below): Arthur, Prince of Wales, *c.* 1499, English School (15th century) (Hever Castle Ltd., Kent, UK / Bridgeman Images).

Page 12 (left): Sketch of Margaret Tudor / Recueil d'Arras / Bibliothèque Municipale d'Arras, France, Ms. 266, (16th century) (Historic Images / Alamy).

Page 12 (right): Detail of Mary Tudor and Charles Brandon, Duke and Duchess of Suffolk, *c.* 1516, attributed to Jan Gossaert (Woburn Abbey, UK / Art Heritage / Alamy).

Page 13 (above): Catherine of Aragon, *c.* 1520, by Unknown Artist (National Portrait Gallery, London, UK (© Stefano Baldini / Bridgeman Images).

Page 13 (right): John Fisher, Bishop of Rochester, *c.* 1532-34, Hans Holbein the Younger (Royal Collection Trust © Her Majesty Queen Elizabeth II, 2019 / Bridgeman Images).

Page 14 (above left): Statue of Margaret Beaufort, at the entrance to St John's College chapel, Cambridge, UK (Charles O. Cecil / Alamy).

Page 14 (above right): St John's College, Cambridge, UK (© Nicola Tallis).

Page 14 (right): Lady Margaret Beaufort's coat of arms on the gatehouse at Christ's College, Cambridge, UK (Andrew Michael / Alamy).

Page 15 (left): Exterior view of the Henry VII Lady Chapel, Westminster Abbey, London, UK (Andrew Michael / Alamy).

Page 15 (below): Detail of the tomb effigies of King Henry VII and Elizabeth of York by Pietro Torrigiano in the Henry VII Lady Chapel, Westminster Abbey, London, UK (Angelo Hornak / Corbis via Getty Images).

Page 16 (left): Portrait of Henry VIII, *c.* 1509, by Meynnart Wewyck (Denver Art Museum, Colorado, USA / Fine Art Images / Heritage Images / Getty Images).

Page 16 (right): Tomb effigy of Lady Margaret Beaufort, Westminster Abbey, London, UK (Granger Historical Picture Archive / Alamy).

THE BEAUFORT FAMILY

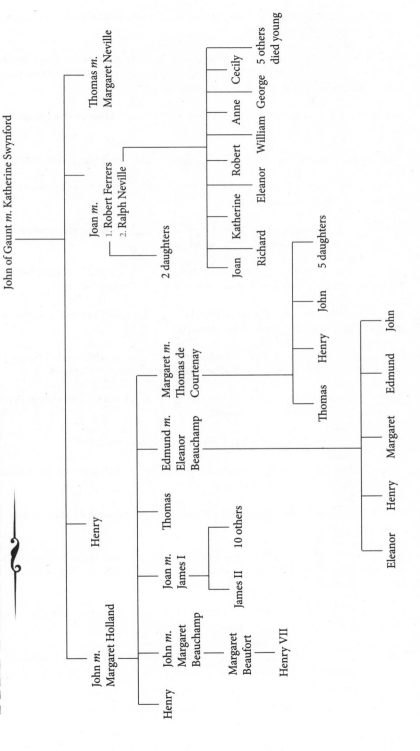

THE TUDOR FAMILY

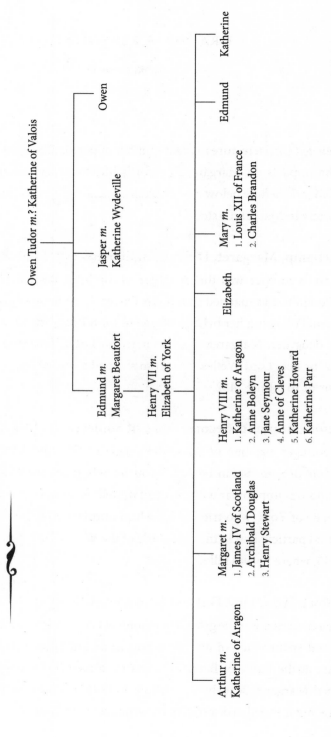

Owen Tudor *m.*? Katherine of Valois

Edmund *m.*
Margaret Beaufort

Jasper *m.*
Katherine Wydeville

Owen

Henry VII *m.*
Elizabeth of York

Arthur *m.*
Katherine of Aragon

Margaret *m.*
1. James IV of Scotland
2. Archibald Douglas
3. Henry Stewart

Henry VIII *m.*
1. Katherine of Aragon
2. Anne Boleyn
3. Jane Seymour
4. Anne of Cleves
5. Katherine Howard
6. Katherine Parr

Elizabeth

Mary *m.*
1. Louis XII of France
2. Charles Brandon

Edmund

Katherine

Uncrowned Queen features a great number of personalities, all of whom had varying impacts on Margaret Beaufort's life. In order to help familiarize the reader, I include below a brief biographical sketch of some of the main characters in Margaret's story.

Beauchamp, Margaret, Duchess of Somerset (*c.* 1420–82)

Margaret's mother was the daughter of Sir John Beauchamp and Edith Stourton. She was married first to Sir Oliver St John, by whom she had six children. Following her brief marriage to John Beaufort, which produced a single daughter, Margaret, she remarried in 1447. Her third husband was Lionel, or Leo, Lord Welles, by whom she had a son. Margaret Beauchamp died prior to 3 June 1482.

Beaufort, Edmund, Second Duke of Somerset (*c.* 1406/7–55)

The younger brother of Margaret's father, Edmund was granted the dukedom of Somerset in 1448. A favourite of both Henry VI and his queen, Edmund was unpopular with many of his fellow nobles – most significantly the Duke of York, who tried to have him imprisoned on several occasions. Edmund participated in the first battle of the Wars of the Roses at St Albans in 1455, where he was killed.

Beaufort, John, First Duke of Somerset (1404–44)

Margaret's father was the grandson of John of Gaunt and Katherine Swynford. Somerset spent much of his youth imprisoned in France, as a result of his capture at the Battle of Baugé. He was ransomed in 1438, and in 1442 he married Margaret Beauchamp. In July 1443 he led a military campaign to France, but it ended in disaster. He returned six months later, in January 1444, and was met with disgrace. In May – just days before his infant daughter's first birthday – Somerset died, possibly at his own hand.

Bray, Sir Reginald (c. 1440–1503)

Margaret met the man who would become one of her most trusted servants and lifelong friends following her marriage to Henry Stafford. Bray acted as receiver-general to the couple, and managed Margaret's estates for around two decades. He served Margaret loyally, and conspired on her son's behalf in the Buckingham Rebellion of 1483. Following Henry VII's accession in 1485, Bray was handsomely rewarded and became one of the King's most influential advisors. He died childless on 5 August 1503.

Cecily of York (1469–1507)

Margaret was extremely fond of the third of Edward IV's daughters, who she is likely to have come to know well during her time at the court of the Yorkist King. It was probably under Margaret's auspices that Cecily was married to John Welles, Margaret's half-brother, in 1487. Following Welles' death, Cecily wed Thomas Kyme without seeking Henry VII's consent. The King was outraged, but Margaret did her best to protect the former Yorkist princess, interceding on her behalf. Cecily lived out the remainder of her days quietly.

Edward IV (1442–83)

The son and heir of Richard, Duke of York, following a victory at the Battle of Mortimer's Cross in February 1461, in March, Edward declared himself king. His victory was consolidated after the bloody Battle of Towton on 29 March. Edward secretly married Elizabeth Wydeville in 1464, and together the couple would produce ten children – eight of whom survived infancy. In 1470 Edward was briefly deposed and fled abroad, but he returned the following year to fight for his throne. After two successful victories at Barnet and Tewkesbury, he regained his crown. Edward died unexpectedly in 1483, the results of which led Margaret Beaufort to spy an opportunity for her son.

Elizabeth of York (1466–1503)

The eldest daughter of Edward IV and Elizabeth Wydeville, Elizabeth was betrothed to the French Dauphin in 1475 as part of her father's peace negotiations. The betrothal was broken off in 1482, and the following year Margaret plotted to marry Elizabeth to her son, Henry. Their marriage finally took place in January 1486, and in September Elizabeth gave birth to the first Tudor heir, Arthur. Together she and Henry sired seven children, four of whom survived infancy. Elizabeth died nine days after the birth of her final child, Katherine.

Fisher, John, Bishop of Rochester (*c.* 1469–1535)

The son of a Yorkshire merchant, Fisher first met Margaret in 1494 when he was Senior Proctor at Cambridge. The two struck up an immediate friendship, and before long Fisher had assumed the role of Margaret's chaplain and confessor. In 1504 Fisher was created Bishop of Rochester, and remained a close friend of Margaret's for the rest of her life. So much so that he was one of the executors of her will, and it is from him that much of the information about her life stems – largely related by Margaret herself.

George, Duke of Clarence (1449–78)

A younger brother of Edward IV, it was to Clarence that Henry Tudor's title of Richmond was given in 1462. Clarence was treacherous, and rebelled with the Earl of Warwick against his brother in 1469. He was later reconciled with Edward IV, and became a recipient of the King's favour. Married to Isabel Neville, the couple had two surviving children: Margaret, later married to Sir Richard Pole, and Edward, Earl of Warwick, executed in 1499. Following the death of his wife in 1476 – probably as a result of childbirth – Clarence's behaviour became increasingly erratic. He was arrested and tried on charges of treason, of which he was found guilty. He was executed on 18 February 1478, reportedly by being drowned in a butt of Malmsey wine.

Henry VI (1421–71)

Margaret's kinsman was the only child of Henry V and Katherine of Valois. Gentle and pious by nature, Henry was completely unsuited to the task of ruling a country. Under his rule, the Wars of the Roses broke out in 1455. Henry was deposed in 1461 and spent the next nine years either in hiding or imprisoned. Though he was briefly reinstated in 1470, the following year he was deposed once more and murdered in the Tower of London on 21 May 1471.

Henry VII (1457–1509)

Margaret's only son was born at Pembroke Castle two months after the death of her husband, Edmund Tudor. His birth was traumatic, but in spite of this Henry grew to be a healthy boy. Much of his early life was spent under the protection of his uncle, Jasper Tudor, but in 1462 Henry became the ward of William Herbert. He was treated kindly, and kept in contact with his mother, though he seems to have seen her but rarely. In 1471, at Margaret's urging, Henry fled abroad with Jasper Tudor, spending fourteen years in exile in Brittany and France. He returned at the head of an army in August 1485, and successfully defeated Richard III at the Battle of Bosworth. In January 1486, Henry married Elizabeth of York, thereby uniting the houses of Lancaster and York. The couple had four children who survived infancy, chiefly his successor, Henry VIII. Henry died at Richmond Palace on 21 April 1509.

Henry VIII (1491–1547)

Henry was the second of Margaret's grandsons, and was raised with his sisters, primarily at Eltham Palace. As with all of her grandchildren, Margaret was fond of Henry, and her accounts show that she sometimes bought gifts for him. Following the death of his elder brother Arthur in 1502, Henry became Henry VII's sole surviving male heir. He succeeded his father as Henry VIII in April 1509 and married Katherine of Aragon soon after. At the time of his death in 1547 he had married six times and produced three legitimate children.

Herbert, William, Earl of Pembroke (*c.* 1423–69)

In 1462 William Herbert, a loyal supporter of Edward IV, became the guardian of Margaret's son, Henry Tudor. The boy was brought to live with Herbert and his family at Raglan Castle, and was treated kindly by his guardian and his wife, Anne Devereux. Herbert eventually hoped to arrange for Henry's marriage to his daughter, Maud. In July 1469, Herbert partook in the Battle of Edgecote, taking young Henry with him. He was captured and executed the day after the battle.

Katherine of Aragon (1485–1536)

The Spanish bride of Margaret's eldest grandson, Arthur, arrived in England in October 1501. The following month, Katherine and Arthur were married in a lavish ceremony in St Paul's Cathedral, but the marriage was cut short when Arthur died in April 1502. Katherine was then betrothed to Margaret's younger grandson, Henry, but he repudiated this in 1505. She nevertheless remained in England, despite being poorly treated by Henry VII and forced to endure a great deal of financial hardship. Shortly after his father's death, Henry VIII resolved to marry Katherine, and the couple were quietly married on 11 June 1509. In spite of numerous pregnancies, Katherine produced just one surviving child, a daughter named Mary. By 1526 her marriage to Henry had begun to fall apart, and she was later forced to endure a very public and painful separation from him. In 1533 Katherine and Henry's marriage was declared invalid, and three years later she died a lonely death at Kimbolton Castle.

Margaret of Anjou (1430–82)

Henry VI's French-born queen was the daughter of René of Anjou and Isabella, Duchess of Lorraine. Married to Henry VI in 1445, it was she rather than her husband who came to be a dominant force in the Wars of the Roses. Following the Lancastrian defeat at Tewkesbury in 1471 that saw the death of Margaret's only child, Prince Edward, Margaret became Edward IV's prisoner. In 1475 she returned to France, having been ransomed to Louis XI, and died there in poverty on 25 August 1482.

Morton, John (*c.* 1420–1500)

Hailing from Dorset, Morton had risen steadily to prominence under Henry VI, and had been appointed Chancellor to his heir, Prince Edward, on 26 September 1456. Following the Lancastrian defeat at Towton, Morton was captured while attempting to flee to Scotland, and was imprisoned in the Tower of London. Incredibly, he managed to escape and hurried to join Margaret of Anjou in France. He remained there until Henry VI's readeption, but after his master's murder he reconciled with Edward IV and was pardoned in July 1471. He became one of Edward's most trusted advisors, but was later imprisoned by Richard III. Morton supported Henry Tudor's claim and was a key conspirator in the Buckingham Rebellion. Following Henry VII's accession, Morton was appointed Archbishop of Canterbury in 1486 and Lord Chancellor the following year.

Neville, Richard, Earl of Warwick (1428–71)

The man who became known as the Kingmaker supported Edward IV during the first years of his reign. He became the most powerful noble in the realm, but was incensed when he discovered that Edward had married Elizabeth Wydeville in 1464. Five years later, he rebelled against Edward and succeeded in capturing him, but an attempt to rule in Edward's name failed. Though he and Edward were reconciled, it was short-lived, and in 1470 Warwick supported the readeption of Henry VI. When Edward IV returned to claim his throne the following year, his army met with that of Warwick at Barnet on 14 April. During the course of the battle, Warwick was killed.

Richard III (1452–85)

The younger brother of Edward IV, Richard – following the King's unexpected death in April 1483 – moved quickly to take control of his nephew, Edward V, and eventually, the realm. He was proclaimed King of England on 26 June, and crowned alongside his wife, Anne Neville, on 6 July with Margaret in attendance. Three months later, Richard was forced to deal with the Buckingham Rebellion, of which Margaret was one of the leading conspirators. The rebellion was a failure, and Richard confiscated all of Margaret's goods. The remainder of his reign was plagued by unrest, and in the summer of 1485 Richard prepared to face Henry Tudor on the battlefield. He was killed in the battle, and his naked body slung over the back of a horse – several humiliation wounds were inflicted after his death. Richard's remains were discovered in 2012 and identified the following year. He was interred in Leicester Cathedral in 2015.

Stafford, Henry (*c.* 1425–71)

Margaret's third husband was the second son of Humphrey Stafford, Duke of Buckingham. He and Margaret were married in January 1458, and seem to have enjoyed a genuinely happy marriage. The couple spent a great deal of time together, but after thirteen years of marriage Stafford died in October 1471 as a result of injuries inflicted at the Battle of Barnet.

Stafford, Henry, Second Duke of Buckingham (1455–83)

As the grandson of Humphrey Stafford, Duke of Buckingham, Henry was Margaret's nephew by marriage and also her cousin through his mother. Following the death of Edward IV in 1483, Buckingham became the chief ally of Richard, Duke of Gloucester, and fully supported his usurpation of the throne in June. Before long though, Buckingham began plotting with Margaret for Richard's overthrow, and planned a rebellion. When this failed, Buckingham was captured and executed on Richard III's orders on 2 November 1483.

Stanley, Thomas, Earl of Derby (*c.* 1433–1504)

Margaret married her fourth husband in June 1472, a match made – as with her other marriages – for political advantage rather than personal preference. Stanley was a man of dubious political allegiance, but following Henry VII's accession he was richly rewarded as the King's stepfather. Though Margaret was declared *femme sole* (a sole person) in 1485 and later took a vow of chastity, she and Stanley remained on good terms and continued to work together. Following his death on 29 July 1504, Stanley was laid to rest in Burscough Priory, Lancashire.

Stanley, William (c. 1435–95)

The younger brother of Margaret's husband Thomas Stanley, William was instrumental in Henry Tudor's success at the Battle of Bosworth. He was rewarded for his good service, being appointed Chamberlain of the King's household, and becoming immensely wealthy. At the beginning of 1495, however, Stanley was arrested on suspicion of supporting Perkin Warbeck. He was executed on 16 February.

Tudor, Arthur (1486–1502)

Margaret and her family had high hopes for the first-born child and heir of Henry VII and Elizabeth of York – Margaret's grandson. In 1493 Arthur was sent to Ludlow Castle to continue his education and prepare for the task of kingship that awaited him. He rarely came to court, and thus Margaret saw little of her eldest grandson. On 14 November 1501, Arthur married the Spanish Princess, Katherine of Aragon, and soon afterwards the newlyweds returned to Ludlow. Tragically, before long Arthur fell ill and died on 2 April 1502.

Tudor, Edmund, Earl of Richmond (1428/30–56)

Through his mother, Katherine of Valois, Edmund was the half-brother of Henry VI. It was thanks to the King that Edmund was granted the earldom of Richmond, and it was under his auspices that Edmund's marriage to Margaret Beaufort was arranged in 1455. The newlyweds moved to Wales, but their marriage was short-lived; on 1 November 1456 Edmund died of plague at Carmarthen Castle, leaving Margaret pregnant at the age of thirteen.

Tudor, Jasper, Earl of Pembroke and Duke of Bedford (c. 1431–95)

The younger brother of Edmund Tudor, Margaret's brother-in-law was a devoted and trusted figure in her life. Not only did he support Margaret throughout the trying days that followed Edmund's death in 1456 – including offering her shelter at Pembroke Castle, where she gave birth to her son – he also guarded Henry Tudor and stayed by his side following their foreign exile in 1471. Jasper remained loyal to Henry following his accession to the throne in 1485, and was greatly loved by both his nephew and Margaret. He died childless in December 1495.

Tudor, Margaret (1489–1541)

Margaret always held an especial fondness for her eldest granddaughter and namesake, and showed great concern for her welfare. In 1503 Margaret left England and travelled to Scotland to marry James IV. Her husband was killed at the Battle of Flodden in 1513, leaving Margaret a pregnant widow with a small son – James V. She endured a turbulent marital history, marrying twice more – as a result of her marriage to Archibald Douglas, she had a daughter, also named Margaret. She died at Methven Castle, Perthshire, on 18 October 1541.

Tudor, Mary (1496–1533)

The youngest surviving daughter of Henry VII and Elizabeth of York joined Margaret in order to entertain Philip of Castile at Croydon in 1506. The following year she was betrothed to his son, Charles, but the negotiations never came to fruition. Instead, in October 1514 Mary married Louis XII of France, but he died after just three months of marriage. Shortly after – probably in February 1515 – Mary clandestinely married Charles Brandon, Duke of Suffolk. Their union produced two surviving daughters, Frances and Eleanor. Frances was the mother of Lady Jane Grey and her two sisters.

Welles, Lionel or Leo (c. 1406–61)

Margaret's stepfather married her mother in 1447, having been previously married to Joan Waterton. He was a strong supporter of the house of Lancaster, and served as Joint Deputy of Calais in the 1450s. Welles was created a Knight of the Garter in 1457, and fought for Henry VI at the Battle of Towton in 1461. It was here that he was killed, and later that year he was attainted by Parliament. Welles was buried alongside his first wife in St Oswald's Church, Methley.

Wydeville, Elizabeth (*c.* 1437–92)

The first commoner to become Queen of England was married secretly to Edward IV in 1464. Though her union with Edward was successful, Elizabeth and her family managed to alienate many of her husband's nobles. The result was that, following Edward's death, the Wydeville family had little support in their attempts to secure power in the name of Elizabeth's son, Edward V. Elizabeth and her remaining children fled to sanctuary, where she plotted with Margaret to overthrow Richard III. Following Henry VII's accession and the marriage of her daughter, Elizabeth of York, to the King, Elizabeth reappeared at court. However, in 1487 she removed to Bermondsey Abbey, and it was here that she died in 1492.

31 August 1422	Accession of Henry VI
31 May 1443	Margaret Beaufort is born at Bletsoe Castle
27 May 1444	John Beaufort, Duke of Somerset, dies in Dorset
23 April 1445	Henry VI marries Margaret of Anjou
22 May 1455	First Battle of St Albans
June–August 1455?	Margaret marries Edmund Tudor
1 November 1456	Edmund Tudor dies at Carmarthen Castle
28 January 1457	Henry Tudor is born at Pembroke Castle
3 January 1458	Margaret marries Henry Stafford
10 July 1460	Battle of Northampton
2 February 1461	Battle of Mortimer's Cross
3 February 1461	Execution of Owen Tudor at Hereford
4 March 1461	Accession of Edward IV
29 March 1461	Battle of Towton
12 February 1462	Henry Tudor's wardship granted to William Herbert
11 February 1466	Birth of Elizabeth of York
26 July 1469	Battle of Edgecote
3 October 1470	Readeption of Henry VI
11 April 1471	Second reign of Edward IV begins
14 April 1471	Battle of Barnet
4 May 1471	Battle of Tewkesbury
21 May 1471	Henry VI is murdered at the Tower of London
2 June 1471	Henry Tudor flees abroad
4 October 1471	Henry Stafford dies at Woking
June 1472	Margaret marries Sir Thomas Stanley
9 April 1483	Edward IV dies at the Palace of Westminster
26 June 1483	Accession of Richard III
6 July 1483	Coronation of Richard III

2 November 1483	Execution of the Duke of Buckingham
7 December 1484	Henry Tudor denounced as a rebel
22 August 1485	Henry Tudor defeats Richard III at the Battle of Bosworth
30 October 1485	Coronation of Henry VII
18 January 1486	Henry VII marries Elizabeth of York
20 September 1486	Prince Arthur born at Winchester
16 June 1487	Battle of Stoke
25 November 1487	Coronation of Elizabeth of York
28 November 1489	Princess Margaret born at the Palace of Westminster
28 June 1491	Prince Henry born at Greenwich Palace
2 July 1492	Princess Elizabeth born at Sheen Palace
16 February 1495	Execution of Sir William Stanley
18 March 1496	Princess Mary born at Sheen Palace
21 February 1499	Prince Edmund born at Greenwich Palace
23 November 1499	Execution of Perkin Warbeck
28 November 1499	Execution of the Earl of Warwick
14 November 1501	Prince Arthur marries Katherine of Aragon
January 1502?	Margaret travels to Calais
2 April 1502	Prince Arthur dies at Ludlow
2 February 1503	Princess Katherine born at the Tower of London
11 February 1503	Elizabeth of York dies at the Tower of London
29 July 1504	Thomas Stanley dies
1505	Margaret founds Christ's College, Cambridge
21 April 1509	Henry VII dies at Richmond Palace
11 June 1509	Henry VIII marries Katherine of Aragon at Greenwich Palace
24 June 1509	Coronation of Henry VIII and Katherine of Aragon
29 June 1509	Margaret Beaufort dies at Westminster Abbey

AUTHOR'S NOTE

I HAVE SPENT months painstakingly transcribing hundreds – if not thousands – of pages of fifteenth- and sixteenth-century material for this book. While this is always an invaluable part of the research and writing process for me, the sheer volume of material has obliged me to seek the services of the excellent team at Transcription Services Limited on occasion. I am extremely grateful for their help. As always, I have modernized all of the spelling and punctuation from contemporary books and documents in order to create a clearer narrative.

All monetary values have been presented with the contemporary amount, followed by the modern-day equivalent in parentheses. All conversions were done according to the National Archives Currency Convertor (www. nationalarchives.gov.uk/currency), and are approximate values. Please also be aware that they may be subject to change.

Finally, for clarity, all dates have been calculated using the modern-day Gregorian calendar, under which the year turns on 1 January.

NOTES ON SOURCES

THE SOURCES FOR Margaret's life are both varied and plentiful, providing us with a wealth of information about this extraordinary woman. One of the most abundant supplies of documents are stored in the archives of St John's College, Cambridge. Here can be found many of her surviving household accounts and inventories, all of which provide compelling details of Margaret's life and the luxury in which she lived. Some of her personal papers are also extant, including copies of her will in which she painstakingly recorded her final wishes over the course of many years. Household accounts belonging to Margaret's third husband, Henry Stafford, survive in the Westminster Abbey Muniments, along with other documents that provide further insights into her life.

Further sources of information come from those who knew her. The account of Henry Parker, Lord Morley, was later presented to Margaret's great-granddaughter, Mary I. Having been a member of Margaret's household during his youth, Parker knew her well, and it was probably by her arrangement that he was married to her great-niece, Alice St John.[1] His account provides some charming details of the sort that can only be gleaned from sources of this personal nature. It must be remembered, though, that it was written many years after his service to Margaret had come to an end. Of equal importance is the account of John Fisher, Bishop of Rochester, who became Margaret's chaplain and close confidante. He knew his mistress well and preached a sermon in her honour at her funeral. Unsurprisingly, both Morley and Fisher paint highly flattering pictures of Margaret, praising her achievements and her generosity. Fisher did, though, claim that 'my purpose is not vainly to extol or to magnify above her merits', but to use her as an example for the bettering of others.[2] Even so, the praise of those who knew Margaret is not unjustified in many quarters, for these accounts are often supported by other sources. They are most useful for their ability to provide personal details from people who actually knew Margaret, thereby offering glimpses into her personality in a way that other sources are unable to.

The sources covering the dramatic and dangerous events of both the Wars of the Roses and Richard III's coup of 1483 are plentiful, for they were relatively well documented by contemporary chroniclers. Margaret features in some of these too, yet, as with all historical sources, they need to be carefully scrutinized in order to establish their reliability. The account of the Croyland Chronicler, for example, is one of the most superior sources for this period and much of the information it provides can be shown to be accurate.[3] Though its author is anonymous, it is likely to have been John Russell, Bishop of Lincoln, a member of the royal Council. Margaret and her family had close links with Croyland Abbey in Lincolnshire, which was one of the richest religious houses in England, and she also knew Russell. Dominic Mancini, an Italian visitor to England in the summer of 1483, is a useful source, whose account was only discovered in 1936.[4] Although he has been heavily criticized and doubts cast upon his reliability, it is clear that he spoke to a number of people who were involved in the mysterious happenings of the spring and summer of 1483, including Dr John Argentine, physician to Edward V. Mancini left England after Richard III's coronation on 6 July, and wrote his account in December – just months after the events that he had witnessed took place. The Italian-born Polydore Vergil was responsible for writing an official history of England, the *Anglica Historia*, which Henry VII commissioned from him in 1507.[5] Vergil claimed to have consulted a wide range of sources when composing his history, and though his work can often be shown to be accurate, it must be remembered that he had to employ tact when writing about his patron. Similarly, Bernard André, a blind French poet, penned an official account of the life of Henry VII, 'the most prosperous and victorious of the kings of England and France', producing a work that was highly flattering not only of Henry, but of Margaret too.[6] He did, however, experience first-hand many of the events about which he wrote, and gleaned much of his information not only from Henry, but also from Margaret.

What we lack is an account from Margaret herself, who, of course, was an eyewitness to many of the events that saw Richard III's usurpation and the disappearance of his two royal nephews in the summer of 1483. From her days at court, she knew both Edward IV and Richard III personally, as well as at least one of the two boys – Prince Richard, the younger of the pair – who have become known to history as the Princes in the Tower. She herself heard the rumours that the Princes had been murdered, and, keeping in mind the events of the autumn of 1483, it is almost certain that she believed them to be dead, although she had no way of confirming this. Contrary, though, to several suggestions that emerged in the seventeenth century and that have inspired some modern interpretations, there is not a shred of contemporary evidence that even hints at Margaret's involvement in the Princes' disappearance. This is the strongest evidence of her innocence, and that she has been mooted as a potential murderer demonstrates the extent to which her reputation has been blackened over time. This, in turn, provides a compelling reason for a fresh appraisal of her life.

Documentary sources are not unique in their ability to fill in the jigsaw of Margaret's life, and there are other clues for those who seek to find them. Westminster Abbey, the splendid Gothic monument so long associated with royal authority, houses the magnificent tomb that was raised to Margaret's memory after her death. This provides the most tangible and lifelike depiction of the woman who determined to be remembered by history as an integral part of the Tudor dynasty. Likewise, fragments of several of the places that Margaret would have known still survive, including Woking Palace, one of her favourite homes, while archaeological digs are currently underway at the site of her once-magnificent palace of Collyweston in Northamptonshire. The tomb of Margaret's parents – created at her own commission – can be seen in Wimborne Minster, and the two Cambridge colleges of her foundation – Christ's and St John's – are still active.

AMID THE MODERN-DAY bustle of Central London, the Palace of Westminster – the seat of government for centuries – dominates the scenery. Adjacent to the Palace stands the imposing Westminster Abbey, the magnificent setting for the coronation of English monarchs since William of Normandy conquered England in 1066. Fifteen monarchs lie buried inside its ancient stone walls, alongside consorts, royal children, and others who have played a pivotal role in shaping England's history.

Prominent both within and without the abbey is the spectacular Lady Chapel, whose fan-vaulted ceiling and stained-glass windows provide a splendid example of late medieval architecture. Begun by Henry VII in 1503 as a permanent and tangible memorial to the Tudor dynasty, the chapel was described by the awestruck Tudor traveller John Leland as 'the wonder of the world'. It is also the final resting place of some of history's most illustrious figures, several of whom were a part of the famous Tudor family: Edward VI, Mary I, Elizabeth I, as well as the chapel's founder, Henry VII, who lies entombed with his wife, Elizabeth of York.

In the south aisle of the chapel, set apart from the grand, tourist-crowded monuments, stands a black marble tomb-chest. Atop the chest lies a skilfully crafted bronze effigy of a woman: she is dressed simply in a widow's wimple with a long mantle, her head resting on two intricately designed pillows that show a portcullis and a Tudor rose. A coronet – long since lost – once lay above her head in an indication of her noble status. Lines and wrinkles that hint at years of stress and anxiety are etched on to her face – probably moulded on a death mask – serving as a permanent and tangible reminder of the extraordinary and perilous events that shaped her life. Her small, delicately crafted hands that show signs of age and the arthritis that plagued her towards the end of her life are raised in prayer, and a mythical yale (a creature with the head of a goat with swivelling horns, body of an antelope, and tail of an elephant) that once boasted horns sits at her feet. The black marble tomb-chest contains sculpted bronze shields with arms that proudly proclaim the woman's heritage. Most prominent among them are the Royal Arms. Adorning the tomb is a Latin inscription composed by the celebrated Dutch humanist scholar, Desiderius Erasmus, which begins with a proclamation of the woman's defining legacy: 'Margaret of Richmond, mother of Henry VII, grandmother of Henry VIII.'

The regal Margaret of Richmond – better known as Margaret Beaufort – lies resplendent, her tomb embellished with symbols that emphasize the identity that she had created. Few of the abbey's visitors recognize that the tomb of this small, simply garbed lady is that of the mother of Henry VII and grandmother of Henry VIII – the notorious Tudor king. By contrast to the awe-inspiring double tomb of her son and daughter-in-law that dominates the Lady Chapel, therefore, Margaret Beaufort's memorial attracts little interest.

Yet, following her son's accession to the throne until her death, Margaret's birthday was proudly celebrated in the abbey each year, in fitting recognition of a woman who was instrumental in founding England's most famous dynasty. Descended from a line of English kings, and the great-granddaughter of a royal duke, Margaret – against quite incredible odds – would raise herself to become the mother of a king. Her life reads like an episode of a modern-day soap opera. War was to be a common theme. Born into the midst of the Hundred Years' War that raged between England and France, Margaret soon saw bloodshed spread to English soil. Political tension spilled over into civil war, destroying families and tearing apart the country and those who sought to rule it. Margaret would not have recognized the terms 'the Cousins' Wars' or the 'Wars of the Roses' by which the conflict became known, for these were the product of a later age, but the bloody twists and turns of the struggle between her own house – that of Lancaster – and her enemy's – York – would dominate and shape much of her life. It was a war in which most of the noble families of England would become hopelessly embroiled. In 1976, J.R. Lander suggested that by 1461 at least forty-nine out of sixty peerage families had been involved in the wars – Margaret's most of all.[1] From the outset, her life was overset with obstacles, all of which she was forced to negotiate. A marital pawn since the earliest days of her childhood, she was just thirteen when she was both widowed and gave birth to her only child. These circumstances forced Margaret to take an active role in seeking a protector both for herself and for her son, while ingratiating herself with kings from a rival house in order to safeguard their futures. It was finally a scheme initiated by Margaret that began to settle the conflict and brought the son of a nobleman born with no expectations of kingship to the throne of England, ushering in – at least in part – an era of peace.

'Henry VII's devout and rather awesome mother', was the description the historian Neville Williams offered of Margaret Beaufort in his 1973 biography of the King.[2] Both adjectives in this statement are true, but neither do full justice to the woman who forms the subject of this book. Williams' assessment does, however, accurately summarize the way in which Margaret has often been portrayed: a religious fanatic who was obsessively ambitious on her son's behalf and dominated his court, an image compounded by the effigy upon her tomb as well as the surviving portraits, which show her wearing widow's weeds and a barbed wimple, on her knees in prayer. This is the image often conjured up when the name Margaret Beaufort is mentioned. Yet it is as two-dimensional as the paintings themselves, frequently used as a convenient short-hand when relating the tales of the period. Margaret's own story and her true character as a living, breathing woman are a far cry from such flat representations.

My first proper introduction to Margaret Beaufort came when I was researching the jewel collections of the queens of England in the period 1445 to 1548. Throughout my exploration I was struck by how different the Margaret that was beginning to emerge from the pages of archival material was to the traditional figure. Her image has been through some revisions over the years since her death, but the popular one has rarely been accurate. Furthermore, in spite of the impact Margaret made on English history, she has often been little more than a footnote, overlooked and ignored. In recent years this has begun to change, and she is now starting to feature more prominently in the narratives that she helped to shape.

In the years following Margaret's death, though she was remembered and her memory revered by those whose lives she had touched, she failed to attract the attention of poets, playwrights and artists. Given the impact she made on her son and his court, it is somewhat surprising that her story did not inspire William Shakespeare enough to consider her inclusion in any of his plays. She was referenced on brief occasions in *Richard III*, in which her husband Thomas Stanley was afforded a role. Considering the part that Margaret had played in the events of Richard's reign, her exclusion as a character in her own right is curious. It can perhaps only be explained by a desire from the playwright not to offend Margaret's great-granddaughter, Elizabeth I, by highlighting the disgrace of her ancestress following Richard's discovery of her treasonous activities – chiefly, her plotting to overthrow the Plantagenet king and replace him with her own son, for which Richard placed her under house arrest.

It would not be until the twentieth century that Margaret would begin to re-emerge from the shadows into which she had been cast following her death. Since that time, she seems to have finally caught the attention of an array of novelists, writers and others. She has appeared regularly in popular culture, and today interest in Margaret persists. Curiously, she has been remembered in two very contrasting ways: sympathetically, as a pious and cultured lady who ought to be celebrated for her achievements and as the mother of the Tudor dynasty, and in an altogether more sinister light as the woman who may have been responsible for the disappearance of the Princes in the Tower – a theory that we shall put to bed once and for all in the pages of this book.

There have been other layers of obfuscation as well, as novels have toyed with the idea of Margaret as a romantic heroine, deeply in love with her second husband Edmund (Margaret's experience of love was never so conventional), while TV series have predominantly chosen to focus on her ruthless ambition.[3] More recently, there has been a wave of enthusiasm and interest in Margaret's story, sparked by Philippa Gregory's series of novels in which she features heavily. Indeed, *The Red Queen* is told from Margaret's point of view. Her portrayal in the accompanying 2013 drama series *The White Queen* is as a fanatic, obsessed with the idea that God intended her son to rule and working tirelessly in order to ensure that he fulfilled his destiny. The series also wove a love story and affair into her relationship with her brother-in-law, Jasper Tudor. By contrast, the 2017 adaptation of Gregory's *The White Princess* saw Margaret smother Jasper to death upon his discovery of her involvement in the murder of the Princes in the Tower, as well as being publicly humiliated by her son. The trend of casting Margaret in a variety of guises depending on the dramatic leanings of the author/producer seems set to continue.

But her true story is far richer than any of these fictions. My impressions while interrogating Margaret's jewel collection only grew as I broadened my investigation. Indeed, the privilege of writing Margaret's story – and it has absolutely been a privilege – has been enhanced by the opportunity to delve into the wealth of source material that is still extant. It has been both extremely challenging and exceptionally rewarding. When handling this treasure trove of Margaret's papers, the overwhelming sensation of experiencing history as it happened envelops the reader, and it becomes easy to immerse oneself fully in the fifteenth and early sixteenth centuries. A similar feeling occurs when studying the handful of Margaret's letters that survive, written in varying contexts to a number of recipients. These allow us to view different aspects of her character, for through these we can see how she conducted her business affairs, how she viewed her family, and her intense affection for her son.

I am not the first scholar who has been drawn to Margaret, and neither will I be the last. The rich abundance of surviving primary source material, details of which can be found in Notes on Sources, has ensured that she has long attracted the fascination of biographers, while her prominent role in television series, such as those mentioned above, has given her considerable appeal among a wider audience. I must, however, take time to highlight the exceptional work of Michael Jones and Malcolm Underwood, whose 1992 joint study is considered – more than justifiably – to be the definitive work on Margaret's life. Following in their footsteps has not been easy. Other scholars have sought to highlight her educational and religious patronage, which, although covered in this book, are not the main focus. Instead, my aim is to dispel the many myths surrounding Margaret's life, and in their place offer a rounder, richer picture.

I have discovered a woman who started life playing by the rules: a marital pawn, defined by her wealth and bloodline. But, early on, the dangerous events that unfolded around her unleashed a new side to Margaret – one that sought a voice and independence. The fifteenth century was an extraordinary time for women and gave them hitherto unprecedented opportunities to make their voices heard: as Sarah Gristwood remarked in her exceptional work on the women of the Wars of the Roses, 'the second half of the fifteenth century is alive with female energy', and Margaret was one of its most potent forces.[4] Over time, Margaret maintained pressure against the constraints imposed by her sex and society, slowly demanding more and more control over her life, until the crown on her son's head allowed her to make the unprecedented move for almost total independence: financially, physically and sexually. This is a woman who learned pragmatism very early on, who knew when to lay aside ego and finer loyalties for the sake of the long game – unlike so many of her male contemporaries. No doubt, the turning point was the birth of her son. His rights and very survival gave Margaret extraordinary energy and zeal, even when her own life was at stake.

Margaret's story is one of tragic lows and unprecedented highs: it is a tale of war and peace told through the eyes of an extraordinary woman who played a leading role and became one of the most influential personalities of the late fifteenth century. Though in material terms she was privileged and never went without, emotionally she suffered heartache and loss, endured struggles and faced perils. Yet she survived: in time she would thrive. In so doing she helped to lay the foundations for England's most famous dynasty. More importantly though, she created a lasting legacy as an individual who ought to be remembered in her own right, thereby achieving more than she could ever have anticipated. Margaret's is, therefore, a life to be celebrated: it is the life of a woman who became a queen in all but name.

Nicola Tallis, Westminster Abbey

PROLOGUE

28 January 1457

AS THE BITTER weather swirled, in the strong stone walls of Pembroke Castle a thirteen-year-old girl was undergoing the worst ordeal of her life. The war that would tear apart the country had not long begun, but here, in the mighty Norman stronghold, situated in the midst of south-west Wales, close to the river estuary that opens into the Celtic sea, two lives hung in the balance.

Lady Margaret Beaufort – a wealthy heiress with royal connections to the house of Lancaster – had been just twelve years old when she married Edmund Tudor, half-brother to the Lancastrian king Henry VI, but her painfully tender age did not prevent the eager bridegroom from consummating the match and Margaret quickly conceived. Her condition was soon fraught with danger and uncertainty when her husband died of plague on 1 November 1456, leaving his young wife alone and terrified of contracting the same disease. The heavily pregnant teenager was far from her family and forced to seek aid from her brother-in-law, Jasper Tudor. She fled to his fortress at Pembroke. It was here that the young Margaret now faced a terrible labour. Her underdeveloped body struggled to endure the strain being put upon it and it was thought that neither mother nor child would survive. Her confessor, Bishop John Fisher, would later declare: 'It seemed a miracle that of so little a personage anyone should have been born at all.' Yet after many traumatic hours, Margaret gave birth to a son. She named him Henry in honour of his Lancastrian forebears. This was the moment when everything changed for Margaret – and ultimately for England. The healthy baby that she had brought into the world must have seemed a true miracle, and as she cared for him over the following days and weeks, a love grew in her like none she had felt before. That love would bring

Margaret once again close to death before culminating in a dramatic twist on Bosworth battlefield in 1485. For in her arms she held the future King of England. A man who would seek to end the bloodshed and unite the rival houses of Lancaster and York. But as Margaret recovered, sheltered for the moment inside the broad walls of Pembroke Castle, there were still many more trials to overcome before she – and her son – would truly be safe.

PART ONE

CHAPTER 1

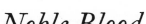

Noble Blood

S URROUNDED BY A moat amid fragrant gardens and situated in the
heart of the pretty Bedfordshire village of Bletsoe, the castle was in
reality more of a fortified manor house than a defensive structure. A
comfortable three-storey house with crenellations added in the fourteenth
century, Bletsoe Castle had come into the hands of the Beauchamp family
in 1359, and it was here that Margaret Beauchamp, Duchess of Somerset,
had spent much of her childhood.[1] With its happy family associations, it
is little wonder that the Duchess had chosen Bletsoe as the setting for the
birth of her child in the spring of 1443. When her daughter arrived on 31
May, she chose to name her Margaret, perhaps after herself and in honour
of the infant's paternal grandmother, Margaret Holland. In her own hand
the Duchess carefully noted the arrival of baby Margaret – her only child
by John Beaufort, Duke of Somerset – in her beautifully decorated Book of
Hours, which had originally been commissioned by her father-in-law. In
time, her daughter, Lady Margaret Beaufort, would inherit and treasure this
book, treating it as a family heirloom and using it to record the momentous
events within her own family.[2]

'She came of noble blood lineally descending of King Edward III.'[3] This
summary by John Fisher, Bishop of Rochester, on the prestigious origins
of the baby born at Bletsoe, to whom he became a close friend in later life,
perhaps pinpoints the most significant detail of Margaret's beginnings.
Indeed, to understand Margaret fully and, in particular, how her sense of
her own place in the world matured and made its mark, it is vital to trace
back the line that links her with Edward III – a lineage that is more colourful
than Bishop Fisher made out. Edward himself had become king at the age

1

of fourteen in 1327 when his father, Edward II, had been deposed, and had ruled England until his death in 1377. The fifteenth century would be defined by the bloody conflicts that took place between his descendants, who came to form two rival houses, both of which stemmed from two of Edward's sons: John of Gaunt, founder of the house of Lancaster, and Edmund of Langley, Duke of York and fourth son of Edward III, the founding member of the house of York.

Margaret – who would be one of the most enduring victors of the conflict – was a member of the house of Lancaster. Her royal blood came courtesy of her father, who was the grandson of John of Gaunt (the name being an English take on Ghent, the place of his birth in 1340), himself the third of five surviving sons born to Edward III and Philippa of Hainault.[4] Although he was a younger son, Gaunt had once been the most ambitious and powerful nobleman in the realm, renowned for his courage and widely admired for his military capabilities. Gaunt made three marriages during his life. The first, a love match to Blanche of Lancaster, through which John became the Duke of Lancaster, produced two surviving daughters and a son – a son who would later turn the face of the English monarchy upside down by usurping the throne as Henry IV, in so doing becoming the first of three Lancastrian kings.[5] The second, after Blanche died in 1368, was to Constance, the daughter of the murdered Pedro I 'the Cruel', King of Castile, which gave rise to Gaunt's ambitious pursuit of Castile's throne.[6] The marriage of Gaunt and Constance was unhappy, and it may have been this that prompted him to seek fulfilment elsewhere.[7] Around 1372 he began a passionate affair with Lady Katherine Swynford, the daughter of a knight from Hainault who had been a member of Queen Philippa's household.[8] She had once served in the Duchess Blanche's household and was now governess to Blanche and Gaunt's two daughters, Philippa and Elizabeth.[9]

Like Gaunt, Katherine Swynford had been married before and widowed Her first husband, Hugh Swynford, a knight hailing from the small Lincolnshire estate of Kettlethorpe, died while campaigning with Gaunt in Aquitaine on 13 November 1371, leaving Katherine with two young children to support. She was already connected to Gaunt's household and thus had regular contact with him: at some point, the two began a relationship. Gaunt and Katherine's adulterous affair was widely known by the mid-1370s and continued for many years, resulting in the births of four children: John, Henry, Joan and Thomas.[10] The nature of their parents' relationship rendered these children illegitimate, and they were given the surname Beaufort after the lordship and castle that Gaunt had once owned in Anjou.[11] Unsurprisingly, her husband's infidelity caused Gaunt's wife Constance great distress, and led to tension within their marriage. Matters came to a head in 1381, when Gaunt agreed to end his relationship with Katherine in order to further his claim to the Castilian throne. Their children, however, rendered him unable to sever all ties with her and he continued to support them.

On 24 March 1394, Constance died.[12] She and Gaunt had long been living separate lives, but her death left the path now open for Gaunt to resume his relationship with Katherine Swynford, and it was not long before he did so.

This time there was no reason why it should not be an honourable coupling, and in January 1396 Gaunt and Katherine were married at Lincoln Cathedral. The marriage received the blessing of Gaunt's royal nephew, Richard II, who had succeeded his grandfather Edward III in 1377, and who was fond of Katherine and her children. Just months after their wedding, the Pope declared the couple's marriage valid, and pronounced all of their children – including any that might be born in the future – legitimate. Closer to home, in the Parliament of February 1397 Richard II 'legitimized my lord John Beaufort, his brothers, and his sister'.[13] In one stroke, Margaret's ancestors were transformed from bastard stock to legitimate descendants of the great King Edward III. Despite the Beaufort siblings now being acknowledged as legitimate by law, and all four of them going on to glittering careers, in the years to come they and their descendants were to discover that the stigma of illegitimacy stuck.[14] Indeed, during the reign of Richard III, when the King was eager to discredit Margaret's son, he took care to emphasize that 'his mother

[Margaret] was daughter unto John Duke of Somerset', whose father had, he claimed, been conceived 'in double adultery'. Therefore, 'no title can or may be in him'.[15]

ON 3 FEBRUARY 1399, John of Gaunt died at Leicester Castle at the age of fifty-eight.[16] His son by Blanche, Henry, Earl of Derby, was in exile in Paris following a quarrel with Thomas Mowbray, Duke of Norfolk, who was also in exile due to the two men's intention to duel. In recent years, the reign of Richard II had twisted into tyranny, and the King now refused to allow Henry to inherit the lands that should rightfully have passed to him at his father's death. It was this that prompted Henry to return to England at the head of a military campaign, and he landed at Ravenspur on the coast of Yorkshire in early July. Richard II was on campaign in Ireland with most of his loyal lords, and before long Henry had gathered enough support not only to assert his rights as Duke of Lancaster, but to make a bid for the English throne. Support for Richard crumbled in the face of Henry's army, and having chased him to Conwy Castle in North Wales, Henry successfully captured his royal cousin, taking Richard to the capital where he was imprisoned in the Tower of London. Henry had himself crowned Henry IV on 13 October, and, before long, Richard was sent north to Pontefract Castle – no longer a king but a prisoner. Three months later, in January 1400, the dethroned Richard died: many believed that he had been starved to death, either by his own choice or by the actions of his jailers.[17]

John, the eldest of the Beaufort sons – Margaret Beaufort's grandfather – born somewhere around 1372 or 1373, had been well favoured by Richard II. In 1397, he was created Earl of Somerset, and later that year elevated further to Marquess of Somerset, Marquess of Dorset and Lieutenant of Aquitaine. Further good news was to come when, on 27 September – two days before his elevation to the rank of marquess – he married the King's niece and wealthy heiress Margaret Holland.[18] It was this marriage that would in time help to enhance Margaret Beaufort's position, for she came to inherit many of her grandmother's manors. These in turn ensured that

Margaret became a wealthy heiress, thereby provoking competition for her hand in marriage in a bid to secure a right to her lands.

Throughout the tumult of 1399, John Beaufort had remained loyal to Richard II. Though he was later reconciled to his half-brother, Henry IV, his position nevertheless reverted from Marquess, to Earl of Somerset. In other ways, however, he was well rewarded by the new regime, first becoming Chamberlain of England in 1399 and then Constable of England in 1404. Three years later, the King clarified John Beaufort's status and that of his siblings. On 10 February 1407, Henry IV reaffirmed the legitimacy of the Beauforts, but this time there was a difference. The words *excepta dignitate regali* – 'excepting the royal authority' – were added to the Letters Patent, thereby dictating that the Beauforts' legitimacy did not entitle them to stake a claim to the throne.[19] Given the manner in which Henry had acquired his crown, his measures are unsurprising. Crucially, however, his additions were never passed through Parliament, and thus would emerge as a matter of contention in later years when the legitimacy of the Beauforts became of paramount importance to Margaret and her son – in Henry VII's first Parliament of 1485 he took care to reaffirm Richard II's statute, but unsurprisingly made no mention of Henry IV's added clause. Returning, though, to John Beaufort, his exhaustive efforts in the King's service eventually undermined his health. He died on 16 March 1410 at the hospital of St Katharine by the Tower in London and was buried in Canterbury Cathedral.[20] When Henry IV died in 1413, he too was buried in Canterbury, with Richard Beke designing both his tomb and that of his half-brother.[21]

Margaret Holland did marry again, to Thomas, Duke of Clarence, second son of Henry IV, but she had no more children, meaning that her wealth remained reserved for John Beaufort's children. Together, they had produced six children: four sons and two daughters.[22] Following the death of her eldest son, Henry IV's godson and namesake, Henry, in 1418, John – Margaret Beaufort's father – inherited the earldom of Somerset.[23] His tragic tale was to have far-reaching consequences for Margaret's early life.

John, Earl of Somerset, had been born in 1404, and much of his life would be dictated by politics and war. In 1337, England had become embroiled in a war that came to be known as the Hundred Years' War against its traditional enemy, France. In 1419, when he was at 'a tender age' of around fifteen years old, the young Earl of Somerset travelled to France to engage in military service with his stepfather, Thomas, Duke of Clarence, and his younger brothers Thomas and Edmund.[24] Matters started well for young Somerset when Henry V – the second Lancastrian king and Henry IV's heir – knighted him at Rouen. However, disaster would engulf the family when, on 22 March 1421, Somerset's stepfather Clarence was killed at the Battle of Baugé. Somerset himself and his younger brother Thomas were 'taken prisoner, and kept in close custody for many years'.[25] Somerset was the most valuable of all of the prisoners taken by the French, but numerous attempts to secure his release came to nothing. This was just the beginning of a series of disasters that were set to hover over his career; he would spend over seventeen years in French captivity. His brother Thomas was set at liberty in 1430, but tragically died the following year in battle at Louvier.[26]

When Somerset had been imprisoned for almost eighteen months, news arrived that would change the whole course of the war. On 31 August 1422, Henry V died unexpectedly of dysentery at the Château de Vincennes to the east of Paris.[27] Henry had been just shy of his thirty-sixth birthday, and his death was met with 'great heaviness of all his people'.[28] This was not only due to the continuing war, but also because his heir was 'an infant still in his cradle'.[29]

The nine-month-old baby who now succeeded his father as King of England was Henry V's only child by the French princess, Katherine of Valois. Henry VI had been born on 6 December 1421 at Windsor Castle, around eighteen months after his parents' marriage. He had never been afforded the opportunity to meet his father, who had been campaigning in France at the time of his birth. Just two months after the death of his father, the unbalanced French King Charles VI – Henry VI's maternal grandfather – also died, leaving the infant Henry the ruler of both England and France; although the French would go on to crown their own choice – Henry's uncle – Charles VII. A child of this age was quite clearly incapable of ruling, and Henry's mother, Queen Katherine, was only twenty years old. This may not have been young in terms of other rulers of the period, but her sex and her foreign roots rendered her an unsuitable candidate for a regent, and her husband's English subjects regarded her with considerable suspicion. Instead, the next fifteen years were dominated by power plays between the young King's three uncles – John, Duke of Bedford, Humphrey, Duke of Gloucester, and Henry Beaufort, Bishop of Winchester – as well as by the shifting fortunes of the war in France. It was not until 12 November 1439 that the King – just shy of his sixteenth birthday – declared himself to have come of age.

AT THE TIME of Henry VI's accession, Margaret Beaufort's father, Somerset, was a French prisoner still in the early days of his captivity. Despite desperate pleas to the King's Council begging for action to be taken in order to secure his release, it was not until 1438 that, after a series of complicated and drawn-out negotiations he 'was ransomed for an immense sum of money', £24,000 (£15,000,000).[30] Unsurprisingly, he would claim that his ransom left him 'impoverished', but it was not only money that he had lost.[31] As he emerged from confinement at the age of thirty-four after seventeen years of imprisonment – the longest period of captivity endured by any English aristocrat over the whole course of the Hundred Years' War – his youth had been irretrievably taken from him and his health seems to have been undermined by the experience.[32]

Somerset's captivity and engagement in military action ensured that there had been no time for domesticity, although he had managed to sire a bastard daughter, Tacyn, during his French imprisonment.[33] In 1442 his thoughts at last turned to marriage. His choice of bride was Margaret Beauchamp, who according to Bishop Fisher was 'right noble as well in manners as in blood'.[34] Though it was by no means the sort of prestigious match that one so closely connected to the Crown might have expected, it was at least a respectable choice. Margaret, born around 1420, was the daughter of Sir John Beauchamp and his second wife, Edith Stourton, who resided at Bletsoe Castle in Bedfordshire.[35] Though Margaret's origins were by no means as noble as those of her husband, she was rendered all the more attractive by the fact that in 1421 she had become the heiress of her only brother, John Beauchamp, who had died unmarried and childless. This meant that Margaret inherited all of his lands, including Bletsoe, Lydiard Tregoze in Wiltshire, and other manors in Dorset and Bedfordshire. Though she was a few years Somerset's junior, she was already a widow; her marriage to Sir Oliver St John had produced six children: two sons and four daughters.[36] Sir Oliver had died in France in 1438 – the same year as Somerset's release – leaving his wife with this large brood of young children to support. The need for a male protector was almost certainly the driving force behind Margaret Beauchamp's decision to remarry, although it is unclear how the match with Somerset came about.

The precise date of Somerset and Margaret Beauchamp's wedding is unknown, but it had certainly been concluded by July 1442.[37] The couple can hardly have known one another, yet in no time at all Margaret had become pregnant. Though he was doubtless pleased with the speed at which his new wife had conceived, Somerset's mind was very much occupied with other matters, chiefly finding ways to pay off his crippling ransom. In an effort to raise funds, he had resorted to pledging some of his jewels: his wife later tried to recover a piece that had been sold to a London tailor.[38]

Another opportunity to bring in funds came about when he was appointed to command the English force in a new campaign in France, following Charles VII's invasion of Gascony in 1443.[39] Despite his limited military experience, Somerset negotiated hard in order to reach a suitable agreement. By the early months of 1443 he was busy making preparations to leave England once more. In April the King appointed him captain general of Aquitaine and Normandy, and there was a further honour to come. By act of Parliament, on St George's Day, 'from an earl he was created a duke, and God so ordaining it, was sent upon an expedition in the parts beyond sea'.[40] The new Duke of Somerset was nevertheless conscious that his wife was shortly due to give birth to his first legitimate child, and his forthcoming absence prompted him to make provisions for his unborn heir if 'anything come to my said Lord of Somerset in the said voyage but good'.[41] It was with this in mind that the King agreed that Somerset's wife would be entrusted with the care of their child as opposed to a potential guardian, since 'she should by nature have it in more tenderness than any other creature'.[42] Matters having been settled as far as was possible, Somerset continued with his preparations.

With her husband preparing to depart for France, it is little wonder that the Duchess of Somerset chose the familiar surroundings of Bletsoe as the setting for the birth of her child. It was in this charming house that the infant Margaret Beaufort – sole legitimate heiress of her father – was born in May 1443, and she would spend the early years of her life there in her mother's care, surrounded by her half-siblings, the St Johns. For Margaret's father, however, life was about to take a heart-breaking turn.

There had been high hopes for the French campaign led by the newly created Duke of Somerset, but in a sign of what was to come, it started badly. Having finally met with his troops after a series of delays – perhaps partially accounted for by the birth of his daughter – Somerset left England in July. On 12 August he had reached Cherbourg with a force of approximately seven to ten thousand men – reports differ on the exact number – and he immediately began marching towards Brittany.[43] The campaign, however, would bring nothing but disappointment. Although Somerset succeeded in taking some minor towns, he did not even come close to achieving the success that had been anticipated, and never once engaged with the French army. To make matters worse, he allowed his men to pillage and plunder French towns and villages, and squandered and misused Crown funds in an attempt to replenish his own coffers. His foremost concern seemed to be recovering some of the money he had lost through his ransom, rather than winning glory for his country, and in so doing his actions deeply angered the King. His mission had never been easy, but the campaign had been a dismal failure.

In January 1444, eight months after the birth of his daughter, Somerset returned home. He travelled to London immediately, but his reception was cold. The usually mild-mannered King was outraged with his kinsman, and forgiveness was not forthcoming. Instead, according to a contemporary chronicler, Somerset 'being accused of treason there, was forbidden to appear in the king's presence'.[44] His career was seemingly in tatters, and it was made clear that he was not welcome at court: he had no choice but to withdraw in shame, and he retired to one of his Dorset estates.[45]

It is unclear whether Somerset's wife and infant daughter joined him in Dorset, but given what may have transpired it seems improbable. It was related by a chronicler that in a state of desperation and despair,

> *The noble heart of a man of such high rank upon hearing this most unhappy news, was moved to extreme indignation; and being unable to bear the stain of so great a disgrace, he accelerated his death by putting an end to his existence, it is generally said; preferring thus to cut short his sorrow, rather than pass a life of misery, labouring under so disgraceful a charge.*[46]

Margaret was just a few days shy of her first birthday when her father died on 27 May 1444, a tragedy that her mother would record in her Book of Hours. Although suicide was considered to be a mortal sin, the Croyland Chronicler – whose author was well placed to know the truth of the matter – shockingly claimed that this was the manner in which the disgraced man had met his death. Other contemporary sources ignore the matter entirely, simply stating that Somerset died without making further comment.[47] This strongly suggests that he did indeed commit suicide, and if this was the case then, given contemporary views, it says much about his tormented state of mind. The manner in which Margaret's father could have met his death was not spoken of openly – another indication of the uncomfortable circumstances – but as Margaret grew, she would have become aware of the rumours, although she never addressed them – in public, at least. Throughout her life, Margaret's deceased father evidently held some place in her heart, for she would later order prayers to be said for his soul at Cambridge. Whatever the true circumstances, the loss of Somerset at such an early point changed the course of his infant daughter's life considerably.

It was in the Saxon minster at Wimborne, burial place of the Saxon King Ethelred and a royal peculiar (a church that falls under the direct jurisdiction of the Crown) since 1318, that Somerset was laid to rest.[48] At his daughter's cost and instruction, a magnificent tomb of Purbeck marble and Dorset limestone was later erected to his memory and that of his widow, still to be seen in the minster today.[49] Fascinatingly, the effigies of Margaret's parents show them clasping hands – clearly indicative of how Margaret herself chose to view her parents' marriage, in spite of its short duration. A memorial window depicting the couple and their daughter could once also be seen in the East Window, but was moved to All Saints' Church, Landbeach, in the eighteenth century. Here the beautiful jumbled glass featuring the only known likeness of Margaret in her youth can be seen.[50] Margaret later founded a chantry within Wimborne Minster, and of the many she endowed, this would be the most personal, giving some indication as to the sorrow she felt for the loss of a father who she had never known.[51]

At the time of his death, the Duchess was once again pregnant, so the couple had clearly been reunited at some point following Somerset's return from France.[52] Possibly the shock of her husband's death caused her to miscarry, or else the child was stillborn or died young, for nothing further is heard of this pregnancy. Though her father was dead, his lineage continued through Margaret, who was proud to be his daughter. As Somerset's only legitimate child, Margaret – though just an infant – became a wealthy heiress. He may have struggled to recover from his imprisonment financially, but in landed terms Somerset's estates had been vast, in large part inherited from his mother, Margaret Holland. Among others, he owned lands in the counties of Kent, Worcestershire, Lincolnshire, Norfolk, Somerset, Essex and Sussex. However, his death left Margaret – and her mother – vulnerable, and without a male protector in the vicious and backbiting world of fifteenth-century politics. The young heiress's inheritance made her a precious – and therefore vulnerable – commodity, and was something that powerful men in the realm would seek shortly to exploit. Moreover, her royal blood that stemmed back to Edward III meant that she held further appeal, although the shaky legitimacy of the Beauforts would follow her in later years when her family became closer to the throne. She was nevertheless proud of her connections, and would later invest money and great energy into proclaiming them. In 1444, though, she was still a little girl, less than a year old. A little girl who had no voice and no say in her own future: a pawn in a much bigger game whose fate – at this time, at least – seemed set to be decided by others. Within no time at all it became clear that the decisions made in Margaret's girlhood would affect the whole course of the rest of her life.

CHAPTER 2

Of Singular Wisdom

T HE 31 MAY 1444 marked Margaret's first birthday. Her father had only been dead for four days, yet in that time the King, residing at the royal castle of Berkhamsted in Hertfordshire, had already made a momentous decision about the infant's future.

And forasmuch as our cousin the Duke of Somerset is now late passed to God's mercy, the which hath a daughter and heir to succeed him, of full tender age called Margaret. We considering the notable services that our cousin the earl of Suffolk hath done unto us, and tendering him therefore the more specially as reason will, have of our grace and especial proper motion and mere deliberation granted unto him to have the ward and marriage of the said Margaret, without anything.[1]

Prior to Margaret's birth the King had agreed with her father that the Duchess of Somerset should have control of Margaret's care-taking, but since then the Duke had fallen into disgrace. Henry VI felt no compunction to uphold the agreement, and Somerset's death was recast as an opportunity – as a direct descendant of John of Gaunt, the child was, after all, a member of the royal family. Though her male Beaufort relatives were regarded as superior in rank by right of their sex, Margaret herself was now the most senior member of the Beaufort family in the female line. Furthermore, her familial relationship to the King – her father's second cousin – and her lack of a male guardian had not gone unnoticed, and there were many who were eager to obtain her valuable wardship in order to secure an interest in her lands. Bishop Fisher later

13

confirmed that as a result of the 'likelihood of inheritance many sued to have had her to marriage'.[2]

The man that Henry VI chose to settle his cousin's wardship upon, William de la Pole, Earl of Suffolk, was one of his great favourites. Described by Fisher as 'a man of great experience', Suffolk had been born in 1396 and was the son of Michael de la Pole, second Earl of Suffolk, and Katherine Stafford.[3] Like Margaret's father, Suffolk had been a soldier who had loyally served Henry V throughout the French campaign.[4] Suffolk's position was bolstered by his marriage in 1430 to the formidable Alice Chaucer, dowager Countess of Salisbury and granddaughter of the famous poet, Geoffrey.[5] Like that of Margaret's parents, their marriage would produce just one child, a son, born in 1442. With a lone precious heir, it was only natural that Suffolk considered his son's marital prospects to be of the greatest importance. Fisher claimed that it was with this in mind that his thoughts turned to Margaret, and he 'most diligently procured to have had her for his son and heir'.[6] This may have been Suffolk's initial thought and it did indeed eventually come to pass, but at one time his plans for his son's future lay elsewhere. In 1446 he successfully obtained the wardship of Anne Beauchamp, the sole heir of Henry Beauchamp, Duke of Warwick.[7] Sadly, Anne died in 1449 while still a young girl, bringing all hopes of a future matrimonial alliance to an abrupt end. These earlier plans would later gain grave significance for Suffolk, but this was all still to come. In the meantime, in 1449, Suffolk's attentions definitively fell upon Margaret, though there is no evidence that he ever even met her or that she left her mother's care.[8] He was conscious, nonetheless, that she was a wealthy young heiress with prestigious connections, and lands that he had been granted the keeping of upon Somerset's death.[9] On Margaret's side, Suffolk's standing with the King made an alliance with the de la Pole family honourable, but the advantage was mostly theirs – unlike Margaret, they had no royal blood, being descended from wool merchants.[10]

AT THE TIME of Margaret Beaufort's birth, her kinsman and king, Henry VI, was twenty-one. To the disappointment of his subjects, as he had grown he had shown none of the attributes of his warrior father, and it had long been clear that, in terms of the standards of the time, he was of weak character. The Tudor historian Polydore Vergil would later state that in adulthood Henry was 'tall of stature, slender of body', and was 'of comely visage', but his temperament did not match his appearance.[11] Vergil explained that he did 'abhor all vices both of body and mind', and as such was 'a condemner of all those things which commonly corrupt the minds of men'.[12] He was learned, and education was one of his greatest passions – it was something he and Margaret would have in common. Neither was this the only interest they shared, for, like Margaret, the King was also exceptionally pious, and his chaplain, John Blacman, later recalled that Henry was 'more given to God and to devout prayer than to handling worldly and temporal things, or practising vain sports and pursuits'.[13] Instead, he was 'continually occupied either in prayer or the reading of the scriptures or of chronicles', preferring scholarly activities to governance.[14] Although Henry's piety was admirable, in other respects he was very different from what the English people had come to expect of a medieval king, and displayed no leadership qualities. Neither did he have any desire for military glory in the same manner as his father had done. He has been described as 'perhaps the greatest disaster ever to occupy the English throne', and the inescapable truth is that he was indeed highly unsuited to the burdens of kingship that had been thrust upon him in his babyhood.[15] He was, nevertheless, an exceptionally kind man, a quality that Margaret cannot have failed to recognize – and undoubtedly appreciated – when she met him for the first time during her girlhood.

John Blacman recalled that his royal master 'was chaste and pure from the beginning of his days', and 'eschewed all licentiousness in word or deed while he was young'.[16] Nevertheless, it was expected that the King should take a wife in order to provide for the future security of the realm, and Henry was enthusiastic about the prospect. In 1441 his thoughts turned to marriage, and he received portraits of several potential brides. In Henry's mind the ideal candidate was one who would bring the opportunity for peace with France, and in the autumn of 1443 his uncle Henry Beaufort – by now a Cardinal who enjoyed huge influence with the young King – seemed to have found the perfect choice. His suggestion was Margaret of Anjou, the niece of Charles VII and daughter of René of Anjou, the titular king of Naples, Sicily and Jerusalem (titular because, although he adopted these titles, they meant nothing and he ruled none of these kingdoms).[17] In May 1444 Suffolk agreed the Treaty of Tours, whereby Margaret of Anjou would be married to Henry VI and the English would hand back the regions of Maine and Anjou. This was hugely unpopular in England, and matters were made worse by René's poverty, which rendered him unable to provide a dowry for his daughter. Regardless of these flaws, the deal had been done.

Margaret Beaufort was just shy of her second birthday when, on 9 April 1445, the *Cock John* – part of an entourage consisting of fifty-six ships – docked on the south coast of England. On board was precious cargo in the form of the King's bride-to-be, Margaret of Anjou, who had been escorted by Margaret Beaufort's guardian, Suffolk, and his wife Alice.[18] Her arrival signified a policy of peace between England and France, but it was not one that was destined to last. It had not been an easy crossing for the fifteen-year-old French princess, who was feeling so unwell upon landing that Suffolk had to carry her ashore. When she had recovered from the treacherous journey, the Princess made her way to thirteenth-century Titchfield Abbey in Hampshire.[19] It was here that, on 23 April, Bishop William Ayscough solemnized her marriage to Henry VI: England had a new queen.

The Milanese ambassador later told his mistress that an Englishman had described the new queen as being 'a most handsome woman, though somewhat dark'.[20] In truth there are few indications as to Margaret of Anjou's looks, but all surviving images of her portray her with blonde hair: whatever the truth, the King was certainly pleased with his new bride.[21] He had spent the princely sum of £200 (£128,600) on Margaret's wedding ring, which he paid his goldsmith Matthew Philip to refashion from the ring that he had been consecrated with at his coronation in Paris.[22] He seems to have felt an immediate affection for his wife and continued to lavish her with gifts, including costly jewels – at Titchfield she had even been presented with a lion, which was later placed in the menagerie at the Tower.[23] An exorbitant sum was laid out in preparation for the Queen's coronation, which included the commissioning of new jewels, and which took place at Westminster Abbey on 30 May. Unusually, Henry it seems was also faithful to his wife; Blacman claimed that 'he kept his marriage vow wholly and sincerely, even in the absences of the lady, which were sometimes very long: never dealing unchastely with any other woman'.[24] It was a mutual feeling, and in personal terms the royal couple got along well and were extremely loyal to one another. A much stronger character than her husband, Margaret of Anjou is undoubtedly one of the most controversial queens ever to have worn the English crown. As Gristwood accurately summarized, 'few queens of England have so divided opinion'.[25] She is frequently portrayed as a woman who dominated her husband in an era when women were expected to be subservient to their male superiors, but, as will become clear, much of Margaret's poor reputation is undeserved. Her hand was ultimately forced by subsequent events, many of which were beyond her control. Though one contemporary wrote that 'the Queen is a great and strong laboured woman', her jewel accounts show a different side to her character and bear testament to her generosity – particularly to her servants and those who were loyal to her.[26] The events of Henry and Margaret's reign would have momentous and surprising consequences for Margaret Beaufort and many of those involved in her story. Even so, her own loyalty to her kinsman and his controversial queen – though masked on occasion – seems never to have been shaken.

Members of Margaret Beaufort's family had been by the young King's side from the moment of his accession, chiefly Cardinal Beaufort, Margaret's great-uncle, who would play a prominent role in the affairs of the realm until his death in 1447.[27] Following Cardinal Beaufort's death, Margaret's uncle, Edmund Beaufort – the youngest and only surviving of Somerset's brothers – assumed the role of head of the family. Edmund was around three years younger than Margaret's father, and during Somerset's French imprisonment had distinguished himself so well in military affairs that he had been made first Earl and then Marquess of Dorset. He also had his own family, for in the 1430s he had been married to the widowed Eleanor Beauchamp, daughter of the Earl of Warwick, by whom he had many children.[28] Following Somerset's death, Edmund maintained contact with his sister-in-law, the Duchess of Somerset.[29] He was steadfastly loyal to Henry VI and, unlike his elder brother, ingratiated himself with the King and managed to retain his trust. Henry relied on him heavily, and Edmund also worked closely with Suffolk: together the two men headed the party in Council that favoured peace with France. On 31 March 1448, when Margaret was four years old, her uncle Edmund was rewarded for his loyalty when he was created Duke of Somerset, the title once held by her father. Though he would become one of the King's staunchest allies during some of his most trying days, he would pay a high price for it.

MARGARET BEAUFORT'S DEVOTION to her family, a quality of character that endowed her with steely resolution and direction throughout the trials of her life, was clearly instilled in her during her youth. Despite the tragic circumstances in which her father died, Margaret does seem to have enjoyed a happy childhood. The family network that surrounded her was always very strong, and remained so until the end of her life. Raised by her mother alongside her half-siblings, the St Johns, and her father's bastard daughter Tacyn, Margaret would always remain close to her half-brothers and sisters.[30] Their appearances in her accounts bear witness to the bond they shared – the names of Edith, John, Mary, Elizabeth, Oliver and Margaret St John all appear at various points. While at Bletsoe, Margaret worked on an embroidery that depicted the lineage of the St John family: she would later present this to her half-brother, John St John, on the occasion of his marriage in 1498.[31] Given her many siblings, Margaret would never have lacked for company during her childhood. Unlike them, however, Margaret alone could boast of her royal lineage and connections: it was her career that had the most potential.

As a small child, Margaret could never have comprehended her own significance. Neither, in her early days, would this have been of great import to her, applying herself to her lessons being her foremost concern. Not all girls in this period were given an education; that Margaret was shows that her mother recognized how important it would be to her daughter's future. Practical skills, such as managing lands and estates – in which Margaret later took such an interest – were a crucial part of a noblewoman's life and would have been expected when Margaret assumed the role of a wife. She was also a skilled embroiderer, and her family were great music lovers. In later life, regular payments for minstrels appear in her accounts – they were not always her own; those of the King, Queen, her granddaughter Princess Mary, and the Abbot of St Albans are mentioned, among others. Singers from the King's chapel sometimes performed for her entertainment, and the children of her chapel at Collyweston often sang for her.

Not all of Margaret's lessons were concerned with the practical. Her friend and admirer Bishop Fisher would later recollect that 'she was of singular wisdom', and that 'right studious she was in books which she had in great number both in English and in French'.[32] This was not mere flattery, for Margaret owned books in both languages and later commissioned them too. An understanding of French was considered to be both desirable and necessary for men and women – particularly those with a future career at court – but Margaret, not content with French alone, was keen to learn another language. According to Fisher, 'Full often she complained that in her youth she had not given her to ye understanding of Latin wherein she had a little.'[33] Margaret's thirst for knowledge was impressive; perhaps she inherited some of the fervour of her paternal grandmother, Margaret Holland, who had been a great literary patron with a variety of scholarly interests. Further evidence of Margaret's intellectual pursuits is given by her later inclusion in the will of her mother-in-law, the Duchess of Buckingham, from whom she had borrowed books on occasion.[34] The Duchess was clearly aware of Margaret's enthusiasm, and bequeathed her several items: 'To her daughter Richmond a book of English, being a legend of Saints; a book of French, called Lucun; another book of French, of the Epistles and Gospels; and a devotional book with clasps of silver gilt, covered with purple velvet.'[35] As the printing press had yet to be established, books were valuable commodities that were all carefully handwritten, and were therefore particularly precious: Margaret would treasure hers. She would later amass an impressive library consisting of all manner of subjects, but she had evidently cherished a love of books since childhood.

Margaret's interests went further than reading in the French language: as an adult she translated works from French to English. The most notable examples of her work are *The Mirror of Gold for the Sinful Soul*, a religious work that had first been translated from Latin to French, and that would earn Margaret great admiration, and Thomas à Kempis's *Imitation of Christ*.[36] Much later, Margaret's great-granddaughter Elizabeth I would skilfully emulate similar projects. Her mother, the Duchess of Somerset, to whom 'she was a very daughter in all noble manners', supervised all of Margaret's lessons and must have been delighted at the attentiveness she had shown in her education.[37]

The primary setting for Margaret's childhood was Bletsoe, the Bedfordshire place of her birth, where – as Margaret's nineteenth-century biographer Caroline Halsted tells us, Margaret's mother lived in 'great pomp'.[38] Margaret would therefore soon have become accustomed with the entertainers that would have graced the Duchess's household – perhaps singing, dancing and performing for the family's amusement. She later also showed a great fondness for finery, no doubt reflecting her mother's enjoyment of luxury fabrics and other expensive items. Margaret would also have become familiar with the medieval church of St Mary the Virgin in the village, which boasted a splendid fifteenth-century wall painting of St George and the Dragon. Her mother was pious, and may have instilled the importance of religion in her daughter. From the beginning of Margaret's life, religion played an integral role that would become increasingly apparent as she grew, offering her both comfort and reassurance. She may also have been influenced by her half-sister, Margaret St John, who became a nun and later Abbess of Shaftesbury.[39]

When not at Bletsoe, Margaret and her mother's household would often reside at Maxey Castle. Located in the village of Maxey in rural Northamptonshire, the castle was another residence that had formed a part of the Duchess's inheritance.[40] Today, all that survives is the partial remains of the double moat that once surrounded it. It was in these residences that the Duchess felt most at home, and chose to raise her growing family.

Just under two years after the death of Margaret's father, the Duchess of Somerset fell in love. The object of her affection was Sir John Neville, and the relationship was serious. So much so that the couple decided to wed.[41] As they had familial ties, they applied for a dispensation from the Pope in which they claimed that they were motivated by 'the ardour of a singular affection'.[42] The Duchess, being a widow, evidently felt vulnerable, as the dispensation stated that the couple were prompted by 'the conserving of the divers domains which the said Margaret holds by right of dower in several dioceses, and for several other reasonable causes'.[43] The dispensation was duly granted on 5 April 1446, but for some unknown reason the marriage never took place. It is possible that Sir John Neville died, for there is no further mention of him in contemporary sources and nothing in regards to the Duchess of Somerset. The personal reasons that prompted the Duchess's desire to marry were ones that her daughter would never experience, for Margaret herself seems never to have fallen in love. Her marriages, instead, were all later made for practical considerations. Young Margaret was witness to her mother's vulnerable circumstances at this time, and would subsequently find herself in a similar position. Unlike her mother, she would be able to use her own power and influence to resolve the situation.

Whatever the circumstances surrounding the Duchess of Somerset's failure to marry Neville, by the following year she had moved on. On 14 April 1447, when Margaret was nearly four years old, her mother was granted a licence to remarry, taking as her third husband Lionel, or Leo, Lord Welles.[44] Margaret grew to be fond of the son – her half-brother – that her mother's third marriage produced, but nothing is known of her relationship with her stepfather. Lord Welles was a loyal supporter of Margaret's paternal uncle, Edmund Beaufort, so it must have been a choice of which he approved and perhaps even had some hand in arranging. Lionel was also close to the King, in whose favour he had risen steadily. In the same manner as many of his contemporaries, he had served in military campaigns before joining the

King's household, and in 1438 he took up the post of Lord Lieutenant of Ireland. Like Margaret's mother, Welles had been married before, to Joan Waterton, the daughter of a trusted retainer of John of Gaunt by whom he had one son and four daughters.[45] At a stroke, therefore, Margaret could add five step-siblings to her growing family, and there is evidence that she retained relationships with some of these in later life. Margaret had always been the baby in her family, but around 1450, when she was seven years old, she was joined in the nursery by a half-brother, John. He was the last child that the Duchess of Somerset would bear, and it seems probable that he was named in honour of John of Gaunt in a proud declaration of the family's connections.

It is unclear how great a role her new stepfather took in Margaret's upbringing, but as he had his own blossoming career to occupy his time, it is unlikely that it was particularly profound. Decisions concerning Margaret's future had been settled upon Suffolk, so there was no reason for Lord Welles to be involved in this. The complexities of her situation, and what her future alliance with Suffolk's heir meant, would have begun to come clear to young Margaret – not yet six years old – when, early in 1450, some time between 28 January and 7 February, she underwent a form of marriage ceremony with John de la Pole. Given the tender years of the bride and groom, who was just a year older than Margaret, the ceremony was never consummated and was instead *per verba legitime de presenti* – what would be termed a common-law marriage in the modern world. This was as far as the relationship would ever go, and in spite of the words that had passed between them, Margaret never classified John de la Pole as her husband; contemporaries instead commonly referred to Edmund Tudor as 'her first husband'.[46] Likewise, John de la Pole, who lived until 1492 and whose descendants became dangerously entangled with Margaret's own, never claimed that the contrary was true. From what would soon transpire, however, it is evident that others thought differently.

THE SAME YEAR that Margaret's wedding ceremony took place, matters in England took a dangerous turn. Henry VI's ineptitude in governing his kingdom effectively was plain for all to see, and he was easily influenced and manipulated by those around him – including Somerset and Suffolk. This had led to huge corruption and greed within the court, and it had not gone unnoticed by the common people. Henry had shown no interest in the military affairs of England, lacking both the understanding and the experience to command his own army in France. Things had been going from bad to worse for the English in recent years: in October 1449, with Somerset in command of the King's forces, disaster had struck when Rouen fell to the French army. It marked the beginning of a serious downward spiral from which there would be no hope of return, for the following July Somerset also surrendered Caen. By the end of August 1450, there were just two remaining English possessions in France: Calais and Aquitaine.

Margaret's guardian Suffolk – now a duke – had long been unpopular in England and had been apportioned much of the blame for England's wars with France by reason of his policy of peace and promoting Henry VI's marriage with a dowerless princess. Although Suffolk retained the King and Queen's favour, Henry was under great pressure from the Duke's enemies to punish him, and the common people were also crying out for his blood. Suffolk desperately protested his loyalty, citing that both his father and his brothers had died in royal service, while he himself had 'borne arms for 34 winters in the time of the king your father and your own time'.[47] He steadfastly declared, 'I may die protesting that I have always been true to you, sovereign lord, and to your land, and to your prosperity and welfare.'[48] At the beginning of 1450, matters came to a head, and in spite of his protestations of innocence, on 28 January Suffolk was impeached by Parliament – the sense of panic as to what his fate might be no doubt hastened the need to ensure the security of his heir, and thus prompted the marriage of his son to Margaret. Outraged that he had not been punished further, the Commons demanded his arrest, leaving the King with little choice but to have his favourite placed in the Tower. Suffolk appeared before Henry on 13 March, accused of having 'falsely and traitorously plotted, contrived, proposed, envisaged, performed and committed various high, great, heinous and horrible treasons', but firmly denied all of the charges brought against him.[49] These included the suggestion that he had intended to overthrow the King and replace him with his own son, John. His accusers claimed that the Duke, having procured Margaret's wardship, was

> *proposing to marry her to his said son, claiming and pretending her to be the next to inherit the crown of this your realm, for want of an heir from you, sovereign lord, in order to accomplish his said traitorous purpose and intention; whereupon the same duke of Suffolk, since the time of his arrest, has caused the said Margaret to be married to his said son.*[50]

There is no evidence to suggest that Suffolk ever had any such intentions, but even in her early years Margaret's royal lineage was well understood, regarded as either an opportunity or a threat. On his knees before the King, Suffolk vehemently denied the accusations made against him, answering that

> *as for the second part of the first article, it is contrary to law and reason to consider the said Margaret so close to the crown; and for his acquittal, he had told to a large number of the lords that if the duke of Warwick's daughter had lived he had intended to marry his son to her and not to the said Margaret.*[51]

He was desperate to do all that he could in order to show that Margaret's lineage was of no interest to him, and that he had certainly not intended to manipulate it to his advantage. Indeed, in order to secure a handsome inheritance for his son, Margaret's lands held far greater appeal to him than her bloodline. This was, though, just one of many charges levelled against him. Neither the King nor his nobles had any wish to drag the matter out in public, which would necessarily ensue if Suffolk were put on trial. Instead, as of 1 May, Suffolk was forced into exile from both England and France for five years.

As the Duke prepared to leave England, across the realm news of his exoneration from capital punishment spread, serving to inflame public anger against him. On 30 April – just a month before Margaret's seventh birthday – he set sail for Flanders, but he did not make it far. Before long a vessel, the *Nicholas of the Tower*, intercepted his ship, and it quickly became clear that those on board were not Suffolk's friends. The unfortunate Duke was taken on board, where he was immediately bade 'Welcome Traitor'.[52] He was then forced to undergo the humiliating spectacle of a mock trial in which the outcome was a foregone conclusion. A correspondent of the Pastons – a Norfolk gentry family through whose copious surviving letters we owe a wealth of information about the tumultuous events of the fifteenth century – reported that Suffolk was 'drawn out of the great ship into the boat, and there was an axe and a stock; and one of the lewdest of the ship bade him lay down his head'.[53] Then, with a rusty sword, he 'smote off his head within half a dozen strokes', before stealing his fine clothes.[54] His mutilated body was thrown overboard and washed up on the shores of Dover on 2 May. The disgraced Duke's mutilated remains were laid to rest in the Church of St Andrew at Wingfield, Suffolk, where his father had also been buried.[55] Though Suffolk's brutal murder shocked many, few of his contemporaries save for the King and the distraught Queen – to whom Suffolk had been somewhat of a father figure – mourned his passing.

Margaret was probably too young to remember much about the fate of her guardian, who it is possible that she had never met. However, in the immediate aftermath of Suffolk's disgrace and murder, she remained married – in name – to his son. On 18 August, three months after the horrendous events that were staged on board the *Nicholas of the Tower*, Pope Nicholas V issued a dispensation to Margaret and her husband. This was in response to their petition – which is likely to have stemmed from their concerned mothers – that 'they formerly contracted marriage *per verba legitime de presenti* in ignorance that they were related in the fourth and fourth degrees of kindred'.[56] Evidently both parties were eager for the youngsters to remain married, for the petition had claimed that if the young couple were to divorce, 'grave dissensions and scandals would probably be stirred up between their parents and friends'.[57] Perhaps there had been concern as to the impact Suffolk's death would have on the marriage of these two young people, and as such it was feared that it would be annulled – which according to the petition was clearly not the hoped-for outcome. As a result of the petition, the Pope decreed that the youngsters were to 'remain in the said marriage, notwithstanding the said impediment. The Pope hereby decrees their offspring, if any, and that to be born legitimate.'[58] For the time being, however, the marriage was to remain as it had been made: *per verba legitime de presenti* – a marriage of words, rather than deed.

SUFFOLK'S MURDER TURNED out to be the first in a series of events in 1450 and beyond that would turn the country upside down. Though the unpopular Duke was now gone, many of the problems for which he had been blamed were not. The Crown was completely bankrupt, resulting in harsh taxation, and corruption and greed around the King remained rife. Henry VI's inability to deal with these issues only made matters worse, and nobody had any faith in his capabilities as a leader. The commoners had had enough, and in May a rebellion broke out in Kent. Led by one Jack Cade, the rebels began to march on London. The rebellion posed a very real threat to Henry VI and his government, and Cade demanded that the King dismiss all of his corrupt advisors.[59] It is highly improbable that Margaret, almost seven years old, would have been in the capital at this time, but she may nevertheless have become aware of the tension spreading across the country. The rebellion was eventually crushed having achieved nothing, many of Cade's men accepting a pardon issued by the King. Cade himself was mortally wounded in the scuffle to capture him, and thus avoided meeting a traitor's death. Order was restored, but tensions in the country were still running high.

The death of Margaret's father-in-law, Suffolk, left the way clear for her uncle Somerset to assume a more powerful role in government. But despite the favour in which both the King and Queen held him, Somerset had a rival:

Richard, Duke of York. York's father, Richard, Earl of Cambridge, was the son of Edward III's fourth son, Edmund of Langley, whilst his mother, Anne Mortimer, was the great-granddaughter of the King's second son, Lionel, Duke of Clarence. Such prestigious ancestry gave York a claim to the throne – and a strong one at that. In appearance York was short and unremarkable, but he was extremely intelligent and well respected, if not particularly amiable. His marriage to Cecily Neville, the mother of Margaret's great-aunt Joan Beaufort, with whom he would sire thirteen children, served to heighten York's power and ambition. Having been appointed Lieutenant General of France on 2 July 1440 – the second time that he had been given a military command there – York had in recent years spent much of his time in France, gaining valuable military experience there. His eldest son, Edward, was born in the French city of Rouen on 28 April 1442 – a son whose future would impact directly not only on Margaret Beaufort, but also on the lives of England's subjects.

York was greatly disliked and feared by Queen Margaret on account of his open opposition to some of the King's policies and favourites. In 1447 he had therefore been created Lieutenant of Ireland – a post that had once been occupied by Margaret's stepfather, Lord Welles – in order to keep him out of the way. He sailed for Ireland in the summer of 1449, but having spent a fortune of his own money during his years in military service – for which he had never been recompensed – he was becoming increasingly alienated from the King's regime. To make matters worse, the Queen's preference for Somerset was clear for all to see, as were her attempts to push York out of a role in government. By the autumn of 1450, like many of the King's subjects, York had had enough. In September he returned from Ireland and demanded that the King's traitorous advisors be removed – chiefly Somerset. York was popular with the common people, who believed that he was genuinely doing his best to restore order to their country. By contrast, the Queen and Somerset suspected that York's motives were more ominous – after all, he had a good claim to the throne in his own right, and the Queen had yet to bear her husband an heir.

York was not alone in his concerns for the government, and there were many who saw that the King had lost any vestige of control. On 1 December Somerset was impeached by Parliament and taken to the Tower. But it would not last long, for both the King and Queen refused to allow this, and soon Somerset was once more a free man. In January 1451 Parliament demanded his removal, but still the King refused to renounce his favourite. Throughout the turmoil, Margaret's family remained unquestionably loyal to Henry VI. By now her stepfather Lord Welles was mostly absent, having been appointed Joint Deputy of Calais in 1451, alongside Richard Wydeville, Earl Rivers. There he would remain until 1455. There is no indication that he took his wife and stepchildren with him or that they even visited, although it is certainly possible.

In 1452 the tension grew worse, and in February York – now desperate to force the King into action – prepared for armed resistance. By this time the Queen and Somerset had been trying to convince Henry VI that York was intent upon taking his throne, and matters were not helped when the Duke began marching with a force towards London. It was an unpopular move, and though Henry pardoned York for taking up arms, the Duke now found himself excluded from politics and utterly humiliated. But that was not an end to his disgruntlement, and matters would soon become far worse.

It was against this backdrop of foreign war and political tension in a country that was swiftly being torn apart by inner strife, bankruptcy and corruption that Margaret Beaufort was raised. Far away initially from the hub of the tension, secluded in her mother's homes, Margaret would before long join her kinsmen and become fully immersed in the intrigues of the court, and with it the problems that were to envelop the country and her family – it was a destiny from which there was no escape.

CHAPTER 3

A Marvellous Thing

WHEN MARGARET WAS just a few months shy of her tenth birthday, in February 1453 the King commanded her mother to attend the court in London, bringing her daughter with her. This is likely to have been the first occasion on which Margaret had visited court, and possibly also London. If so, its bustling, overcrowded streets would have come as a great contrast to the quiet and peaceful existence she had been living in the Bedfordshire and Northamptonshire countryside. Dominating the skyline was the cathedral of Old St Paul's where her ancestor John of Gaunt lay entombed, and which had one of the tallest spires in Europe. Elsewhere, the banks of the Thames were lined with the resplendent houses of the nobility, with sprawling gardens that stretched down to the river, while the rest of the city was a maze of twisting streets bursting with houses and shops where the Londoners peddled their wares. The Palace of Westminster was the King's primary residence, located next to the magnificent abbey where England's monarchs were traditionally anointed. It is likely to have been here that Margaret was brought for what was almost certainly the first occasion on which she met her royal kinsman.

As Margaret was brought into the King's presence, she was confronted with a kindly thirty-one-year-old man who did not conform to the typical vision of a king. A sixteenth-century portrait of Henry that appeared in Henry VIII's inventory (perhaps based on a lost original) shows a richly dressed man with a thin face and dark hair.[1] Though the allures of fine clothes and costly jewels had once appealed to Henry, it was well known, as Blacman tells us, that from the King's youth 'he always wore round-toed shoes and boots like a farmer's'.[2] These were coupled with 'a long gown with a rolled hood like a townsman, and a full coat reaching below his knees', and he rejected all of the fashionable and costly garments that were available to the highest ranks of society.[3] Even on the feast days of the year, when custom dictated he should don his crown, Henry was known to wear a hair shirt 'that by its roughness his body might be restrained from excess'.[4]

The King's reason for summoning his child cousin to court was simple: though Margaret had been married to the heir of the Duke of Suffolk, it had been a marriage of words only – easily dissolvable. The King had now decided – almost certainly at his own instigation – that the young couple should divorce, and so Margaret parted ways with John de la Pole, the child husband whom she had never known.

Intriguingly, however, a story later relayed by Bishop Fisher, who learned of it from Margaret herself, indicates that she may have had some choice in the matter. Being 'not fully nine years old', as Fisher remembered, Margaret was still a child.[5] He related that another candidate for her hand had been presented, for Henry VI 'did make means for Edmund his brother, then the Earl of Richmond'.[6] Margaret, however, being 'doubtful in her mind what she were best to do', had 'asked counsel of an old gentlewoman whom she much loved and trusted'.[7] The identity of this gentlewoman is unknown, but it suggests that Margaret had a choice in the identity of her groom. If this story is true, then she was clearly torn between John de la Pole and the other candidate. Accordingly, the unnamed gentlewoman advised her to 'commend herself to Saint Nicholas ye patron and helper of all true maidens, and to beseech him to put in her mind what she were best to do'.[8] This was, so Fisher says, advice that the young and pious Margaret took to heart, and so 'she followed and made her prayer so full often, but specially at night when she should ye morrow after make answer of her mind determinedly'.[9] He continues, 'A marvellous thing that same night as I have heard her tell many a time, as she lay in prayer calling upon Saint Nicholas, whether sleeping or waking she could not assure, but about 4 of ye clock in the morning one appeared unto her arrayed like a bishop, and naming unto her Edmund had take him unto her husband.'[10] Margaret's reason for appealing to St Nicholas could be explained by the fact that he was believed to be the patron saint of children, as well as being known for performing miracles. Whatever the rationale, it is unsurprising in the light of later events that she would tell such a tale, in so doing constructing a narrative around this time in her life whereby her fate was led by both God and destiny. It was also a story that would later be recounted by others, so was evidently well known. While the narrative was clearly of use in supporting Margaret's ambitions, her own piety lends strong credence to her genuinely believing she had indeed had a vision. Even at this point in her life, she was deeply committed to her religion. And it pointed her very firmly in one direction. For it was 'by this means she did incline her mind unto Edmund ye King's brother and Earl of Richmond'.[11] In truth, whatever spin Margaret later added, it is improbable that the King would have allowed her to make any other choice: he now arranged for her wardship to be reassigned to his half-brothers, Edmund and Jasper Tudor.

Henry VI was well aware of Margaret's worth as a marital pawn, and with Suffolk now dead and Margaret's marriage to his son unconsummated, there seemed to be no reason why that arrangement could not be broken without complications. Margaret evidently agreed. The plan was that Margaret was to wed one of the Tudor brothers, who were both in their early twenties, and the one chosen was Edmund, the elder. Edmund would thus accumulate all of the lands that Margaret had inherited upon the death of her father. It is unclear from where the impetus for Margaret's second marriage stemmed – whether from Henry VI or Edmund Tudor himself – but it was advantageous for all parties. Marriage to an heiress was often a convenient means of boosting one's income and power; Margaret would have benefited from securing her future to one so personally close to the King.

Both Edmund and his younger brother Jasper were to play pivotal roles in Margaret's life. Edmund's would be brief, but Margaret would ensure that his legacy was never forgotten. The Tudor brothers were Henry VI's younger half-brothers, for though they shared the same mother in Katherine of Valois, on their father's side their blood was neither royal nor noble. Following the death of her husband Henry V in 1422, Katherine of Valois had been left a young widow and soon became a willing participant in a dalliance with a squire named Owen Tudor. It has been claimed that the couple were married, but there is no evidence to confirm this. In the Parliament of 1427 it was declared that 'no man of whatever estate or condition make contract of betrothal or matrimony to marry himself to the queen of England without the special licence and assent of the king'.[12] The consequences for those who disobeyed were dire: 'duly convicted' such a one would 'forfeit for his whole life all his lands and tenements'.[13] If Katherine had married Owen Tudor or was considering marrying him, then there was good reason for them to keep the marriage quiet. Polydore Vergil would later claim that, following the death of Henry V, his widow 'being but young in years', fell for Owen, 'a gentleman of Wales, adorned with wonderful gifts of body and mind, who derived his pedigree from Cadwallader'.[14] In truth, Owen Tudor was a Welshman who could trace his lineage from the prominent Tudor family that resided in Penmynydd in Anglesey, and counted Gronw Fychan ap Tudur – once the lord steward of Llywelyn the Great – among his ancestors.[15]

Vergil would subsequently write of a prophecy that spoke of the descendants of the Welsh king Cadwallader recovering the land of England – a prophecy that, conveniently, had materialized in Margaret Beaufort's son Henry at the time when Vergil wrote.[16] It is highly likely that this tale came from Henry VII, who may have learned of it from Margaret herself. Whatever the truth of the matter, as the daughter, wife and mother of kings, the French Queen Katherine was certainly far superior in rank to Owen Tudor. Nevertheless, their liaison resulted in the births of several children – three or four, according to *The Great Chronicle of London* – of which Edmund and Jasper were two.[17] Edmund, the eldest, had been born at Much Hadham in Hertfordshire between 1428 and 1430, while Jasper was born at Hatfield around 1431. Their lives were to be tinged with tragedy when they were still young boys, for on 3 January 1437 their mother Queen Katherine died at Bermondsey Abbey, six years before Margaret's birth.[18] Fortunately, their half-brother Henry VI took a keen interest in their welfare, as Blacman

– a man who knew the King well – confirmed. Henry, he tells us, had provided for them 'most strict and safe guardianship', and by the summer the young Tudor brothers had moved to the royal monastery at Barking Abbey, one of the most important religious foundations in England.[19]

At the time of the brothers' arrival, the Abbess of Barking was Katherine de la Pole, sister of Margaret's former guardian, Suffolk. It was she who was given the responsibility of caring for the Tudor boys, and she would do so for several years. In 1440 she petitioned the King's Council for money for their maintenance, and was granted £53 12s. (£34,465) to cover their expenses – a substantial sum that shows they were living extremely comfortably.[20] Blacman observed that the brothers had been placed in the care of 'virtuous and worthy priests, both for teaching and for right living and conversation, lest the untamed practices of youth should grow rank if they lacked any to prune them'.[21] It is safe to assume, then, that both Edmund and Jasper were raised with principles that echoed the King's own morals; they were told, for example, to 'eschew vice and avoid talk of the vicious and dissolute, and to lay hold on virtue'.[22] Such values were similar to those that Margaret cherished – chiefly that family was of the utmost importance. Their father was staunchly loyal to the house of Lancaster, and his sons likewise would remain devoted to its service for the entirety of their lives.

Aside from the personal grief the family felt following the death of Queen Katherine, it left Owen Tudor exposed and vulnerable. Before long he was summoned to appear before the Council, and though he had been promised safe passage, Tudor instead sought sanctuary in Westminster Abbey. He was later captured while hurrying towards Wales, where his safety could be better assured, and immediately returned to London, where he was thrown into the infamous prison at Newgate.[23] Though he managed to escape in early 1438 after less than a year of incarceration – according to the author of the *Chronicle of the Grey Friars* 'by the help of his priest' and injuring his jailer in the process – he was soon recaptured.[24] In July 1439 Tudor was finally released, being pardoned for all of his ostensible offences in November. He then joined the household of his stepson Henry VI, who treated him well and appears to have been fond of him.

Henry VI greatly favoured his younger half-brothers, both of whom were described as being 'sincerely beloved' in the Parliament of 1453.[25] In 1442 they seem to have left Barking Abbey, and ten years later both brothers – now men – were at their half-brother's court. In the spring they joined the Queen on progress, and later that year both received great rewards as a result of their 'nobility of birth and proximity in blood'.[26] On 23 November 1452, Edmund and Jasper Tudor were raised to the peerage. Edmund was created Earl of Richmond, while Jasper was made Earl of Pembroke. New lands were given to the brothers in order to support their heightened status, in Jasper's case centring in South Wales where he would become immensely popular. The King may already have had young Margaret Beaufort in mind as a bride for his elder half-brother, for what better way to reward Edmund than with the hand of a wealthy heiress with drops of royal blood? There has also been some suggestion that at this time Henry VI, with no male heir of his own, was considering naming Edmund his heir. Though this is unlikely to have been the case – after all, the Duke of York had the strongest dynastic claim and Edmund's royal blood came solely from his French-born mother, who had no claim to the English throne – Margaret's blood stemming from John of Gaunt, would undoubtedly have strengthened any claim of Edmund's. Regardless, it would not be long before such a measure proved to be unnecessary.

Having spent a merry Christmas at Greenwich, where the entertainments included an elaborate disguising (a masque or entertainment in which the participants wore costumes and were disguised), on 5 January 1453 the King knighted both Edmund and Jasper in an extravagant ceremony at the Tower. This could have been in preparation for what lay ahead: just two months later and within weeks of Margaret's divorce from John de la Pole, on 24 March she became the ward of 'the king's uterine brothers'.[27] Her lands were immediately divided between the Tudor brothers, making them both wealthy men.

Following the summons of the Duchess of Somerset to London, her daughter Margaret received her first introduction to court life. As an impressionable young girl of nine years old, the person of the Queen, who was now twenty-three and a powerful figure at court, would have left her awestruck. Despite the crippled Crown finances, Queen Margaret was fond of finery, and frequently appeared bedecked in the richest clothes and jewels, surrounded by her loyal damsels. Young Margaret Beaufort was certainly in attendance for the Garter celebrations at Windsor Castle on 23 April, and would have been dazzled by the splendours of the court and the sumptuous red costume worn by the Queen. At around this time or shortly after, Margaret is also likely to have been afforded the opportunity to meet Edmund Tudor – her future husband – probably for the first time. This could have been what prompted the King to make his 'right dear and right well beloved cousin Margaret' a gift of 100 marks for clothes on 12 May, in order to make a splendid impression at a time when outward display meant everything.[28] In later life Margaret was exceptionally fond of clothes and a keen follower of fashion, and her interest was probably sparked during her youth. Even as a young girl, her wardrobe would have contained items made from the costliest of materials in a sign of her status.

Though she was not yet ten years old, for the second time in her life Margaret's marital prospects had been settled, but there were no immediate plans for her wedding. Given her young age, it had probably been agreed that she could remain with her mother until she was old enough to fully cohabit with Edmund and fulfil her duties in every sense. It was not long though before once again events took an unexpected turn.

Henry VI's ongoing troubles swiftly turned into a crisis as matters both in France and at home spiralled out of control. In the autumn of 1452, John Talbot, Earl of Shrewsbury, had successfully retaken Bordeaux from the French, but it was clear they were not going to give it up lightly. In order to build upon his success, Talbot needed money and supplies, but as a result of England's bankruptcy, neither were forthcoming. In July 1453, terrible news arrived: the English army had suffered a crushing defeat at Castillon in Gascony. Talbot had been killed, and worse still, Calais was now the only remaining English possession in France. This latest disaster finally signified the end of the Hundred Years' War. It was a humiliating defeat.

That August, devastated by the summer's events, the King travelled to his palace at Clarendon to the east of Salisbury.[29] Clarendon had been a popular residence with Henry's predecessors, and was often used as a hunting lodge. It was here that the King, complaining of extreme fatigue on the evening of 15 August, collapsed into what *John Benet's Chronicle* described as 'a major illness'.[30] Henry seems to have fallen into a stupor from which he could not be roused, leaving him seemingly conscious but unable to communicate and unable to walk – he had no awareness or understanding either of himself or of those around him, and completely lost all ability to feed or care for himself. This left his attendants both mortified and perplexed. His illness has been the subject of debate among modern historians, with some believing he was suffering from what we would now term a mental breakdown, others suggesting it was catatonic schizophrenia. To Henry's doctors there seemed to be just one explanation: insanity.

For Queen Margaret, the news of her husband's illness was particularly distressing: after eight years of marriage, in April she had been able to deliver him the happy news that she was pregnant with her first child, due in the autumn. Yet it soon became clear there was going to be no quick recovery for the King. The situation became desperate, and in an attempt to conceal his condition from his subjects Henry was sent to the relative seclusion of Windsor Castle. His absence left the pregnant Queen Margaret to face the challenges of governing the realm – and those in it – alone. England had already emerged from the Hundred Years' War in a state of humiliation, but with the King's illness the country was descending into chaos.

Queen Margaret's primary objective was to ensure that the Duke of York learned nothing of the King's incapacity, for she was fearful he would once more attempt to seize the reins of government. But matters were soon beyond her control, for on the morning of 13 October, at the Palace of Westminster, she was finally 'delivered of a fair Prince, whose name was called Edward'.[31] On a dynastic level, the birth of Prince Edward immediately settled the question of the succession, for the King now had a legitimate male heir. But what should have been an occasion of great joy was marred by Henry VI's continuing state of unresponsive breakdown. Secluded at Windsor under the supervision of his doctors and servants, the

King had no idea that he was now a father. Matters were not helped by the circulation of rumours suggesting that the Prince was actually the result of his mother's adulterous affair with Margaret Beaufort's uncle, Somerset.[32] It was not the first occasion on which Somerset's name had been linked with that of a queen, for it had once been rumoured that he had conducted an affair with Katherine of Valois. There was certainly no truth in the accusations of his involvement with Queen Margaret, which stemmed purely from the favour in which the Queen and her husband held him. As the political crisis grew, so too did the long-standing divide in the political structure. Two rival factions had now clearly emerged: on the one side, the court party was headed by Queen Margaret and Somerset, while York and his two key allies, the Earls of Salisbury and Warwick – father and son as well as Salisbury being York's brother-in-law – lay on the other. There was no question as to where the loyalties of Margaret Beaufort's family lay.

Early in the new year of 1454, Henry VI was presented with his baby son. It was crucial that he should acknowledge the Prince, for until he did so vicious rumours about the infant's paternity would continue to circulate. Unfortunately, the King remained unresponsive and showed no signs of recognizing the child, let alone acknowledging him. With no improvement in Henry's health, action needed to be taken in order to safeguard the government of the realm. By this time York had won some further support among the nobles, but in the Queen's mind she alone was the obvious candidate to head a regency, so she now made a bid for power. However, her arrogance and her contemptuous demeanour, coupled with the repugnance with which many viewed the idea of female rule, lost her a great deal of valuable support. The Queen's foreign origins also worked against her, and it was obvious that nobody would rest easy with her at the forefront of affairs. Other arrangements would have to be put into place, but the Queen was adamant that York should play no part in them.

When Parliament opened at Westminster on 14 February, the atmosphere was tense. Then, much to Queen Margaret's horror, on 27 March York was appointed Lord Protector of the realm during the King's incapacity. Most people recognized York's genuine concerns for the state of the country and believed he was capable of restoring good order. But it was disastrous for Margaret Beaufort's family, and her uncle Somerset was promptly sent to the Tower. This time, Queen Margaret was utterly powerless to prevent it. Indeed, she was now sent to Windsor to join her husband: the stage of power seemingly belonged to York alone. The wheel of fortune had turned in his favour, and he proved himself to be a strong leader. Widely admired by the commons for his strenuous efforts to restore good government, he did his best to repair the bankruptcy of the Crown. Though their loyalty remained wholeheartedly with Henry VI, both Edmund and Jasper Tudor fully supported York. Unlike many of Henry VI's nobles who were primarily motivated by self-interest, the Tudors seem to have been driven by a commitment to the fair governance of their half-brother's realm as well as his wellbeing, willingly complying with York's attempts to reduce the numbers of the royal household in an effort to restore Crown finances. They did not complain when this affected their own households, which were reduced to a chaplain, two esquires, two yeoman and two chamberlains each.[33] Throughout York's protectorate, Jasper appears to have been particularly conscious of maintaining a presence in London, attending both Parliament and meetings of the Council.[34] His brother Edmund was often absent for reasons that are unclear – possibly he was suffering from poor health.

Just as good order was being restored, once again life took an unexpected turn. On Christmas Day, to the elation of the Queen and her supporters – among them Margaret's family – Henry VI made a recovery. Prayers were immediately offered up in thanks, with the King – who had no memory of what had happened to him – dispatching his almoner to Canterbury to make an offering on his behalf.[35] He was by no means restored to full health though: recovery was gradual and he continued to suffer with bouts of ill health for the rest of his life. The court party were ecstatic that their King seemed to have regained his wits – after he had spoken to some of his lords 'as well as ever he did', the men were so overwhelmed that 'they wept for joy'.[36] Henry was at last able to meet – and more importantly acknowledge – his young son, Prince Edward, much to Queen Margaret's pleasure. To the relief of Margaret's family, Prince Edward's birth signified the continuation of the Lancastrian royal family, yet unbeknown to them all hopes that the arrival of an heir would bring security for the future were sorely misplaced.

With the King's recovery it was clear that York's nine-month protectorate would soon come to an end. Accordingly, on 9 February 1455, much to Queen Margaret's delight, he was formally discharged. Although he had made some positive changes, many of the country's problems still remained, and much of his good work would soon be undone. Five days before York's protectorate was dissolved, Margaret's uncle Somerset was released from his imprisonment in the Tower and quickly restored to his former place by the King and Queen's side, as were his supporters.[37] York was furious, and withdrew to his stronghold of Sandal Castle, near Wakefield.[38] Though his power had dissipated, the Queen's hatred of him had not. Intent on destroying him, she and Somerset began plotting the demise of their enemy.

Henry VI may have been on the road to recovery, but he continued to display a lack of interest in the affairs of his realm. He turned more than ever to religion to find solace, leaving Queen Margaret and Somerset holding the reins of power. Her position had been immeasurably strengthened by the birth of her son, which gave her more reason than ever to safeguard the Crown. She turned her attention to trying to rally as much support as possible, as well as persuading her husband that York was vying for the throne. York, meanwhile, knew that his enemies would soon try and move against him and was not prepared to wait for them to strike. Together with Warwick and Salisbury, he began raising an army with which to confront them. All three men owned extensive estates in the north, and combined were a force to be reckoned with.

A great meeting of the King's Council was planned for 21 May at Leicester, but York and his allies were deliberately excluded. Instead, they were all summoned to present themselves in front of the Council, but York was wary. Fearing the consequences now that Somerset was free, and suspecting that charges would be brought against him and his supporters, he took matters into his own hands: he and his army began to march south, intent on securing his own restoration to power and destroying Somerset for good.

On 1 May, Jasper Tudor left London with the King on the first stage of their journey to Leicester. When word reached them that York and his supporters were travelling south with an army, Somerset convinced Henry that York was coming to claim the throne. He immediately raised a force in readiness to defend the monarch, fully aware that he, himself, was York's real target. A violent outcome seemed impossible to avoid: the Wars of the Roses were about to begin.

On 22 May, the political tension between the court party and the Duke of York and his supporters finally erupted into violence. Accompanied by Jasper Tudor, Somerset and 'many lords', Henry VI had reached St Albans, twenty-two miles north of London, when York intercepted them.[39] Though he had the bigger force, neither he nor the royal party really wanted to fight. Instead, York attempted to persuade Henry to hear his complaints, and in so doing left him in no doubt as to his wishes: chiefly the removal and punishment of Somerset. His efforts were in vain, for the King – however weak – was not prepared to be dictated to and steadfastly refused to hand Somerset over. His men were heavily outnumbered, but his unyielding response made it clear that if York wanted to settle the matter, he would not be able to do so peaceably.

Feeling that there was no alternative, York made the drastic decision to attack. According to a Milanese envoy, informed by a messenger, when the King's party 'were outside the town they were immediately attacked by York's men'.[40] By taking such an aggressive stance, York was fully aware that many would believe he had taken up arms against his lawfully anointed king – and in so doing committed treason. The King's forces, led by Humphrey, Duke of Buckingham – a man who would later be closely connected with Margaret Beaufort – were badly prepared and taken aback by the full ferocity of York's charge. Despite being caught by surprise, the royal party initially held their own, but they were defeated when Warwick managed to lead a force into the town by unguarded back lanes. The result was disaster for the royal army, many of whom fled when they perceived the direction that the battle was taking. Although Henry's men, including Jasper Tudor, fought valiantly, in less than an hour York had won the day thanks to the Earl of Warwick's successful routing of the royal forces. The casualties on the King's side were heavy and included the Earl of Northumberland and Lord Clifford. Many were also badly injured, among them Margaret's cousin, Henry Beaufort, Somerset's heir. He would survive his injuries, though his father would not be so fortunate.

Realizing that the battle was lost and that York was out for his blood, Margaret's uncle Somerset attempted to take refuge at the Castle Inn in the town. It was not long, however, before York's men had surrounded it: for Somerset – so long protected by the King and Queen – this time there would be no escape. Though he attempted to fight his way out and did so bravely, killing four men in the process, he was soon struck down. As *John Benet's Chronicle* reported, 'all of the Duke of Somerset's party were killed, wounded or at the least despoiled'.[41] With his death, the battle ceased. The head of Margaret's family was now dead, and Vergil later claimed that

> *king Henry conceived great and incredible sorrow for the loss of the duke of Somerset, because he had reposed all his hope in him, and for that such a noble captain, who had fought valiantly so many years against the French men, should now finally be killed of his own countrymen.*[42]

But for the King, who had stood watching the violence that was playing out around him, there were to be more direct consequences. On Warwick's orders, Yorkist archers began to shoot at his bodyguard, killing and injuring several in the process – the injured included Jasper Tudor, the Duke of Buckingham and the King himself. Although Henry 'was hurt with the shot of an arrow in the neck', his injuries were not serious, but that was not an end to the matter.[43] More alarming was that York succeeded in capturing him. Having gained control of the King's person, according to the Milanese ambassador, 'the Duke of York went to kneel before the king and ask pardon for himself and his followers, as they had not done this in order to inflict any hurt upon his Majesty, but in order to have Somerset. Accordingly, the king pardoned them.'[44] York had successfully eliminated his enemy, and in so doing knew that he had taken a huge step in securing his return to power.

Margaret's uncle Somerset was laid to rest in the abbey at St Albans.[45] She herself not only later made offerings to the abbey, but also on one occasion rewarded the minstrels of the abbot. Whether the links with her uncle gave her an extra sentimental tie to St Albans is unclear, but she would certainly have been aware that he had lost his life in the King's service there. Somerset's death meant that the head of Margaret's household – and a potentially powerful protector for her – was now gone. Thus far, Margaret's short life had been punctuated by the deaths of some of the leading male figures in her life: her father, Suffolk, and now her uncle. In their place, Somerset's eldest son – Margaret's injured cousin Henry – was the new head of the family. Like his father, Henry harboured a bitter resentment against the Yorkist regime – exacerbated by Somerset's murder – and would continue his family's struggle to fight York's power.

Blood had now been shed, and as those involved digested what had been the first battle in the conflict between the houses of Lancaster and York, the following morning York and his supporters escorted the King back to London. A contemporary chronicle claimed that Henry returned to the capital 'as king and not as a prisoner', but in the eyes of many the reality seemed otherwise.[46] The conclusion of the Milanese ambassador that 'now peace reigns' could not have been further from the truth.[47]

CHAPTER 4

At War Together in Wales

WHILE THE SWORDS clashed at St Albans, Margaret Beaufort had probably remained with her mother and siblings in the Bedfordshire and Northamptonshire countryside. On 31 May – nine days after the Battle of St Albans – she reached her twelfth birthday, and it was probably soon afterwards that her marriage to Edmund Tudor was celebrated – it had certainly taken place by September. Margaret was not even a teenager, yet her marriage made her Countess of Richmond. It was a title that she retained even after Edmund's death, and the result of the marriage would determine the entire course of the rest of her life.

No details of Edmund and Margaret's wedding are known, and it is unclear precisely where and when it took place – possibly at Maxey or Bletsoe, Margaret's childhood homes. Her mother was probably present, with perhaps Owen and Jasper Tudor in attendance too. The experience must have been all the more daunting for Margaret given that she had only met Edmund once – or at the most no more than a handful of times – prior to the ceremony. By the same token, given the age difference – Edmund was more than ten years Margaret's senior – they are unlikely to have had much in common. This was not unusual by contemporary standards, but does give some insight into how the twelve-year-old Margaret must have felt as she promised to love, honour and obey a man that she barely knew. The conclusion of her marriage brought Margaret one step closer to Henry VI, who was already her kinsman by blood. Now, Henry also became her brother-in-law. It meant that Margaret was now drawn even more into the brewing conflict – and thus the fate of the royal house – for she would no longer be able to live at home, distant from events, under her mother's protection. She was the wife of the King's half-brother, and as such would become directly involved in and witness first-hand the political turmoil that lay in store.

In spite of her adolescence there was no question of Margaret's second marriage following a similar course to her first. From the start, Edmund Tudor fully intended that his young wife should fulfil her marital duties without delay. Chief among them was the consummation of her marriage, which took place either immediately or soon after the couple's wedding. The Church declared that twelve was the age at which a girl was permitted to have sexual relations with her husband and cohabit, while fourteen was prescribed for boys. Nevertheless, many of Margaret's contemporaries still considered this to be painfully young and often chose to wait a few years. Mary de Bohun, for example, had been a similar age when she was married to Henry, Earl of Derby (later Henry IV), but had not given birth to her first child until six years after her wedding, indicating a delay in consummation.[1] So eager, though, was Edmund to secure an interest in Margaret's inheritance through consummation and the production of an heir that this was not an option. Despite being in his mid-twenties and between thirteen to fifteen years older than his bride, he wasted no time in making Margaret his wife in the fullest sense of the word. To the modern eye, Edmund's determination appears both horrific and brutal: indeed, Jones and Underwood have described his actions as 'ruthless and inconsiderate'.[2] He certainly showed a reckless disregard for Margaret's wellbeing heightened by her physical underdevelopment, which meant that she had yet to reach sexual maturity. The trauma that Edmund's decision caused would later manifest itself in the deep emotional scars – and possible physical ones too – that Margaret was left with.

In spite of what happened, it is nevertheless possible that Margaret harboured fond feelings towards her second husband. She did of course frequently tell the tale of her having chosen his suit by means of divine guidance, and she would later go to great lengths to identify herself with him. In her first will dated 2 June 1472, she left instructions for Edmund's remains to be removed from their resting place in Carmarthen and moved to Bourne in Lincolnshire, where she intended to be laid to rest beside him.[3] Later, she also gave orders that prayers were to be said for her husband's soul at her foundation of Christ's College, Cambridge. Margaret's thoughts on her own memorial later changed as her position transformed, and as such this never transpired. She did, however, request that Edmund's arms should be incorporated on her tomb, where they remain to this day. It is worth considering how far her initial request was based on the desire to be associated with Edmund – a desire intensified by the fact that their union led to the foundation of the Tudor dynasty – and how far, if at all, on true warmth of feeling, given that their marriage lasted for less than eighteen months, not all of which was spent together. The truth is that we know frustratingly little of Margaret and Edmund's relationship and thus can never know for sure.

It is also difficult to get a true sense of Edmund's character or appearance, not helped by the fact that there are no surviving portraits of him. The brass that adorns his tomb provides the only clue as to what he looked like, and shows a rather harsh-looking man with shoulder-length dark hair fully bedecked in armour – thereby emphasizing his military prowess – his hands raised in prayer. But as this was created at a later date, it cannot be taken as an accurate reflection.[4]

Margaret's husband had not participated in the fighting at St Albans, but in the aftermath of the battle he was keen to be seen supporting his half-brother the King. Four days after the battle and prior to Margaret's marriage, Parliament had been summoned: convening in July, it opened 'with the lord king sitting on the royal throne in the Painted Chamber'.[5] Edmund had returned to the capital in order to attend, and was there on 9 July to witness York and his supporters renewing their oath of allegiance to Henry VI. The purpose of the Parliament was to find a way in which the government could move forward inclusive of York. Immediately after St Albans, the Milanese ambassador was of the belief that York 'will take up the government again, and some think that the affairs of that kingdom will now take a turn for the better'.[6] The Duke had already taken steps to ensure his return to power, building a strong network of support. He had also been appointed Constable of England. By the same token, his ally the Earl of Warwick had been created Captain of Calais, thereby strengthening the position of York's supporters further. Queen Margaret, meanwhile, had been left devastated by the death of Somerset, which only served to deepen her hatred of York. Like him, she now attempted to rally support, and she could certainly be assured of the loyalty of Margaret – though still a child – and her husband.

By the autumn, Margaret had bidden farewell to her mother, and with her husband travelled to the heart of Pembrokeshire in West Wales. In September the newlyweds had taken up residence at the luxurious Palace of Lamphey, a bishop's palace that had been largely constructed by Henry de Gower, Bishop of St David's, in the fourteenth century. Featuring two courtyards, it was a regal and spacious residence that boasted an impressive 82-foot-long Great Hall that provided the perfect space for entertaining. There was also a chapel, of which Margaret would have made full use, as well as comfortable apartments. Coupled with its lavish interiors, Lamphey's copious grounds contained orchards, fragrant herb gardens, and fishponds. Set in the vast and beautiful Welsh countryside, Lamphey had always been intended as a rural retreat, and thus it provided an idyllic setting for a newly married couple to get to know one another. Edmund, however, had more than recreation on his mind.

On 12 November, Parliament met again, but this time neither Edmund – in Wales with Margaret – nor his brother Jasper were present.[7] The King was also absent 'for certain just and reasonable causes', and it is wholly possible that he was once again suffering from a mental breakdown.[8] Soon after it had been convened, York was once more appointed Protector of England by Parliament. Yet again he made a concerted effort to resolve some of the realm's problems, particularly the improvement of Crown finances. His hard work paid off in terms of winning public opinion, and the commons loved him for it. Yet the Queen and her supporters remained suspicious as to his true motives, and were convinced that he had set his sights on the throne. Whatever her feelings, for the moment Queen Margaret was powerless to oppose York's rule. The fate of Margaret Beaufort's house, therefore, appeared to rest in the hands of another – one who had great personal ambitions of his own: it would only be a matter of time before he chose to pursue them.

THE ARRIVAL OF the Earl and Countess of Richmond in Wales had never been intended purely as an opportunity for leisure. Instead, Edmund had been tasked with overseeing the King's authority in the area, though he was also prepared to lend his support to York in London once more. He had not been in Wales for long when he made his presence felt, and it was soon apparent that to some it was unwanted. The most powerful magnate in the region was Gruffudd ap Nicholas, and friction immediately arose between the two men, presumably as a result of Edmund's determination to assert his authority. Thus far, Nicholas had always been loyal to the house of Lancaster, but as a result of their defeat at the Battle of St Albans he seems to have lost some of his possessions. Edmund's presence in Wales served to further intensify his resentment. So much so that by the late spring or early summer of 1456 the tension had erupted into violence: at the beginning of June a correspondent of the well-informed Paston family reported that the two men 'are at war together in Wales'.[9]

Margaret, living in unfamiliar territory with a husband she barely knew, must have found the conflict unnerving at the very least. Despite her luxurious surroundings, it would have been a far cry from the relative serenity of her upbringing. Her husband was not prepared to back down in his war with Nicholas, and before long his efforts reaped a satisfying reward. At the beginning of August, he had successfully taken control of Carmarthen Castle from his rival – a mighty twelfth-century stronghold that was key to government in that part of Wales, and of which York was constable.[10] Little did he know that his actions were to have damaging consequences.

That summer Margaret had just passed her thirteenth birthday, and while Edmund was busying himself with military matters, she would have become aware that she was pregnant with her first child. Tradition has it that she conceived at Caldicot Castle in Monmouthshire, but there is little evidence to support this. Given that Caldicot was over a hundred miles from Lamphey, it seems unlikely that she would have travelled this far.[11] The news would have come as a source of joy to Edmund, whose determination to secure an heir had been the driving force behind the early consummation of their marriage, but Margaret's own response is less clear. Her lack of bodily development and small build had not prevented her from conceiving, but there was a long way to go. Medicine and midwifery were still in their early stages, and Margaret would have known the terrifying risks that childbirth brought with it at any age. Mother and infant mortality was high and took no account of rank. While a woman might survive labour, she ran the risk of becoming afflicted with a postnatal infection for which there was no cure. Likewise, possibly more than 30 per cent of children died before the age of seven as a result of disease or malnourishment. It was a terrifying reality.

While Margaret was undergoing her first experience of pregnancy in the heart of the Welsh countryside, she was far from the court in London and news took some days to travel. She may not, therefore, have been immediately aware of the state of the government. In February, Henry VI – now seemingly recovered – had dissolved York's protectorate in Parliament. The Duke nevertheless remained a member of the Council, despite the protestations of his bitter enemy the Queen. Queen Margaret had ample reason to be wary of York, for he had already demonstrated that he was prepared to resort to warfare in order to retain his grip on the reins of power. But of greater concern to her was the dynastic threat he posed, for she was fearful that, given the opportunity, he would not hesitate to press his claim to the throne and in so doing would do all he could to disinherit her son Prince Edward.

Margaret's cousin Henry Beaufort, who had succeeded his father to the dukedom of Somerset following Edmund's fall at St Albans, had now ingratiated himself in the Queen's favour and was one of her key supporters. In the summer, the King and Queen moved with the court to Coventry, accompanied by Margaret's brother-in-law Jasper. Throughout that spring and summer, Jasper had been in almost constant attendance on the King, who clearly enjoyed his company and knew that he could trust him implicitly. It is not inconceivable that Jasper was keeping his brother Edmund abreast of affairs at court; if this were the case, then Edmund would have known that though there was an uneasy peace between the Queen and York, tensions between them had by no means been quelled. York, however, was quietly waiting for Queen Margaret to make the next move.

WHEN WORD REACHED York that Edmund Tudor had successfully captured Carmarthen, of which he was constable, he was alarmed. Edmund's unshakeable loyalty to Henry VI was well known, and York was not prepared to risk him becoming too powerful a force in Wales where he himself commanded support. With this in mind he immediately assembled a force to take back Carmarthen and reassert his authority. Two thousand men led by Sir William Herbert and Sir Walter Devereux, brothers-in-law who were both York's steadfast supporters, marched to the Welsh town and made straight for the castle. Edmund's men were unable to withstand such an attack, and on 10 August the castle was seized. Edmund was captured and imprisoned.

Back at Lamphey, Margaret – married for only about a year, and in the early months of pregnancy – was suddenly in fear for her husband's life, as well as the safety of herself and her unborn child in this unknown country. But her distress would be of short duration, for before long Edmund was released. However, he remained at Carmarthen and, as the autumn approached, showed no signs of returning home. It may be that he was simply eager to remain and ensure that the King's interests were being upheld, or else he was showing signs of illness that rendered him unable to travel. Whatever the circumstances, at some point Edmund did become unwell. It became alarmingly clear that he had contracted the plague, which had been mercilessly ravaging Wales. It was a deadly disease that swiftly claimed the lives of its many victims, which explains why there was no time for Edmund to prepare a will. Tragically, he soon succumbed, dying on 1 November at Carmarthen Castle.

Edmund's death left his pregnant teenage wife alone and vulnerable. Her residency in Wales rendered her completely isolated from her family in England, with no one to turn to for support. The timing could hardly have been worse and Margaret was consumed with fear. Not only had she lost her husband, but she was also about to embark on the most perilous experience of her life – with no guarantee of survival.

CHAPTER 5

My Good and Gracious Prince, King and Only-Beloved Son

AS THE BITTER winter winds swirled, Margaret was ensconced at Lamphey when word reached her of the death of her husband at Carmarthen Castle. There is no indication as to how or precisely when Margaret was told of Edmund's death, or of her reaction to the news. She was, though, consumed with anxiety and compelled by a sense of urgency to ensure her wellbeing and that of her unborn child. Her second husband was laid to rest in the Grey Friars at Carmarthen, but, later, more than two decades after Margaret's own death, his remains would be moved to St David's Cathedral during the Dissolution of the Monasteries on the orders of his grandson, Henry VIII. The inscription on his tomb offers little insight into Edmund's life or character, instead highlighting simply that he was the 'father and brother to kings'.[1]

Later, Edmund's son would order ceremonies annually at Westminster Abbey in order to commemorate his father, and similarly money was sent each year to Carmarthen in order to pay for daily prayers to be said for his soul. But here in 1456 Edmund's death left Margaret a widow at the age of just thirteen, and alone at Lamphey in the midst of an unknown Welsh region, ravaged by plague. Left to fend for herself at a time when she was already fraught with anxiety, she now showed her true strength of character and would shortly prove that she was a survivor.

There was no time for Margaret to grieve for the husband she had barely known, for she was nearly seven months pregnant and fearful for the safety of her unborn child. She was terrified of the plague, and in later years Bishop Fisher would explain to her son that 'while your mother carried you in the womb you narrowly avoided the plague of which your illustrious father died, which could so easily have killed an unborn child'. Given the fate of her husband and the virulence with which the plague spread, Margaret's fears were both understandable and fully justified. It was against a backdrop of fear from disease and political unrest that Margaret was forced to consider her future – and quickly. Not only did her youth and pregnancy make her vulnerable to the plague; also her sex and widowhood made her a potential target for power-hungry men: it was evident that she could not remain alone at Lamphey. Her advanced pregnancy and the bleak winter weather ensured that there was no question of her undertaking the gruelling journey to her mother's estates in England, and thus she was forced to turn elsewhere.

THOUGH AN UNEASY peace had ensued, the divide between the Lancastrian court party and the Yorkists still ran deep and showed no signs of healing. It was clear that there was no middle ground, and that choices would have to be made. For Margaret's brother-in-law Jasper, the decision was simple: though he had done his best to work with York and understood that his actions were for the good of the country, he had never wavered in his loyalty to Henry VI. Familial ties won the day, and there was no question of Jasper abandoning his half-brother now. This was all the more important given that the death of Margaret's husband Edmund deprived the King not only of his half-brother, but also of a loyal and valuable ally whose allegiance had been unshakeable. At some point in November, word reached Jasper of the death of his beloved brother, and the news doubtless came as a bitter blow. Many years later, in a touching sign of his devotion to his family, Jasper would leave instructions in his will for four priests to sing perpetually in Keynsham Abbey for 'the well of my soul', and those of his parents and brother.[2] But in the winter of 1456 he was at once made aware of the plight of his sister-in-law – alone in Wales, heavily pregnant and fearful of plague. Laying aside his personal grief, Jasper wasted no time: it would be him who came to the pregnant Margaret's aid.

Margaret's relationship with her brother-in-law had always been amicable, and at twenty-five years old he was both strong and brave. He was not yet married, and thus had no family of his own with which to occupy his time. Jasper was therefore an ideal choice of protector for Margaret, and although she did not know him well, she knew that she could trust him with her safekeeping and that of her unborn child. It was a task that he in turn approached with the utmost seriousness. Probably it was during this time that a bond of trust was forged between them – one that would endure for the rest of their lives and be of the utmost consequence in the coming years.

In normal circumstances, Margaret's thoughts at this time would have been occupied with plans for her confinement – plans that she later helped to ensure were put into practice with meticulous detail for the births of her grandchildren – but there was no time for that now. Similarly, the idea of travelling in winter through an unfamiliar landscape would have been unthinkable for a woman so advanced in her pregnancy. But in the circumstances, it was essential that she do so. As Jasper's horse pulled into the courtyard at Lamphey – the date unknown, but probably some time in mid-November – Margaret prepared to bid farewell to the comfortable home in which she had spent much of her brief marriage.

Jasper's main seat was the mighty stronghold of Pembroke Castle, situated on the banks of the river estuary in the town of Pembroke: André described it as being near to 'the source of a violent stream'.[3] At a little over two miles from Lamphey, it was a short journey, though given her pregnancy it would have been far from comfortable for Margaret. She nevertheless arrived at Pembroke safely.

Of Norman origin, the towering five-storey stone keep built by the mighty William Marshal and dating from 1204 dominated Pembroke.[4] The castle was surrounded by thirteenth-century stone walls, encasing an impressive Norman Great Hall and a whole host of other buildings, including a dungeon – a gruesome reminder of Pembroke's violent past.[5] Its position on a high rock made it more easily defendable against potential attackers, and, given the uncertainty of the times, it was a wise choice of location for Margaret to spend the remainder of her pregnancy. The castle had been granted to Jasper in 1452 as part of the earldom of Pembroke, although his frequent presence at court makes it unlikely that he had been afforded an opportunity to spend much time there. He had nevertheless spent a great sum of money in an attempt to maintain Pembroke's defences as well as to ensure that it was a congenial residence. There was a fine chapel, accommodation for Jasper and his household, and a solar (an upper chamber commonly found in medieval homes) into which he had inserted a splendid oriel window.[6] Although not as luxurious or as peaceful as Lamphey, Pembroke was a secure and comfortable alternative.

The circumstances surrounding Margaret's arrival at Pembroke made the prospect of giving birth all the more terrifying for the teenage girl, with unrest continuing to rage throughout the land. And because Jasper was unmarried, there is likely to have been a distinct lack of noble female company at Pembroke – Margaret's own servants and the female household staff would have been all there were – making the experience even more isolating for her.

As Christmas, New Year and the onset of 1457 were celebrated at Pembroke, Margaret's due date quickly approached.[7] It was to be the first Christmas Margaret ever spent away from her family. At least, under Jasper's protection, she could feel relatively safe within its walls, Pembroke – as André tells us – being a 'heavily fortified castle'.[8] Given that childbirth was an exclusively female process, Margaret would have been attended by at least one midwife, but no other details of the preparations put in place are known. Some women relied on holy relics in order to help them through the ordeal of childbirth, while others employed special amulets to protect them. In later life Margaret is known to have owned jewels featuring the likenesses of saints thought to aid pregnant women. However, she may simply have relied on prayer: a prayer book she later commissioned for her fourth husband, Thomas Stanley, contains a number of prayers aimed at protecting the user from all manner of dangers, including childbirth.[9]

At the end of January, Margaret's labour pains began, and she was confronted with the agonizing reality of childbirth. Always a pious woman whose religious enthusiasm shone through for the rest of her life and provided her with a great source of comfort – Margaret would need all of her faith to get her through this most difficult time. But it would not have been enough to ignore the fact that her undeveloped body was ill equipped to deal with the strain that childbirth placed on it. Given that she was 'not yet fourteen' and had not encountered all of the changes that puberty brings, even the most skilled of midwives would not have been able to make the process any easier. It is little wonder, therefore, that her experience was both difficult and traumatic.

On 28 January the exhausted Margaret at last gave birth to a son. A tower still called the Henry VII Tower has always traditionally been cited as the place of birth of Margaret's child, but recent excavations at Pembroke have shown that he is more likely to have been born in a lavishly decorated building that once lay inside the castle's outer walls.[10]

Bishop Fisher recalled the outcome of Margaret's labour:

Like Moses, [Henry] was wonderfully born and brought into the world by the noble Princess his mother, who was very small of stature, as she was never a tall woman. It seemed a miracle that, at that age, and of so little a personage, anyone should have been born at all, let alone one so tall and of so fine a build as her son.

Given that Margaret was 'so much smaller at that stage', the birth of her son was even more remarkable.

Henry's biographer Neville Williams rightly observed that Henry's 'arrival in the world was not heralded by national rejoicing', for he was born as nothing more than the son of a deceased nobleman.[11] Nevertheless, André later did his best to emphasize his master's parentage, describing it as 'most noble'.[12] He took particular care to highlight Edmund Tudor's connections, boldly, and falsely, stating that it stemmed all the way back to the Roman politician Brutus, one of the key conspirators in the murder of Julius Caesar. When it came to Margaret, whom André described as Henry's 'most illustrious royal mother', he was careful to stress that she was 'a very noble woman, endowed with uprightness and virtue from above'.[13]

Though she had done her duty and produced a living child, the experience had been so difficult that, to begin with, both Margaret's life and that of her infant were believed to be at risk. But it was not long before the danger passed. The day of the birth was one that Margaret celebrated for the rest of her life, and in later years she wrote to Henry on his birthday remembering that it was 'this day of St Agnes, that I did bring into this world my good and gracious prince, king and only-beloved son'.[14] Margaret had suffered great trauma, and she was now faced with the reality that – although just embarking on her teenage years – she had a new and important role to play: that of a mother. Yet this did not faze her, for from the moment of Henry's birth an extraordinary bond was forged between mother and son: one that would endure for the rest of their lives, perhaps later heightened by the knowledge that Henry was to be Margaret's only child – whether through choice or circumstance.

Rather than naming her son after the father who had died before he was born, in a proud declaration of her own heritage and loyalty to the royal family into which he had been born, the baby was christened Henry in honour of Margaret's kinsman Henry VI – the child's uncle and probable godfather. The only association with his father and the Tudor family was the title, Earl of Richmond, with which Henry was styled in right of Edmund Tudor from the moment of his birth. In the sixteenth century, however, the Welshman Elis Gruffydd, who hailed from Flintshire, recorded in his chronicle that the infant had first been christened Owen – probably at the request of his uncle Jasper as a compliment to his own father – but that during the course of the ceremony Margaret had insisted that the bishop should alter this to Henry. No other source makes any reference to this incident, so it is impossible to corroborate, but knowing Margaret's character, her insistent independence and fierce familial loyalty, there is certainly more than a hint of truth to it.

There is a possibility that the physical and psychological trauma of her son's birth caused Margaret permanent damage. It has often been said that the harm inflicted as a result of childbirth rendered her physically incapable of bearing another child. It is true that despite two further marriages, she is not known to have experienced any further pregnancies, and certainly produced no more children. More than five hundred years later, it is impossible to know what the true long-term physical implications of Henry's birth were, if indeed there were any. It is possible that Margaret had scar tissue or a damaged uterus that prevented her from carrying another child, but consideration must also be given to other possibilities.[15] Clearly, the experience made its mark on her psychologically: in years to come she would urge her son not to allow her granddaughter and namesake to be sent to Scotland for her marriage to James IV too early, in case in his haste to consummate their union he might 'injure her, and endanger her health'. Margaret was speaking from experience. With this in mind, it is hardly surprising that childbirth left Margaret emotionally scarred – so much so that it is possible she made a conscious decision not to become pregnant again. Such a prospect can only ever be speculative, but there is evidence in her later life, in particular as regards her choice of third husband, that gives us good reason to consider such a possibility seriously. That Margaret actively chose not to have another child has never been mooted, but given what we know of her character, her circumstances and her later behaviour, it ought not to be ruled out. Unsurprisingly, there is evidence that her experience of sex at such an early age made the thought of it completely abhorrent. A religious book that she later bequeathed to Christ's College, Cambridge, contained a section on frigidity. This was annotated, possibly in Margaret's own hand, with a poignant question: was it a sin to loathe sex?[16]

In spite of the physical and psychological impact of Henry's birth – whether temporary or permanent in either sense – from the start Margaret adored him. She 'wisely attended to the care of her son', nursing Henry devotedly in his early days.[17] Nevertheless, in the same manner as all noble children, her baby would have been entrusted to the care of nurses – presumably including a wet-nurse to suckle him – who were responsible for his everyday care. Margaret knew all too well, though, that these precious days at Pembroke were not destined to last for long.

Shortly after Henry's birth, thoughts turned to Margaret's future. Though she was now a mother and fell under the protection of her brother-in-law, her age and position as a widow made her vulnerable. This was only exacerbated by the growing tension within the realm in which Jasper knew that he as well as Margaret and her son would become inextricably tangled. It was imperative, in order to safeguard her future – and that of her son – that she should marry again, and there was no time to be lost. Though the impetus seems to have been Margaret's own, Jasper also appears to have recognized the importance of his sister-in-law taking another husband, and played an important role in making arrangements. Margaret was still just thirteen, but on the third occasion on which she would be wedded she was determined that it should be to someone of her own choosing who would also be prepared to consider the interests of her infant son. This time, Margaret would take full responsibility for shaping her own future.

PART TWO

CHAPTER 6

Lady Stafford

M ARGARET SPENT THE first weeks of motherhood bonding with
her son – a bond that is likely to have been all the stronger
given that, like Henry, she had also never known her father.
Having lost her husband, Margaret was her son's sole parent, which may
have intensified not only her love for him, but also the need to keep him
safe. This was undoubtedly a strong consideration when she made her
next move. Likewise, the isolation from most of her peers in the early
weeks of Henry's life would surely have rendered Margaret's need to keep
him close stronger still. Though he would undoubtedly have remained
at Pembroke in the aftermath of Margaret's ordeal, it is unlikely that her
brother-in-law Jasper would have seen much, if anything, of her during
this time due to the protocol known as churching, which dictated that a
woman could not re-enter society until she had gone through a religious
ceremony of purification.

It was around this period that Jasper began to associate more closely
with Humphrey Stafford, Duke of Buckingham, who was also a kinsman
and loyal supporter of Henry VI.[1] Buckingham was one of the most
powerful noblemen in England, and throughout the political turmoil
that came with the King's descent into mental illness, he had attempted
to mediate – unsuccessfully – between the Lancastrian court party and
the Duke of York. The circumstance was even more uncomfortable for
Buckingham given his personal ties: his wife was York's sister-in-law.[2]
York wielded only moderately more power than Buckingham, who was
an extremely wealthy landowner with estates that spanned Staffordshire
and the Welsh Marches among others. As a rich and powerful magnate

with unshakeable allegiance to her own house, Margaret found the idea of Buckingham's protection greatly appealing, and following her churching in March 1457 – two months after Henry's birth – she turned her attention towards his family when looking to form her next matrimonial alliance. The arrival of her son signified a momentous change in Margaret's outlook, for no longer was her own future her sole consideration – her decisions would affect the course of Henry's life too, and that made them of even greater import. Though he had his uncle Jasper, she considered that another male figure who could offer protection in the uncertain political climate was essential. Margaret recognized that in order to safeguard Henry's interests she needed an ally and protector, and the way to obtain one was through marriage. If she were to avoid another husband not of her own choosing being thrust upon her, then the matter had to be undertaken as one of urgency.

Once again, there would have been many who were eager to secure Margaret's hand. Elizabeth Norton has suggested that the obvious choice of husband would have been Margaret's brother-in-law, Jasper, who was still unmarried.[3] Yet many at the time would probably have felt her marriage to his brother Edmund rendered them too closely related, if indeed the pair ever considered one another as potential spouses. Jasper's support for Margaret's next marriage was nevertheless essential, for his familial relationship with her young son Henry ensured that their interests would always be closely aligned. It is unthinkable that he and Margaret would not have discussed the matter of her marriage, and it is plausible that an alliance with Buckingham's family came at Jasper's suggestion.

The level of Margaret's own involvement in her marital arrangements is extraordinary, considering her youth and all that she had been through in so short a space of time. Henry's birth had had a profound impact on her, imbuing her with a new sense of purpose. The experience of childbirth in a land full of political unrest forced Margaret to grow up quickly, and she emerged as a stronger and more determined character who would put her son's interests above all else. Henry's future wellbeing then, was the motivation that drove her when considering her marital arrangements.

Shortly after she had been churched, Margaret probably left her infant son in the care of his nurses at Pembroke; one, a Welsh woman by the name of Joan ap Howell was later rewarded by Henry with an annuity of 20 marks.[4] Accompanied by Jasper, she now began the journey to Greenfield, the Duke of Buckingham's estate in Newport. Situated over a hundred miles from Pembroke, it was a gruelling journey that cannot have been comfortable for Margaret given her recent experience of childbirth. That she chose to undertake it is a testament to her own insistence on being involved in the negotiations concerning her future. After all, as Margaret had already experienced, marriage negotiations did not require the person of the woman to be present – or indeed out of the nursery. Having arrived safely at Greenfield, where she and Jasper were greeted by Buckingham's hospitality, talks regarding Margaret's third marriage began.

Henry Stafford was Buckingham's second son, and at around thirty-one years old he was almost two decades Margaret's senior.[5] In spite of this, he had never been married, ironically making Margaret the more experienced of the two in this quarter. This was perhaps because Stafford's father had placed primary importance on arranging the nuptials of his elder brother, Humphrey, who had been wedded to Margaret's own cousin – incidentally also named Margaret Beaufort – the daughter of her late uncle Edmund, Duke of Somerset.[6] Thus, the valuable bonds of allegiance that marriages brought had already been forged with Margaret's family. Alternatively, Stafford's accounts reveal that he suffered from ill health at various points in his life, which may also account for his delay in taking a wife.

Although Henry was a second son, his father's powerful position made him a good match for Margaret, but the greatest advantage was undoubtedly his on account of Margaret's landed wealth. The couple were related through Henry's mother, Anne Neville, who was a granddaughter of John of Gaunt and Katherine Swynford, and his noble blood may also have helped to enhance the match's appeal to Margaret.[7] It is unclear from where the impetus for Margaret's choice of third husband originally stemmed; though a girl with her inheritance and connections would undoubtedly have had other options should she have wished, there is no evidence to suggest that she looked elsewhere for a husband of which she approved. It is possible that one thing especially attracted her to Stafford: his age. That a man of Stafford's years and standing had not been married thus far was unusual, but if indeed, as has been speculated, Margaret had made a conscious decision not to become pregnant again, she was probably aware that a man in his thirties would have been considered rather old by contemporary standards to be fathering his first child.

As a second son, the need for Henry to produce an heir to continue his line was also less pressing than if he had been his father's heir – his elder brother had already produced a son, thereby securing the future of their family for at least another generation. Henry's ill health may also have made the possibility of fatherhood less likely. There is some evidence that he may have suffered from a skin complaint known as St Anthony's Fire (also called Holy Fire), which was relatively common in the medieval period.[8] The symptoms were similar to those experienced by sufferers of leprosy, and in 1466 Henry and Margaret joined the confraternity of the leper hospital at Burton Lazars in Leicestershire. Margaret would, in turn, show a devotion to St Anthony, the patron saint of lepers.[9] Further hints that Stafford may have been a sufferer come in March 1470, when he was travelling north with the royal army and his chaplain, John Bush, was busy distributing alms to places that housed lepers.[10]

Although there is no evidence to suggest that Margaret and Stafford's union was not consummated – by all accounts their marriage was happy – consideration must also be given to the possibility that Stafford may have been infertile. His accounts show that on several occasions physicians were called for and medicines received from London, and although the nature of his ailments is not known, his health evidently caused concern.[11] In the past, many historians have looked no further than the birth of Henry Tudor when examining Margaret's lack of further children, citing that the physical damage to her body as a result of this experience must have been the cause. Rarely have other causes – such as infertility on the part of Stafford – been considered.

The agreement for Margaret to wed Henry Stafford was settled swiftly, but given their familial relationship, a papal dispensation was required – it would be Margaret's second. This too was applied for promptly, and on 6 April the Bishop of Coventry and Lichfield granted the dispensation – plans for Margaret's marriage could now proceed.[12] Yet it would be some months before the wedding could take place, for she was still in the prescribed year of mourning for Edmund Tudor.

In the space of just four months, Margaret's life had changed unalterably: she had lost her husband, been obliged to abandon her home, given birth to a son in traumatic circumstances, and negotiated a third marriage. It was more than some of her contemporaries would go through in a lifetime, yet Margaret was still just thirteen. That she not only survived all of the changes she had been forced to endure, but emerged from them with a determination to secure her own future, is a testament to her strength of mind and her ability to adapt and cope with the unpredictable circumstances with which she was faced.

ELSEWHERE, DISORDER IN the realm remained rife. In an attempt to prevent him from taking a role in government, the Duke of York had been sent to Ireland to resume his post as Lieutenant. Even from a distance, though, the Queen remained fearful of him and his faction. Jasper is likely to have been one of the few people whom she could truly trust, and in April – the same month as Margaret's dispensation to wed Henry Stafford was issued – Jasper was appointed Constable of Carmarthen Castle, among other titles, thereby replacing York. Given the association of his late brother with Carmarthen, it would have been understandable if this role carried some sad associations for him, but he undertook it admirably. He successfully managed to tame Gruffudd ap Nicholas, once more firmly demonstrating his loyalty to the Lancastrian dynasty. While Jasper was in Carmarthen, Margaret returned to Pembroke Castle to observe her year of mourning for Edmund Tudor and to be with her son. Unbeknown to her, these few months were to be the only ones she would spend with her son while he was a baby.

On 3 January 1458, almost a year after Henry's birth, Margaret was married to Henry Stafford. The Duke of Buckingham's favoured red-sandstone residence of Maxstoke Castle in Warwickshire may have provided the setting for the wedding, and given that in later years the couple would regularly celebrate their wedding anniversary, often with a sumptuous meal crammed with luxury items, we can assume it was a happy occasion. Unfortunately, there are no clues as to what Stafford looked like, but whatever his appearance, in character at least he was kindly and amiable, if perhaps somewhat weak – he would later actively try and avoid participating in the conflict that racked the country. In spite of his father's position, Stafford himself had little in terms of personal wealth and income, and he and Margaret lived primarily from the revenues that came from her estates. Neither did he have a grand title, so Margaret, formerly Countess of Richmond, now became Lady Stafford. She nevertheless continued to use the title of Countess of Richmond for the remainder of her life, valuing the prestige associated with it. That Margaret was yet to reach her fifteenth birthday by the time of her third marriage was extraordinary even by fifteenth-century standards, but of all her marriages, this one seems to have brought her the most happiness in personal terms. Though their marriage was first and foremost a business arrangement in the same manner as many other fifteenth-century marriages, made for the mutual benefit of both families, Margaret and Stafford seem to have genuinely felt affectionate towards one another. After the tumultuous happenings of Margaret's youth, her third marriage – although only the second that she would acknowledge – would provide her with exactly the kind of stability that she craved.

According to Norton, on 8 January – five days after Margaret's wedding – Henry VI granted Henry Tudor's wardship to Jasper and the Earl of Shrewsbury.[13] However, the grant issued made no mention of Henry's wardship, and instead stipulated that the men were to have 'the keeping of all possessions in England, Wales and the marches' that had once been Edmund's during Henry's minority – except for his possessions in Lincolnshire.[14] This was, as Norton indicates, in response to Margaret's marriage to Stafford, but the reason for splitting the lands between Jasper and Shrewsbury remains a mystery. Shrewsbury had been created a Knight of the Garter alongside Margaret's stepfather Lord Welles, so it is certainly possible that he was a friend of the family. Alternatively, he was the King's Lord Treasurer, so the grant could simply have been a reward for his loyalty. What is unclear, though, is who would retain custody of Margaret's son.

There is no evidence that Henry remained in his mother's care following her marriage to Henry Stafford, and in what was doubtless a heart-wrenching move, it was probably before her marriage was solemnized that Margaret was forced to bid him farewell. Most likely, it was agreed that Henry would remain in the care of his uncle Jasper at Pembroke. Here his safety could be better assured throughout the seemingly never-ending days of uncertainty caused by the turbulent political climate. Margaret would have been left in no doubt that Jasper would safeguard her son's best interests, and indeed for the rest of his life Jasper would treat Henry as his own son. In turn, Margaret, too, remained close to her former brother-in-law, who she trusted implicitly.

Following her marriage, Margaret and her husband took up residence at Bourne, in the Fens, which formed a part of her inheritance from her father. Bourne had once been a possession of the Holland family, and Edward III had been entertained there in 1330.[15] Set in beautiful parkland with fine rooftop views overlooking the Fens, the house in which Margaret and Stafford lived was of Norman origin – a large motte-and-bailey castle that featured a keep, and was entered through a medieval gatehouse that may have led into a courtyard. There was ample room to accommodate their household, as well as to entertain visitors, most probably in the Hall. There was also an abbey nearby in which Margaret's great-grandfather, Thomas Holland, Earl of Kent, lay buried. Margaret was evidently fond of Bourne: in the first of her wills, dated 1472, she stipulated her desire to be buried there. Though her wish later changed, she retained her affection for the place until the end of her life, making a bequest of a mass book to the abbey in her will.

At the beginning of Margaret's marriage, the separation from her son must have been difficult for her, and she would undoubtedly have sought solace in her religion as a means of comfort. Her pain as a mother separated from her child would only have been exacerbated by the fact that – as André would later observe – young Henry was 'often sickly at a tender age', and as such was 'tenderly educated by his caretakers, men upright and wise'.[16] Throughout his life, Margaret was eager to retain as much contact with Henry as possible, and Stafford also took an interest in his new stepson. Though he saw him infrequently, the surviving evidence suggests that he grew fond of the boy. This may have been heightened by the fact that – for whatever reason – in what transpired to be a fourteen-year marriage, Stafford sired no children of his own by Margaret.

Margaret was living apart from her son, yet in all other respects her domestic arrangements had provided her with the security she needed in order to safeguard both of their futures. Once more, she had married into a family whose head had power and influence matched only by York, but they were living in uncertain times.[17] Ultimately, the outcome of these testing and unpredictable days meant that it would not be long before the stability that Margaret's marriage had hitherto provided her with was shattered.

THE SAME MONTH as Margaret's marriage in 1458, Henry VI had ordered all of his nobles to attend upon him at Westminster. In the interest of a longer-standing peace, the King was eager to reconcile both sides. On 24 March – Lady Day – a reconciliation was staged between the King and Queen, on one side, and York and his supporters on the other: it would become known as Loveday. The Queen and York followed the King hand in hand as they processed through London for all to see, but few believed that it was more than a superficial show. Tensions continued to rise, and in anticipation of further violence, both sides had been busily recruiting men to their cause.

On 23 September 1459, Lord Audley, acting on Queen Margaret's orders, ambushed some of the Yorkist forces at Blore Heath in Staffordshire as they were making their way to Ludlow to join their main army. The result was a Yorkist victory, but a rout at Ludford Bridge the following month turned the tables and York, Salisbury and Warwick fled. York managed to evade capture and cross to Ireland, taking his second son Edmund, Earl of Rutland, with him. Salisbury and Warwick fled to Calais, taking York's eldest son, Edward, Earl of March, with them. With York and his supporters out of her reach, Queen Margaret began consolidating royal power and taking full control of the government. A bill of attainder was drawn up in Parliament against York and his followers, who were found guilty of high treason against the Crown. This resulted in the loss of their estates, which were swiftly handed out to Lancastrian supporters by way of reward. Among the beneficiaries were Owen and Jasper Tudor, as well as Margaret's stepfather. On 19 December, Lord Welles was granted lands in Essex formerly owned by Salisbury, which were now forfeit, 'for good service against the rebels'.[18]

Across the Irish sea, York was working hard to drum up support, and sympathy for his cause was also growing across the Channel. On 26 June 1460, Warwick, Salisbury and the Earl of March landed in England. They immediately marched to London, where the citizens joyously welcomed them. They nevertheless took care to declare that they had only come to lay their grievances before the King in person, and to ensure that good government was restored. Henry VI was in Coventry with the Queen and Prince Edward. He swiftly began preparing for an armed confrontation. Thanks to the Queen's efforts, Henry now had a sizeable army of around twenty thousand men at his command, and he began to lead his men towards Northampton. The Queen, meanwhile, took her son to Eccleshall Castle in Staffordshire, where she waited anxiously for news.[19]

Warwick and March had led their army – double the size of the King's force – towards Northampton, and promptly sent a message to Henry in which they pleaded with him to hear their grievances in person. Henry, who was joined by his commander Buckingham – Margaret's father-in-law – steadfastly refused, and in so doing underlined that there was no other choice but to resort to armed conflict. Both he and Buckingham, however, had underestimated Warwick and the Yorkist army.

On the afternoon of 10 July, the two armies engaged in battle. In a repeat of St Albans, it was to be of short duration, and would prove to be a decisive

Yorkist victory 'without a serious fight or much slaughter' as the Milanese ambassador had been told.[20] The majority of the casualties were sustained by the Lancastrians, and in the process of trying to defend the King from the advancing Yorkists, Buckingham and several others, including the Earl of Shrewsbury, were killed. To make matters worse, Henry VI was captured by a Yorkist archer, named Henry Mountfort. It was a disastrous outcome for the Lancastrians, and many of those who had survived the battle fled into hiding. But for the King there was to be no escape: the *Croyland Chronicle* reported that Henry was taken 'in solemn procession', with the Earl of Warwick 'bearing the sword before the king, bare-headed and in all humility and respect'.[21] There was to be no repeat of the deference shown in the wake of St Albans. This time, he returned to London as a Yorkist prisoner, and once more Margaret's family was in the power of others.

It had been a mere two years since Margaret had married. Now, the death of the Duke of Buckingham meant that the head of Margaret's marital family was gone, and the security that such a powerful magnate had seemingly promised was shown to be as unreliable as that offered by so many of the other men in Margaret's life. Her father-in-law was buried in the Grey Friars in Northampton, which no longer survives. Stafford's elder brother, Humphrey, had died in 1458, meaning that the dukedom of Buckingham passed to Stafford's nephew – Humphrey's son. His name was also Henry Stafford, and the young boy now became the second Duke of Buckingham. The new Buckingham was not only Margaret's nephew by marriage, but also her cousin, and in later years the now five-year-old little boy would come to play an intriguing and pivotal role in her life. As Buckingham was still a minor, Margaret's husband Stafford temporarily became the figurehead of the family. What was more, his loyalty to the house of Lancaster remained unshaken.

WHEN NEWS OF the Lancastrian defeat and her husband's capture reached Queen Margaret at Eccleshall Castle, she was utterly horrified. Flight was her only option, and after a brief stop in Wales she sailed to Scotland, where the Queen Dowager, Mary of Gueldres, welcomed her.[22] Meanwhile, on 8 September York arrived in England from Ireland, where he had been drumming up support since his flight there following the rout at Ludford Bridge the previous year. Landing in North Wales, he set out for London, but this time there was a profound difference: he made no pretence of wishing for a role as the King's advisor – he was here to claim the throne. On 7 October, Parliament met, but Henry VI – though he attended the opening – was otherwise notably absent. Three days later, on 10 October, York reached the capital. He immediately made his way to Westminster, where he marched into Parliament. According to Croyland, in a purposeful gesture, York 'approached the royal throne and claimed the seat as his own'.[23] If he was hoping for an enthusiastic response though, he was sadly mistaken. Whatever Henry VI's shortcomings, he was still an anointed king, and one to whom most of the nobles had sworn allegiance. Many people, including York's own supporters, felt that he had overreached himself. But York thought otherwise, and on 16 October he staked an official claim to the throne by right of his bloodline, which he believed to be superior to that of Henry VI. Nobody could deny that he had a good claim: he was, after all, descended from two of Edward III's sons – paternally, he was related to Edward's fourth son, but through his mother he claimed kinship with Edward's second son, Lionel of Clarence. This was not enough to convince the nobles to accept him as an alternative to Henry VI. After much debate, it was finally agreed that Henry VI should remain king, but that York would be named his heir – thereby displacing Prince Edward. On 24 October the Act of Accord by which this became law was drafted, but it was not an end to York's ambitions. As Alison Weir has highlighted, it was now evident that the divisions between Lancaster and York had escalated into a struggle for the throne itself rather than power between the two rival sides.[24]

When Queen Margaret learned of the Act of Accord she was outraged. There was worse news: on 8 November York had not only been declared Henry VI's heir apparent, but also Protector of England once more, thereby exercising power in the King's name. The Queen and her supporters immediately marched south with a Scottish army provided by Mary of

Gueldres. She was also able to attract the support of a substantial chunk of the English nobility including northern lords such as Percy and Clifford who, like Somerset, were thirsting for revenge for the deaths of their fathers at St Albans. York, accompanied by Salisbury, prepared to journey north to meet her, and the two left London on 9 December. They made it to Sandal Castle, York's impregnable stronghold near Wakefield, where they intended to spend Christmas. By now Lancastrian forces had regained control over the area, and this time it was York's turn to underestimate their strength. It would lead to his undoing.

On 30 December, York ventured out of the security of Sandal for reasons that are unclear. His forces soon became engaged in battle with the Lancastrian army, commanded by the Duke of Somerset. The Milanese ambassador was subsequently told that the Yorkists, 'although they were three times stronger, yet from lack of discipline, because they allowed a large part of the force to go pillaging and searching for victuals, their adversaries, who are desperate, attacked the duke and his followers'.[25] During the ensuing Battle of Wakefield, York was slain, as was his seventeen-year-old son, Edmund, Earl of Rutland, while Salisbury was captured and later killed. It was a crushing blow for the Yorkists, and the severed heads of all three men were placed on spikes above the Micklegate Bar in the city of York – York's wearing a paper crown.

Save for his family and the commons, with whom he had been popular, few mourned York. Indeed, for Margaret Beaufort and her family, it would have been cause for much celebration. However, though he was dead – his ambitions for the throne never realized – the wars were by no means over. His eldest son, Edward, Earl of March, now emerged as his father's successor, and he was determined to avenge the savagery and disgrace that had been inflicted upon his father and brother. It was evident that more violence would soon follow, and it was only a matter of time before Margaret's husband, Stafford, would be forced to become involved.

CHAPTER 7

Like a Fugitive

I N JANUARY 1461, Margaret and Henry Stafford had been married for three years. Thus far they had remained largely uninvolved in the drama of the Wars of the Roses, bearing the damage from a distance. In particular, Jasper Tudor's role ensured that Margaret was in a constant state of anxiety over the welfare of her son.

Jasper and his father Owen were intent on causing trouble for York's son and successor, so, leaving the young Henry Tudor at Pembroke, in January they moved with their men towards Herefordshire. On 2 February they engaged in battle with the Yorkist army at Mortimer's Cross, close to the Welsh border. The Yorkists had a strong force that included Sir William Herbert, who had once ousted Edmund Tudor from Carmarthen. The Battle of Mortimer's Cross was one of the most savage of the Wars of the Roses, and the Lancastrian losses were heavy. When it became clear that the Yorkists had the victory, Jasper fled from the battlefield. His father was not so fortunate, for Owen was captured. The following day he and several others were taken to the marketplace in Hereford and executed.[1] According to the contemporary author of *Gregory's Chronicle*, it was not until he saw the block and the axe that the realization of impending death set in, causing Owen to declare 'that head shall lie on the stock that was wont to lie on Queen Katherine's lap'.[2] His head was set upon the market cross, but *Gregory's Chronicle* claimed that a mad woman took it and 'combed his hair and washed away the blood of his face'.[3] With her father-in-law dead and Jasper a fugitive, Margaret was in a state of panic – her son was still at Pembroke Castle and now he had no protector.

In the aftermath of Mortimer's Cross there was no time to be lost. On 17 February the two armies once more crossed swords at the Second Battle of St Albans as Warwick and his men attempted to prevent the Lancastrian army from reaching London. Henry VI had been in Warwick's train, and was 'placed under a tree a mile away, where he laughed and sang' while the battle was fought.[4] This time the Lancastrians were victorious, and Henry was set at liberty. He was reunited with his wife, and the royal couple intended to march to London. However, to Queen Margaret's dismay she quickly discovered that they were not wanted in the capital, forcing them to retreat. Instead, at the end of February, York's son and heir, Edward of March, entered London to the great elation of the citizens. Shortly afterwards, a meeting took place at Baynard's Castle on the Thames: here some of the lords agreed that Henry VI ought to be deposed; in his place, Edward IV was declared King of England.

The news was largely met with celebrations. Henry's former subjects were disenchanted with his rule and had lost all patience with his lack of control, which had in turn created many of the country's problems. Like his predecessor, Edward had a legitimate claim to throne – one technically stronger than that of Henry VI. Nevertheless, though Henry IV had set the precedent following his usurpation of the throne in 1399, the deposition of a monarch was still an extraordinary move, and one that was not taken lightly by the nobles of the realm. Margaret, who was just seventeen years old and had known no other king than Henry VI, met the news of her kinsman's deposition with horror. But all hope was not yet lost. Henry and his queen were still at liberty, and there was every chance they would continue to fight for their thrones: this was exactly what they intended to do.

Following the Second Battle of St Albans, Henry VI and his men began marching towards York. Somerset and many other lords who remained loyal, including Margaret's stepfather Lord Welles, accompanied him. This time, however, her husband Stafford would also be joining them, leaving Margaret behind at home – probably at Bourne. The newly established Edward IV, who recognized the need for swift action if he was to crush his rival, soon followed them. Edward had been hastily recruiting men to his cause, and within a short time his forces had closed in on the Lancastrian army close to the Yorkshire village of Towton. Eager to avoid further bloodshed if possible, Henry VI requested a truce, but Edward steadfastly refused: he was determined to destroy his enemies permanently. As dawn broke on the morning of Palm Sunday, 29 March, both armies awoke on the brink of a bitter snowstorm. The treacherous weather conditions did not prevent a battle that was 'great and cruel' from ensuing, during which the crisp white snow became stained with blood.[5] In what may have been the bloodiest battle ever to have been fought on English soil, the meadow on which the Battle of Towton took place would become known as the Bloody Meadow.[6] The atrocities to which Henry Stafford bore witness that day can only be imagined, for the sounds of clashing swords, flying arrows and the screams of the dying were rife. Thousands were mercilessly slaughtered in the ten hours of fighting over which the battle was staged, including Lord Welles, Margaret's stepfather. The appalled Croyland Chronicler reported that 'The blood, too, of the slain, mingling with the snow which at this time covered the whole surface of the earth, afterwards ran down in the furrows and ditches along with the melted snow, in a most shocking manner, for a distance of two or three miles.'[7] The Bishop of Salisbury was later told that 'the heralds counted 28,000 slain, a number unheard of in our realm for almost a thousand years, without counting those wounded and drowned'.[8] It eventually became clear that the Yorkists had won the field, but so huge was the slaughter that this was no great victory, despite the Yorkists claiming it as such. Even so, it was enough to establish Edward IV firmly on the throne … for now.

With the news of their defeat, Henry VI, Queen Margaret and their son fled across the border into Scotland. Other Lancastrians – including Margaret's cousin, Henry Beaufort, Duke of Somerset – soon joined them, but, for some, flight was not an option. Having actively taken up arms against the new king, the life of Margaret's husband Henry Stafford was in danger.

WHEN WORD OF Edward IV's victory at Towton reached London, 'all the city were fayne, and thanked God'.[9] Soon after replacing the Yorkist heads on Micklegate Bar with those of his defeated foes, the new King returned to the capital, where he received a rapturous welcome from his subjects. A Milanese observer reported that Edward had become 'master and governor of the whole realm. Words fail me to relate how well the commons love and adore him, as if he were their God.'[10] It was little wonder that he was so adored, for he provided a stark contrast to Henry VI.

Edward had been born in Rouen in 1442, and at eighteen he was 'young and more handsome than any man then alive', although he would later become very fat.[11] Thomas More, who received his account from one who knew him, would describe Edward as 'a goodly personage, and very princely to behold', while another contemporary referred to him as being 'tall of stature, elegant in person, of unblemished character, valiant in arms, and a lineal descendant of the illustrious line of king Edward the Third'.[12] Physically, then, Edward IV had many of the qualities that people expected of a medieval king, but he possessed other important attributes. He was of 'sharp wit', and 'bountiful to his friends'.[13] He was also 'of heart courageous, politic in counsel, in adversity nothing abashed, in prosperity rather joyful than proud, in peace just and merciful, in war sharp and fierce, in the field bold and hardy'.[14] Like his father he was a natural leader, and unlike Henry VI his very presence commanded respect and admiration. He was certainly incredibly popular, and the people had high hopes for his reign. Accordingly, on 28 June a proclamation was issued in the King's name in which Edward promised his people both strong rule and good government. In this he did not disappoint, although for the first few years of his reign he was ably assisted in much of the government of the realm by the Earl of Warwick, who was by Edward's side from the start. It seemed that few among the commons were sad to see the back of Margaret's house.

The nobility had more reason to be fearful – especially those who had taken up arms against the new King. Many of their worries proved to be unfounded, for Edward quickly showed that he was eager to heal the wounds of the past. Fortunately for Margaret, his clemency extended to Henry Stafford, who was also his cousin by reason of their mothers being sisters. On 25 June he issued a pardon to Stafford for 'all offences committed by him' – one that extended to his younger brother, John, who had also fought for Lancaster at Towton.[15] The King's pardon ensured that the lands Margaret had inherited from her father were saved from confiscation, much to her relief, but there were to be other consequences for her. Edward IV's victory seems to have been enough to convince Stafford and his younger brother to abandon the Lancastrian cause permanently. From now on he would be a loyal – although often reluctant – adherent of York. It is difficult to comprehend how Margaret felt about her husband's decision, or indeed if she had any hand in it. Her personal sense of loyalty to her own house is beyond question, yet though she had only just passed her eighteenth birthday she had enough experience to recognize that the balance between expressions of loyalty and the likelihood of survival required a temperate approach. This was to be just the beginning of a period of her life that saw her ingratiating herself with those who were considered enemies to her house. In so doing, she proved that she was wise enough to know when a cause was lost – at least for the time being – and to adapt to a new regime. Her conduct throughout the reign of Edward IV shows her to have been both a realist and a pragmatist, while her pride about being the kin of kings was dominated by a canny ability to adapt to the changing political climate. In this, Margaret showed, in the words of her biographers Jones and Underwood, 'political astuteness rather than blindly partisan allegiance'.[16] Whatever her personal feelings – and given how events unfolded, these must have been strong indeed – she repeatedly mastered them. Her primary motivation over the coming years once again appears to have been the safety of her son and his interests rather than seeking preferment and personal gain for herself.

On 9 May, the news that Margaret had been dreading became a reality. Edward IV issued a commission to his loyal supporter Sir William Herbert and his brothers to 'take into the king's hands the county and lordship of Pembroke', together with all of the other lands belonging to Jasper Tudor.[17] A similar commission was issued on 10 August, which termed Jasper 'a rebel'.[18] This was followed, on 7 September, by Herbert and his brothers, along with Sir Walter Devereux, being tasked with taking over 'all castles, lordships, manors, lands and possessions late of Humphrey, Duke of

Buckingham, in South Wales', on account of the minority of his son – Henry Stafford's nephew.[19] The Herberts wasted no time in fulfilling both commissions. Margaret and her family were powerless to prevent them, and on 30 September Sir William Herbert successfully captured Jasper's home of Pembroke Castle just as he had once overtaken Edmund Tudor at Carmarthen. On 4 October a Paston correspondent reported that 'all the castles and holds in South Wales and in North Wales are given and yielded up into the king's hand. And the Duke of Exeter and the Earl of Pembroke are flown and taken to the mountains, and divers lords with great puissance are after them.'[20] Jasper had fled, leaving his four-year-old nephew Henry Tudor at Pembroke to the mercy of the Yorkists. For Margaret, the years of endless agitation as she agonized over Henry's welfare had begun.

ON 1 NOVEMBER Edward IV convened his first Parliament. Acts of Attainder were passed against 150 Lancastrians headed by Henry VI and Margaret of Anjou, and included Somerset and Margaret's deceased stepfather Lord Welles.[21] Though the King had pardoned her husband, Margaret had good reason to feel concerned, given the treatment received by her kinsmen. To her relief, though, provision was made to secure her lands, presumably as a result of Edward's show of reconciliation towards her husband. It was officially stated that

> no act made or to be made in this present parliament shall extend or be prejudicial to Margaret, countess of Richmond, daughter and heir of John, late duke of Somerset, with regard to any lands, tenements or other possessions, whatever they may be, which she holds in dower, of the endowment of Edmund, late earl of Richmond, her late husband, and by assignment of Henry VI, late in deed and not by right king of England; or to any lands, tenements, rents or other hereditaments which descended or ought to descend to her from the said John, late duke of Somerset, her father.[22]

Margaret was not unique, for in a further extension of Edward's attitude of clemency, Parliament also secured the lands of other leading noblemen and women, including her mother the dowager Duchess of Somerset.[23] Others were not to be so fortunate. The estates of those who had been attainted for 'falsely and traitorously against their faith and allegiance there raised war against the same King Edward, their rightful, true and natural liege lord' – whether alive or dead – were now taken from their families.[24] They provided rich rewards, which Edward IV distributed to his faithful supporters. Although Margaret's lands were not affected by the King's redistribution, it would not be long before those of her son were.

Immediately after the capture of Pembroke Castle, young Henry became the King's ward. There is no evidence, though, that he left Pembroke at this time. Nor is there any indication as to who oversaw his care, but given Margaret's later conduct, it seems plausible that she would have petitioned for him to be returned to her, or at the very least attempted to communicate with Henry. Whatever her hopes may have been, the decision was not hers to make. On 12 February 1462, Edward IV granted to Sir William Herbert 'the custody and marriage of Henry son and heir of Edmund, earl of Richmond, tenant in chief of Henry VI, in the king's hands by reason of his minority'.[25] Henry's wardship was a valuable prize, and in order to secure it, Herbert paid the huge sum of £1,000 (£643,000).

With his uncle branded a traitor, five-year-old Henry now bade farewell to the place of his birth and childhood home, and started on the long and arduous journey across the breadth of Wales to the imposing Raglan Castle that was his new guardian's main seat. One of the last medieval castles to be built in England and Wales, the site had long been fortified, perhaps as far back as the Norman conquest of Wales. It had only recently become Herbert's home, having been granted to him in 1461.[26] Herbert himself, however, had a long-standing record of loyalty to the Yorkist cause as well as military experience. Like many magnates, he had fought in France during the Hundred Years' War, during which he had been captured at the Battle of Formigny in 1450.[27] He was knighted two years later, and soon became an important figure in Wales, where he kept semi-regal state and wielded great power. He had strong ties to the Duke of York, whom he had openly declared his support for by August 1460 in the aftermath of the Battle of Northampton. His allegiance was later transferred to Edward IV. Having fought bravely for Edward's cause, he would become increasingly powerful in the coming years. For Margaret, losing her son to the man who had been responsible for routing his father at Carmarthen six years earlier must have been bitterly painful, but she had no choice in the matter. Her prudent efforts to position herself in a powerful family so that she could provide her son with a secure future had come to nought, crushed in a battle between kings.

Margaret would have at least drawn some solace from the knowledge that Henry was comfortable at Raglan Castle. Herbert would spend a vast sum on improvements to the fortress, firmly putting his own stamp on his recently acquired home. These included magnificent suites of new apartments in order to accommodate his family, and an impressive gatehouse that inspired awe in Raglan's visitors. A luxurious setting for Henry's upbringing, it was also the main administrative centre of Herbert's lands, and thus would have been a constant hub of hustle and bustle as Herbert and his staff worked to keep these in good order.

To Margaret's relief, Herbert took his role as guardian with great seriousness, and he and his wife would prove to be kindly, taking genuine concern in Henry's welfare. In 1449, Herbert had been married to Anne Devereux, the daughter of Sir Walter Devereux of Weobley, and she was particularly fond of Henry.[28] He in turn formed a close bond with her, and years later would not only remember her but also welcome her to his court. At Raglan – for the first time – Henry would have been able to enjoy the company of other noble children, for the Herberts had young children of similar ages, including sons William and Walter.[29] There were also several daughters, and in his will Herbert subsequently set out his hope that the eldest of these, Maud, should 'be wedded to the Lord Henry of Richmond'.[30] Whether Herbert ever consulted Margaret about this is unknown. For a time Henry was able to enjoy some semblance of a normal childhood under the Herberts' supervision, and in later years he would not forget their kindness, but he was still left in no doubt of his status. He would later recall that 'since the age of five he had been guarded like a fugitive or kept in prison'.[31]

Though she was separated from him, Margaret and her husband still took a keen interest in Henry's welfare. She was able to retain contact with him through letters and messengers and took care to do so regularly, probably referring to him in terms such as 'my dear heart', as she did when he reached adulthood. Perhaps she even sent gifts on occasion. Given the importance she placed on her own education, she would have been gratified to hear that Henry was doing well in his lessons, which were supervised by the Oxford graduate Andrew Scot. Another former Oxford pupil, Edward Haseley, was later described as 'instructor of the king in grammar in his tender age', while Sir Hugh Johns may have been on hand to assist with some early military training.[32] Unsurprisingly, André was full of praise when it came to young Henry's academic abilities, and claimed that Scot had told him that 'he had never heard of a boy at that age with such great mental quickness and capacity for learning'.[33] Henry was, André said, 'endowed with such sharp mental powers and such great natural vigour and comprehension' that he grasped his lessons quickly.[34] He apparently 'surpassed his peers', and 'possessed such becoming noble manners, such charmful grace of royal expression, and such great beauty'.[35] He was, in short, a son to be proud of, though to her sorrow Margaret would not be the one to raise him.

On 20 September, it appeared that Henry's lineage and education would be all that he had to commend him, for on that day, to Margaret's horror, the King issued a grant. In it, 'the lordship of Richmond, which Edmund Hadham, late Earl of Richmond, lately had of the grant of Henry VI', which had then passed to his son Henry, was taken from him.[36] Instead, the earldom and the lands that came with it were conferred upon the King's brother, George, Duke of Clarence.[37] In a show of defiance, and demonstrating a resolute determination to acknowledge what she truly believed to be his birthright, Margaret continued to refer to Henry as 'Lord Richmond', as indeed did Lord Herbert. What was more, she was not prepared to give up hope of getting them back, even if it meant humbling herself before her enemies.

NORTH OF THE border, others of Margaret's family were not so set on appeasement. Having lost his lands, Jasper had almost certainly made his way to Scotland to join Henry VI and his family in exile. He continued to work tirelessly for the Lancastrian cause, though it now seemed hopeless and he had lost several of his family members in active service to Henry VI. In 1462 he joined Queen Margaret as she sailed to her homeland of France in an attempt to beg for Louis XI's aid in restoring her husband to his throne. On 28 June Louis signed the Treaty of Tours, the terms of which agreed a one-hundred-year truce between himself and Henry VI, as well as both parties promising not to support the other's enemies.[38]

Not all of Henry VI's supporters were as loyal as Jasper Tudor. By 1463 Margaret's cousin Somerset had had enough of being an exile, and decided to throw himself on Edward IV's mercy. As a leading Lancastrian, by submitting himself to Edward, Somerset became a figurehead for those who were willing to accept a monarchy without a Lancastrian king at the head. Edward IV was delighted by this turn of events, and in an attempt to win Somerset's friendship he made a point of lavishing attention on him: they hunted together, Somerset became captain of Edward's guard, and, in a sign of great favour, he even shared the King's bed.[39] The King evidently recognized the need to broaden his support network, realizing that he could not rely on Warwick and his affinity alone. This reconciliation with the Yorkist regime also led to a positive outcome for other members of Margaret's family: her aunt, Eleanor, dowager Duchess of Somerset (wife of Margaret's deceased uncle Edmund) was pardoned, and members of the family circle were accepted back into the fold.[40] Margaret may well have deemed this a wise move; it was a similar course of action to the one taken by her husband, and in time she too would become a figurehead of Lancastrian submission. On 10 March, Somerset was granted a general pardon, and the King made several gifts of money to him and his family.[41] But it was not a course that Margaret's cousin would sustain, for at heart he was a true Lancastrian; in December Somerset abandoned Edward IV and fled to join Queen Margaret, then in France. Though he had betrayed his house, the Queen was relieved to have him once more back on side, and forgave Somerset for his earlier desertion.

Edward IV was outraged by Somerset's treachery, and Margaret would have been fearful of the potential consequences for her family. She had good reason to be, for the furious King wasted no time in imprisoning Somerset's mother to whom he had so recently granted a pardon. The dowager Duchess seems to have been kept in relatively stringent conditions. Somerset's double betrayal meant that Edward IV was in no mood to be merciful or reconcile with the Beaufort family.[42] On 24 April 1464, the duke having returned to England, Somerset's forces were defeated by the Yorkists at Hedgeley Moor. But he was not ready to give up, and on 15 May the two armies met again at Hexham in Northumberland. Once again, the result was victory for the Yorkists, and for Somerset himself there were to be no more chances. After the battle, he was captured and immediately executed.[43]

In the aftermath of Hexham, Henry VI, who had been present, was now a fugitive, and would spend the next year relying on the charity of Lancastrian sympathizers while his wife and son were safely abroad in France. Throughout all of this, Margaret and her husband had remained living quietly at Bourne, doing their best to avoid any further involvement in the conflict in the aftermath of Towton. However, they may have been as alarmed as the rest of the country when in the autumn of 1464 some surprising news came to light.

FOR THE FIRST few years of his reign, Edward IV had devoted himself primarily to enjoying the pleasures of kingship that he had fought so hard to obtain. The chronicler Philippe de Commynes claimed that he 'thought of nothing else but women (far more than is reasonable), hunting and looking after himself'.[44] He was extremely athletic but he also loved finery, particularly jewels, in which he indulged heavily. There is certainly truth that he took particular pleasure in women, and he sired several illegitimate children.[45] By 1464, however, the King's lack of a wife had drawn comment among his subjects: his biographer Charles Ross described him as being 'Europe's most eligible bachelor'.[46] Eager to secure an alliance with France and thus put an end to Louis XI's support of the Lancastrians, for months Warwick had been carefully negotiating a marriage for Edward with Louis' sister-in-law, Bona of Savoy.[47] Unbeknown to Warwick, Edward had made his own marital arrangements.

In September, Warwick was left completely stunned when the King announced to his astonished councillors that he was already married. Writing about Edward's new wife, the chronicler Dominic Mancini recalled that one of the ways in which Edward 'indulged his appetites was to marry a lady of humble origin, named Elizabeth'.[48] This Elizabeth was no foreign princess who would bring her husband a valuable European alliance, but the daughter of a Northamptonshire knight, Sir Richard Wydeville.[49] Though her mother was Jacquetta of Luxembourg, the widow of John, Duke of Bedford, such a connection did nothing to improve Elizabeth Wydeville's suitability as the wife of a king.[50] To make matters worse, Elizabeth was also 'a widow and the mother of two sons by a former husband'.[51] According to Mancini's account, 'when the king first fell in love with her beauty of person and charm of manner, he could not corrupt her virtue by gifts or menaces'.[52] Determined to have his way with her, 'when Edward placed a dagger at her throat, to make her submit to his passion, she remained unperturbed and determined to die rather than live unchastely with the king'.[53] This display of womanly virtue only served to inflame Edward's passion for her, and as a result he 'judged the lady worthy to be a royal spouse'.[54] Knowing, however, that such a marriage would be unpopular with his supporters, the wedding took place 'in a secret place' with only the bride's mother, the priest, two gentlewomen and a man who helped the priest to sing being present.[55]

Edward was now forced to deal with the consequences of his secret marriage, the news of which infuriated the nobles and members of his own family. Mancini records that the King's mother, the Duchess of York, 'fell into such a frenzy, that she offered to submit to a public inquiry, and asserted that Edward was not the offspring of her husband the Duke of York, but was conceived in adultery, and therefore in no wise worthy of the honour of kingship'.[56] Most significantly, however, Warwick was 'greatly displeased with the king; and after that rose great dissension ever more and more between the king and him'.[57] This would later have serious consequences for their relationship, but for the time being – in public at least – Warwick was forced to put on a display of unity as Queen Elizabeth was presented to the King's nobles for the first time.

Margaret would have been as stunned as the rest of the King's subjects when she learned that the new queen was a commoner, and the Milanese ambassador reported that the marriage 'greatly offended the people of England'.[58] Like the rest of her contemporaries, however, it would not be long before Margaret, too, was forced to bend her knee to Queen Elizabeth.

In July 1465, news reached London that Henry VI had been captured in Lancashire. The deposed king was returned to London 'without all honour like a thief or an outlaw', and paraded through the streets bound to a horse, wearing a straw hat.[59] His former subjects jeered and taunted the fallen man as he was taken to the Tower, where he would spend the next five years as a prisoner. Here, Blacman later reported, the conditions in which he was kept were harsh, and 'he patiently endured hunger, thirst, mockings, derisions, abuse, and many other hardships'.[60] His capture served as a great blow to Lancastrian morale, yet this did not prevent Queen Margaret, who was still in France, from continuing her tireless efforts for his restoration. As for Margaret and Stafford, for the next few years they would do all that they could in order to ingratiate themselves with the Yorkist king.

CHAPTER 8

A Long Gown for My Lord

THE MANOR AT Woking was idyllic in the summer: its gardens blooming with fragrant flowers, orchards heavy with plump fruits, and fishponds that were regularly used to supply the household.[1] Located on the banks of the River Wey and surrounded by a moat, it stood in a large deer park that provided excellent hunting and recreation. Nearby stood the ancient church of St Peter's, to which Henry Stafford would later bequeath money in his will.[2] It was also the ideal place from which to enjoy the Surrey countryside, while it provided easy access to London. This tranquil spot became Margaret and Stafford's new home in 1467, when Edward IV made them a grant of the former Beaufort property in December 1466. Such a grant was a sign of his determination not to treat Margaret – now twenty-three – with the same antipathy he had displayed to other members of her family following the treachery of her cousin, Somerset; indeed, Woking had once belonged to the disgraced duke. It was not only a sign that Margaret and Stafford were reconciled with the house of York, but also the result of their display of allegiance to the new King. Their favour with the monarch would only continue to grow.

Woking had once been the property of Edward the Confessor, but the first mention of a house on the site comes from 1272.[3] In the fourteenth century, the manor passed into the hands of the Holland family, and remained with them until Margaret Holland married Margaret's grandfather John Beaufort, thus beginning the start of its Beaufort ownership.[4] Perhaps because of its resonance with her own family, Woking quickly became Margaret's favourite home and would remain so for many years. It was a grand house that was entered via a gatehouse, which led into a large courtyard. The house boasted a chapel, hall, kitchen quarters that included a bakehouse and a laundry, as well as apartments that both Margaret and Stafford could enjoy. It was sumptuously decorated with beautifully patterned tiles adorning the floors. Archaeological finds from Woking have shown that blue and white glazed tiles originating from Valencia were used – luxury items indeed – and these probably date from the time of Margaret's residence.[5] The couple's steward, Gilbert Gilpyn, who hailed from Westmorland, oversaw life at Woking, and it was his responsibility to ensure that all ran smoothly.[6] He was highly trusted by his employers, and often carried out tasks on their behalf, as Stafford's account books testify.[7] Similarly, their receiver-general, Reginald Bray (sometimes called Reynold), was an important member of the household; he not only managed Margaret's estates for around twenty years, but also became a lifelong friend.[8] Bray would come to play an integral role in some of the most significant events of Margaret's life, risking his own safety in the process. His wife, Katherine, also served in Margaret's household and is referenced at various points in her accounts.[9]

Stafford's accounts show that he and Margaret spent a great deal of their time in the late 1460s at Woking.[10] Works were undertaken to improve their domestic arrangements, and they lived very comfortably there. They soon became important magnates in the area, and may have been seen on occasion in the local church of St Peter's. The couple were rarely apart, and together they visited the nearby towns frequently, including Guildford from where they regularly obtained household supplies, and Windsor where they are known to have hunted.[11] Hunting appears to have been a favourite pastime, for references to Margaret's participation in this sport appear regularly in Stafford's accounts – on one occasion the couple killed a buck at Henley. Similarly, in later years her own accounts show payments for hawks; clearly hawking was another sport that she enjoyed.[12]

Margaret and her husband were neither important nor regular figures at Edward IV's court, yet at Woking they were living a life of luxury and wanted for nothing. Despite not having the care of her son, Margaret clearly adored life at her Surrey manor. With a staff of around fifty servants to wait on them, the household consumed meat, fish, and red and white wine in large quantities, and often sent to London for other luxury items such as salmon.[13] Fruits such as strawberries and cherries also appear in their accounts. They often used Woking as their base from which to travel to the capital, something that as the 1460s progressed they did with increasing regularity. While in London they would frequently purchase clothes, such as fur for 'a long gown for my lord', black velvet for Margaret and material for a kirtle (part of a woman's gown) to name but a few.[14] Contrary to the dour image conveyed in most of her portraits, Margaret was fond of fashion and took a great interest in her appearance. Later in her life, her inventories reveal the extent of her love of clothes and jewels, but earlier evidence also shows that she was purchasing expensive materials and was conscious of creating an outward impression of splendour as her rank demanded.

Sometimes Stafford would travel to London alone. He did not have an official role at court, but the King sometimes summoned his cousin, clearly eager to keep Stafford on side. Once he travelled to Windsor, and in May 1467 he attended a Council meeting at Mortlake Palace.[15] From his infrequent appearances, it is clear that in spite of their familial ties, Stafford was not a part of Edward IV's inner circle and played a minimal role in his affairs. He does not appear to have been an ambitious man, but there is no way of knowing whether the King's failure to promote him rankled with Stafford or his wife. It is certainly possible, given that the interests and alliances of the rest of Stafford's family were meanwhile becoming increasingly Yorkist. His Bourchier half-uncles were well favoured by Edward IV: Thomas Bourchier (created a Cardinal in 1473) had crowned both Edward IV and his queen; Henry Bourchier had been made Earl of Essex and his son was married to one of the Queen's sisters; and John Bourchier, Lord Berners, was Queen Elizabeth's Chamberlain.[16] Stafford had some contact with these relatives, for Thomas is known to have visited his nephew and his wife at Woking, while in July 1470 Stafford dined with Lord Berners in Guildford. By late 1467 Stafford also had a stepfather, Walter Blount, who was the King's Lord High Treasurer.[17]

As the 1460s progressed, Margaret would often join Stafford on his visits to London. In May 1468, for example, the couple travelled to the capital so that Stafford might attend Parliament, where it had been anticipated that Edward IV would announce an expedition to invade France, led by Stafford's stepfather. The announcement was, however, delayed. Margaret and Stafford had arrived in London by boat, taking up lodgings at The Mitre in Cheapside.[18] Cheapside, despite its name, was a wealthy area of medieval London, and was also one of the main shopping streets, with a market and a vast array of shops and stalls. It was, therefore, the perfect place for Margaret to pick up her luxury items while in the city. She may also have taken the opportunity of her visit to socialize with family and friends. On one occasion, for example, a boat was hired when she paid a visit to the Bishop of Chichester, a man who had formerly served as Henry VI's chaplain and confessor.[19]

Stafford's lack of position at court meant that he was in turn able to accompany Margaret on her travels. She showed a genuine desire to feel involved in the running of her lands, and toured some of these estates to check that everything was in good order.[20] In 1467, she and Stafford viewed some of her West Country lands in Somerset and Devon, including Langport, where the Beaufort portcullis was proudly carved into the battlements of All Saints Church. This is likely to have been an interest that stemmed from her youth.

It was also during this time that Margaret became close to her husband's family, including Stafford's mother and his brother John, who regularly visited the couple at Woking to hunt and play cards. Margaret was fond of cards, and in later life she once sent a man from Buckden to deputize for her on a pilgrimage while she played.[21] Likewise, she enjoyed both chess and gambling, so much so that she was known to place bets on the results of games of chess. These may have been pastimes that Margaret had in common with her husband, for she and Stafford appear to have been genuinely close, and throughout the course of their marriage they were rarely apart. Ordinarily they travelled together, and in spite of the age difference a picture emerges of a couple who enjoyed one another's company. Given their closeness, Margaret's later decision not to include Stafford's arms on her tomb is a mystery. The Stafford knot does, however, appear on the surviving strip of bronze effigy-plate of the tomb, in a more subtle acknowledgement of their union. Though their marriage is unlikely to have been a love match, it became one of heartfelt companionship. As a couple they retained contact not only with Stafford's family members, but with Margaret's too. They spent the Christmas of 1466 as the guests of Margaret's mother, the dowager Duchess of Somerset, at Margaret's childhood home of Maxey. Maxey was located at a convenient distance from their home at Bourne, so it is certainly possible that prior to their move to Woking Margaret saw her mother at fairly regular intervals, as well as spending time together at the Duchess's London residence, Le Ryall. They also corresponded regularly.[22] That Christmas they were joined by Margaret's half-sister, Elizabeth St John.[23] Such was the merriment enjoyed by the party during that festive season that they remained at Maxey for six weeks.[24] Mother and daughter had a close relationship, and in 1465 they both joined the confraternity of the Abbey of Crowland (or Croyland) in Lincolnshire.[25] This was a religious community that promoted solidarity through religion, and that practised both devotional activities and acts of charity. Bishop Fisher would later recall that Margaret 'so studiously in her life was occupied in good works', and it is wholly possible that this stemmed from this period and before.[26] Demonstrating a further link with her family, it was the abbey's chronicler who recorded many of the details of those involved in Margaret's story – including the potentially tragic end of her father. It is unknown whether Margaret's son Henry was ever given the opportunity to meet his grandmother, but no doubt he would frequently have been the subject of conversation between mother and daughter.

Her son was still a constant in Margaret's thoughts, and in a sign both of her own piety and of her concern for Henry's moral welfare, in 1465 she had arranged for the two of them, and Stafford, to be admitted to the confraternity of the Order of the Holy Trinity at Knaresborough.[27] At this time Margaret was only in her early twenties, but the level of religious devotion she was already displaying was extraordinary. The intention in this instance may have been to strengthen her family bonds by allying her husband and son in a common interest. Later in her life, her piety and the

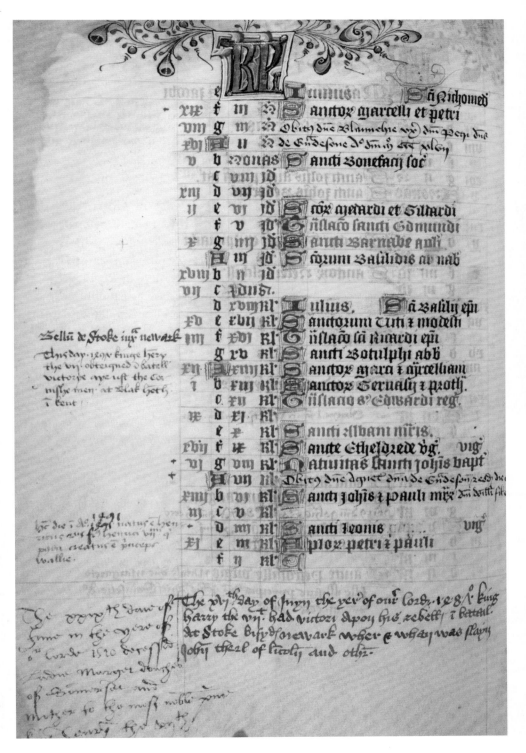

ABOVE: The Beaufort Book of Hours. Margaret used this book to record momentous events in her family, including births and deaths. This page notes Henry VII's victory at the Battle of Stoke.

LEFT: John of Gaunt. It was through Margaret's great-grandfather that she inherited her royal blood.

BELOW LEFT: Young Margaret Beaufort depicted in stained glass at All Saints Church, Landbeach, Cambridgeshire.

BELOW RIGHT: Tomb of Margaret Beaufort's parents in Wimborne Minster. Created on Margaret's orders, the couple are shown clasping hands in an indication of how Margaret perceived their marriage.

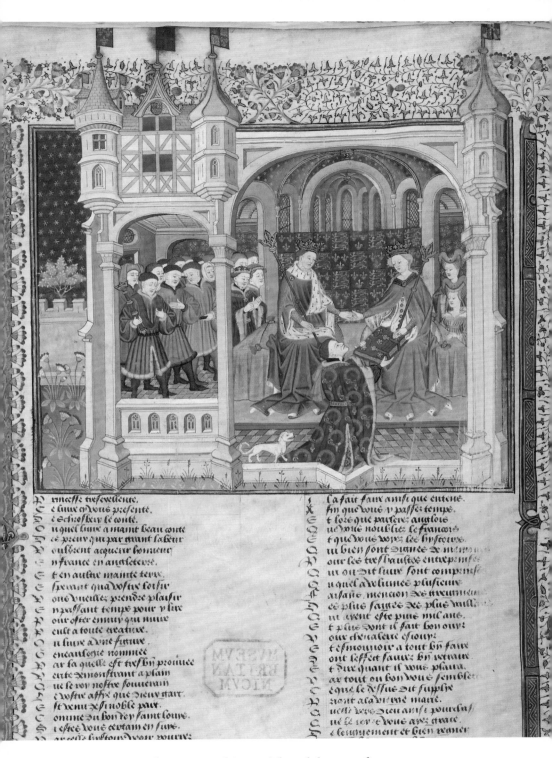

ABOVE: Henry VI and Margaret of Anjou. Though he was of weak character, Margaret Beaufort and her family were loyal to her kinsman and his wife.

LAMPHEY PALACE.

ABOVE: Lamphey Palace. Margaret spent much of her short marriage to Edmund Tudor at Lamphey.

RIGHT: Tomb of Edmund Tudor, St David's Cathedral. Margaret's marriage to Edmund lasted little more than a year before it was cut short as a result of Edmund's death from the plague.

ABOVE: Pembroke Castle. It was at Pembroke, the stronghold of Margaret's brother-in-law Jasper Tudor, that Margaret gave birth to her only son on 28 January 1457.

LEFT: Edward IV. For years Margaret attempted to ingratiate herself with the Yorkist king in her efforts to secure her son's safety.

ABOVE: Raglan Castle. Following Edward IV's accession Henry Tudor came to live at Raglan as the ward of Sir William Herbert. Margaret visited him there in 1467.

LEFT: Elizabeth Wydeville. Edward IV's controversial queen later plotted with Margaret in an attempt to place Henry Tudor on the throne.

LEFT: Richard III. Soon after Richard's coronation Margaret began plotting against him. When Richard discovered her involvement he confiscated her lands and placed her in the custody of her husband, Lord Stanley.

RIGHT: The Princes in the Tower. It was as a result of the disappearance of Edward IV's sons in the summer of 1483 that Margaret perceived an opportunity for her son to become king.

LEFT: Elizabeth of York. The plan for Henry Tudor to marry Edward IV's eldest daughter probably came from Margaret, and she certainly encouraged it. It is likely that she had a good relationship with her daughter-in-law, with whom she spent much of her time during Henry VII's reign.

RIGHT: Merevale Abbey, Leicestershire. It was here that Henry Tudor and part of his army camped on the night before the Battle of Bosworth in 1485.

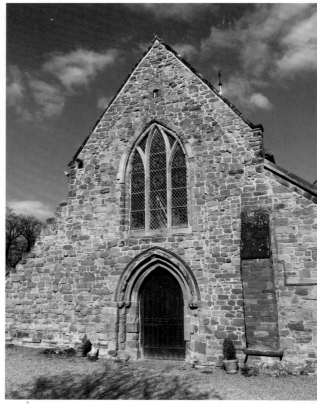

observances she made were recorded in greater detail, but it seems highly likely that these were rituals she had begun much earlier. They clearly afforded a great deal of strength during difficult times, and may have stemmed from her mother and her links to the various confraternities with which she became involved. It seems plausible that Margaret's piety may have increased as a result of her separation from her son, with prayer helping to sustain her.

In September 1467, twenty-four-year-old Margaret was finally afforded the opportunity to see Henry. It is unclear when she had last seen him, but certainly this was the first recorded occasion in her husband's account books. The previous month she and Stafford had been touring her estates, which took them as far as Sampford Peverell in Devon. As they reached Bristol, they paid 10 shillings (£321.50) for a ferry to take them to Chepstow, from whence it was a short distance to Raglan Castle.[28] The couple were evidently made welcome by Lord Herbert and his family, as they remained at Raglan as his guests for a week. Thus Margaret was given a rare chance to spend some time with her son, who was now ten years old. It was probably all the more precious because she is unlikely to have seen Henry, 'my dearest and only desired joy in this world', for some years – mother and son barely knew one another. It may also have been the first occasion on which Stafford met his stepson. The boy was clearly being well cared for. There was comfort to be had, but perhaps also a touch of jealousy. The visit would have been all too short for Margaret, and it would doubtless have come as a huge emotional wrench for her when she was ultimately left with no choice but to bid Henry farewell, not knowing when she would be afforded another opportunity to see him.

'MY LORD OF Pembroke, brother of the deposed King Henry of England, with some armed ships has entered the country of Wales', the Milanese ambassador reported in July 1468.[29] Supplied with money and a fleet provided by Louis XI, Jasper took the opportunity to begin raiding the land where he had always been popular. 'The old Lord Jasper', as *Gregory's*

Chronicle referred to him, succeeded in capturing Denbigh Castle and was soon holding court 'in King Harry's name', in spite of the fact that Henry VI remained a prisoner in the Tower.[30] This convinced Edward IV that he would have to take control of Harlech Castle, which remained the only Welsh castle in Lancastrian hands. The author of *Gregory's Chronicle* believed that Harlech 'is so strong that men said that it was impossible unto any man to get it'.[31] Sir William Herbert and his brother Richard were sent to secure its fall, and it may be that they were joined by Herbert's ward, Henry Tudor.[32] If Henry did accompany his guardian, he would have witnessed as the garrison surrendered to Herbert's forces on 14 August, forcing his uncle Jasper to flee into exile once more. But, there was one final humiliation left for the die-hard warrior to endure: on 8 September, Herbert was created Earl of Pembroke – the title previously held by Jasper – in grateful thanks for his loyalty. With Jasper in exile again, Henry Tudor remained in the custody of the newly ennobled Earl of Pembroke.

With every Lancastrian incursion, Margaret's position became once again precarious. She was politically astute enough to recognize that Edward IV was a strong king and she never sought to join forces with her rebellious house, whatever her personal feelings. But Margaret bore Lancastrian blood, and her unwavering obedience to Edward's rule was not enough in the King's eyes. In what may have been a test of their loyalty, on 20 December Edward paid the Staffords the honour of a visit at Woking. The couple placed great emphasis on the occasion, and costly preparations were put in place. Every detail had been considered, including the pewter dinner service – brought from London – from which the King would eat the five dozen dishes on offer.[33] This is certainly likely to have been Margaret's first meeting with Edward IV, and in honour of the occasion she purchased a sumptuous velvet dress.[34] Brookwood, the hunting lodge that lay next to their home, had been chosen to host the visit. It was here that Margaret remained on the appointed day, busily overseeing the preparations in the hope of making a splendid impression. It was left to Stafford to ride to Guildford to meet the King, and having first enjoyed the hunt together, he escorted his royal guest to Brookwood to indulge in his wife's hospitality.

The chronicler Philippe de Commynes observed that during the hunting season Edward would often have 'several tents brought along for the ladies. All in all, he had made a great show of this.'[35] The King would therefore have been pleased at the sight of the elaborate purple tent of sarsenet (a fine fabric) that had been specially erected for the occasion. No expense had been spared when it came to the refreshments the King was to enjoy, and the meal was eaten to the sound of strumming minstrels. There was an assortment of seafood that included hundreds of oysters, as well as eel and lampreys, all of which were washed down with ale. What Margaret's impressions of the man who had ousted her family from the throne were as she entertained him at her home can only be imagined, but on the surface at least she maintained the appearance of the perfect hostess. The King's visit was a success, although it did nothing in terms of improving Stafford's standing.

By the time of the royal visit, Margaret and Stafford would have known of the growing rift between the King and the Earl of Warwick. Warwick's annoyance with Edward had increased throughout the 1460s, first as a result of Elizabeth Wydeville's rapaciousness and her determination to promote the interests of her family, and then when Edward chose to treat with Burgundy rather than allying with France as Warwick had hoped. By 1469, Warwick had had enough.

In July 1469 the disgruntled Earl sailed for Calais with his family and one notable addition: George, Duke of Clarence – the King's brother and recipient of Margaret's son's title of Richmond. On 11 July, Clarence was married to Warwick's eldest daughter, Isabel, in Calais – a match that the King had expressly forbidden. The following day the two men issued a manifesto in which they urged men to rise up and support their attempts to free the King from those around him – chiefly the hated Wydevilles. Warwick also resented the influence of the recently created Earl of Pembroke, Henry Tudor's guardian William Herbert, and he was a direct target in the manifesto. Having laid the groundwork, Warwick and Clarence set sail for England, intending to take up arms against the King.

Edward IV was unprepared for battle, and immediately summoned his supporters. Chief among them was William Herbert, who did not hesitate to come to the King's aid. Having gathered a force of men, Herbert left Raglan and hurried to meet Edward in the north. His brother, Richard, and his twelve-year-old ward, Henry Tudor, joined him. Herbert's reasons for taking Henry with him are unclear, but he may have been fearful lest he should be snatched from Raglan during his absence. Whatever the circumstances, Henry was about to witness the devastation wreaked by the Wars of the Roses at first-hand.

The Herbert brothers had yet to reach the King when, on 26 July, their heavily outnumbered army engaged with the rebels at Edgecote Moor, north-east of Banbury. The rebels had the victory, and both William Herbert and his brother were taken prisoner. Led before Warwick and Clarence at Northampton, the fate of the two men was a foregone conclusion: the following day they were both executed.[36] In what had been his first taste of warfare, Henry Tudor had lost his guardian: unprotected, Margaret's son was in great danger.

CHAPTER 9

Divine Prophecy

MARGARET AND STAFFORD were enjoying their favourite pastime of hunting in the forests surrounding Windsor when news of Warwick's victory at the Battle of Edgecote was brought to them.[1] They were told nothing further, for there was no news of either Henry or Herbert – or indeed the King. Evidently aware that Henry had accompanied his guardian, Margaret was frantic with worry: Stafford's accounts provide a glimpse of her panic as the couple urgently dispatched their servant William Bailey with messages in an attempt to discover Henry's whereabouts.[2] There was an agonizing wait for news.

Though his army had been advancing south from Nottingham, Edward IV had not been present at Edgecote. When he heard not only of the defeat of his army but of the execution of his staunch ally William Herbert, he was shocked. Worse was to come when his men began to desert, and a jubilant Warwick and Clarence soon captured him. Yet their plan was ill thought through. Edward was sent to Warwick's stronghold of Warwick Castle – a prisoner – while the Earl attempted to rule in his name, punishing his Wydeville enemies.[3]

Finally the news that Margaret had been waiting for arrived: though she was horrified to learn of Herbert's execution, her young son was safe. According to the later petition of Sir Richard Corbet, it was he 'that brought your grace out of the danger of your enemies'.[4] Corbet was married to Anne Herbert's niece, and it was to the wife of his deceased guardian Anne Herbert that Henry was returned.[5] In the aftermath of Edgecote, she was to be found at Weobley Castle on the Gower Peninsula, the home of her brother Sir Walter Devereux, a significant distance from where the battle had taken place.[6] That Henry was conveyed such a distance shows that his rescuers were eager to ensure that he was as far away from danger as possible, but the journey – over a hundred and fifty miles – must have been exhausting for the twelve-year-old boy. Even so, he was safe, and as Margaret digested this welcome news, the immediate concern of her husband seems to have been to ensure that his stepson was kept entertained. Henry was evidently fond of archery, for a payment in Stafford's accounts notes the purchase of bows and arrow shafts 'for his disports' while at Weobley, a touching insight into his stepfather's caring nature.[7] In spite of this attempt at normality, Henry understood that once again he had lost a guardian, and he was old enough to wonder where his future lay.

With Herbert dead and Edward IV seemingly unseated, Margaret had only one thought. On 24 August she and Stafford travelled to London, intent on gaining an audience with Clarence. Her purpose was to petition for Henry to be returned to her care and to have his title restored. The title currently belonged to Clarence, and with him at the forefront of affairs alongside Warwick, it seemed like the ideal opportunity to negotiate on her son's behalf. To her disappointment, upon visiting Clarence's London residence alone, she learned that he was at Middleham Castle in the north.[8] Margaret's determination to re-establish Henry's birthright overruled her good sense, for the realm was still greatly unsettled. Yet it is also a sign of her desperation to regain what she felt was her son's due, and throughout her life she demonstrated a fierce resolve to do what she felt to be right, never giving up in spite of the obstacles that confronted her. In this circumstance, however, attempting to communicate with Clarence was a risk, and one that would prove to be a mistake.

Though Edward IV was in Warwick's custody, ruling England in the King's name was no easy feat and few were responsive to Warwick's efforts. On 10 September, Warwick was left with no choice but to release his captive, and the following month Edward was warmly welcomed back to London. Meanwhile, Margaret and Stafford had consulted their lawyers in regards to Henry Tudor's custody, and with the help of the trusted Reginald Bray, a copy of the original wardship document had been purchased.[9] However,

Herbert had invested an exorbitant sum in Henry's wardship, and his widow was not prepared to simply give this up. On 21 October, The Bell in Fleet Street was chosen as the setting for a meeting between the legal councils of the Staffords and Anne Herbert and her brother. To investigate Margaret's case, the services of London lawyer Humphrey Starkey had been employed, but in their desire to be kept abreast, characteristically Margaret and her husband also joined the meeting. As the party dined on a meal of cheese, bread and mutton washed down with ale, Henry's future was discussed. The outcome of the negotiations is unclear, but they were evidently complicated, as a resolution had still not been reached early the following year.[10] During this time Henry remained with Anne Herbert at Weobley, and once more Margaret was forced to take a back seat in her son's life.

BOTH HIS COUSIN and his brother had risen up against him, yet Edward IV did not seek to destroy them. Though he would trust neither of them again, in December the three men were formally reconciled. But tensions still simmered underneath the surface, and it would not be long before they boiled over. Given her swift action on behalf of her son following Edward's imprisonment, Margaret had good reason to be worried by his re-establishment. Although, in a show of loyalty, Stafford had ridden to meet Edward as he returned south, joining his brother and stepfather when the King returned to London, Margaret's rash behaviour in treating with Clarence had not helped matters. Edward was more wary of them than ever, and their disfavour was evident when, on 5 January 1470, Stafford's younger brother John was created Earl of Wiltshire while Stafford was ignored.[11] It was a clear sign of the King's scepticism towards them.

By February the treacherous Warwick and Clarence were plotting once more, and this time they involved a member of Margaret's own family. Following the slaughter of Margaret's stepfather Lord Welles at Towton, his eldest son Richard inherited his title.[12] Her stepbrother had been a young adult at the time of her mother's marriage to his father, but in spite of their difference in age they had almost certainly had some contact as Margaret grew. Like the rest of her family, Richard was a loyal Lancastrian who had fought at Towton, but he had later been reconciled with Edward IV, who pardoned him on 5 February 1462. Furthermore, as a result of Richard's petition in Parliament in 1467, Edward had graciously reversed the attainder of Welles' father, which had left him 'so deprived of livelihood that he may not do your highness such good service as his heart particularly desires, nor such as his status requires'.[13] Coupled with the previous grant of his father's goods, this helped him to steadily rebuild his life.[14] At the beginning of 1470, however, Welles was summoned before the King to explain his part in a private feud, but was pardoned on 3 March.[15] Unbeknown to Edward, though, Welles was already in league with Warwick and Clarence in a plot to overthrow him and replace him with Clarence. Welles' son Robert was raising troops in Lincolnshire in preparation, an action that Warwick and Clarence wholly encouraged. Yet the rising was doomed, and on 12 March Edward's forces defeated the rebels at Stamford. Margaret's stepbrother Richard Welles was executed the same day, and a week later his son Robert was too, bringing further shame on her family. Stafford and a small force of his men had joined the King at Stamford, and as Norton has emphasized, such a demonstration of his loyalty was needed in the aftermath of Margaret's hasty actions during Edward's imprisonment.[16] It was left to him to break the news of her stepson's treachery to Margaret's mother, the dowager Duchess of Somerset, and Stafford rode to nearby Maxey to inform her.[17] The Duchess had her own reasons to be alarmed, for it seems that she had been in some way involved in the rebellion and had perhaps aided her stepson. Much to her relief – and Margaret's – Edward later chose to pardon his 'kinswoman' for 'all offences committed by her'.[18] Her involvement nevertheless served to underline that the true loyalties of many of Margaret's family members lay elsewhere. With the country so unsettled though, Margaret herself could not afford to do anything that might put her son or his inheritance at risk; neither is there any evidence that suggests she wished to.

Following what became known as the Battle of Losecoat Field at Stamford – named so because many of the rebels discarded items of clothing as they fled from the battlefield – letters were discovered that proved Warwick and Clarence's involvement. Suspicions had already been raised on the battlefield when several of the rebels had made cries of 'A Clarence!' 'A Warwick!' but their complicity was now confirmed. Edward IV was furious at this latest betrayal, and having returned from Maxey, Stafford joined the King as they raced towards Exeter in a determined effort to apprehend them as they took flight, arriving on 14 April. But the treacherous duo were too quick for Edward, and having gathered up their families they sailed for Calais. Denied entry there, soon after the party sailed for Normandy, where they were able to dock in Honfleur.[19] It was from here that Warwick attempted to seek the support of Louis XI. The French King made his guests most welcome, but Warwick now realized that in order to restore his fortunes the only option left was reconciling with the house of Lancaster. To this end Louis XI was keen to heal the rift between the Earl and Margaret of Anjou, who was still residing in France with her son. It was a steep challenge given their background – they had been bitter and implacable enemies for years – and when Louis first approached the subject with Queen Margaret he found her to be 'very hard and difficult'.[20] It was their mutual ambition that won the day, for the Queen was persuaded of the necessity of allying with Warwick if the restoration of her husband were to stand any chance of success. Three days later, Warwick was gratified when his youngest daughter, fourteen-year-old Anne, was betrothed to sixteen-year-old Prince Edward of Lancaster in Angers Cathedral.

When the extent of Warwick's treachery came to light, Edward IV began canvassing support. In September he was in the north when word arrived that Warwick had landed in the West Country at the head of an invasion fleet supplied by the French King. It had been agreed that Queen Margaret and Prince Edward would remain in France until Warwick had secured the realm, but both Clarence and Jasper Tudor joined him. No sooner had he landed than Warwick, urging the people to rise up and support Henry VI, began gaining men, while Jasper set out for Wales in an attempt to recruit more. The Earl was certainly determined, to the extent that it was reported that 'Warwick has pursued his enterprise with spirit and has practically the whole of the island in his power'.[21] Warwick was gaining further men by the day, and his success caused many of Edward's men to desert, for the King was no longer as popular as he once had been, partially on account of the greed of the Wydeville family. His only option was to flee. With just a handful of his supporters, including his youngest brother Richard, Duke of Gloucester, Lord Hastings and Queen Elizabeth's brother Anthony, Earl Rivers, Edward took a boat from King's Lynn to Flanders.[22]

Meanwhile, a confident Warwick made his way to London, 'where he was received in most friendly fashion'.[23] He immediately set the bewildered Henry VI at liberty from the Tower, where he had spent almost five years in quiet imprisonment. He was taken to Westminster, where he was once more 'proclaimed through all the town of London with the greatest festivities and pomp as the true king and lord of England'.[24] This period became known as the Readeption, and though Henry VI was king once more, it was Warwick who was pulling the strings. It is therefore unsurprising that Thomas More later wrote that Warwick 'made kings and put down kings almost at his pleasure', earning him the nickname of 'Kingmaker'.[25]

Margaret was delighted at the reversal in her family's fortunes, yet the haste with which she had conducted herself the previous year had made her all too aware of the swiftness with which fortune's wheel could turn. Likewise, she was enough of a realist to recognize that the Wars of the Roses were not over: though Edward IV had fled, he would not give up on his throne.

Having been forced to flee from his realm and his family 'with seven or eight hundred followers who possessed no other clothes than the ones they were fighting in', the fallen Edward IV was a desperate man.[26] The party landed in Flanders, but the exiled King did not even have the money to pay the ship's captain; he could only offer him a fur-lined robe with the promise of a better reward in the future. Commynes observed that 'there never was such a beggarly company'.[27]

JASPER TUDOR HAD spent most of the 1460s as a fugitive in Wales, Scotland and France, and thus had missed out on almost as much of his nephew's life as Margaret. Now, with the house of Lancaster restored to the throne, Henry, once again a member of the royal family, was afforded an opportunity to reconnect with the relatives he barely knew. Parliament was due to convene in November 1470, and having collected his nephew from Hereford whence he had been delivered by Sir Richard Corbet, Jasper took Henry to London. They arrived at the end of October, and here Margaret was briefly reunited with her son for what was almost certainly the first time in three years. Henry was fast approaching his fourteenth birthday and, according to André, he had been summoned into the presence of his kinsman and king, Henry VI.[28]

Much emphasis was later placed on Henry Tudor's meeting with the newly restored monarch, which took place at Westminster on 27 October. Its significance was perhaps intensified because – unbeknown at the time – it was to be both the first and last occasion on which Margaret's son ever met the man whom he would later go to strenuous efforts to revere. According to André's account, which probably came from Henry Tudor, on his first appearance at court the King held 'a splendid feast with the nobles and best men of the kingdom'.[29] As the King was washing his hands, Henry was brought before him. It was then, so said André, that 'the king prophesied that some day the boy would undertake the governance of the kingdom and would have all things under his own power'.[30] Given that Henry VI had his own son, it seems unlikely that he would make such a statement, but with his nephew being the posthumous son of his dearly loved half-brother Edmund, it was only natural that he would have been eager to meet Henry. This is, though, unlikely to have stemmed from anything other than a familial interest in the boy, for prior to 1483 nobody considered the prospect of a Beaufort/Tudor claimant to the throne. Nevertheless, in light of later events, it suited the Tudors to relay this tale as one of 'divine prophecy'.[31]

Whatever transpired during Henry's meeting with the King, he later dined with his mother, stepfather, uncle Jasper and Sir Richard Tunstall, the King's Chamberlain.[32] The party were doubtless eager to discuss Henry's impressions, but probably also his future.[33] In the meantime it had been agreed that Jasper would retain custody of his teenage nephew, but not before he had first spent some time with his mother.

Before the end of the month, Margaret and Stafford returned to Woking, bringing Henry with them. For nearly two weeks Margaret was given the opportunity to spend time with the son from whom she had been cruelly parted for years, and she was determined to make the most of it. Having spent most of his life in a handful of Welsh castles, Henry was unfamiliar with the Surrey countryside surrounding London. His mother and stepfather took him on a brief tour of some of the towns surrounding their home, including Guildford, which boasted a Norman castle and fourteenth-century guildhall, Maidenhead and the market town of Henley.[34] This afforded Henry a short opportunity to travel that he had hitherto never experienced. His visit also provided Margaret with a chance to get to know her son, who was now at the impressionable age of thirteen. It is not unreasonable to suppose that it was during this time that the strong bonds of trust between mother and son were forged deeper, and that Henry's respect for his mother grew – it would later become apparent that he trusted her judgement implicitly, and was willing to listen to her advice. They may also have enjoyed games of cards together for, like Margaret, Henry also grew to be fond of the pastime.[35] But it was once again over all too soon. On 11 November, Henry bade his mother and stepfather farewell, and joined his uncle Jasper. Though neither Margaret nor Henry could have known it, they would not see one another again for almost fifteen years.[36]

On 26 November, Parliament met, and though Henry VI was present it was Warwick who was in control. He had regained all of his former power, though many loyal Lancastrians were wary of him and distrusted his motives. Jasper Tudor was elated when his attainder was reversed and he was restored to the earldom of Pembroke that had previously been unceremoniously snatched from him. Margaret also had hopes of recovering her son's inheritance, and she now felt secure enough in the political climate to approach Clarence about the matter. Though

Clarence had been afforded a place on Henry VI's Council, in other terms his treachery to his brother had not paid off and he had gained little. On 27 November he agreed to meet with Margaret and her husband at Baynard's Castle – his mother's residence – well aware of what they wanted.[37] Stafford had already approached him about the matter, but he was not obliged to relinquish the Richmond title in spite of Henry VI's restoration. To Margaret's disappointment he would not comply with her wishes. Despite several further visits made by Stafford, there was nothing further Margaret could do: she would have to bide her time.[38]

Across the Channel, Queen Margaret and Warwick's family remained in France. It was there that, on 13 December, a marriage took place between Prince Edward and Warwick's daughter, Anne Neville. Once the wedding celebrations were over, the Queen prepared to return to her recently restored husband – and her realm. She was not the only one who was planning a return: in Flanders Edward IV was ready to reclaim his throne. Once more, the Crown – and the future of England – were all to play for.

CHAPTER 10

Heaven Protects him who has No Burial Urn

O N 14 MARCH 1471, the deposed Edward IV landed at Ravenspur. With the aid of the Duke of Burgundy, he had managed to assemble a force, hoping to gather more men upon his arrival. He was not to be disappointed, for according to Commynes, 'there were more than two thousand of his supporters' who had gone to ground following his flight, and men soon began rallying to his banner.[1] Edward was particularly heartened when his brother Clarence led his men to join him, meeting them at Banbury on 3 April. Clarence had finally realized that he had nothing to gain by supporting Henry VI and Warwick, and Edward was only too willing to forgive him. Warwick was in the north when he heard of Edward's landing, and he was 'greatly distressed' when he discovered that Clarence had abandoned him.[2] He had no choice but to continue raising men, for on 24 March Queen Margaret had at last set sail from France and was on her way to join him.

The forthcoming violence placed Stafford in a predicament. Throughout the Wars of the Roses he had done his utmost to avoid the conflict wherever possible, and this time was no different. However, on 3 March a visitor arrived at Woking. Though it was not Margaret he had come to see, she nevertheless took care to extend her cousin, Edmund Beaufort, Duke of Somerset, a warm welcome. A younger son of her uncle, the same Edmund Beaufort who had been slain at St Albans, and whose brother had been killed in the aftermath of Hexham, it was as a result of his brother's death that Edmund had since inherited the dukedom of Somerset. He had been raised primarily in France since 1461, and as a result Margaret had not seen him since childhood. Yet now was not the time for a family reunion.

As it was Lent, Margaret sent especially to London for an array of fresh fish for her guest to enjoy as he spoke with her husband.[3] The purpose of Somerset's visit was to persuade Stafford to declare his support for Lancaster – he was aware that Stafford had previously fought for York, but was also conscious of his background and connections. Stafford was reluctant, and either refused to commit himself or was left to ponder the matter, because on 24 March Somerset returned to Woking – this time for four days. The length of his visit suggests that he was either given some positive sign or that he was confident of persuading his host. Margaret's feelings on the matter are unknown: did she urge her husband to take up arms and fight for her own house, or did she advise caution? Whatever she felt, Somerset left Woking without an affirmative answer from Stafford. It would not be long, though, before he was forced to make a choice.

On 11 April, Edward IV arrived in London. Warwick had hoped that the capital would remain loyal to Henry VI, but Edward had always been popular there, and as he entered he was 'very joyfully received by the whole city'.[4] He immediately went to Old St Paul's, where he declared Henry VI to be deposed. A prisoner once more, Henry was sent to the Tower. Edward then gave orders for his wife and children to be escorted from the Sanctuary in Westminster Abbey, to where they had fled following his hasty departure abroad. Here the Abbot of Westminster, Thomas Milling, who was sympathetic to Queen Elizabeth's plight, had given up his own rooms for her; she had been otherwise wholly dependent on charity. In order to feed them, William Gould, a London butcher, had donated meat to the destitute Queen and her children on a weekly basis.[5] It had been 'at Westminster within the Sanctuary' that Queen Elizabeth had given birth on 3 November: her baby was a boy.[6] After presenting Edward IV with three daughters, Elizabeth had at last provided her husband with a male heir, but the circumstances surrounding his arrival were a far cry from those of her daughters. Margaret's own half-sister, Elizabeth St John – now Lady Scrope – had been present at the Prince's birth, having been sent to assist the deposed queen by a sympathetic Henry VI. She even stood as godmother when the infant – named Edward after his father – was christened 'with little pomp'.[7] Though he had been born in the poorest of circumstances, this was a baby whose existence would have life-changing consequences for Margaret and her son.

Prince Edward was five months old when Edward IV was reunited with his family, during which emotional encounter he was at long last afforded the opportunity to meet his baby son. In spite of that, it was time to turn his attention to crushing the Lancastrians permanently, and the arrival of his male heir gave him even greater impetus. It was probably the news of Edward's warm reception in London – so close to Woking – that swayed Stafford into joining him, thereby bringing him into direct combat with his wife's kin. He reluctantly arrived in London on 12 April accompanied by a small group of men including Gilbert Gilpyn, the steward of Woking. That it was a hesitant decision is clear, for he had made no preparations – the following day, parts of his armour had to be brought to him, and he hastily prepared a will that he ordered to be delivered to Margaret. He evidently feared the outcome.

Edward IV recognized that there was no time to be lost. Taking Henry VI with him, he left London on 13 April, encountering Warwick's forces at Barnet. He was heavily outnumbered, but this did not stop him from engaging with Warwick's army the following morning – it was Easter Sunday. 'A great mist' had descended and was so bad that it hampered the fighting; in the confusion, Warwick's men started fighting their allies.[8] The battle was 'most bitterly and strenuously fought', and had disastrous consequences for the Lancastrians.[9] Croyland described the battle as 'a terrible conflict', during which 'various nobles fell on both sides'.[10] Among them was Warwick: the Kingmaker was gone. 'The same day after noon, the King came riding through the City and offered at Paul's, and so unto Westminster; and after him was brought King Henry, riding in a long blue velvet gown; and so to Westminster, and from thence to the Tower, where he remained prisoner as he had done before.'[11] Edward had the bodies of Warwick and his brother returned to the city too, 'which he caused to be placed in St Paul's Church, so that all the people might see them'.[12]

Though word of Edward's victory had probably soon reached Margaret at Woking, she had heard nothing of Stafford's welfare – it must have reminded her of those terrible days after Edgecote when she had been forced to endure the agonizing wait for news of her son. She may have sought comfort from her faith, and Bishop Fisher later recalled that she often wept 'tears sometimes of devotion sometimes of repentance'. What may have gone through her mind, it is tempting to wonder, in terms of the latter. More than five hundred years later, it is impossible to know. With no reports of her husband forthcoming and unable to endure the suspense any longer, on 17 April she travelled to the capital herself. Though it was only a short distance, it was a risky decision given the unrest, and bedraggled and injured soldiers from both sides were steadily trickling back into the city. Margaret, though, was desperate, and when times called for it she was always ready to be a woman of action. To her dismay, upon her arrival there was nothing. She immediately sent a rider to Barnet to try and discover her husband's fate, and was relieved to learn that he was alive. However, he had been injured, and to such an extent that he was unable to continue in active military service. The nature of Stafford's injuries is unknown, as are the details of how they were inflicted. But they were serious enough to ensure that he returned to Woking where Margaret oversaw his care.

Queen Margaret, meanwhile, landed at Weymouth on the day of Edward IV's victory at Barnet, having endured a terrible crossing. She had been delayed by bad weather, and was seriously disheartened when she was told of the recent Lancastrian defeat, Warwick's death and her husband's imprisonment. So much so that her first instinct was to return to France. Her supporters, though, including Margaret's cousin Somerset, persuaded her that all hope was not lost. Jasper was raising support in Wales, and if they could meet with his forces, a Lancastrian victory seemed possible. Thus the Queen, accompanied by Prince Edward and his wife Anne Neville, began travelling through the West Country, attempting to rally men to their banner along the way.

When Edward IV learned that Margaret of Anjou had landed, he immediately planned to pursue her in the hope of capturing her before she had an opportunity to meet up with Jasper in Wales. By 30 April the Lancastrian force had reached Bath and were travelling towards Gloucester, where they planned to cross the River Severn. The Queen's army 'grew daily', but Edward was hot on her tail.[13] When the Lancastrians arrived at Gloucester, they found the city gates closed against them, leaving the exhausted army to head for Tewkesbury. It was unseasonably warm for the time of year, and when they arrived on the afternoon of 3 May, they set up camp. It was here that Edward's army caught up with them, and though both sides were 'too weary of foot and from thirst to march any further', it was clear that a fight would soon ensue.[14]

On the morning of 4 May a merciless battle took place in Tewkesbury. Supported by his brothers and his loyal friend Lord Hastings, Edward was determined to destroy the Lancastrians and their leaders for good. The battle was fought with great savagery, and resulted in 'a famous victory' for Edward IV.[15] The victorious king resolved to show no mercy, and as the Lancastrian forces fled the field, many of them were cut down. Some attempted to take refuge in Tewkesbury Abbey, including Margaret's cousin Somerset. The Yorkist army took no account of this and forced their way in, dragging Somerset out.[16] Edward ordered his execution in the town marketplace on 6 May.

The Lancastrians faced further devastating consequences. At almost eighteen, Prince Edward had been partially responsible for commanding the Lancastrian army. Yet at Tewkesbury he met his end, the young man being slaughtered there.[17] He, Somerset, and Somerset's brother John, were all laid to rest in Tewkesbury Abbey.[18]

While the Battle of Tewkesbury raged, Queen Margaret and her daughter-in-law took refuge nearby, apprehensively awaiting news. She was soon delivered the crushing pronouncement of the disastrous Lancastrian defeat, but received no word of her son's fate. The Queen's party fled, but they did not get far. On 7 May, Sir William Stanley discovered them hiding at Little Malvern Priory in Worcestershire. It was here that the Queen was dealt a devastating blow: when she was told of her son's death, she collapsed into a torment of grief. With Prince Edward 'died the hopes of the House of

Lancaster' which now seemed lost.[19] For Margaret, the future of her house had been deprived of its heir, leaving a trail of uncertainty in its wake. Commynes accurately summarized the situation when he stated that 'in eleven days the earl of Warwick had won all of England, or at least got it under his control. In twenty-one days King Edward reconquered it, though there were two desperate and bloody battles.'[20] Margaret's house had been utterly annihilated.

On 21 May the victorious Edward IV entered London in triumph. With him came the fallen Queen Margaret, who was 'brought to London in a chariot, and after sent home into her own country'.[21] She was subjected to a torrent of abuse from the Londoners as she was conveyed through the streets of the city that she had once ruled. Her career was at an end, and she would eventually be ransomed to the French King and returned to her homeland. She died in poverty in France in 1482.[22]

For Henry VI there was to be no such outcome. Tradition has it that on the evening of 21 May – the same day that Edward IV returned to London – as Henry knelt at prayer in the small oratory within the Wakefield Tower, he was dealt a heavy blow to the head. Various stories circulated, and Vergil would later write that 'the continual report is, that Richard duke of Gloucester killed him with a sword'.[23] André also laid the blame at Gloucester's door, dramatically claiming that he was 'thirsty for human blood', and was sent by his brother 'to slaughter King Henry himself'.[24] Writing later, More too held Gloucester responsible, reporting that 'He slew with his own hands King Henry the Sixth, being prisoner in the Tower, as men constantly say.'[25] Gloucester is known to have been at the Tower on the evening of Henry's murder, so it is likely that he was present even if he did not slay the deposed King with his own hand. By contrast, the author of the *Arrival of King Edward IV* related that when the news of his son's death was conveyed to Henry, 'he took it so great' that 'of pure displeasure, and melancholy, he died'.[26] Croyland refused to comment, but did state that Henry's body was displayed at St Paul's.[27] This took place the morning after his death, and there the chronicler John Warkworth remarked that 'his face was open that every man might see him; and in his lying he bled on the pavement there; and afterward at the Black Friars was brought, and there he bled new and fresh'.[28] Edward IV was taking no chances, and in order to quell any future unrest it was essential to prove that Henry was dead. The late King's body was taken to Chertsey Abbey for burial, but that would not be an end to Henry's role in Margaret's story.

Margaret was among those who mourned Henry VI's passing. His death, together with those of Prince Edward, Somerset, and his brother, meant that the direct male Beaufort line was now extinct: just the female line survived, of which Margaret was the most senior.[29] Though this may have gone unremarked upon by her contemporaries, it was a circumstance that Margaret could not have failed to recognize. She dared not mourn her kinsmen openly, for the house of York reigned victorious. There was no figurehead to challenge Edward IV's authority, and his power seemed unassailable. Though the Lancastrian heirs were dead, Margaret still had reason to be fearful of Edward. Indeed, her son who, like her, possessed Lancastrian blood, was now in the greatest danger of his life.

JASPER TUDOR HAD been unable to reach Margaret of Anjou's army prior to Tewkesbury, and he was at Chepstow with his nephew Henry when he heard of Lancaster's defeat. Though Jasper had not partaken in the fighting, he was fully aware that his allegiances rendered Edward IV's attitude towards him far from conciliatory. This was highlighted by Edward's behaviour to those at Tewkesbury, which had shown that he could be cruel and untrustworthy, and was determined to crush those in possession of Lancastrian blood. Jasper could therefore see that 'matters were past all hope of recovery'.[30] Realizing that neither he nor his nephew were safe, Jasper and Henry hurried west to Pembroke Castle.

Yet even here Jasper was conscious that his fortress was no longer able to provide the same level of safety it once had, and knew that another plan was needed. The best course of action was to take flight: according to André, the impetus for this came from Margaret, who 'pondered long over many aspects of the proposal, both for and against'. Realizing that her son was in potentially grave danger, 'she came to understand that she must bear his departure with sorrow'.[31] Margaret's 'firm and constant resolve toward him, which demanded more than a woman's frailty, was manifested to several of his most proven counsellors'.[32] Foremost among these was Jasper, and André claimed that as Margaret approached him, she expressed the opinion that it 'seems better and safer to yield to the wrath and raving of the tyrant and go abroad'.[33] If Henry were to remain, then she feared for his safety,

And unless my imagination or maternal instinct deceives me, the great distance of the sea will help us avoid all perils. I know that the hazards of the sea will be great; yet his life will be safer on the ocean's waves than in this tempest on land. But if it turns out otherwise, heaven protects him who has no burial urn. I would prefer that God keep him from harm rather than see him killed by the bloody sword of a tyrant.[34]

Jasper listened carefully to her worries, answering that 'I shall gladly undertake this office, and shall take as good care of my nephew as if he were my own son.'[35] Henry and Jasper's exile was agreed, but Margaret was left with the realization that she might never see her son again.

Leaving Pembroke Castle behind, Jasper and Henry travelled the short distance to the harbour town of Tenby. It was from here that 'a time and place were arranged and ships provided' with the purpose of aiding their escape.[36] One of the few people who had been entrusted with helping them was the Mayor of Tenby, Thomas White. With his aid, on 2 June Henry and his uncle 'sailed into France' with 'certain other his friends and servants'.[37] As the Welsh coastline grew more distant, Henry and Jasper had no idea if or when they would see their homeland again: they were exiles. As for Margaret, she was about to embark on almost fifteen years of endless stress and agitation as the ability to keep her son safe now seemed beyond her control.

Though the sailing party had been heading for France, 'blustery south winds drove them ashore in Brittany'.[38] Duke Francis II, 'a kind and good prince', ruled the kingdom, and having heard of the fugitives' arrival he 'welcomed Henry with great joy'.[39] Jasper duly 'submitted himself and his nephew to his protection', and their reception was warm.[40] Duke Francis, '[w]ith such honour, courtesy, and favour entertained them as though they had been his brothers, promising them upon his honour that within his dominion they should be from thenceforth far from injury, and pass at their pleasure to and fro without danger.'[41] Jasper and Henry were safe – but it was nevertheless made clear to them that they would not be permitted to leave: they were now Francis's prisoners.

Margaret was relieved to learn that her son had succeeded in reaching foreign shores, but she also knew that the danger had far from passed. For now though, Margaret had other things to worry about. The injuries that Henry Stafford had sustained at Barnet had left him in a seriously weakened state, and though initially it was hoped that he would recover, by the beginning of October it was evident that the end was quickly approaching. Stafford had first drafted a hasty will prior to the Battle of Barnet, but on 2 October he made his final will. Two days later, he died. Margaret and her household at Woking were immediately plunged into mourning.

Stafford's death brought Margaret's third marriage – arguably the most successful in personal terms – to an end, and at the age of twenty-eight she became a widow for the second time. Stafford's feelings towards her can be gauged from his final will, in which he referred to Margaret as 'his entirely and best-beloved wife'.[42] Though most of their income had derived from her estates, he nevertheless took care to ensure that she was generously provided for. He also demonstrated his affection for his exiled stepson, to whom he bequeathed a trapper of four new horse harnesses of velvet.[43] Other bequests were made to his brother and to the faithful Reginald Bray, who would continue in Margaret's service. Interestingly, the latter were all horse related, perhaps reflecting a passion of his. Everything else was left to 'my beloved wife Margaret, Countess of Richmond'.[44] In a further testament to his faith in her abilities, Stafford made his young wife the executor of his final wishes. It was left to Bray to make the arrangements for his master's burial, and Margaret's husband was laid to rest in the Church of Holy Trinity at Pleshey in Essex, where other of his family members lay entombed.[45]

Just a year earlier her son had enjoyed his first audience with the King –
now, that king was dead and his family destroyed, Margaret had lost Henry
Tudor to foreign exile, and her husband whom she had cared for deeply was
dead as a result of the conflict. The tragedy was almost too much to bear.

CHAPTER 11

———◆———

Grace and Favour of the King's Highness

FOLLOWING STAFFORD'S DEATH, taking three of her ladies with her, Margaret briefly joined her mother's household at Le Ryall, the Duchess's London residence.[1] It was probably from here that feelers were put out on the subject of her next move: marriage. She was not obliged to remarry, but ever the realist, she recognized her weakness: with no protector, her family allegiances and her son's exile made them both vulnerable. This time it was essential that she choose a husband who could not only offer her protection, but who also had strong links to the house of York coupled with the ability to use these to the advantage of her and her son.

Thomas Stanley was the eldest son of Thomas Stanley, first Baron Stanley, and his wife Joan.[2] The Stanleys hailed from a family whose power base lay largely in Lancashire and Cheshire, where they were powerful magnates. Though the Stanleys had served at Henry VI's court and become embroiled in the wars, it quickly became clear that their priority was to align themselves with the winning side. In a similar manner to Margaret's third husband Stafford, Stanley was a cautious man who was wary of committing himself, and did his best to retain some middle ground. Yet despite this he had successfully managed to retain the favour of Henry VI, and later Edward IV. He was nevertheless a man of dubious political allegiance, and had critically failed to lend his support to Edward IV during the crucial and bloody battles of 1471. Keen to promote reconciliation rather than bloodshed, however, the King had forgiven Stanley for his lack of action,

114

and the same year had appointed him Steward of the King's Household. His position may have been bolstered by the support of his younger brother, William, who had fought for Edward and had probably assured him of his brother's loyalty. This was to be a familiar pattern in the coming years, which would see the Stanley brothers working together during times of crisis. Like Margaret, Stanley was also a pragmatist who was able to put his personal feelings to one side, though for largely different reasons to Margaret: he was primarily motivated by self-preservation and a wish to curry favour. That he was also a member of the King's Council suggests that he was intelligent and politically able, and he had and would continue to demonstrate an abundance of acumen. He was slightly older than Margaret, and like her had been married before. His first wife, Eleanor Neville, was the daughter of the Earl of Salisbury and sister to the Kingmaker, providing Stanley with prestigious connections.[3]

By the end of 1471 Stanley's position with Edward IV, though growing, was still not solid. Even so, he was determined to win the King's trust and served him loyally. His place in the royal household meant that he had a strong presence at court, with close access to the King. It was strengthened by his links with those within Edward's circle. His heir George, for example, would later be married to the Queen's niece.[4]

Though she was a Lancastrian, for Stanley a marriage with Margaret presented many advantages, not least her wealth. For Margaret, marrying someone closely allied with the Yorkist court had obvious benefits. It effectively helped to neutralize Edward IV's suspicions about her loyalties by aligning her to a man who was an integral part of his court. It is even possible that the King had a hand in organizing the match, but the arrangements were very much made by Margaret's agents: the trusted Bray was to play a key role. Like her previous marriages, the match was very clearly one of mutual convenience. The marriage contract made no provision for future children, and this may have been a deliberate strategy on Margaret's behalf: she would present her husband with a prayer book that she had commissioned in 1478, and which is now in the collection at Westminster Abbey, containing prayers that highlighted all of her fears.

Within the beautifully illuminated book, on which the badges and coats of arms of both Margaret and Stanley appear, were prayers intended to protect the user against death in battle, plague, and protection for women during pregnancy.[5] Similarly, the results of Stanley's first marriage meant that he had no need to attempt to sire further children with Margaret, for with three sons to inherit, his line seemed secure. Love and the production of children were not, therefore, a consideration on either side, but this is unlikely to have been a concern for Margaret. She seems never to have experienced a romantic attachment in the same manner that her mother once had for John Neville, for none of her marriages had been made for personal reasons of the heart. She and Stanley seem nevertheless to have lived harmoniously together, and later remained on good terms when their marriage underwent a dramatic change. Margaret also had good reason to hope that her marriage to Stanley would benefit her son too, for through him she was provided with a means of approaching the King in order to petition on Henry's behalf. In 1482 this was precisely what she did.

Margaret's fourth wedding took place at one of the Stanley estates in early June 1472 – certainly by the 12th.[6] That she was prepared to marry before the prescribed year of mourning had been undertaken – before Stafford had even been buried – is a sign of her vulnerability and the urgency with which she perceived her situation. Stanley owned several properties in Lancashire, including Knowsley and Lathom, the latter of which would in time become a grand residence replete with impressive towers and surrounded by moats.[7] Lathom stood around twelve miles north of Liverpool, and in a poem written by Stanley's grandson he later claimed that it influenced the building of Henry VII's Richmond Palace: 'King Henry the Seventh, who did lie there eight days, And of all the houses he gave it the most praise, And his haul at Richmond he pulled down all To make it up again after Lathom Hall.'[8] Margaret came to spend time at both of these properties – particularly prior to 1485. Additionally, Stanley also had a London residence, which was later known as Derby House.[9] From the onset of her marriage, Margaret and her husband moved regularly around these properties, and also stayed at Woking, which she had retained after

Stafford's death. For many of the coming years though, Margaret is likely to have spent much of her time in the capital. Unlike with Stafford, Stanley's presence was often required at court, and as the 1470s progressed, Margaret too became an increasing presence. Given her background, this cannot at first have been a comfortable experience for her, surrounded by a court of Edward IV's supporters who had fought against her own house, and those who were now reconciled with his rule. Likewise, the King's brother Clarence would not have forgotten Margaret's eager petitions to him on her son's behalf just a few years previously. However, as time passed, Edward's attitude towards her began to thaw. He could afford to be lenient, as in the aftermath of Tewkesbury for the first time in his reign he had good reason to feel secure on his throne: not only was he in good health, but he now also had a male heir. But his goodwill did not extend to everyone.

Having reached the safety of Brittany, as the years passed so too did the conditions of Henry Tudor's exile begin to change. Occasional references to him appear in Duke Francis's accounts, such as in the spring or summer of 1472 when new clothes were purchased for him.[10] Uncle and nephew were moved between palaces until around 1474, when Henry was separated from Jasper and taken to the chateau at Largoët – also known as the Tour d'Elven – away from the coast.[11] Here the chateau's owner, Jean IV de Rieux, Marshal of Brittany, who seems to have treated him well, oversaw his custody.[12] Nevertheless, Henry and Jasper's English servants were taken from them and replaced with Breton guards. It had become clear that they were less honoured guests, and more prisoners. There is no evidence to suggest that either Henry or Jasper were the victims of poor treatment, for Commynes claimed that Francis 'treated them very gently as prisoners'.[13] Notwithstanding this, it was made plain to them that they were not permitted to leave.

The change in Henry's conditions came as a result of pressure that Francis was receiving from both France and England, and coincided with Edward IV's desire to invade France in 1475. Margaret and Stanley had celebrated the Christmas of 1474 in London, and she had no doubt learned of the King's plans from her husband, for Stanley was to be actively involved in Edward's pursuit of military glory. The following year, Margaret was among those who gathered in London as Edward made his preparations to invade France. Commynes reported that the King had amassed 'the biggest army with which any king of England had invaded France', and he had good reason to feel confident.[14] In July the English forces crossed to France from Dover, but there was to be no military action on this campaign. Instead, a peace treaty was negotiated with Louis XI, and Stanley was one of those chosen to participate in the discussions, which were concluded at Picquigny on 29 August. Few were pleased with the outcome of the campaign, for rather than achieving a glorious victory in the same manner as that of Henry V, Edward had instead been pensioned off by Louis. As a result, the King became 'so rich no one was able to rival him'.[15] Additionally, he had earned a seven-year truce between the two countries, as well as agreeing a marriage for his eldest daughter, Elizabeth, with the Dauphin.

With the onset of peace between England and France, Edward IV now attempted to lay hands on Henry Tudor. His agents were sent to Brittany in an effort to persuade the Duke to hand over his guest, and Edward offered him 'fine promises, bribes, and entreaties'.[16] He also claimed to be proffering Henry the hand in marriage of an English noblewoman, perhaps one of his daughters. However, André reported that Margaret, 'a most cautious woman, saw through the ruse, and through secret addresses by messengers and in letters she continually forbade him to return'.[17] She was right to be wary, for Edward's promises seem to have been nothing more than a ploy to lure Henry to England, and there is no evidence to suggest that they were sincere. Duke Francis, though, was left to ponder.

While her son's future hung in the balance, Margaret did all that she could to please Edward IV and his unpopular queen. As with her predecessor's, Elizabeth Wydeville's reputation was subjected to a propaganda campaign that has persisted to this day. Though there can be little doubt that she was greedy and eager to enhance her own status, Elizabeth's household was run less extravagantly than that of Margaret of Anjou and she seems to have been more savvy.[18] In personal terms, her marriage to Edward IV was both successful and happy. She was extremely fond of her children, and in total she and Edward would have ten – eight of whom survived infancy.[19] Prior to the birth of Prince Edward, born in sanctuary in 1470, the couple's eldest daughter, Elizabeth of York, had been born on 11 February 1466 at the Palace of Westminster. Her birth was followed by that of Mary in 1467, and Cecily in 1469. The King and Queen also had another surviving son, Prince Richard, who had been born on 14 August 1473 in Shrewsbury. Thus, the future of the Yorkist kings seemed to be both solid and secure. In addition, Elizabeth had two sons from her first marriage, Thomas Grey, Marquess of Dorset, and Sir Richard Grey, who played prominent roles at court. It is highly likely that Margaret knew many of the royal children well during her time at court: she would certainly have become familiar with Elizabeth of York, and as the Princess was of gentle and kindly nature it is probable that they got along well. There is good evidence from a later period that they had a warm relationship. By the same token, Margaret also became close to Princess Cecily, and it is possible that this stemmed from this time in their lives. While Margaret left no evidence of how she truly felt towards the Yorkist queen, she seems to have been successful in charming her, as by 1476 Elizabeth and Edward afforded Margaret a prominent role in court affairs. The significance of such was to be realized in a highly symbolic ceremony.

The village of Fotheringhay in Northamptonshire had once been the main seat of Edward IV's family, and several of his siblings had been born in the castle where 'there be very fair lodgings'.[20] It was the church, though, that dominated the village, and John Leland declared that 'The glory of it standeth by the parish church of a fair building and collegiate.'[21] It was in this magnificent building that the King had known since childhood that he envisioned building a magnificent tomb for his father and brother, who had been slaughtered at Wakefield. Edward had never forgotten the pain and humiliation that had been caused when the heads of his father and younger brother Edmund had been impaled above the Micklegate Bar in York, before their remains were unceremoniously buried at Pontefract. Indeed, the *Croyland Chronicle* stated that Edward remembered the 'very humble place of his father's burial', and was determined to honour him and his brother with due ceremony.[22]

In the summer of 1476, the King and Queen travelled to Fotheringhay with their court in order to attend the reburial of the Duke of York and Edmund, Earl of Rutland. Margaret and her husband accompanied them, for Margaret had been appointed to wait upon the Queen and two of her daughters.[23] The remains of York and Rutland had been brought ceremonially from Pontefract, and on 29 July the procession arrived at the church. The following day, funeral masses were celebrated for the souls of the dead, and Margaret joined the princesses in making offerings at the altar rail.[24] She and her husband then watched as the King gave orders and 'translated the bones of his father, as well as those of his brother Edmund, earl of Rutland, to the fine college of Fotheringhay'.[25] A splendid tomb was later erected to York's memory.[26] Following the ceremony, the whole court feasted at Fotheringhay Castle in lavish style on a huge array of dishes that had been prepared especially. Margaret's presence as the closest member of the Lancastrian affinity symbolized not only reconciliation with the past, but also her acceptance of Edward IV's rule. It was a public display of Edward's desire for her to be seen within the folds of the Yorkist regime. Edward was righting the wrongs of the past, as he saw them, and Margaret was one of his figureheads. It was a position she was happy to publicly humble herself to. In secret, however, she would continue to counsel her son to be wary of the King she now knelt before. It was wise counsel and Henry knew it.

BY NOVEMBER 1476, Duke Francis had become sick of Edward IV's persistent efforts to convince him to hand over Henry Tudor. Yet his treasurer, Pierre Landais, 'a man both of sharp wit and great authority', eventually persuaded him that if he did so then Edward would treat the young man – now approaching his twentieth birthday – with respect.[27] It was this that finally swayed him. Handing Henry over to the English envoys, they wasted no time in conveying the young man to St Malo off the north coast of Brittany, where a ship was waiting to carry him to England. But, perhaps by means of an urgent message from Margaret, Henry recognized that it was a trap. Claiming to have fallen ill, he sought sanctuary – possibly in the Cathedral at St Malo – but the English envoys were not about to give up their recently won prize easily.[28] They tried to remove Henry from the church, but the townsfolk came to his aid. Furious that such a violation was being made on a house of God, they turned on the envoys in an attempt to protect Henry. In the meantime, Jean du Quélennec, the admiral of Brittany, was able to persuade Francis of the danger Henry faced if he was transported back to England. Francis now changed his mind and offered Henry his protection once more. For the time being, Henry was safe. He was taken to Vannes, where he was reunited with his uncle Jasper. They were kept honourably, and were also welcome guests at Francis's court. Edward IV's attempts to gain custody of Margaret's son had been thwarted, but he was not about to give up. For now, however, there were other matters with which to occupy his mind, for it soon became clear that Edward faced greater danger from one much closer to home.

Since their reconciliation prior to the violence of 1471, the relationship between Edward IV and his brother, George, Duke of Clarence, had remained strained. The Queen also loathed Clarence, for Dominic Mancini claimed that 'she concluded that her offspring by the king would never come to the throne, unless the Duke of Clarence were removed'.[29] In 1472 Clarence was furious when his sister-in-law Anne Neville married his own brother, Richard, Duke of Gloucester, forcing him to share the inheritance the Neville sisters had received by right of their mother.[30] His behaviour became increasingly erratic following the death of his wife on 22 December 1476 – probably as a result of childbirth.[31] Incensed when Edward IV quashed his hopes to marry Mary of Burgundy, Clarence began to plot, and at the beginning of 1478 he was put on trial, having been accused of 'conspiring the king's death by means of spells and magicians'.[32] Found guilty of treason, the death sentence was pronounced by the Duke of Buckingham. On 18 February, Clarence was put to death in the Tower. Croyland, who was perhaps uncertain as to the manner in which the Duke met his end, would say only that the execution was 'carried out secretly', but Mancini offered an alternative explanation. According to him, Clarence was 'plunged into a jar of sweet wine' and drowned.[33] It was a deed that Edward IV seems to have deeply repented.

The destruction of the King's family by his own hand was an unexpected turn of events, but for Margaret it created an opportunity. The Richmond title that she believed was rightfully her son's was now available, and Margaret would later seek to get it back. Having almost certainly learned from her haste in her past dealings with Clarence and her desperation to regain Henry's title, she wisely did not seek to do so immediately. Perhaps recognizing that she would need further time to assure Edward IV of her loyalty and earn his confidence, Margaret employed caution and chose to wait.

Margaret continued to rise in royal favour, further evidence of which appeared in 1480. On 10 November the Queen was at Eltham Palace when she gave birth to her final child. It was a girl, named Bridget, and Margaret was probably at Eltham on the day of the baby's arrival. She was certainly there the following day, as she participated in the Princess's christening. In what was a singular honour, Margaret was given the privilege of carrying the new-born baby to the font, where the Bishop of Chichester performed the ceremony. Following this, it was reported that 'the godfather and the godmothers gave great gifts to the said Princess'.[34] The Princess's godmothers were her paternal grandmother, the Duchess of York, and her elder sister, Elizabeth of York. Elizabeth was fourteen years old and was growing into an extremely beautiful young woman. Though she was betrothed to the Dauphin of France, there would later be other suitors for her hand, one of whom she could never at this time have envisaged.

PRIOR TO 3 June 1482, Margaret's mother died. On a personal level, the death of the dowager Duchess of Somerset came as a great blow, for she had been the only parent Margaret had ever known. It had been she who had raised Margaret and supervised her early lessons, and she who had accompanied her daughter on Margaret's first trip to court. She may also have been responsible for instilling much of Margaret's sense of piety, which Margaret could now turn to for comfort. The Duchess was laid to rest beside her second husband – Margaret's father – at Wimborne.[35]

Though devastated by the death of her mother, as always, practicality was at the forefront of Margaret's mind. She now attempted to negotiate with the King.

Throughout Henry's exile, Margaret seems to have been a faithful correspondent, keeping her son abreast of affairs in England. Though none of their letters from this period have survived, it is highly probable that they contained sentiments similar to those she expressed in her later letters to him: she often gave him her blessing, and on one occasion, in a reflection of her affection towards him, she assured Henry that 'I trust you shall well perceive I shall deal towards you as a kind, loving mother'. At this time, however, Margaret was clearly considering the possibility of bringing about his return, though she also recognized that she would need time to achieve this. As her standing with Edward IV improved, so too did her confidence to effect a reconciliation. If she could continue to win the King's trust, Henry's foreign exile could potentially be brought to a swift end.

By the beginning of June 1482, her efforts appeared to have produced some results when Edward agreed that Henry could receive a share of his grandmother the dowager Duchess of Somerset's lands to the value of £400 (£276,500) if he were to return 'to be in the grace and favour of the king's highness'.[36] Edward signed the agreement on 3 June, attaching his official seal. A draft still survives and can be found among Margaret's papers.[37] The groundwork for Henry to return home had been laid. Edward's grip on the reins of power was unchallenged, and with two surviving sons, his dynasty appeared to be assured. His attempts to lay hands on Henry had been unsuccessful, but by now he felt secure enough not to view Margaret's son as a threat. His attitude towards Henry had therefore changed, and he had better reason to be conciliatory than hostile. Thus it was that, on an unknown date, Edward – curiously, using the same piece of paper on which Margaret's second husband had been created Earl of Richmond – drafted a pardon for her son.[38] Margaret began to hope that she and Henry would soon be reunited.

The Christmas season of 1482 was passed with much cheer at court, where it was observed that the King 'very often dressed in a variety of the costliest clothes'.[39] Given her earlier negotiations with Edward IV, Margaret had good grounds to feel hopeful about what 1483 might bring. Yet the year did not begin well, for early on the King received word that on 23 December Louis XI had signed the Treaty of Arras with Emperor Maximilian. By its terms the Dauphin was to marry Maximilian's daughter, Margaret of Austria, jilting Elizabeth of York in the process.[40] Edward was so outraged that he immediately declared war on France. All thoughts of pardoning Henry Tudor were set aside.

But just as violence was on the horizon, at the beginning of April 1483, very suddenly, Edward fell ill. His malady was destined to be of short duration: on 9 April the King, 'who ruled England with great renown', soon 'rendered up his spirit to his Creator' at Westminster.[41] He had been just short of his forty-first birthday, and though Thomas More would relate that in the latter years of his life the King's indulgence had led him to become 'somewhat corpulent and burly, and nevertheless not uncomely', the death of the man who had secured his throne so energetically by right of his sword came as a devastating shock both to his court and his subjects.[42]

Various stories arose about the manner in which Edward met his death: Mancini, who arrived in England at the end of 1482, had heard that he fell into 'the greatest melancholy' over events with the French, or that 'being a very tall man and very fat though not to the point of deformity, allowed the damp cold to strike his vitals, when one day he was taken in a small boat, with those whom he had bidden go fishing, and watched their sport too eagerly'.[43] Whatever the reason, as usual, Margaret's first thoughts were for her son. Henry's return had yet to be finalized, and with Edward dead, who knew if he would still be able to return home?

CHAPTER 12

***

A Boar with his Tusks

ON 16 APRIL Edward IV's corpse was conveyed from Westminster with 'all pomp and solemnity' to Windsor Castle.[1] It was here that, in St George's Chapel, which he had 'raised from the foundations' but was yet to complete, the King was laid to rest.[2] More stated that at the time of Edward's death, 'this realm was in quiet and prosperous estate', but within the court the situation was vastly different.[3]

As he lay dying, Edward's thoughts had turned to the future of his kingdom. His heir, Prince Edward, was just twelve years old, meaning that some kind of regency would be necessary until he reached his majority. This task, Edward decided, was to fall upon his younger brother, Richard, Duke of Gloucester, who was to be appointed Lord Protector until the Prince was old enough to rule for himself. Gloucester seemed like a solid choice, for he had always been steadfastly loyal to his elder brother, and had fought by his side during the decisive battles of 1471. Born on 2 October 1452 at Fotheringhay Castle, Gloucester was an experienced and brave military commander who had led a brief invasion of Scotland in 1482, accompanied by Margaret's husband, Lord Stanley.[4] During the later years of Edward's reign, Gloucester had effectively been responsible for governing the north of England in his brother's name, and it was here that he had established his power base and had a great affinity. The Earl of Warwick's former stronghold of Middleham Castle in Wensleydale was his primary residence, and it was here that his only child by Anne Neville, Edward, was born – possibly at the end of 1473.[5] Gloucester's estates did not lie at too great a distance from those of Stanley, but he is nevertheless unlikely to have been someone who Margaret knew well. In physical terms, More described Gloucester as being 'little of stature, ill-featured of limbs, crook-backed, his left shoulder much higher than his right, hard-favoured of visage'.[6] Though More was highly critical of him, thanks to the discovery of Richard's skeleton we now know that parts of this unflattering description are true.[7] Since the execution of his brother Clarence, Gloucester only rarely appeared at court, and instead 'kept himself within his own lands and set out to acquire the loyalty of his people through favours and justice'.[8] He did so successfully, and was both popular and highly respected in the north. However, he was now on the verge of making his presence felt in the south – in the most dramatic sense.

Gloucester may have been Edward IV's choice of protector, but he had enemies. Crucially, despite his best intentions, Edward had failed to unify the two factions within his court, and the divides within the political framework now became glaringly obvious. Queen Elizabeth and her family were anxious to retain their grip on power, and intended to use the young Edward V – declared king on 11 April – as their puppet. In order to do so, they were determined to ignore Edward IV's wishes and exclude Gloucester from all vestiges of power. Mancini explained that they were afraid that 'if Richard took unto himself the crown or even governed alone, they, who bore the blame of Clarence's death, would suffer death or at least be ejected from their high estate'.[9] In so doing, they may have forced his hand.

At the time of Edward IV's death, his heir was at Ludlow Castle. Here Mancini tells us that 'he devoted himself to horses and dogs and other youthful exercises to invigorate his body'.[10] Edward was a bright child with a special understanding of literature, and Mancini believed that he was cleverer than his years. Now that her son was king, Queen Elizabeth recognized that in order to secure her own power it was essential that she should obtain his custody as swiftly as possible. She wasted no time in sending word to her brother, Earl Rivers, her son's guardian, with orders to convey him to London immediately – they set out on 24 April. With the rest of the King's Council she then began making plans for the King's coronation;

eager that this should take place without delay, the date was set for 4 May. In a sign of gross discourtesy, she neglected to inform Gloucester, then in the north, of his brother's death. Edward IV's close friend Lord Hastings 'had a friendship of long standing with the duke, and was hostile to the entire kin of the queen'.[11] He was horrified by this disrespect, and as he was utterly loyal to the wishes of Edward IV, he disapproved of the Queen's plans to cut Gloucester out. In the same way that she felt unable to cooperate with Gloucester, the Queen also knew that she would be unable to work with Hastings, partially on account of her jealousy over his friendship with her late husband. Hastings sent word to Gloucester conveying the news of his brother's death, and urged him to come to London with a force to 'avenge the insult done him by his enemies'.[12]

According to Croyland, when Gloucester learned that the King was dead and that the Queen intended to exclude him, he 'wrote the most pleasant letters' to her in which he assured her of his loyalty to her son.[13] But he recognized that she was eager to exclude him, and in order to prevent his downfall he knew that he had to move quickly. He began journeying south, and when he reached Northampton on 29 April he met with the man who was to be his key ally during the events that followed: the Duke of Buckingham. As the grandson of Humphrey Stafford, Margaret's one-time father-in-law, Buckingham was Margaret's cousin and former nephew, and she had known him for most of his life. It was to him that Gloucester complained of 'the insult done him by the ignoble family of the queen'.[14] He could not have chosen a better ally, for Buckingham had his own reasons for loathing Elizabeth; in February 1466, when he was still a youth, 'he had been forced', Mancini reports, 'to marry the queen's sister, whom he scorned to wed on account of her humble origin'.[15] Though his marriage to Katherine Wydeville caused him great disgust, it had served to bind Buckingham's allegiances and those of his family to Edward IV.[16] Now, though, he threw in his lot – and his loyalty – with Gloucester.

Shortly after their arrival, the two men were joined in Northampton by Edward V's uncle, Earl Rivers, who had been escorting his nephew to the capital.[17] Leaving the King at Stony Stratford, Rivers had ridden to pay his respects to Gloucester, and before long the Queen's son Sir Richard Grey also arrived. Neither Rivers nor Grey had any reason to believe that anything was amiss, but the following morning both were locked into the inns in which they had been staying while Gloucester and Buckingham rode to meet the King. Edward V was preparing to leave Stony Stratford when his uncle Gloucester and Buckingham caught up with him. He was shocked when Gloucester informed him that his kinsmen were bad advisors who had been conspiring the Duke's death, causing Gloucester to issue orders for their imprisonment. The helpless men were 'taken to the North in captivity', and were later executed at Pontefract.[18] The young King was now in Gloucester's control.

In London, when word arrived that Gloucester had intercepted the King and imprisoned the Queen's family, 'the unexpectedness of the event horrified every one'.[19] Before long, for the second time in her life the Queen gathered her youngest son Richard, Duke of York, and her five daughters and fled to the Sanctuary at Westminster Abbey.

On 4 May – the day scheduled for the coronation – Edward V arrived in London accompanied by Gloucester and Buckingham. Gloucester had already sent word to the Council that he had rescued his nephew from the hated Wydevilles, and had himself proclaimed Protector of the realm. There were, nonetheless, already many who feared his motives: Mancini reported that a rumour was circulating that 'the duke had brought his nephew not under his care, but into his power, so as to gain for himself the crown'.[20]

Edward V, meanwhile, was taken to lodge in the Bishop's Palace near St Paul's, but it was agreed that an alternative residence would need to be found. While deliberating the matter in Council, claims Croyland, some suggested 'the Hospital of St John, some Westminster, but the duke of Buckingham suggested the Tower of London and his opinion was accepted verbally by all, even by those who did not wish it'.[21] In the Tudor period, the Tower would gain a terrifying reputation as a place of imprisonment and brutal execution, but it held no such associations in 1483. It was instead a royal palace that had been much favoured by Edward IV, and contained luxurious apartments for the king and queen. It was here that Edward V was now sent in order to prepare for his coronation, while Gloucester made plans to assume further power.

MARGARET'S PRECISE WHEREABOUTS at the time of Edward IV's death are unknown, but it is certainly likely that she was close to the heart of the events that followed. After all, she and her husband were to be directly involved with what happened next, and the events of spring and early summer 1483 laid the foundations for what would prove to be a turning point in Margaret's life. There is no knowing how she may have felt about Gloucester's wresting of power from the Wydevilles, but perhaps of greater concern to her was the fact that with Edward IV's death, all possible plans for her son to come home had ground to a halt. The uncertain nature of the future now meant that there was no way of knowing whether this would still be an option; a cruel twist of fate that must have left her feeling frustrated at the very least. Throughout May the Council met regularly to discuss business and plans for the coronation. As a Council member, Stanley was actively involved, and probably related some of the happenings to his wife who was almost certainly with him in London. Margaret would therefore have known that Gloucester was in complete control, loyally supported by Buckingham. She was probably as stunned as many others at the way in which events were transpiring. Buckingham, in turn, was being handsomely rewarded for his services: on 15 May he was created Constable of England, and the following day he was granted the offices of chief justice and Chamberlain of North and South Wales.[22] Stanley was given no such reward, suggesting that he had no role in Gloucester's schemes. At the end of May, as Gloucester's power grew, there were many who were becoming increasingly suspicious of his motives, and Stanley may have been among them. By now, most were in agreement that Gloucester planned to take the throne for himself.

Having assumed control of the Council, Gloucester then set about removing all of those who were loyal to Edward IV, including Hastings and John Morton, Bishop of Ely. Morton had been involved in the negotiations for Margaret and Stanley's marriage settlement, and would soon become even more closely entwined in her story. These were all men who had been well trusted by Edward IV, but the same could not be said for his brother. Though Hastings had proved himself to be a useful ally to Gloucester, he was also unswervingly loyal to the memory of Edward IV and his children. On this basis, Gloucester decided that Hastings would have to go.

On the morning of 13 June, the Council met at the Tower. It was not long before Gloucester arrived and 'cried out that an ambush had been prepared for him, and they had come with hidden arms, that they might be first to open the attack'.[23] Chaos ensued as a group of armed guards under Gloucester's command entered the room and began attacking Hastings and his supporters. More had heard that 'another let fly at the Lord Stanley, which shrunk at the stroke and fell under the table, or else his head had been cleft to the teeth, for as shortly as he shrank, yet ran the blood about his ears'.[24] This may have been exaggerated, for there is no indication that any injuries inflicted upon Stanley were serious. It was Hastings who was Gloucester's main target. Taking his opportunity to destroy him, Gloucester made his move. Having accused the man of plotting against him, Gloucester declared that 'I will not to dinner till I see thy head off.'[25] The helpless Hastings was dragged out and 'brought forth into the green beside the chapel within the Tower, and his head laid down upon a long log of timber, and there stricken off'.[26] His remains were later interred in St George's Chapel, Windsor, near those of his friend and master Edward IV.[27] Everyone agreed that his unceremonious execution without trial was an act of tyranny, and one that sent shockwaves through the city: 'Thus fell Hastings, killed not by those enemies he had always feared, but by a friend whom he had never doubted.'[28]

According to More, after suffering from 'so fearful a dream, in which him thought that a boar with his tusks so raced them both by the heads that the blood ran about both their shoulders', Margaret's husband Stanley had suspected that Hastings was in danger – the boar was Gloucester's well-known badge.[29] The dream supposedly had such an effect on him that he attempted to warn Hastings of what was afoot. Sending a 'trusty secret messenger unto him at midnight' the evening before his death, Stanley urged that 'he was thoroughly determined no longer to tarry, but had his horse ready, if the Lord Hastings would go with him to ride so far yet the same night, and they should be out of danger ere day'.[30] Clearly he was fearful for both of their lives. But Hastings paid Stanley's fears little heed, sending a message assuring him to 'be merry and have no fear'.[31] His confidence was misplaced.

Stanley's life may have been spared, but according to Vergil, on Gloucester's orders he was forced to endure a spell of brief imprisonment.[32] However, he was released 'safe and sound', for Gloucester feared 'lest if he should have done him any wrong George, Lord Strange his son should have stirred up the people to arms somewhere against him'.[33] The shock of the events of 13 June was evidently enough to convince Stanley to declare his allegiance to Gloucester. Margaret would have been left both horrified and fearful as a result of the unexpected brutal treatment that her husband had received, and would now have become aware of what Gloucester was capable of. She would thus have had good reason to loathe him as a result.

Though Edward V was in the Tower, his younger brother Richard, Duke of York, had joined their mother in sanctuary. Mancini says that Gloucester foresaw that York 'would by legal right succeed to the throne if his brother were removed', and so it was to this end that he 'resolved to get into his power the duke of York'.[34] He sent word that he wished for the younger of the Princes to join his brother in the Tower, where the two could prepare for Edward's coronation. By the same token, Edward would be pleased to see York, 'to whose grace it were as singular comfort to have his natural brother in company'.[35] Yet Gloucester realized that the Queen would not willingly surrender her youngest son, and so 'with the consent of the council he surrounded the sanctuary with troops'.[36] Gloucester was prepared to use force. Knowing that she was trapped, Elizabeth 'surrendered her son, trusting in the word of the cardinal of Canterbury, that the boy should be restored after the coronation'.[37] York was sent 'to be kept with the Prince, his brother'.[38]

At the Tower, Gloucester now had both of his nephews in his keeping, and 'after that day they never came abroad'.[39] Initially, the author of the

Great Chronicle of London related that the boys 'were seen shooting and playing in the garden of the Tower by sundry times'.[40] Such occasions, though, appear to have become increasingly less frequent, and Mancini was told that 'all the attendants who had waited upon the king were debarred access to him. He and his brother were withdrawn into the inner apartments of the Tower proper, and day by day began to be seen more rarely behind the bars and windows, till at length they ceased to appear altogether.'[41]

Even Edward's physician Dr Argentine was now forbidden from treating his young master, and had reported that the young King, fearful for his life, 'like a victim prepared for sacrifice, sought remission of his sins by daily confession and penance, because he believed that death was facing him'.[42] Equally disturbing was More's claim that 'when the protector had both the children in his hands, he opened himself more boldly, both to certain other men, and also chiefly to the Duke of Buckingham'.[43] This was a view that was supported by Croyland, who stated that 'both these dukes showed their intentions, not in private but openly'.[44] These intentions were about to become shockingly clear.

Edward V's coronation had been rescheduled for 22 June, but as that day arrived there were no signs of celebration. Instead, Dr Ralph Shaa, 'a divine of great reputation', made his way to St Paul's.[45] There he preached a sermon, the text of which was 'bastard slips shall not take root' from the Bible.[46] He claimed that Edward IV was 'never lawfully married unto the Queen', because he had in fact been contracted to marry another woman: her name was Eleanor Butler.[47] The unfortunate lady had since conveniently died, so was unable to corroborate the story.[48] Yet by preaching such a sermon, Shaa was attempting to cast doubt on the legitimacy of Edward V. The nature of Edward IV's relationship with Eleanor Butler has been hotly debated, but however unpopular his marriage to Elizabeth Wydeville, most people – Margaret included – believed it to be legitimate and valid. Thus nobody was fooled by Shaa's speech, in which he also took great care to extol the merits of the Duke of Gloucester.

Many of the nobles had arrived in London for Edward V's coronation, and were summoned to Westminster by Buckingham on 25 June. Here he reiterated Edward V's illegitimacy as a result of the invalidity of the Wydeville marriage, as well as rendering Clarence's son, the Earl of Warwick, unfit to rule on the grounds of his father's attainder.[49] Buckingham therefore claimed that 'the only survivor of the royal stock was Richard, Duke of Gloucester, who was legally entitled to the crown'.[50] Gloucester would, Buckingham said, be hesitant to accept such a burden, but might be persuaded if petitioned by the lords. It was clear that there was no real choice, and that same day Edward V was declared illegitimate and deposed: the legacy that Edward IV had fought so hard for had crumbled. The following day, the lords gathered at Baynard's Castle, where they invited Gloucester to take the throne. After a show of reluctance, he accepted. Thus, on 26 June, the reign of Richard III officially began.

Historians still debate whether Richard intended to usurp the throne from the moment of Edward IV's death, or whether his hand was forced by the hostility of the Wydevilles and subsequent events. Vergil was unsurprisingly in no doubt, and claimed that Richard immediately 'began to be kindled with an ardent desire of sovereignty'.[51] More concurred, expressing the view that 'certain it is that he contrived their destruction [the Princes], with the usurpation of the regal dignity upon himself'.[52] Margaret's feelings about Richard III's usurpation would soon become clear, and she had good reason to feel concerned. Richard's treatment of the Wydevilles, his nephews and Hastings – as well as her own husband – had shown that he would not scruple to resort to violence if he felt threatened, and this may have made Margaret fearful for her son Henry. She had bent her knee to a Yorkist king in the past, but there was no guarantee that this one would be as willing as his brother had eventually seemed to allow Henry to return home. After all, the circumstances in which Richard had acquired his throne meant that he would not enjoy the same sense of security as Edward IV had done, so he might well have viewed Henry Tudor as more of a threat. However, it would not be long before Margaret was prepared to risk Richard's wrath in order to gain a higher prize.

The coronation of Richard III was set for 6 July, and there was much to be done. Margaret's husband had remained in London throughout the dramatic events of June, and if she had not been there before, then Margaret had certainly joined him by the beginning of July. On 4 July the new King and his queen, Anne, took up residence in the Tower – the same fortress in which their disinherited nephews languished. That same day, Stanley was appointed steward of the household in an attempt to secure his loyalty. The following day, the royal couple rode through the city 'attended by the entire nobility and a display of royal honours', presumably including Margaret and her husband. At some point that day, Richard took the time to grant Margaret and Stanley an audience at Westminster in order to help settle a dispute that had been lingering since the death of her mother. It was a stark contrast to the ruthless treatment he had meted out to Stanley just three weeks earlier, and he seems now to have been motivated by a desire to win them over and bind their loyalties to him by assuring them of his good intentions. The matter concerned an outstanding debt owed by the Orléans family, to which Richard and his chief justice, William Hussey, agreed to lend their support in attempting to secure the repayment of. It seems plausible that Margaret also took the opportunity of her audience with the King to beg for clemency on her son's behalf; Sir Francis Bacon, who referred to Margaret as 'this cunning countess', said that she knew well 'to dissemble great love to the king, to desire and to effect the love of King Richard', so she 'came in all humility and besought him to call home her son and to be gracious to him'.[53] If she indeed did so, nothing came of it. It had, though, been agreed that she and her husband were to play a prominent role in the events of the following day.

On 6 July, 'the said Duke was with Queen Anne his wife at and in Westminster Church crowned with great solemnity'.[54] Both the King and Queen were magnificently dressed in sumptuous clothes of the most costly materials. Many of the ladies and gentlewomen attending the Queen had been delivered beautiful robes, and like them Margaret had been gifted 'a long gown made of six yards of crimson velvet', which contained six yards of 'white cloth of gold'.[55] This made a magnificent impression on observers, and there was a further privilege. As Queen Anne processed into Westminster Abbey, 'on her head a rich circlet of gold with many precious pearls and stones set therein', Margaret came bearing her train.[56] Stanley had also been given an important role, for as the King entered the abbey it was Stanley who walked before him, bearing the mace. The couple looked on as the Archbishop of Canterbury, 'albeit unwillingly, anointed and crowned him king of England'.[57] Margaret had also been given 'a long gown made of six yards of blue velvet' containing the same amount of crimson cloth of gold – she may have worn this to the celebratory banquet that followed in Westminster Hall, for which she was sat next to the Duchess of Norfolk.[58] The royal kitchens had been busy preparing an enormous selection of sumptuous dishes: roast crane and cygnet were followed by courses including peacock, venison, carp, 'fresh sturgeon with fennel', and pike, all of which had been fragranced with spices such as cinnamon, saffron and ginger.[59] These delights were all washed down with copious amounts of ale and red and white wine.

Within the space of just a few short months, the entire shape of fifteenth-century England had changed. But behind the masks of outward loyalty that were displayed to Richard III at his coronation, there were many who were already opposed to his rule. None were better than Margaret at masking their true feelings. She had spent Edward IV's reign biding her time and employing all of her pragmatism in order to move closer to the heart of power. All in an attempt to keep her son from harm and achieve the ultimate prize of his restoration. Her goal had been within touching distance when, suddenly, Edward's death cast doubt on Henry's future. Now Margaret was faced with a new king whose intentions towards Henry were uncertain, but whose actions in acquiring his throne had shown that he could be a man without scruple. Margaret once again sought to use events to create an opportunity for her son. Her plan would risk great danger, but having had Henry's restoration so cruelly snatched from her, she was no longer prepared to play the long game – or to wait upon Richard's actions.

CHAPTER 13

The Head of that Conspiracy

I N THE AFTERMATH of Richard III's coronation, life is likely to have resumed much of its normal routine for Margaret. With the celebrations at an end, many of his nobles had returned home, but Richard was anxious to keep Stanley by his side as he made preparations for the first progress of his reign. This was not borne out of a desire for his company, but as a security measure. Though Stanley had assured the King of his loyalty, Richard was still wary – perhaps of Margaret, too. This was undoubtedly partially influenced by the manner in which he had acquired his throne, which made him naturally suspicious, but there was more to it than that. Stanley had, after all, been one of the integral members of Edward IV's household, and, combined, he and Margaret had much influence across their lands in the north and elsewhere. Additionally, Margaret was one of the key surviving members of the house of Lancaster, and the mother of a male member of that family who had spent years in foreign exile as a result of his bloodline. On 22 July, Richard rode out of London on the first stage of his journey north, taking Stanley with him. The events of the spring and summer had thrown the future into a torrent of uncertainty: Richard III's usurpation had been profoundly unpopular throughout the realm, and many recognized that his actions were unlawful.

As he left, London was abuzz with speculation as to the fate of the deposed Edward V and his brother – popularly remembered as the Princes in the Tower. People were whispering in the streets, in the inns and in the stews, and rumours had begun to circulate that the Princes were dead – murdered on the orders of their uncle Richard. When Mancini left England shortly after the coronation, he had learned nothing of Edward's fate, but had seen 'many men burst forth into tears and lamentations when mention was made of him after his removal from men's sight; and already there was a suspicion that he had been done away with'.[1] There were, though, some who still believed the Princes to be alive, and when the King left his capital a plan was hatched to set them free. What was more, Margaret may have been involved.

The details of the plot are sketchy and derive largely from the chronicler John Stow, who had access to sources now lost. The outline of the plan – initiated by former members of Edward IV's household – appears to have been to set fire to parts of the city, thereby distracting the King's men while the Princes were rescued.[2] Margaret's role in the conspiracy is uncertain, but she was probably motivated by a desire to improve her son's prospects, for Jasper and Henry Tudor had been invited to participate.[3] Presumably she felt that Henry's future would be better assured under Edward V's rule than that of Richard III, and that she was prepared to throw caution to wind and involve herself in such a plot can perhaps be taken as a sign of her desperation and frustration at having any immediate hopes for her son's return thwarted. It was a huge turning point for her, for hitherto she had displayed both patience and caution in her former dealings with Edward IV. But there was none of that now. The conspiracy was ill thought out and failed, and on 29 July Richard issued a warrant to his Lord Chancellor referring to 'certain persons of such as of late had taken upon them the fact of an enterprise'. As Margaret was not punished it seems likely that the King was unaware of any involvement she may have had. The result, though, was that the Princes were immediately moved to the inner confines of the Tower. Furthermore, Richard recognized that his own security could not be assured while the boys lived: it was almost certainly this that prompted him to make a chilling decision.

Thomas More related that while Richard was on progress, he summoned John Green 'whom he specially trusted'. It was through Green that he sent word to the new Constable of the Tower, Sir Robert Brackenbury, that he should 'in any wise put the two children to death'.[4] But although loyal to Richard, Brackenbury was an honourable man, and 'plainly answered that he would never put them to death'.[5] In frustration Richard turned elsewhere. On 30 August he arrived in the city of York with his wife and son, where the citizens warmly received the royal party. While he was there, Croyland reported that Richard 'arranged splendid and highly expensive feasts and entertainments to attract to himself the affection of many people', but he had always been popular in the north.[6] Having pondered the problem posed by his nephews, Richard's attention, claims More, was drawn to Sir James Tyrell, a man who was eager for promotion.[7] Approaching him about the possibility of murdering the boys, he 'found him nothing strange', and Tyrell left York for London and the Tower.[8] On Richard's orders, upon his arrival Tyrell was sent to Brackenbury 'with a letter by which he was commanded to deliver Sir James all the keys of the Tower for one night, to the end he might there accomplish the king's pleasure in such thing as he had given him commandment'.[9] Brackenbury must have known what was afoot. It was probably the evening of 3 September when, with the assistance of several accomplices, Tyrell arrived at the Tower.[10] More's account relates that, having entered the chamber where the two princes slept, the men

suddenly lapped them up among the clothes – so bewrapped them and entangled them, keeping down by force the featherbed and pillows hard unto their mouths, that within a while, smored and stifled, their breath failing, they gave up to God their innocent souls into the joys of heaven, leaving to the tormentors their bodies dead in the bed.[11]

Once the deed was complete, the assassins 'laid their bodies naked out upon the bed and fetched Sir James to see them'.[12] The lifeless Princes were then buried 'at the stair-foot, meetly deep in the ground, under a great heap of stones'.[13] The sons of Edward IV were dead.

Having completed his task, Tyrell returned to Richard in York and 'showed him all the manner of the murder'.[14] He was well rewarded for his services, but later in life his actions may have returned to haunt him: in 1502 he apparently confessed to the Princes' murder before his execution for treason.[15] On 8 September, meanwhile, Richard III's young son Edward was formally invested as Prince of Wales in the spectacular York Minster: his line seemed set to continue, just as he had plausibly destroyed that of his brother.

More's account of the murder of the Princes in the Tower was not the only one in circulation, but as Weir has shown in her excellent book on the subject, there are good reasons for believing in its credibility.[16] Following the coronation, nobody had seen the Princes and hopes for their survival faded fast. Many people in England believed them to be dead, and in Europe, too, people were murmuring as to their fate. Numerous stories emerged as to the manner in which the two boys had met their deaths; the *Great Chronicle of London* reported that opinion was divided, 'for some said they were murdered between two feather beds, some said they were drowned in Malmsey and some said they were sticked with a venomous poison'.[17] When André wrote that Richard 'cruelly murdered his brother Edward the Fourth's two sons', he said that the King had given orders that 'his unprotected nephews secretly be dispatched with the sword'.[18] The *Grey Friars Chronicle* simply stated that they were 'put to silence', and Commynes confidently declared that it was Richard who was responsible.[19]

Not one contemporary or near contemporary source accused Margaret of complicity in the disappearance or murder of the Princes, and her name was never linked with theirs. In the seventeenth century, however, the first claims emerged. First William Cornwallis and then Sir George Buck, who claimed to have read 'in an old manuscript book' that it was 'held for certain that Dr Morton and a certain countess, conspiring the deaths of the sons of King Edward and some other, resolved that *these* treacheries should be executed by poison and by sorcery'.[20] Buck was often unreliable, and other parts of his story can be proven to be untrue. The suggestion that Margaret was in any way involved in the murder of the Princes is frankly ludicrous, yet it is one that has persisted to this day. There is not a shred of contemporary evidence to connect her with their disappearance – let alone their murder – and this is surely the most definitive indication of her innocence. Even had Margaret wished to, an opportunity for her to arrange entry for an assassin was highly unlikely to occur; though entry to the Tower would have been possible, it is clear that the Princes were extremely well guarded, with even Edward V's physician debarred access.[21] Only one who had the power and authority of the King behind them could have arranged for such a chance. Had Margaret visited or attempted to do so, contemporary chroniclers would certainly have noted it. Practicalities aside, it makes no sense that Margaret would have wished them dead when mere months earlier she may have been involved in a plot to free them. Quite simply, she had no motive. On the other hand, Richard, as the popular phrase goes, had both motive and opportunity. Similarly, it is worth considering Margaret's character. Though she could be politically ruthless, she was a woman of immense religiosity and great kindness who had known and witnessed at least the younger of the boys growing up. Could she realistically have countenanced their death? Would such a thing even have crossed her mind? Her later accounts reveal nothing that could be taken as a show of remorse for such a terrible deed, and with very good reason. Whatever the fate of the Princes, the insinuation that Margaret was in any way involved is nothing short of preposterous and an unfair slur on her character.

Though confirmation had not been given, the popular belief in the Princes' murder meant that Richard 'lost the hearts of the people', as one London chronicler reported.[22] Given Margaret's subsequent actions, she too clearly believed that they were dead. Elsewhere, Buckingham, Richard's chief ally, had joined his master on progress, but had bidden farewell to him at Gloucester. He returned to his castle of Brecknock in Wales, where he had in his custody Dr John Morton, Bishop of Ely.[23] Following the events that witnessed Lord Hastings' cruel beheading, Morton – himself spared the horrors of execution – had been sent into Buckingham's keeping.

More described Morton as being a man 'of great natural wit, very well learned, and honourable in behaviour, lacking no wise ways to win favour', and much of this transpired to be true.[24] Though his loyalties had always been Lancastrian, following the defeats of 1471 and Henry VI's murder, reconciling with Edward IV seemed to be the only viable option. Before long, Morton had ingratiated himself with his new master, and Edward came to rely on his advice – so much so that Morton was appointed one of the executors of his will, and he was one of those who Richard III knew to be loyal to his brother's memory. It was now that Morton supposedly helped to plan Richard's downfall.

By the time he left Richard at Gloucester, Buckingham had become disaffected. Several reasons for his estrangement have been suggested, with Vergil claiming that he was 'partly repenting that hitherto of himself he had not resisted King Richard's evil enterprise' and had thus 'resolved to separate himself from him'.[25] It is certainly plausible that Richard had told him of his intentions to kill the Princes, a step that Buckingham considered to be too far.[26] Having returned to Brecknock by the middle of August, Buckingham spoke with Morton and 'waxed with him familiar'.[27] He told his prisoner that in consideration of his own royal descent he was considering pressing his own claim to the throne, which stemmed from Thomas of Woodstock, the youngest son of Edward III. Morton, who had no difficulty in recognizing the Duke's pride, flattered him. He also perceived an opportunity for Buckingham to join forces, for Margaret too was plotting. Vergil claimed that with the Duke's consent, Morton summoned Margaret's trusted servant, Reginald Bray, 'to come unto the duke into Wales'.[28] Buckingham had evidently informed Bray of his thoughts in regards to his own claim, and Bray was able to report them to his mistress. For now, though, Buckingham did nothing further. Intriguingly, however, Margaret already had her own plan in place: 'for she was entered far into them, and none better plunged in them and deeply acquainted with them. And she was a politic and subtle lady.'[29] Her plan was for Henry to bear the crown once worn by his Lancastrian forebears, and to become King of England.

This dramatic change in Margaret's mind-set and ambitions was undoubtedly triggered by her belief that the Princes in the Tower had been murdered. Though her son Henry was 'a member of the house of Lancaster', Commynes correctly acknowledged that 'he was not the closest claimant to the crown, whatever one may say about it'.[30] Margaret was also aware of this, and prior to 1483 the future of the house of York had appeared secure – Edward IV had been strong and robust with two male heirs, and thus there was no reason to even consider the possibility that Henry Tudor might one day stand a chance of becoming England's ruler. Even after Richard's coup, there were several York boys in line with a possibility of succeeding him, foremost of which was his own son, Prince Edward.[31] Moreover, Margaret's actions in the aftermath of Richard's coronation and the attempt to rescue the Princes show that she had not considered her son's claim to be a strong one at this point. Henry's Lancastrian blood was not enough to stake a claim to the throne, particularly as many still considered the Beauforts to be bastards. By the same token, having spent most of his life in exile, Henry was an unknown entity in England. He needed something – or someone – to strengthen his claim, and Margaret did not have far to look. Elizabeth of York, the eldest of Edward IV's daughters, was beautiful, charming and intelligent. Despite her proclaimed bastardy in light of the so-called revelations about Edward IV's marriage, in the wake of her brothers' disappearance many were of the opinion that she was the legitimate heir to the throne. What better way, then, to promote Henry's own claim than a marriage with the Yorkist heiress?

According to Vergil,

after the slaughter of King Edward's children was known, [Margaret] began to hope well of her son's fortune, supposing that that deed would without doubt prove for the profit of the commonwealth, if it might chance the blood of King Henry the Sixth and of King Edward to be intermingled by affinity, and so two most pernicious factions should be at once, by conjoining of both the houses, utterly taken away.[32]

It is probably true that the impetus for Henry's marriage to Elizabeth of York came from Margaret, and she was certainly the chief manoeuvrer behind what came next. Margaret trusted her Welsh physician, Dr Lewis of Caerleon, implicitly. Likewise, 'because he was a grave man and of no small experience, she was wont oftentimes to confer freely with all, and with him familiarly to lament her adversity'.[33] It was to him that Margaret suggested the possibility of a marriage between her son and Elizabeth of York, in order that Richard 'might easily be dejected from all honour and bereft the realm'.[34] For such a plan to stand any chance of success, the connivance of Elizabeth Wydeville would be essential. Elizabeth still languished in penury in the Sanctuary at Westminster Abbey, and it would be impossible for Margaret to approach her directly – Richard's men watched the Sanctuary closely, and visitors were regarded with suspicion. Margaret needed an intermediary, and Dr Lewis was the ideal candidate.

Conveniently, being 'a very learned physician', Dr Lewis also served Elizabeth Wydeville.[35] It would not appear strange or unusual for him to enter the Sanctuary on the pretext of visiting his patient, and on Margaret's orders this was precisely what he did. Elizabeth was incredibly vulnerable, for it was either on an earlier occasion or during the course of Lewis's visit that she had been told that her sons were dead. The news 'drove her into such passion as for fear forthwith she fell in a swoon, and lay lifeless a good while' before descending into hysteria.[36] As Lewis approached the Sanctuary, his arrival drew no more than a glance from the guards, and he was able to enter unmolested. When he broached the subject of Margaret's plan with the fallen queen, the response he received was enthusiastic. That Elizabeth agreed to the plan confirms that both she and Margaret believed her sons to be dead, and though, to her sorrow, Elizabeth would never assume the role of the king's mother, she at least had hope of becoming the mother of a queen. She instructed Lewis to return to Margaret with a favourable answer, and promised to do all that she could in order to rally Edward IV's supporters. Thus it was that a new conspiracy was laid between the two women.

Margaret waited anxiously at her husband's London townhouse for news, and when it arrived she tasked Reginald Bray, 'a man most faithful and trusty, to be the chief dealer in this conspiracy'.[37] Bray was to begin recruiting men to Henry's cause, and within a few days he had successfully enlisted a number of gentlemen who had once been members of Edward IV's household, including Giles Daubeney, Richard Guildford, Thomas Ramney, John Cheyney 'and many more'.[38] Additionally, Elizabeth Wydeville had secured some valuable support, and plans were taking shape. It was at this time that Vergil related that Margaret, 'careful for the well doing and glory of her son', charged her chaplain, Christopher Urswick, with travelling to Brittany to inform Henry of what was afoot.[39] But before he could depart, Margaret received word from Buckingham, who had decided that he was intent 'of the same practice'.[40] It was at this point that the two plots – originally separate enterprises – became one.

It is unclear on what basis the two sides agreed to combine forces. Vergil noted that when Margaret received Buckingham's message, she 'altered her intent', and instead of sending Urswick to Brittany she sent her servant, Hugh Conway, 'with a good great sum of money' to deliver to Henry.[41] André later said that Henry had been informed of recent events in England 'through his mother's messengers' – Thomas Ramney was not far behind Conway with a similar purpose – so she had presumably conveyed her belief that the Princes were dead.[42] Margaret further commanded her son to sail to Wales, where he would find aid awaiting him. Croyland says that Morton urged Buckingham to send a message to Henry 'inviting him to hasten into the kingdom of England as fast as he could reach the shore to take Elizabeth, the dead king's elder daughter, to wife and with her, at the same time, possession of the whole kingdom'.[43] Buckingham never, in fact, made any mention of Henry taking the crown when he wrote to him on 24 September. Jones and Underwood have underlined the possibility that Margaret recruited Buckingham under false pretences, suggesting that he ought instead to claim the throne for himself.[44] This would explain why Vergil said that Margaret had changed her intent – she was, after all, 'a wise woman'.[45] However, it is equally likely that it was a double bluff, and that Buckingham's intention was to claim the throne while feigning support for Henry's cause.

Margaret, 'commonly called the head of that conspiracy', began to further her plans and by late September they were almost complete.[46] It had been agreed that all sides would rally their troops in a bid to topple Richard, and they planned to rise on 18 October. Throughout the plotting, Margaret's husband Stanley had remained with the King, and though apart from his wife in physical terms it is hard to believe that he had no knowledge of the plans that were being formulated in his own house. It is unlikely that he supported them though, and he certainly did not join the conspirators. Conveniently, his presence by Richard's side provided him with a watertight alibi as well as serving as a useful tool if the rebellion did not go to plan – Richard believed him to be guiltless when it came to light. On the other hand, Margaret's role of conspirator was fraught with danger. Henry VII's biographer S.B. Chrimes referred to her as 'the chief spinner of plots', but she was aware that her actions carried great risks.[47] They were risks that she was prepared to take, and spurred on by ambition for her son, with Buckingham's support she had high hopes of the plot's success. After all, not only was Richard's former key ally prepared to back the plot, but Buckingham was also a powerful magnate who had both money and men. Coupled with Wydeville support, which had been engineered under Margaret's auspices, there was good reason for her to feel confident about developing her plans.

Upon receiving word from his mother, Henry immediately sought the assistance of Duke Francis. He willingly offered his support, and agreed to provide him with 'a large force of men and boats'.[48] Feeling optimistic, Henry sent Conway and Thomas Ramney back to England in order to prepare his supporters: by 2 October he was ready to sail.

Elsewhere, 'This whole conspiracy was known well enough, through spies, to King Richard', Croyland reported.[49] By 11 October, while in Lincoln he had learned of what was afoot, yet the disaffection of his former ally, Buckingham, came as a shock. It is unclear whether Richard was aware of Margaret's involvement at this point, as Vergil stated that he believed that Buckingham was 'the head of the conspirators'.[50] He was determined to crush his enemies, and began raising a force. Requesting men from his loyal city of York, Richard declared that 'the Duke of Buckingham is traitorously turned upon us contrary to the duty of his allegiance, and intends the utter destruction of us'.[51] It soon became clear though that luck was against the Duke.

Everything went wrong for the conspirators: those who rose in Kent at the command of the Wydeville faction had risen too early and were easily suppressed, and for Buckingham in Wales matters fared far worse. Heavy rain relentlessly pounded the land that autumn, and it proved impossible to cross the River Severn into England. Though Buckingham and his men had risen up as planned on 18 October, the conditions made many of the roads treacherous. Within a short time, most of his army had deserted him, and the Duke was forced to flee 'in secret wise unto a servant's place of his' in the Forest of Dean.[52] Unpopular among his tenants, when the King issued a reward for his capture the game was up. Buckingham was betrayed and taken to Salisbury, where 'the king had arrived with a great army'. He was beheaded on 2 November in the marketplace. It was a Sunday, but in spite of the fact that it was the Lord's day Richard was not giving any quarter. Buckingham had begged for an audience with Richard, but his request was refused.

Unaware of what had transpired, on 3 October Henry Tudor set sail for England. The treacherous weather forced his ships back, and it was not until 18 October that he sailed again. Though aiming for the Devon coast, a storm drove his ships near to Poole in Dorset. Here he came close to landing, for those who had gathered on the shore tried to convince him that they were Buckingham's men and that the rebellion had been a success. Yet he was suspicious and his good judgement soon set in. Turning back, he returned to Brittany once more. For the moment all hope for his cause appeared lost.

Buckingham's execution served as a horrifying example of the way in which Richard III dealt with traitors. It is unclear precisely how or when the King became aware of Margaret's involvement, but it would not remain a secret for long. Her fate now lay in the hands of her enemy. Her kinsman Buckingham was dead at the executioner's hand, her son had returned to exile, Elizabeth Wydeville remained in sanctuary, Dr Lewis was probably imprisoned in the Tower, but Margaret had nowhere to flee.[53] Having committed high treason, she must have been terrified for her life as she awaited the consequences of her plotting – almost certainly in London. When the punishment came, it was remarkably lenient. Though in the eyes of the law Margaret had committed the most heinous of crimes by conspiring against the King, it was his own vulnerability that saved her. Richard III was aware of his diminished popularity, and could not afford to risk alienating Lord Stanley – who had grown in power and prestige over the years since his marriage to Margaret – by ordering the execution of his wife. He was therefore left with no option but to spare Margaret the death penalty, but that did not mean she would go unpunished.

CHAPTER 14

Mother of the King's Great Rebel and Traitor

ENRY TUDOR HAD returned safely to Brittany, where he took up residence in the medieval walled city of Vannes, but he had not given up on his ambition: with Margaret's support, the seed had been planted in his mind, and Henry was determined to ensure that it grew. Upon his return he had been joined by a number of those who had been involved in the rebellion, and over the course of the next year and more, a steady trickle of exiles continued to arrive – all of whom were disaffected with Richard III. These included Margaret's half-brother, John Welles, who had conspired against Richard in August, the Marquess of Dorset, and Elizabeth Wydeville's brothers Richard, Lionel and Edward.[1] Morton, meanwhile, had managed to escape from Brecknock and fled to Flanders. Reginald Bray, Margaret's devoted servant and friend, escaped punishment and on 5 January 1484 was pardoned for his role in the conspiracy.[2] The conspiracy may have failed, but its very existence permanently altered the political landscape. No longer was Henry Tudor attempting to reconcile with the house of York in the same manner as his mother had been negotiating during the reign of Edward IV; he was a contender for the throne. On Christmas Day Henry and his supporters had gathered in Rheims Cathedral. It was here that he solemnly pledged to overthrow Richard III and marry Elizabeth of York, thereby uniting the houses of Lancaster and York as his mother had intended. At the same time, his supporters 'swore unto him homage as though he had been already created king'.[3]

Across the Channel, Richard III recognized that the threat posed by

Henry had not been vanquished, and Buck later claimed that he 'feared and suspected Jasper, Earl of Pembroke, and his nephew Richmond, and not without good cause, and as was apparent to all the world afterward'.[4] For the time being, they were destined to remain thorns in Richard's side, but he was determined that Margaret would not.

In January 1484 the only Parliament of Richard III's reign convened: it was here that Margaret's fate was decided. Bills of attainder against Henry and Jasper Tudor were passed, as well as against Morton, Dorset and Welles, who were all 'denounced traitors to their country'.[5] Then there was Margaret. Referring to her as 'mother of the king's great rebel and traitor, Henry, Earl of Richmond', it was declared that she had

> *lately conspired, leagued and committed high treason against our sovereign lord King Richard III in various ways, and in particular by sending messages, writings and tokens to the said Henry, urging, instigating and stirring him by them to come into this realm to make war upon our said sovereign lord; to which urging, instigation and stirring the said Henry applied himself, as experience has recently shown.*[6]

Additionally, she had 'supplied great sums of money within the city of London as well as elsewhere in this realm to be employed in the execution of the said treason and malicious purpose'. In so doing, Margaret had 'conspired, leagued and plotted the destruction' of King Richard, and 'knew of and assented to, and assisted in the treason planned and committed by Henry, late duke of Buckingham'.[7] The evidence was damning, and Margaret's guilt had been proclaimed in the most public and shameful manner. Yet the King,

> *of his special grace, mindful of the good and faithful service which Thomas, Lord Stanley, has given and intends to give our said sovereign lord, and for the sincere love and trust which the king has in him, and for his sake, remits and will forbear the great punishment of attainting the said countess, which she or anyone else doing the same has deserved.*[8]

She had been spared the dishonour of attainder on account of her husband's standing with Richard, but there were to be other consequences:

> *the said countess henceforth shall be legally unable to have, inherit or enjoy any manors, lands or tenements, or other hereditaments or possessions whatsoever, and also henceforth shall be unable to bear or have any name of estate or dignity; and that the said countess shall forfeit to our said sovereign lord the king and his heirs all the castles, manors, lordships, lands, tenements, rents, services, reversions and other hereditaments and possessions, whatsoever they may be, of which the said countess, or anyone else to her use, is now seized or possessed of estate of fee-simple, fee-tail, term of life, in dower or otherwise.*[9]

All of her lands and wealth were taken from her and passed to her husband, who was entitled to keep them for the remainder of his life, thence to revert to the Crown. If Stanley died prior to Margaret, there would be no question of them being returned. Margaret's lands had been an integral part of her inheritance, and indeed had added significantly to her appeal from a suitor's perspective. Not only had she always taken a great interest in the administration of her estates, but she seems to have genuinely cared about their smooth and efficient running. So much so that she had taken the time to visit some of them, and would continue to do so later in life. That they were now stripped from her therefore came as a hefty blow, for it was these lands that added to her very identity. She would later ensure that nobody would ever take her lands from her again. But her punishment did not end there:

> *for as much as the working of a woman's wit was thought of small account, the council therefore set down and commanded that Thomas, who proved himself guiltless of the offence, should remove from his wife all her servants, and keep her so straight with himself that she should not be able from thenceforth to send any messenger neither to her son, nor friends, nor practice any thing at all against the king.*[10]

With her husband entrusted with the role of jailer, she was to be placed under house imprisonment. Margaret was a traitor.

Margaret's confinement was probably spent at Stanley's northern residences, Lathom and Knowsley. She was no longer permitted to attend court or travel; although her husband treated her leniently. This was the lowest point in her life – after years of careful political manoeuvring and outward loyalty to the house of York, she had taken the most dangerous gamble of her life only to see it end in bloodshed and dismal failure. She had been publicly disgraced and shamed as an enemy to the King, with all of her hopes and ambitions in tatters and her wealth taken from her. This can only have intensified her sense of loathing towards Richard. In spite of the treatment that had been meted out to her, the later statement of her servant Henry Parker reveals much about her approach to it. Though 'in King Richard's days, she was often in jeopardy of her life, yet she bear patiently all trouble in such wise', a testament to both her peril and her faith.[11] It is plausible that she believed that God had kept her safe thus far, and this may also help to explain her numerous religious offerings in later life, by way of thanks. It was perhaps her faith and the knowledge that her son was safe abroad that gave Margaret the strength to carry on, for, more significantly, the consequences of her actions did not deter her from continuing to support Henry. Neither had she any intention of forgoing contact with him. The Buckingham Rebellion had revealed that there were those in the realm who were prepared to take up arms against Richard, and though it had been unsuccessful Margaret was not prepared to give up. In her eyes, it was all still to play for.

IN THE SAME Parliament that had witnessed Margaret's humiliation, the Act of Settlement – also known as *Titulus Regius* – was passed, establishing Richard III's sovereignty. This also confirmed the illegitimacy of Elizabeth of York and her four sisters, who remained in sanctuary. Before long though, Richard had turned his attention towards their removal, which Vergil believed was an attempt to thwart Henry Tudor's pretensions of marriage with Elizabeth. Croyland claimed that Elizabeth Wydeville had been 'urged by frequent intercessions and dire threats' to release her daughters, until after much persuasion she finally agreed to 'yield herself unto the king'.[12] Much has been made of her decision to do so, with revisionists suggesting that she would never have come to terms with Richard if she believed that he had been responsible for the murders of her sons. Yet there is no escaping from the fact that she did precisely that. Even without the consideration of the Princes, Elizabeth knew that Richard had ordered the unlawful execution of her brother, Earl Rivers, and her son Sir Richard Grey, and that she was prepared to come to terms with him was a sign of her desperation. She had been in sanctuary for months, and had her daughters' futures and that of her remaining son, the Marquess of Dorset, to consider. Nevertheless, she refused to allow them to leave without Richard first offering some assurance as to their safety. It was with this in mind that on 1 March Richard swore a public oath at Westminster:

> I, Richard, by the Grace of God King of England etc., in the presence of you my lords spiritual and temporal, and you, Mayor and aldermen of my City of London, promise and swear on the word of a king, and upon these holy evangelies of God, by me personally touched, that if the daughters of Dame Elizabeth Grey, late calling herself Queen of England, that is, Elizabeth, Cecily, Anne, Katherine and Bridget, will come unto me out of the Sanctuary of Westminster, and be guided, ruled and demeaned after me, then I shall see that they shall be in surety of their lives, and also not suffer any manner hurt in their body by any manner [of] person or persons to them, or any of them in their bodies and persons by way of ravishment or defouling contrary to their wills, not them or any of them imprison within the Tower of London or other prison.[13]

In light of the imprisonment – and probable murder – of the Princes in the Tower, the reference to the Tower is particularly significant. It was enough to convince Elizabeth, who 'forgetting her faith and promise given to Margaret, Henry's mother', gave up her daughters to Richard.[14] The five princesses emerged from sanctuary, and Vergil reported that they were welcomed at court. It was not until later that year, however, that their mother left Westminster, though she would never attend Richard III's court.[15] Her reconciliation with him, nevertheless, prompted her to send word to her son Dorset 'to forsake Earl Henry, and with all speed convenient to return into England'.[16] Though he attempted to do so the following year, he was apprehended and persuaded to return. But Henry would never trust him again.

Following Parliament, Vergil claimed that Richard continued to be 'vexed, wrested, and tormented in mind with fear almost perpetually' of Henry Tudor's return.[17] On account of this he had 'a miserable life'.[18] His life was about to become worse and his position considerably weakened when on 9 April his son Prince Edward died at Middleham Castle 'after a short illness'.[19] The King and Queen were at Nottingham when they heard the news, and were so distraught that they became 'almost out of their minds for a long time when faced with the sudden grief'.[20] Edward had been their only child, and since the Queen had experienced no further pregnancies it was widely believed that she was now unable to bear children.[21]

Meanwhile, in Brittany Henry enjoyed considerably more freedom than he had done during Edward IV's lifetime. This period of Henry's life is poorly documented, and little is known about his time abroad.[22] As historians Griffiths and Thomas suggest, that he and his supporters were making offerings at Vannes Cathedral indicates that he was no longer under guard.[23] He was also busy doing all that he could to persuade Duke Francis to back a second invasion attempt. Though he agreed to do so, nothing transpired. Francis, though, was under a great deal of pressure, for in the same manner as his brother, Richard III made several attempts to regain Henry's custody. Not only did he promise Francis 'great gifts', but he also offered him the yearly revenues from Henry's confiscated lands and those who were with him.[24] But Francis 'by reason of sore and daily sickness' was too unwell to negotiate.[25] Pierre Landais was far more responsive. Motivated by a desire to gain the respect of his countrymen through the conclusion of the negotiations, Landais reached an agreement with Richard. Unbeknown to Henry, he was on dangerous ground.

In September, Christopher Urswick arrived in Flanders. He had come to seek Morton, carrying news of Richard's plans to lay hands on Henry. This came 'from his friends out of England' – feasibly Margaret or members of the Council.[26] Morton wasted no time in dispatching Urswick to Henry, urging him to flee without delay. The message caught Henry by surprise, and he immediately sent the faithful Urswick to France to discover whether he would be afforded safe passage there. Louis XI had died the previous August and had been succeeded by his thirteen-year-old son, Charles VIII.[27] During his minority, Charles's sister, Anne de Beaujeu, ruled France, and Henry was relieved when he learned that he would be welcomed at their court, safe passage being 'easily obtained'.[28]

Sending his uncle Jasper on ahead, Henry planned to flee Brittany. Few were entrusted with the plans for his escape, and two days after Jasper's departure Henry 'feigned to go unto a friend'.[29] Accompanied by just five servants, he made his way towards the French border. Having changed into 'a serving man's apparel' in some woods, Henry and his men galloped across the border into Anjou.[30] Having discovered that Henry had fled, Landais sent Breton soldiers in pursuit, who were within an hour of catching him. When Duke Francis recovered and learned what had happened, he was outraged with Landais' actions, and paid for the remainder of Henry's supporters to join him in France. Having evaded danger once more, Henry travelled to Angers, where the court was in residence. He was made very welcome, and wasted no time in begging Charles VIII for assistance in his pursuit of the English crown. André reported that, when he did so, Charles, 'As if advised by a divine oracle, marvelled at Henry's graceful and distinguished countenance, his natural prudence, and his remarkable fluency in French.'[31] His pleas fell on open ears, for 'so much did they abhor the tyranny of king Richard, King Charles promised him aid.'[32]

With French backing, it was probably in November that Henry attempted to canvass greater support for his cause. It may have been now that he wrote to his friends in England, pushing himself forward as a rival candidate to the throne:

Being given to understand your good devoir and entreaty to advance me to the furtherance of my rightful claim, due and lineal inheritance of that crown, and for the just depriving of that homicide and unnatural tyrant, which now unjustly bears dominion over you, I give you to understand that no Christian heart can be more full of joy and gladness than the heart of me your poor exiled friend, who will, upon the instant of your sure advertising what power you will make ready, and what captains and leaders you get to conduct, be prepared to pass over the sea with such force as my friends here are preparing for me.[33]

Nobody was left in any doubt that he was preparing to make another bid for the Crown. Richard knew it too, and on 7 December he issued a proclamation in which he denounced Henry and his supporters – chiefly his uncle, Jasper, Dorset, and others – as 'rebels and traitors'.

THE CHRISTMAS FEAST of 1484 was celebrated with much merriment at court. Among those who were there to enjoy the revels was the King's niece, Elizabeth of York. At eighteen years old, Elizabeth's beauty was beginning to attract admirers, and the 'vain exchanges of clothing between Queen Anne and Lady Elizabeth, eldest daughter of the dead king, who were alike in complexion and figure', had not gone unnoticed.[34] By January it was whispered that Richard harboured romantic feelings towards his niece; 'it was said by many that the king was applying his mind in every way to contracting a marriage with Elizabeth', either after his wife had died, or by means of a divorce.[35] These rumours must have alarmed Margaret, and they certainly unnerved Henry – so much so that he began to consider other potential brides should his plan to marry Elizabeth fail to materialize.[36] It was Margaret, though, who recognized the need for him to continue to pursue Elizabeth if his campaign were to stand a chance of success.

Richard was well aware that across the Channel, Henry was planning an invasion, and in an attempt to humiliate and discredit him, he intensified his flirtation with Elizabeth with the aim of 'dispelling the hopes of his rival'.[37]

Soon it was widely rumoured that the King would discard his wife, Queen Anne, and replace her with his niece. Elizabeth herself also seems to have harboured some romantic feelings towards her uncle.[38] But as Richard's attentions to his niece grew more apparent, so too did the hostility with which his courtiers viewed it. A startled Croyland reported that the 'people spoke against this and the magnates and prelates were greatly astonished'.[39]

Richard's behaviour caused his wife great distress, and already sorrowful following the death of their son, Anne became gravely ill. According to Croyland, 'her sickness was then believed to have got worse and worse because the king himself was completely spurning his consort's bed'.[40] She would not have to endure such treatment for much longer. On 16 March, during an eclipse of the sun, Queen Anne died – it would not be long before rumours began to circulate that her husband had had her poisoned.[41] Anne was buried in Westminster Abbey 'with honours no less than befitted the burial of a queen'.[42]

Richard was now at liberty to remarry, but there was great opposition to a potential match with Elizabeth of York. His Councillors, in particular Sir Richard Ratcliffe and William Catesby, informed him that if he were to proceed with such a course 'in order to complete his incestuous association with his near kinswoman', he would lose many of his supporters – particularly in the north where he had always been popular and where the Nevilles – the family of Richard's deceased queen – had held sway.[43] Such was the force of the gossip and the protestations that Richard was compelled to declare that 'such a thing had never entered his mind'.[44] It may have been this that turned a spurned Elizabeth's hopes elsewhere.

According to a contemporary ballad, *The Song of the Lady Bessy*, Elizabeth of York joined Lord Stanley's London household following the death of Queen Anne. Written during the reign of Henry VII by Stanley's esquire, Humphrey Brereton, the accuracy of the piece has been questioned. While some parts can be shown to have been fictionalized, it is plausible that there are elements of truth to parts of the story it portrays. It does seem unlikely that Elizabeth would have taken up residence with Stanley, for after all there would have been no female figurehead in his household: in light of the recent scandal, it would have been out of the question for her to do so had Margaret been residing in London, but she was far away in the north. It seems highly probable, nevertheless, that Elizabeth and Stanley were in contact.

The ballad undoubtedly exaggerated Elizabeth of York's role in the events of the spring and summer of 1485, yet if it is to be believed, then Elizabeth now stirred Stanley into taking action to support his stepson's bid for the throne:

> *Good father Stanley, remember thee!*
> *It was my father, that king royal,*
> *He set you in that room so high.*
> *Remember Richmond banished full bare,*
> *Any lieth in Britain behind the sea,*
> *You may recover him of his care,*
> *If your heart and mind to him will gree:*
> *Let him come home and claim his right,*
> *And let us cry him King Henry!*[45]

According to the ballad, initially Stanley was reluctant, but then he and his brother William soon began to plot on Henry's behalf. If this was true, then at some point Margaret became aware of it and doubtless encouraged him. If Stanley was planning on supporting his stepson, he must have been partially convinced that he stood some chance of success, but he also knew that he was taking a huge personal risk: if Richard discovered the truth, he was doomed.

Margaret's house imprisonment had not deterred her from continuing to promote her son's claim to the throne, albeit in the utmost secrecy – perhaps with the connivance of her husband. She must have recognized that, in spite of any suspicions the King may have harboured towards her, he could not risk alienating her husband, and this may have given her the confidence to continue with her plans. Richard III's unpopularity was becoming increasingly apparent, and soon 'man of name passed over daily unto Henry'.[46] However, Margaret, more than most, knew that nothing was certain and there was still far to go.

AWARE THAT AN invasion would soon be upon him, Richard III set up headquarters in Nottingham in June. He now stepped up his campaign to discredit Henry, issuing a further proclamation in which he took care to highlight the latter's dubious lineage, claiming that Henry 'is descended of bastard blood both of father side and of mother side'. Henry's mother, he went on to say, was the eventual product of John of Gaunt's adulterous liaison with Katherine Swynford.[47] Margaret was Henry's route to the throne, so it was she who bore the brunt of the slurs. Richard must have been pleased to have a convenient opportunity to humiliate the woman who had plotted against him.

In France, Henry was preparing his force. He had been joined by an increasing number of English exiles, including the priest Richard Fox, 'a man of an excellent wit, a man learned', whom Henry immediately admitted to his Council.[48] Another important ally was John de Vere, Earl of Oxford, who had hurried to Henry's side having escaped from Hammes Castle, where he had been imprisoned for ten years.[49] When Henry saw him, 'he was ravished with joy incredible that a man of so great nobility and knowledge in the wars' had joined him.[50] Oxford would remain loyal to him for the rest of his life. Crucially, Henry also had the backing of Charles VIII, for 'an army was immediately provided for, and foot soldiers and mounted knights were levied'.[51] Commynes said that Henry's force consisted of 'some three thousand of the most unruly men that could be found' in France, a number that he hoped would grow once he landed in England.[52] It seemed that 'God suddenly raised up against King Richard an enemy who had neither money, nor rights, so I believe, to the crown of England, nor any reputation except what his own person and honesty brought him.'[53]

Ignoring the strictures that had been placed upon her, Margaret was exchanging messages with her son during this time, although sadly none have survived. She would later write to him that she prayed to 'Almighty God to give you as long, good, and prosperous life as ever had prince, and as hearty blessings as I can ask of God', and there is every reason to believe that her feelings were similar at this time. Her prayers during this period probably carried an increased fervency, because Margaret was painfully conscious of the fact that – unlike Richard III – her son Henry had no military experience. It is likely that Stanley was also participating in the correspondence with Henry, and had probably given his stepson some indication of his support. Husband and wife were both aware that 'rumours grew daily that those in rebellion against the king were making haste' with their plans, and it was only a matter of time before Henry arrived.[54]

On 1 August, Henry and his army set sail from Harfleur. He had left the untrustworthy Dorset behind as surety for his debts, and was accompanied by many of the followers who had shown him devoted service. It was 'with a favourable breeze' that the party made their way towards the Welsh coast.[55] From now on, Henry would not only be fighting for the throne, but also for his life.

CHAPTER 15

The Priceless Crown

'A LITTLE BEFORE SUNSET' on the evening of 7 August, Henry's ship dropped anchor in Milford Haven in Pembrokeshire, an event that Margaret would record in her Book of Hours.[1] For the first time in almost fifteen years, he set foot on Welsh soil; the circumstances were a far cry from those in which he had left. The following morning, his army began the first stage of their journey east, making their way 'along wild and twisting tracks'.[2] Henry was delighted when news arrived from Pembroke, the town of his birth, declaring their support for him, but more was needed. One of the first to join him was Sir Richard Corbet, who had once saved Henry from the battlefield at Edgecote.[3] David Owen, the illegitimate son of Henry's grandfather Owen Tudor, also offered his allegiance.[4] They marched through Wales unopposed, but men did not rally to Henry's banner in the numbers that he had hoped. In order to secure a victory over his enemy, he would need his stepfather's aid.

Shortly before Henry's arrival in Wales, knowing what was afoot, Lord Stanley 'received permission to go across to Lancashire, his native county, to see his home and family from whom he had long been away'.[5] The King had been greatly concerned about Stanley's loyalties, and would only permit him to go on condition that he sent his heir, George, Lord Strange, to him at Nottingham as surety for his good behaviour. Stanley complied, but in so doing he found himself in a predicament.

Since the beginning of her house imprisonment, Margaret had remained in the north, but like Richard III she had been well aware that the arrival of her son's invasion force was imminent. When she received word that Henry had arrived on Welsh soil, she knew what was at stake. For more than two decades Margaret had played the dutiful subject to a monarchy headed by a rival house, and for the past fourteen years had been seeking out every opportunity to bring her son home safely. It had all culminated in this moment, but Margaret was aware that there was no certain outcome. Henry was on home soil, heading an army, ready for battle with the King. The Wars of the Roses had claimed many Lancastrian lives, whether on the battlefield or the executioner's block. Margaret knew that failure could well mean death for both of them. It was their greatest and last chance, and she gave all she had to ensure his success. She seized on the opportunity of her husband's return to speak with him about what lay ahead. Richard 'feared (what in fact happened) that the Earl of Richmond's mother who was the wife of Lord Stanley might induce her husband to support her son's party'.[6] We will never know exactly what passed between Margaret and Stanley on the subject of Henry's invasion, but with his son in Richard's custody it was clear that he would not openly declare his support for Henry whatever promises he had made. Margaret knew that it was not just she and Henry's whose lives might be forfeit by their daring actions.

It was 11 August when word reached Richard III of Henry Tudor's landing. Having been carefully preparing his army in readiness for the invasion, 'on hearing of their arrival, the king rejoiced', so ready was he to vanquish the threat to his throne.[7] He began commanding his lords to come to his aid, including Stanley, who he ordered to appear without delay. He was furious when he did not do so, Stanley alleging that he was lying dangerously ill at Lathom with the sweating sickness. Croyland claimed that Lord Strange had 'secretly prepared to escape from the king', but as he attempted to do so he was apprehended.[8] It was then that Strange revealed 'a conspiracy to support the party of the Earl of Richmond' between himself, his uncle Sir William Stanley, and Sir John Savage.[9] Both William and Savage were immediately proclaimed traitors, but interestingly Strange did not name his father as a conspirator. On the contrary, having written to Stanley 'announcing the danger he was in together with the urgent need of presenting help of this sort', he begged Richard for mercy, promising 'that his father would come to the king's aid'.[10] Stanley faced a terrible dilemma.

As Henry marched east via Shrewsbury, he was disappointed to find that men were not hurrying to join his ranks. He had sent Christopher Urswick to his mother and stepfather to inform them of his plans and to ask for their aid, and similar messages were sent to Holt Castle, the Wrexham residence of Stanley's brother, William. The response was encouraging, and it is highly likely that Margaret had also sent her son money to help his cause. As Henry approached Stafford, Gilbert Talbot rode to meet him with a small force.[11] He was heartened further when, upon arrival in the town, Sir William Stanley greeted him 'with a small retinue'.[12] William's support was of vital importance to Henry's cause and Vergil later recalled that he had noted William's 'loyalty and devotion'.[13] They did not remain in Stafford for long, and continued to Lichfield, where they camped outside the city walls. The following day, Henry was 'honourably received' in the city, but he did not linger.[14]

Quickly recovering from his supposed sickness, Stanley had left Lathom – and Margaret – on 15 August. It is unthinkable that the two would not have shared a conversation about his strategy before his departure, and Margaret could only pray that her husband would lend her son the support that he so desperately needed. With his own son as Richard's hostage, though, he was still unable to do so openly. Stanley had reached Lichfield when he first made contact with his stepson, around 20 August. Learning that Henry was not far away, he marched with his five thousand well-armed men the sixteen or so miles to Atherstone to wait for him. Vergil says that he did this 'to avoid suspicion', fearing that if his actions were to become known then Richard 'might kill his son George'.[15] It was to Atherstone that Henry rode to meet with his stepfather and his brother privately, and according to Vergil a joyful reunion ensued. Stanley doubtless conveyed messages of support from Margaret, one of which was later imagined by William Shakespeare. Although Margaret does not feature as a character in any of the Bard's plays, she is referenced during the talks held by Henry and Stanley on the eve of the Battle of Bosworth in *Richard III*:

Richmond: All comfort that the dark night can afford
Be to thy person, noble father-in-law!
Tell me, how fares our loving mother?
Stanley: I, by attorney, bless thee for thy mother,
Who prays continually for Richmond's good.[16]

According to Vergil, once pleasantries had been exchanged a discussion of battle tactics followed. What was said will never be known, but Henry is likely to have been left with some assurance that the Stanley brothers were committed to supporting his cause. Before long, further men arrived to join Henry's army at their camp near Merevale Abbey. In later years Henry made a return visit to the abbey, and so too did his son, Henry VIII with Katherine of Aragon.[17] Presumably both visits were in grateful remembrance of the events that later transpired. The arrivals in Henry's camp not only swelled his numbers, but 'greatly replenished him with good hope'.[18] He also had the support of the faithful Oxford, Margaret's half-brother John Welles, Urswick, Fox, and numerous others who had supported him during his exile. Curiously, no source refers to Jasper's presence at the ensuing battle, but he is generally presumed to have been there. The *Chronicle of the Grey Friars* refers to him landing in Wales alongside his nephew, with whom he had sailed from France.[19] On the evening of 21 August, they prepared to do battle on the morrow: it would be here that Margaret's fortunes and those of her family would be decided in the most dramatic manner.

MEANWHILE, THE HASTE with which Henry was moving necessitated Richard's growing army to leave Nottingham and march south towards Leicester. Richard was confident, and indeed the odds seemed stacked in his favour: in spite of his unpopularity 'there was a greater number of fighting men than there had ever been seen before, on one side, in England'.[20] This is supported by the account of Richard Bygot, who served Richard III and later became Margaret's carver – he claimed that Richard 'had three men for one'.[21] Richard was also the more experienced soldier for, after all, Henry had never before fought a battle, the closest he had got to that being witnessing one in his youth. Richard was prepared to do battle, and on 21 August 'the king left Leicester with great pomp, wearing his diadem on his head', and accompanied by many of the great lords of his realm.[22] Among them were the Duke of Norfolk, Sir Robert Brackenbury and 'other great lords, knights and esquires'.[23] But there was one notable absence: Lord Stanley.

Richard's army marched towards the town of Market Bosworth, setting up camp on Ambion Hill close to the village of Sutton Cheyney. Here, having refreshed his soldiers, the King 'with many words exhorted them to the fight to come'.[24] Yet in spite of his numbers he was full of anxiety that evening as the prospect of the battle loomed ahead: this would be the first battle fought on English soil since the bloody scene at Tewkesbury more than a decade earlier, and in order to secure his crown it was crucial that Richard should win. But he did not rest easy, for Croyland reported that the King 'had seen that night, in a terrible dream, a multitude of demons apparently surrounding him'.[25] It was an inauspicious start.

As morning dawned on 22 August, the two sides made their final preparations. Aside from his disturbed sleep, the day had not started well for Richard, who had risen so early that his chaplains were unprepared to celebrate mass. Bygot apparently recalled that when the chaplain had one thing ready 'evermore they wanted another; when they had wine they lacked bread, and ever one thing was missing'.[26] Neither was there any breakfast 'to revive the king's flagging spirit'.[27] None knew more than Richard that the day's events would have monumental consequences, and Croyland 'affirmed that the outcome of this day's battle, to whichever side the victory was granted, would totally destroy the kingdom of England'.[28]

The sources for what followed are slender, for there are no surviving eyewitness accounts. Both sides were drawn up in battle order, but Henry's forces were severely outnumbered. He needed the support of his stepfather, but Stanley's army stood to the north and avoided taking either side. According to Bygot, it was Henry 'coming on apace' that made the first move, thereby ensuring that 'King Richard was constrained to go to the battle'.[29] Within no time, 'there now began a very fierce battle between the two sides'.[30] Henry's French, Welsh and English troops fought valiantly, yet still the Stanley brothers and their men remained apart, uncommitted to either side. Richard was furious, and gave the order that Stanley's son Lord Strange 'should be beheaded on the spot'.[31] But those to whom the task had been entrusted 'failed to carry out that king's cruel command', and instead released him.[32]

Oxford was in command of Henry's vanguard, and within less than two hours Richard was dismayed as, against all odds, the tide of the battle turned very much in Henry's favour thanks to the defeat of his own vanguard under the Duke of Norfolk. Not only had Stanley remained on the sidelines, but so too had the Earl of Northumberland despite Richard's signal for assistance. The King was urged to flee but steadfastly refused to do so, declaring his intention to be victorious or die in the field. Even his enemies commended his courage, and the Tudor chronicler John Rous exclaimed that 'he bore himself like a gallant knight'.[33] Placing his crown upon his helmet, Richard prepared to join the battle himself. Spotting Henry separated from his main army with but a 'small force of soldiers about him', Richard decided to make one final charge in an attempt to bring down his rival.[34] Accompanied by a small band of his loyal followers, he spurred on his horse and pressed himself into the thick of the battle. He came dangerously close to Henry, and in the process successfully cut down his standard bearer, William Brandon.[35] It was now that William Stanley's men 'came to the rescue' rushing to Henry's aid.[36] Richard's men were pushed back, and the King's horse stumbled on the edge of a boggy marsh. Realizing that he had been abandoned by his former allies, he continually cried out that he had been betrayed, shouting 'Treason! Treason!'[37] Before long, William Stanley's forces cut Richard down: he 'received many mortal wounds and, like a spirited and most courageous prince, fell in battle on the field and not in flight'.[38] The last Plantagenet king of England had been slain on an English battlefield; it was time for a new dynasty.[39]

IN WHAT SEEMED like a miracle given his smaller army, Margaret's son had succeeded in winning the crown: he was King Henry VII of England, and his elated men cried out 'God save King Henry, God save King Henry!'[40] Croyland exclaimed that a 'glorious victory was granted by heaven to the earl of Richmond, now sole king, together with the priceless crown which king Richard had previously worn'.[41] André went further, claiming that Henry 'liberated the land by divine and human right, with divine power vindicating, willing, and assisting, as from a most brutal enemy'.[42] He 'swiftly overcame and slaughtered Richard as he deserved and drove his tyranny from the island. After the death of Richard, which pleased the whole kingdom, he began his reign.'[43] Commynes, who stated that Henry was crowned on the battlefield with Richard's crown, posed an interesting question that undoubtedly reflected Margaret's own thoughts on the outcome: 'should one describe this as Fortune? Surely it was God's judgement.'[44]

Following the battle, Henry, 'adorned with the crown which he had so remarkably won', entered the city of Leicester in triumph.[45] It was from here that he issued the first proclamation of his reign, in which he informed his new subjects of Richard III's death and ordered men to return home. Many of Richard's supporters had been killed alongside him in the field, including Sir Robert Brackenbury, Sir Richard Ratcliffe, and the Duke of Norfolk. Several had survived, and on arriving in Leicester Henry gave orders for their executions, most notably William Catesby 'as a final reward for excellent service'.[46] Henry was resolved that none of Richard's key adherents be left at large.

Following the battle, the body of the dead King Richard was stripped naked and unceremoniously slung over a horse. Croyland attests that, in a shocking display of disrespect, 'many other insults were offered'. The discovery of Richard's corpse confirmed the extent of the humiliating wounds that were inflicted upon him after death. His remains unceremoniously accompanied Henry VII to Leicester, 'a miserable spectacle in good sooth, but not unworthy for the man's life', as Vergil put it.[47] There he was buried 'without any pomp or solemn' funeral in the church of the Greyfriars.[48] It was not until 1495 that Henry would pay £10 12d (£6,700) for Richard's tomb.[49]

When news of Henry's victory reached Margaret, she was both overwhelmed and elated. It seemed like a miracle, and was surely a sign of God's divine intention. Suddenly, the future that neither Margaret nor Henry could ever have envisioned as a possibility until 1483 had transpired into a reality: her enemy was dead, and her son victorious. With her usual attention to detail she took care to note in her Book of Hours: 'this day King Henry the VIIth won the field where was slain King Richard the third'.[50] Some of Henry's first thoughts following his triumph were for his mother, and with the news of his success came, too, a very personal gift: the Book of Hours that had once been Richard's own – taken from his tent on the battlefield, and containing his signature.[51] Margaret immediately erased the name of the man whom her son had slain and whose dynasty was at an end – whom she herself had regarded as an enemy and had plotted to overthrow. Instead, she added her own words:

For the honour of God and St Edmund
Pray for Margaret Richmond.[52]

For years Margaret had been forced to serve a rival house and had managed to successfully adapt to the situation. Yet the reign of Richard III had thrown everything into uncertainty and left her feeling desperate. Her actions throughout his reign could have led to her death, but her experiences highlight her extreme courage and show that she was a survivor. Most significantly, they did not deter her from rallying support for Henry's cause, underlining that her chief motivation was for the bettering of his future, even if it led to her own peril. Her determination to support her son confirms that she was a strong-minded woman who was prepared to risk her own safety in order to try to secure his future. The result was that, with Margaret's support, Henry now stood victorious on a battlefield as King of England. At the time of Bosworth though, neither she nor any other could have been sure that Henry – a man much changed from the fourteen-year-old boy Margaret had urged into exile – would be successful as a king, or even keep hold of his throne. It was in large part thanks to his mother that he went on to establish a dynasty that would become the most famous in English history: the Tudors. In the same manner as she had worked for his rise, she would now strive to help her son establish his own bloodline. In so doing, she would pave the way for her own power.

PART THREE

CHAPTER 16

My Lady the King's Mother

O N 30 OCTOBER – two months after his victory at Bosworth –
Margaret was full of emotion as all of her ambitions for her son
came to fruition in one tangible moment. It was a day that she
would cherish for the rest of her life, proudly recording in her Book of
Hours that 'this day King Harry the VIIth was crowned at Westminster'.[1]
The preparations for the coronation had been undertaken with the utmost
care, and provided the perfect outlet for Henry to indulge his love for finery.
Costly materials had been ordered especially for the occasion, including
powdered ermine, rich crimson velvet and decadent crimson cloth of gold.
All of this was intended to make a dazzling impression on the King's
subjects, and his tailor George Lovekyn had done his utmost to ensure that
his robes did just that. Thus it was that, bedecked in the most sumptuous
of materials that made him appear every inch a magnificent king, Henry
VII entered Westminster Abbey amid the cheers of his subjects, who had
gathered in their thousands to catch a glimpse of him. The abbey had been
beautifully decorated with symbols of Henry's heritage, including the red
rose of Lancaster, and Welsh dragons that proudly proclaimed his descent.
Henry's lords were given the honour of carrying the coronation regalia,
with his stepfather bearing the sword of state through the crowds of Henry's
nobles that had been invited into the abbey. Meanwhile, the ultimate honour
of carrying the crown – St Edward's Crown, which had been used at the
coronation of male monarchs for centuries – was given to Henry's faithful
uncle Jasper. This was the magnificent sight that Margaret was confronted
with as she watched the ceremony, surrounded by a wealth of colour and
splendour. The coronation chair – the same one that had been in use since

1308 – stood before the High Altar in the abbey, and it was here that Henry was to be officially crowned and anointed.[2] It must have been a scene that she could scarcely have imagined would ever be possible. At forty-two, Margaret was no longer the mother of a fugitive held in house imprisonment and viewed with suspicion by a paranoid king: she was the mother of King Henry VII of England. Yet 'when the king her son was crowned in all great triumph and glory, she wept marvellously'.[3] Her tears were a mixture of the greatest pride and fear, for as Fisher later recalled, 'dare I say of her she never yet was in that prosperity but the greater it was the more always she dread the adversity'.[4] Given the emotional trauma that had overtaken every decade of her life, Margaret's fears were understandable: she knew that though Henry had successfully won his crown, he must now begin the fight to keep it.

IMMEDIATELY AFTER HIS victory at Bosworth in August, Henry left Leicester and hastened south. His journey took him through Coventry, where he was presented with a gold cup and a gift of money, Northampton, and St Albans, where the forces of his uncle, Henry VI, had endured defeat exactly thirty years earlier. Upon receiving the glorious news of her son's success, a joyful Margaret had immediately begun making hurried preparations to join him. They had been apart for fifteen years, and she was eager to be reunited. At the beginning of September, the new king, 'accompanied by a great host of nobles, joyfully entered the city of London'.[5] It is unclear whether his mother had already reached him or was yet to do so, but when she did it is sure to have been an emotional reunion. The son that now stood before Margaret was no longer the teenage boy whom she had last seen during the two weeks they had spent together at Woking in 1470, whose future she had agonized over as the Wars of the Roses had raged. At twenty-eight, Henry was a man who had endured great hardship and uncertainty. In physical terms Vergil would describe his appearance as 'remarkably attractive and his face was cheerful, especially when speaking'.[6] Isabella of Castile later referred to him as a 'Prince of great virtue, firmness, and constancy'.[7] He also bore similarities to Margaret. Her portraits do not reveal all of the details of her physical appearance, such as her hair colour – Henry had thinning fair hair – but her son certainly inherited his hooded eyes from Margaret, though his were blue in colour while hers were dark. Both were also of slender frame. From now on, Margaret would take every opportunity she could to be by his side: for much of the next fourteen years, she was an almost constant presence, and Henry in his turn – her 'most humble and loving son' – would welcome it.[8]

Before long there were more arrivals in London, and one of those who had come to celebrate Henry's success was Anne Herbert, the wife of his former guardian.[9] More poignant, though, was the arrival of the ten-year-old Earl of Warwick and his cousin, nineteen-year-old Elizabeth of York, 'accompanied with many noblemen and ladies of honour'.[10] While the Battle of Bosworth raged, both had been ensconced in Sheriff Hutton Castle in Yorkshire 'in safe custody', on Richard III's orders.[11] Before leaving Leicester, Henry VII had sent Sir Robert Willoughby north to escort them to the capital. Upon their arrival, Warwick was immediately given into the safekeeping of one whom Henry trusted implicitly: his mother. As a male Plantagenet contender for the throne, although still very young, securing Warwick's custody was of the utmost importance. He was not to remain with Margaret for long, though, for he was soon removed to the Tower, where 'he was shut up close prisoner'.[12] He would never emerge from its walls as a free man. Elizabeth, whom Henry had pledged to marry, and her mother, Elizabeth Wydeville, were also ordered to take up residence with Margaret, who had just been granted the Thameside palace of Coldharbour by her son. Henry though, was in no hurry to marry.

Coldharbour had once been the residence of the Mayor of London, Sir John Poultney. It later belonged to John Holland, Duke of Exeter – a paternal relative of Margaret's – who had entertained his half-brother, Richard II, in the house.[13] Margaret of York, Duchess of Burgundy, had stayed in the house during her visit to England in 1480, and Richard III had later given it to the heralds for their college. Henry VII, however, was determined that his mother ought to have full use of the property – which offered easy access by river to the royal palaces of the capital – and took it back.[14] Margaret wasted no time in putting her own stamp on Coldharbour, and alterations and improvements took place without delay. All of the principal rooms in the house overlooked the river, including the splendid Great Hall. It was almost certainly here that the new glass displaying Margaret's arms was inserted, leaving nobody in any doubt of her ownership.[15] There was also a Little Hall and a Great Chamber, which contained Dutch glass, and chambers for Margaret's servants – the room of the devoted Reginald Bray was re-glazed with Normandy glass.[16]

A chamber was also prepared for Elizabeth of York. During her stay with Margaret, Elizabeth would not lack for company, for at Coldharbour she was to be joined by other royal children – her sisters and probably her cousin Margaret of Clarence, Warwick's sister.[17] Margaret herself had been granted £200 (£138,260) for the care of these children, and there is every reason to believe that she was fond of them. She had, after all, known these children since her days at Edward IV's court, as well as the former queen Elizabeth Wydeville. Likewise, she had schemed for the marriage of Elizabeth of York to her son – a marriage that now appeared to be within touching distance – and thus Elizabeth had every reason to be grateful to her. Rooms were also prepared for the young Duke of Buckingham and his younger brother, Henry, whose wardship she was granted on 3 August 1486.[18] The boys were the sons of her kinsman, and Margaret seems to have been fond of them. Henry Parker later remembered that Buckingham had visited Margaret one Christmas, and she had given him a jewel worth £100 (£66,600).[19] Such generosity was not unusual from Margaret, for her friend Bishop Fisher remembered that she was 'bounteous and liberal to every person of her knowledge or acquaintance'.[20] Nevertheless, her gift can be taken as a sign of affection. Perhaps she also felt some guilt at the manner in which the boys had lost their father.

Margaret did not spend all of her time in Coldharbour, and in September 1485 she welcomed her son back to Woking, where they had once spent a happy week together before Henry's flight into exile. He was clearly fond of the place. So much so that in 1503 he would later insist that an extremely reluctant Margaret exchange it with him; it was one of the few known occasions on which mother and son would clash, in spite of the fact that, in return, she was granted the use of Hunsdon in Hertfordshire. She was still permitted to use Woking occasionally, but was unhappy with the trade.[21] On this first visit back, Henry remained at Woking for several weeks, almost certainly taking the opportunity to indulge in a favoured pastime that he shared with his mother: hunting. For Margaret, too, the return to Woking would have been welcome, for given all that she had endured during Richard III's reign she is unlikely to have spent much if any time there. It says much of Henry's relationship with Margaret that he chose to stay with her during these early weeks of his reign. Clearly the love and affection that Margaret had poured into her son in childhood and that had maintained her through their years of separation was gladly reciprocated. But their partnership was more than a familial bond. It was Margaret who had helped to sow the seed of Henry's ambition for the throne. It was her support, material and emotional, and her counsel that had guided him, kept him safe and ultimately ensured that he had crossed to England in an attempt to place the crown upon his head: an enterprise in which he had succeeded. Now, in these pivotal early days of his rule, when much groundwork was needed to stabilize this most unlikely of monarchs, he turned to Margaret once again. It was a role that Margaret had been in training for all her life. Whereas Henry knew only what letters and visitors had told him over the years, Margaret had been in among the action, watching the political manoeuvrings as kings and queens lost and gained the throne. She had played her hand expertly, and as Henry's reign progressed, her new strategies would prove just as shrewd. Henry would have been grateful to have an advisor whom he could trust implicitly. Misplaced trust had cost his forebears dearly and he had already experienced the duplicity of men, so while he could continue to rely on faithful supporters such as Jasper, he would never trust anyone more than Margaret.

MARGARET WAS NOT the only one to benefit as a result of her son's accession. In grateful thanks for their loyalty, Henry soon began to reward his supporters. Margaret's cousin, Charles Beaufort – a bastard son of Henry, Duke of Somerset – was high in the King's favour, and in the first year of Henry's reign his surname was changed to Somerset in a rather interesting twist.[22] Another of those who received generous grants was Reginald Bray. After his long and loyal (and sometimes perilous) service to Margaret, he would go on to become an integral part of Henry's government and one of the most influential men in the realm. Christopher Urswick, Margaret and Henry's faithful go-between, and Edward Wydeville were also rewarded, as was Dr Lewis of Caerleon, who had earlier worked with Margaret to plan the marriage between Henry and Elizabeth of York, and who would later become her physician.[23] Even Gilbert Gilpyn, Margaret's steward at Woking, was remembered, being granted 'the office of the swans, and master of the game on the Thames and its streams and creeks'.[24] Similarly, one John Robinson was rewarded 'for good service to the king's father', although precisely what this was is unknown, while David Owen – Henry's illegitimate uncle – was knighted.[25] On 6 March 1486, John Morton was created Chancellor of England and later became Archbishop of Canterbury: he would play a leading role in Henry's government for many years, and he and Margaret were close. Indeed, many of the men whom she trusted, befriended and employed wound their way into Henry VII's circle eventually. This was undoubtedly as a result of Margaret's influence.

The greatest recognitions, though, were reserved for Henry's family. William Stanley, who had come to his rescue on the battlefield, was made the King's Chamberlain, and the following year would be appointed to the role of 'office of justice' in North Wales.[26] Margaret's husband was also well rewarded: he already had his fair share of war trophies, for following Bosworth he had been given permission to take the hangings from Richard III's tent. These were put on display at Knowsley in a proud declaration of the role the family had played in Richard's fall. Now, in further recognition of 'his labours and expenses for the king and as in time past and recently in the conflict of England', Thomas Stanley was awarded with grants of land,

and 'the king's father' was given the 'offices of master forester and steward of all the king's game north of Trent'.[27] Early the following year he would become Constable of England and Chief Steward of the duchy of Lancaster. There were greater rewards to come.

While at Woking, Henry and Margaret had almost certainly discussed the King's promise to wed Elizabeth of York and his forthcoming coronation. Before the former could place, it was essential that *Titulus Regius* – through which Elizabeth had been declared illegitimate – be repealed – and in any case Henry seems to have been eager to establish himself firmly as king in his own right first. There were many who were conscious of Henry's dubious claim to the throne.

On 28 October, Henry took up residence at the Tower in keeping with the custom that a monarch should do so prior to their coronation, and it was here that he made some notable elevations to the peerage. The first of which was the ennoblement of 'his most dearly beloved uncle', Jasper Tudor.[28] Beside Margaret, Jasper had been Henry's most loyal companion and had endured as much suffering as Margaret and her son during the uncertain times of the past three decades. He was rewarded with the dukedom of Bedford.[29] At some time before 7 November he would also take a wife for the first time, marrying Katherine Wydeville, the widow of the executed Duke of Buckingham and mother of two of Margaret's wards. His ennoblement was followed by the creation of Margaret's husband as Earl of Derby, one that allowed Margaret to begin styling herself as the Countess of Richmond and Derby. Two days later, Henry's ultimate moment of triumph had arrived, and he was crowned in Westminster Abbey.

ON 7 NOVEMBER, Henry VII's first Parliament convened. It was to be of the utmost significance for Henry, for many of those who had fought at Bosworth, and for Margaret, too. *Titulus Regius* was repealed, and the Acts of Attainder that had formerly been passed against Jasper, Henry VI, Margaret of Anjou and their family were all reversed. Elizabeth Wydeville also had her lands restored. By reason of his exile, Henry was an unknown

entity in his kingdom, and had not been raised as a prince of the blood – even the majority of his youth had been spent in Wales rather than England, and thus he was unfamiliar with the layout and affairs of the realm. It was therefore essential that he should both secure his claim and strengthen it. Margaret was also acutely aware of this – as it was said of her, echoing the words of Fisher mentioned earlier, 'either she was in sorrow by reason of the present adversities, or else when she was in prosperity she was in dread of the adversity for to come' – and she was resolved to be there to guide her son.[30] By the same token, it may have been now that she began to recall how God had guided her towards a union with Edmund Tudor – not only did it reflect well on her piety, it implied that the union which produced the first Tudor king was ordained by God.

Henry was determined to accentuate his right to rule by establishing that 'his coming to the right and crown of England was as much by lawful title of inheritance as by the true judgment of God in giving him victory over his enemy in battle'.[31] Inaugurating his own – and thus his mother's – legitimacy was a critical part of this. He was Margaret's only heir, and she was directly descended from John of Gaunt. Crucially, therefore, Parliament reaffirmed Richard II's statute of 1397, which removed the stigma of bastardy from the Beauforts. Unsurprisingly, no mention was made of the 1407 clause that barred the Beauforts from claiming the throne – this had never been passed through Parliament in any case. In a sign of the pride he took in his origins, Henry also adopted the portcullis that was the emblem of the Beaufort family. Technically, Margaret had a stronger claim than her son, but no mention was made of it. The only other precedent for female rule in England had been that of the Empress Matilda in the twelfth century, and it had not ended well. Margaret not only knew this but had always prioritized Henry's interests over her own – in any case, to her, they were one and the same thing. There was never any consideration in her mind that she ought to hold the throne for herself. But that did not mean that Margaret was content to claim nothing.

In the days since Margaret and Henry had been reunited, they had spent much time talking: preparations for the coronation and Henry's marriage would have been important topics of conversation, but Margaret's own position was clearly also a matter she was keen to table. Parliament naturally restored all of her former lands to 'the most noble princess Margaret', but she wanted more.[32] Her son's accession had already transformed her relationship with Stanley. As the king's mother she was now the superior and he the inferior in their partnership. But this reversal was not enough for Margaret. It was undoubtedly at Margaret's instigation that Parliament declared her to be a *femme sole* (usually, but not always an unmarried woman, a widow or a divorced woman; also used – as in this case – of a married woman who has sole control of her property, estates and finances). This extraordinary move gave her full and sole control over her estates, 'which shall be vested and remain in her alone by the same entry, as if she were single and unmarried'.[33] She had the power to act independently of Stanley. There is no indication as to how he felt about this, but as 'the king wills it' there was nothing that he could do.[34] Given that in many ways the couple continued to work together – for example, they later jointly hosted a visit from the King and Queen to Lathom and Knowsley – it would seem that whatever reservations he may have had were soon forgotten. The change does, however, highlight that theirs was a marriage of mutual convenience rather than love, which is confirmed by what happened next.

Margaret's bold move was both momentous and unprecedented: *femme sole* status was usually only found in unmarried women, which served to underline the level of power and independence that Henry was prepared to allow his mother, all as a result of his newly acquired kingship. Up to now, Margaret had been forced to seek security as a wife. Each marriage had been taken with great urgency, husbands selected intelligently, always with an eye to her and her son's protection. But the success of each marriage and its consequences had been unpredictable. Margaret had experienced the deaths of two husbands. In her current marriage she had suffered the ignominy of her lands being handed over to Stanley. The position had been intolerable to Margaret, but she had had no choice. Now, as the most powerful woman in England, she would ensure that such dishonour would never happen again.

Having herself declared *femme sole* marked a hugely significant moment for Margaret. From now on, despite having a husband still living, she would stake her independence. She had no need of a husband. With her son's support, she was able to break free of the ties with which society had bound her, and establish herself as an authority in her own right. And as the records show, she relished it. All of her life she had played a supporting role as a wife and mother, and had thrown herself wholeheartedly into Henry's attempts to win the throne: she was now eager to establish herself as the leading lady of the realm, and, following a precedent that had formerly been set by Cecily Neville during the reign of Edward IV, she took the title of 'My Lady the King's Mother'.[35] Her legal independence signified a turning point in her life, and from this moment she took control of her life and her identity. It was with this in mind that in 1499 Margaret adopted the signature 'Margaret R', which can be seen in her surviving letters, and this has been a source of controversy. Did she intend for it to represent 'Richmond', or was it supposed to be interpreted as 'Regina'? Her earlier letters were often signed 'Margaret Richmond', and so it seems evident that the 'R' was a deliberate attempt to emphasize her royal status and authority in keeping with her new role.[36] Likewise, in official documents and accounts she was frequently referred to as 'princess', further underlining her association with royalty.

Although Margaret was now an independent woman in financial terms, her relationship with Stanley did not deteriorate. Indeed, Stanley appears to have been proud of his wife's status. At Lathom, he even went as far as to have his wife's arms added to the windows, along with the inscription 'our Lady the King's Mother'.[37]

In 1499 Margaret would take another step that signified a further change in their marriage. She 'obtained of him license and promised to live chaste, in the hands of the reverend father my lord of London, which promise she renewed after her husband's death in to my hands again, whereby it may appear ye discipline of her body'.[38] In the presence of Richard FitzJames, Bishop of London, and with her husband's consent, Margaret took a vow of chastity. From that time on, she and Stanley maintained separate households, although they continued to visit one another and rooms were reserved in Margaret's homes for Stanley's use. We cannot be sure how long Margaret had been pondering her decision, which was in all likelihood a formality – she and her husband are unlikely to have been living as man and wife for some time, if at all, and the vow was probably prompted by Margaret's increased independence. This allowed her to make such a choice, and though Stanley had given his consent, in reality it is unlikely that Margaret needed it. Her position as the King's Mother now gave her the opportunity to mould herself in whichever way she chose, and religion – always an important and decisive factor in Margaret's life – was one of the threads that she chose to emphasize.

ON 10 DECEMBER, Parliament made a final request of Henry. They begged him to fulfil his earlier promise to 'take to himself that illustrious lady Elizabeth, daughter of King Edward IV, as his wife'.[39] With Elizabeth restored to her rightful legitimacy, the following day Henry gave orders for preparations for the wedding to begin. In so doing, he took the first step in healing the breach between Lancaster and York, thereby ensuring that the foundations of the new Tudor dynasty were firmly laid.

As the New Year of 1486 dawned, so too did the approach of Henry's wedding. It is uncertain when he first met his bride, and given that he and Elizabeth were within the forbidden degrees of consanguinity as a result of their shared descent from Edward III, a papal dispensation was required. This was authorized on 16 January: two days later, the couple were married at Westminster Abbey. In a nice although perhaps not purposeful link with the past, the ceremony was conducted by the elderly Thomas Bourchier, Archbishop of Canterbury – half-uncle of Henry's former stepfather, Henry Stafford. Surprisingly few details of the wedding survive, but according to André, 'Gifts flowed freely on all sides and were showered on everyone, while feasts, dances, and tournaments were celebrated with liberal generosity to make known and to magnify the joyful occasion and the bounty of gold, silver, rings, and jewels.'[40] It is inconceivable that Margaret did not attend

– it had been she, after all, who had instigated it, so it is only natural that she would have wished to witness its conclusion. In her typical style, she took care to note in her Book of Hours 'this day king Harry the VIIth wedded the queen Elizabeth'.[41] The result was monumental: as the chronicler John Stow observed, 'the two families of York and Lancaster, which had long been at great division, were united and made one'.[42]

On the brink of her twentieth birthday, the new queen was a beauty, with fair blonde hair and a gentle countenance. André wrote admiringly that 'Marvellous piety and fear of God, remarkable respect toward her parents, almost incredible love toward her brothers and sisters, and noble and singular affection toward the poor and ministers of Christ were instilled in her from childhood.'[43] There is good evidence to suggest that this was more than mere flattery, and Elizabeth's surviving accounts bear witness not only to the generosity she displayed to her sisters, but also to her extraordinary piety.[44] She always made offerings on religious days: in November 1502 she gave money 'at the obit [obituary] of the King's father holden at Westminster'.[45] This would have given her at least one thing in common with her mother-in-law; indeed, less than three weeks after her marriage was solemnized, the King granted his wife and mother, along with Thomas Bourchier, Reginald Bray and several others, a licence to found a perpetual chantry in the church of the Holy Trinity in Guildford.[46] Such chantries were the most popular tangible sign of medieval piety, and Margaret was responsible for the endowment of several, including at Wimborne and in Cambridge.[47] Given her fondness for Woking and the frequency with which she had visited Guildford, it is tempting to speculate that the location may have been Margaret's suggestion.

It has long been said that the relationship Margaret shared with her daughter-in-law was strained, primarily as a result of Margaret's relationship with her son and dominance at court. Much of this stems from the comments made by the Spanish ambassador in 1498 that 'the King is much influenced by his mother and his followers in affairs of personal interest and in others. The Queen, as is generally the case, does not like it.'[48] The same ambassador also claimed that the Queen, 'a very noble woman, and much beloved', was 'kept in subjection by the mother of the King'.[49] There is no corroborating evidence that this was the case, and most reports suggest that the two women had a good relationship. It must be remembered that Margaret had been the greatest advocate of her son's marriage, and there are several surviving examples of her working harmoniously with Elizabeth. She certainly took a great interest in her daughter-in-law, and spoke very warmly of her in her later correspondence. Margaret was always a stickler for etiquette and eager to ensure that everything ran as it should, and it may have been this that prompted her to have 'a remembrance of the Queen's servants for my Lady's Grace' drawn up in 1501 – a list of all of those in Elizabeth's service.[50] By this time she was spending more time away from court, and was presumably anxious to keep herself well informed.

Following her son's accession, however, for more than a decade Margaret was an almost constant presence at court. Apartments were set aside in each of the royal palaces for her use, and they were always close to those of the King – particularly at Woodstock and the Tower. Given the time that she had spent apart from Henry, her desire to be close to him was understandable, for she clearly did not wish to miss a single moment. He in turn evidently craved her company. His affection can be seen in one of the rare surviving letters between them, in which he wrote: 'I shall be as glad to please you as your heart can desire it, and I know well, that I am as much bounden to do so, as any creature living for the great and singular motherly love and affection that it hath pleased you at all times to bear towards me.'[51]

Margaret's desire to always be on hand to advise him may occasionally have placed some strain on Elizabeth – as may his eagerness to accept this advice. From the start, although Elizabeth's role was largely passive and she played little part in politics, Margaret made it clear that she was not prepared to do the same: though she was not the queen, she took care to ensure that she was closely identified as one, and many of Henry's contemporaries rightly believed her to be the most important woman in England. She and Elizabeth were often listed as though they were one person in official reports, and this in turn is reflective of how Margaret was viewed by her contemporaries. She was frequently in her daughter-in-law's company, and was reported to walk just half a pace behind her. More often than not her name appeared alongside that of the King and Queen on royal ceremonial occasions, leaving nobody in any doubt of her position. Margaret was small of stature, but she was certainly not lacking in presence. Though this may have caused Elizabeth occasional irritation, had there been true cracks in her relationship with Margaret then surely after a time these would have become difficult to hide – no other contemporary ever remarked on any friction between the pair.

Vergil relates that Margaret was 'a most worthy woman [whom] no one can extol too much or too often for her sound sense and holiness of life. Henry allotted [her] a share in most of his public and private resources, thus easing her declining years.'[52] This was certainly true, and in 1498 Margaret was listed foremost among those who the Spanish ambassador believed to have 'the greatest influence in England'.[53] Most of the men who were included in the ambassador's report were Margaret's friends and associates, including Morton and Bray. Clearly, therefore, Margaret and those close to her were believed to have the King's ear. Given that we have no way of knowing how far she was responsible for influencing Henry's decisions, her impact on the politics of Henry's reign can never be fully gauged, but Bacon's statement that 'his mother he reverenced much, heard little' is certainly untrue.[54] The point was that those at court *believed* that she was important. Neither were they alone, for the Pope was also of the understanding that she held great sway. On 8 December 1498, Pope Alexander wrote to Margaret on behalf of one Adriano, asking that she do all that she could to encourage the King to promote him.[55] Despite such assumptions, Henry was far from being Margaret's puppet; she could never have gained the power and influence that she did throughout the course of his reign without his consent. That he was willing to give her this is a testament not only to their close bond, but also to his recognition of Margaret's abilities.

Equally scrutinized is the relationship between Henry VII and his wife: in the seventeenth century Sir Francis Bacon claimed that the King 'was nothing uxorious; nor scarce indulgent; but companionable and respective, and without jealousy'.[56] Henry was certainly faithful to Elizabeth, and in spite of Bacon's statement that he 'showed himself no very indulgent husband towards her though she was beautiful, gentle and fruitful', the marriage was happy.[57] His accounts reveal that he made his wife regular gifts of money: in 1492 there was one for the purchase of gold wire, in 1497 there was £31 10s (£21,000) for jewels, and on other occasions there was cash.[58] The royal couple were frequently together, and there is nothing to suggest that their marriage was anything other than harmonious.

It is possible that Henry and Elizabeth began sleeping together prior to their marriage; either this or, to the joy of her family and the realm, Elizabeth immediately conceived. The hoped-for birth of a prince through which to secure the Tudor dynasty was eagerly anticipated, and every detail of the Queen's confinement was considered. In the spring, Henry VII set out on a progress across his newly conquered land, leaving Margaret and his wife in London. He travelled as far north as Yorkshire in what was an attempt to stamp out disaffection in what had traditionally been Yorkist territory. Many of the towns and cities he entered presented him with gifts of 'gold, silver, wine, beads', but not everyone was pleased to see him.[59] While he was in the north, Sir Francis Lovell, Humphrey Stafford and his brother Thomas – all loyal supporters of Richard III – attempted to raise an army with which to crush him. The rebellion faded away and Lovell fled to Lancashire, while the Stafford brothers sought sanctuary at Culham Abbey. Henry had them forcibly removed, and while Thomas was pardoned, Humphrey was executed on 8 July at Grafton. It was not the last of Francis Lovell though.

IN A DESIRE to emulate the Arthurian legend, Henry VII was determined that his first child should be born in the old city of Winchester. Margaret was not alone among her contemporaries in her belief in King Arthur's kingdom of Camelot – which was thought to have once stood in Winchester – and supported Henry's choice. She accompanied the King and Queen when they moved with the court to Winchester for Elizabeth's confinement, probably arriving in the last week of August. The Queen and her mother-in-law took up residence in St Swithin's Priory, in the close next to the cathedral. Also present was the Queen's mother, Elizabeth Wydeville. For the first time, the court found itself with a queen and two queen mothers, as well as the elderly Cecily Neville, mother of Edward IV and Richard III, who lived until 1495.[60] The nature of Margaret's relationship with Elizabeth Wydeville at this time is unclear, but given that Elizabeth had abandoned her support of Henry in the aftermath of the Buckingham Rebellion, Margaret's feelings towards her are unlikely to have been warm. As Fisher recollected, Margaret 'was good in remembrance and of holding memory a ready wit she had also to conceive all things', so it is impossible that she would have forgotten Elizabeth's betrayal.[61]

In light of her own harrowing experience of childbirth, Margaret and her son were determined to ensure that Elizabeth of York's was remarkably different. The days that saw Margaret fleeing her home in the depths of winter in terror for her life seemed a far cry from the arrangements put in place for Elizabeth, who was to be surrounded by all of the trappings of royalty. Image meant everything to Henry VII – and indeed to Margaret – and thus everything was conducted against a backdrop of splendour.

Quite how far Margaret was involved in all this we cannot be sure. She was once credited with having drawn up the household ordinances in December 1493, but some scholars have recently questioned her involvement in this. Rebecca Olson, for example, notes that there is no contemporary evidence to confirm that the ordinances were drawn up at her instigation, the tradition of Margaret's involvement dating back to Leland's *Collectanea*.[62] That is not to say, though, that she did not take any interest in their creation, for she certainly began to pay close scrutiny to the way in which the court was organized. Implemented before their final ratification, the ordinances were intended to cover all aspects of royal protocol: the coronation of a king and queen, royal births, christenings, and the way in which food was served among many other aspects of court ritual.[63] They clearly convey the importance that Henry VII placed on ceremony and etiquette, stating that the birthing chamber was to be hung with rich cloth of arras, with a royal bed and a pallet bed, while carpets were to line the floor. Four cushions made of crimson damask cloth of gold would be needed, alongside items embroidered with the King and Queen's arms, while the size of the sheets and their fine material was also carefully considered.[64] Every detail was taken into account.

As she entered the perilous time of childbirth, Elizabeth's every need was given the greatest attention and Margaret was probably on hand to ensure that everything ran smoothly. On 20 September, 'in the morning afore one o'clock after midnight', as Margaret proudly recorded in her Book of Hours, the longed-for prince was born.[65] Her first grandson, named Arthur after the legendary king, was 'strong and able', and both Margaret and the infant's parents were elated.[66] The King immediately dispatched messengers to announce the joyous tidings across the realm, and the celebrations that followed were profound: in Winchester, bonfires were set ablaze on the streets as people rejoiced at the arrival of the King's heir. André later claimed that the Prince was 'blessed with such great charm, grace, and goodness, that he served as an example of unprecedented happiness to people of all times'.[67] An elaborate christening was planned for Henry's 'first begotten son', in the cathedral, and in this child were invested all of the hopes of the Tudor dynasty: 'Arthur himself enhanced the sweet and shining roses, those red and white flowers blossoming on one and the same branch.'[68]

On Sunday 24 September, the magnificent Winchester Cathedral had been gorgeously decked out in costly fabrics and decorations in anticipation of this most important of christenings. It had to be delayed for several hours as a result of the late arrival of the Prince's godfather, the Earl of Oxford, who had travelled from Lavenham. The baby Prince, wrapped in 'a mantle of crimson cloth of gold furred with ermine', was carried to the cathedral in procession by his aunt, the Queen's sister Cecily.[69] Most of the nobility of the realm were present, but in keeping with tradition, neither the King nor Queen attended. Curiously, neither did Margaret, and instead it was the Queen's mother, Elizabeth Wydeville, who was chosen to stand as godmother to the young Prince. Sir David Owen, the King's uncle, delivered her christening gift of 'a rich cup of gold'.[70] In what was a great honour, Margaret's husband was also invited to share the role of godfather with Oxford, making his godson a gift of 'a rich salt [cellar] of gold', which Reginald Bray delivered.[71]

Unsurprisingly, Henry VII intended the upbringing of his heir to be vastly different from his own. Prince Arthur's nursery was to be established at the twelfth-century Farnham Palace in Surrey, just nine miles from Woking. Here he was to be cared for by Elizabeth Darcy, who had served as a nurse both to his own mother and to her brother Edward V. Margaret naturally took a keen interest in the upbringing of her first grandchild, and given Farnham's distance from Woking it is not inconceivable that she may have paid the occasional visit there.

When the Queen had been churched in mid-October, Margaret accompanied her and Henry as the court removed to Greenwich to celebrate the feast of All Hallows. There they remained for Christmas and New Year, at which time Margaret distributed rewards to the servants of all of those who had brought gifts. The year 1486 had been a triumphant one for her family, and she was now the proud grandmother of a Tudor heir. However, as 1487 dawned, such a propitious start was quickly tinged with insecurity and danger.

CHAPTER 17

———— ❦ ————

Preservation of Your Most Noble and Royal Estate

'Y OUR SAID MOTHER and the said earl shall heartily pray to God for the preservation of your most noble and royal estate, long to endure in felicity.'[1] These had been Margaret's words to her son at the end of a petition presented to him in the Parliament of 1485. In 1487 her prayers would be needed, for the New Year's celebrations were barely at an end when news reached Henry VII of the first serious threat to his throne.

In what was to be a continuous theme throughout Henry's reign, from the beginning he had been plagued by an array of rumours: the fates of the Princes in the Tower had not been confirmed, for though they were generally believed to be dead no bodies had been found. This left Henry vulnerable, and it was not long before his enemies seized on this as an opportunity to strike. In the summer of 1486, the young son of an Oxford joiner, known as Lambert Simnel – although the *Heralds' Memoir* referred to him as 'John' – came under the tutelage of a priest, Richard Symonds.[2] Symonds was 'a man as cunning as he was corrupt', who was also a loyal Yorkist.[3] He was not alone, for he had become embroiled in a plot to topple Henry VII from his throne and replace him with Simnel, who he was coaching to impersonate Clarence's son, the Earl of Warwick. The real Warwick was incarcerated in the Tower, where he had spent most of his time since Henry's accession. By the end of 1486, Simnel had been taken to Ireland, which was rife with Yorkist sympathizers. The instigators of the plot, though, were much bigger – and more dangerous – fish. Francis Lovell had managed to escape following his attempt to raise arms against Henry VII in 1486, and he had far from given up. He gained the support of a valuable ally – one that was not yet known to Henry, and who he could not have expected: John de la Pole, Earl of Lincoln.

In a strange twist, Lincoln was the eldest son of Margaret's first husband, John de la Pole, Duke of Suffolk. He had been born in around 1460 to Suffolk and his wife Elizabeth Plantagenet, the sister of Edward IV and Richard III, and thus had a trickle of royal blood. Lincoln had been well favoured by his uncle Richard – so well favoured that it is possible that he may have been Richard's intended heir following the death of his son, Prince Edward, in 1484. He had been appointed Lord Lieutenant of Ireland, and fought bravely for Richard at the Battle of Bosworth.[4] He had, though, since reconciled with the Tudor regime. Not only had he attended Prince Arthur's christening, but he was also a trusted member of the King's Council: such trust proved to be ill placed.

On 2 February 1487, Henry VII's Council convened: Vergil reported that by reason of her past agreement with Richard III it was decided that Elizabeth Wydeville should be deprived of all of her possessions, which were instead granted to her daughter the Queen.[5] On 12 February, having been allotted a small pension, she was removed to Bermondsey Abbey, where she would live out the rest of her days. Was this in response to support that she had shown to the Pretender, or did it merely provide an opportune moment for Henry to remove the burden of supporting a queen dowager in addition to his own wife? Elizabeth's role in the Lambert Simnel conspiracy has been disputed, but it is difficult to believe that she would have countenanced a rebellion to overthrow not only her daughter, but also her grandson. The timing of her removal to Bermondsey is certainly suggestive of something more than coincidence, and if nothing else she was, as Henry VII's biographer Neville stated, 'a useful figurehead for traitors'.[6] Neither was Henry taking any chances with the loyalties of her son, Dorset, who was safely ensconced in the Tower until matters came to a head.

On 29 February, in what must have been a welcome change of scene, the Earl of Warwick was removed from the Tower and paraded through the streets of London to St Paul's. Here he was given the opportunity to speak with Henry's courtiers, and through his so doing Lambert Simnel was shown to be an imposter. Meanwhile, abandoning all pretence of loyalty to Henry, Lincoln fled England. The King had been completely unsuspecting of his complicity, but Lincoln now 'went into Flanders to the Lord Lovell and accompanied himself with the king's rebels and enemies'.[7] It was a gross betrayal of trust, made all the more poignant by his father's continuing loyalty to Henry. Arriving in Flanders, Lincoln travelled to the court of his aunt, Margaret of York, Duchess of Burgundy – the sister of both Edward IV and Richard III – who wholeheartedly offered the enterprise to depose Henry her support.[8] Vergil acknowledged that the Duchess Margaret 'pursued Henry with insatiable hatred and with fiery wrath' and 'never desisted from employing every scheme which might harm him'.[9] Her hostility towards him stemmed from her belief that he had usurped the throne from her own house, and Henry himself later wrote of the 'great malice that the Lady Margaret of Burgundy beareth continually against us, as she showed lately in sending hither of a feigned boy, surmising him to have been the son of the Duke of Clarence'.[10]

Within a short time after Lincoln's flight it became apparent that an invasion attempt would be forthcoming, precipitated by his arrival in Ireland to join the Pretender, Simnel. On 24 May the boy was crowned Edward VI in Dublin Cathedral. Yet it is highly likely that Lincoln's support of Simnel was a front, and that, having successfully toppled Henry VII, he intended to assume the throne for himself. Soon afterwards, the rebels set sail for England, landing in Furness in Cumbria on 4 June.

Having been accompanied by 'a great number of knights and esquires' that included Margaret's husband, Oxford and Lincoln's father Suffolk, Henry was at Kenilworth Castle in the Midlands – the former mighty stronghold of Margaret's great-grandfather, John of Gaunt – waiting for news of his enemies. He was greatly concerned for the safety of his family, who remained in the south, and gave orders that Margaret and his wife were to be conveyed to the greater security of Kenilworth. On 13 May he dispatched a letter to the Queen's Chamberlain, Thomas Butler, Earl of Ormond, advising him that 'we have sent for our dearest wife and for our dearest mother to come unto us'.[11] Wishing to consult Ormond on how best to deal with the rebels, he continued, 'we pray you that, giving your due attendance upon our said dearest wife and lady mother, ye come with them unto us'.[12] Margaret and her daughter-in-law were thus escorted to Kenilworth. Many of the men in Margaret's life had died on the battlefield and her fears may well be imagined when one remembers Fisher's comment that 'I pass over ye perils and dangers innumerable which daily and hourly might have happened unto her whereof this life is full.'[13]

Before long, word reached Kenilworth that Lincoln and 'his enemies were landed in the north parties'.[14] Henry immediately set out to confront the rebels, making his way first to Coventry. As he travelled, 'daily his true servants and subjects drew towards his grace'.[15] Henry then journeyed to Leicester, which must have aroused memories of Bosworth less than two years earlier. Having learned that his enemies were approaching Newark, the King's forces marched to meet them, and it was there on the outskirts of the village of Stoke that the two armies engaged in battle on 16 June. Lincoln's forces were led by a German mercenary named Martin Schwarz, but though 'both sides fought with the bitterest energy', the result was a resounding victory for the King. In what is often considered to be the last battle of the Wars of the Roses, Lincoln was killed alongside 'divers other gentlemen', although the fate of Francis Lovell was uncertain.[16] Lambert Simnel was captured, but Henry was merciful. Rather than ordering the boy's execution, in a sign of extraordinary clemency he instead set him to work in the royal kitchens. Simnel later became a falconer, and continued his royal service into the reign of Margaret's grandson, Henry VIII.[17]

Margaret was overwhelmed with relief when she learned that her son had succeeded in crushing his enemies. Characteristically, she triumphantly recorded in her Book of Hours the day when 'King Henry VII had victory upon the rebels in [the] battle of Stoke'.[18] In October she was back in London to witness her son's return. As Henry rode through his capital city,

all the houses, windows and streets as he passed by were hugely replenished with people in passing great number that made great joy

and exaltation to behold his most royal person so prosperously and
princely coming into his city after his late triumph and victory against
his enemies; and so to behold the fair and goodly sight of his so coming
the Queen's grace and my Lady the King's Mother, with other divers
ladies and great estates in their company.[19]

But this was Henry's moment, and Margaret and the Queen watched discreetly from a house besides St Mary Spital in Bishopsgate. The King who had until recently been an unknown in his realm revelled in the love of his people, in what can have been nothing other than a moment of sheer elation for Margaret: it seemed as though the success of 'my sweet king' was God's divine judgement. However, it would not be long before a more serious threat presented itself.

Following his brief respite from captivity, which had served to reassure Henry's subjects that he was alive, Warwick had been returned to the Tower. There he would remain for the next twelve years. It was now, though, that Henry took steps to neutralize others who posed a potential threat to his throne. Almost certainly with some input from Margaret, he arranged for two of the Plantagenet princesses to be married to his own kinsmen. Princess Cecily, Elizabeth of York's younger sister and a favourite of Margaret, who she became close to, was the first of these, and was wed to Margaret's half-brother, John Welles.[20] The second marriage, which may have taken place at the same time, was that of Margaret, the daughter of the executed Duke of Clarence, and again a favourite of Margaret's. She was married to Margaret's nephew, Richard Pole, the son of her half-sister Edith St John.[21] This marriage has been described as Margaret's 'most serious political misjudgement' as a result of the problems that the issue of this marriage caused her grandson, Henry VIII, on account of their opposition to his divorce from Katherine of Aragon: one son was executed, another imprisoned and pardoned, while Reginald Pole stirred up trouble for the King abroad.[22] Margaret Pole herself met a bloody end on the executioner's block as a consequence of the strife in 1541. A misjudgement the marriage may have been, but the outcome was one that Margaret could not possibly have envisaged and that she would not live to see. Both of these marriages not only aligned Margaret's family with royal blood, but were also intended to bind further the houses of Lancaster and York. The remaining three daughters of Edward IV were too young to be married, and it was not until 1495 that Anne would wed Thomas Howard, while Katherine was married in the same year to William Courtenay.[23] Bridget, who had been carried to her christening font by Margaret, became a nun, and at some point following Henry's accession had been removed to Dartford Priory.[24]

⁓

HAVING ALREADY PRODUCED the first heir of the Tudor dynasty, in November the moment of Elizabeth of York's triumph had arrived – delayed as a result of the earlier unrest. Margaret had taken a great interest in the coronation of her daughter-in-law, which was to be conducted on a grander scale than that of her son in an attempt to highlight Elizabeth's role in the new Tudor dynasty.[25] Margaret was listed first among the ladies in attendance. Leaving Greenwich on 23 November, the Friday before St Katherine's Day, 'the Queen's good grace, royally apparelled and accompanied with my Lady the King's Mother and many other great estates, both lords and ladies richly beseen, came forward to the coronation'.[26] They were conveyed by water to the Tower in 'barges freshly furnished with banners and streamers of silk richly beseen' – one of which, *The Bachelor's Barge*, boasted 'a great red dragon spouting flames of fire into [the] Thames' in reference to Henry's Welsh lineage.[27] It was a magnificent sight, and Margaret must have enjoyed the revelry as they were entertained on the journey by trumpeters and minstrels. When the party landed at Tower Wharf and entered the Tower, the King was waiting to welcome his wife in a manner that was both 'joyous and comfortable to behold'.[28] There followed the customary creation of the Knights of the Bath, undertaken by the King, and among those who were afforded this honour were the Queen's Chamberlain, the Earl of Ormond, and Hugh Conway – the servant that Margaret had once used to convey messages to Henry during his exile. As the banners blew and the music played, those uncertain times must have seemed a world away.

The following day, 'her grace being at the Tower of London after dinner was royally apparelled, having about her a kirtle of white cloth of gold damask and a mantle of the same'.[29] 'Her fair yellow hair hanging down plain behind her back with a calle of pipes over it', was adorned with a 'circlet of gold richly garnished with precious stones upon her head'.[30] It was in this state of magnificent adornment that the Queen left the Tower and rode through the streets of the capital to Westminster. Margaret's name is not mentioned alongside those who accompanied her, which included her sister Cecily and her aunts the Duchesses of Bedford and Suffolk, so it can be assumed that she did not participate in this spectacle. Presumably she had either decided to let Elizabeth have her moment, or was preparing herself for the main event the following day. Margaret certainly understood the power of the common gaze and was always astute enough to know when to concede it to others. She was in any case already well represented. As Elizabeth travelled through London in great state, passing the huge crowds of her subjects who had thronged to see her, Jasper and Stanley accompanied her, while Sir David Owen and Sir Richard Pole also participated in the procession.[31] That evening the royal party stayed at the Palace of Westminster, where Margaret probably joined them.

On the morning of Sunday 25 November, Elizabeth's coronation dawned. The Queen was exquisitely dressed in 'a kirtle and mantle of purple velvet furred with ermines', while on her head she wore 'a circlet of gold richly garnished with pearl and precious stones'. [32] Thus apparelled, with her sister Cecily carrying her train, Elizabeth made her way from the Palace to Westminster Abbey. A great deal of ceremony ensued as the nobles of the realm filtered into the abbey ahead of the Queen, who was escorted on either side by the Bishop of Winchester and the Bishop of Ely. As with his nephew's coronation, Jasper – who walked ahead of the Queen – was given the honour of 'bearing a rich crown of gold'.[33] The majesty of the occasion was only marred by the press of people who had gathered to see the Queen – no sooner had she stepped upon the carpet than a surge of people attempted to cut it for souvenirs. Such was the crush that in so doing 'certain persons were slain', ensuring that 'the order of the ladies following the queen was broken and disturbed'.[34]

In his role as Archbishop of Canterbury, Morton conducted the ceremony according to the stipulations of the *Liber Regalis*, which set out the protocol for the crowning of monarchs and consorts. Accordingly, the Queen was anointed and given the ring, and then the Archbishop, having first blessed it, 'set the crown upon her head'.[35] She was handed her rod and sceptre, fully bedecked as Queen of England. Within the abbey, 'on the right side betwixt the pulpit and the high altar, was ordained a goodly stage covered', which offered a perfect view of the proceedings. It was here that the King, 'my lady his mother and a goodly sight of ladies and gentlewomen attending upon her', were able to watch the coronation discreetly.[36] These included the recently married Lady Margaret Pole, whose husband was attending on the Queen. Margaret and her son must have been delighted by the splendour of the occasion, and by Elizabeth's evident piety throughout the ceremony.

Once the service was completed the Queen was afforded a brief time to rest while the coronation banquet was prepared. In what was a magnificent sight to behold, Jasper was

> *in a gown of cloth of gold richly furred, mounted on a goodly courser richly trapped with a trapper embroidered with red roses, a border of goldsmith's work encompassed with red dragons, a long white rod in his hand, a rich chain about his neck. The Earl of Derby, Lord Stanley Constable of England also in a rich gown furred with sables, a marvellous rich chain of gold many folds about his neck, mounted also his courser richly trapped.*[37]

It was left to these two men and the Earl of Nottingham, who joined them, to oversee proceedings and ride their steads proudly about Westminster Hall before the Queen's arrival. As she took her seat in preparation for the banquet, trumpets sounded the entrance of the first course. Elizabeth was presented with the usual assortment of sumptuous dishes: 'kid reversed', crane, swan, and a range of fruit puddings.[38] The second course was equally decadent, consisting of peacock, partridge, quails, and 'castles of jelly in temple wise made'.[39] Once again, neither Margaret nor Henry publicly attended the lavish feast, and instead 'there was made a goodly stage out of a window on the left side of the Hall, richly beseen with Cloth of Arras, and well latticed', where the King and 'the high and mighty princess his mother' could 'privily at their pleasure see that noble feast and service'.[40] As the minstrels played and the banquet eventually came to an end, the Queen retired 'to the rejoicing of many a true Englishman's heart'.[41] Margaret had not played a public role in Elizabeth's coronation, but had instead allowed her to bask in the glory and admiration of her subjects. It was a brilliant piece of spectacle that displayed not only the wealth and status of the house of Tudor but also the happy embrace that had been offered to its Yorkist branch. But spectacle it would remain. In particular as far as Margaret was concerned, as the next day testified.

On the morning following the coronation, Margaret accompanied her son and daughter-in-law as they heard mass in St Stephen's Chapel. They were not alone, and were joined by around forty 'duchesses, countesses, viscountesses, baronesses, and other ladies and gentlewomen'.[42] The setting may have been bittersweet for Elizabeth, calling to mind memories of her younger brother, Richard, who on 15 January 1478 at the age of four, had been married here to Anne Mowbray.[43] This, though, was a day of thanksgiving, and following mass 'the queen kept her estate in the Parliament Chamber, and my lady the king's mother sat on her right hand', with Princess Cecily and the Duchess of Bedford nearby on the left.[44] Margaret was no longer prepared to remain in the background, and this display left nobody in any doubt of how she perceived her status. Having for years remained behind the scenes, subservient to another royal family, she wanted this moment to serve as a visual reminder of the origins of Henry's royal blood and ancestry. This occasion was one of many, and she continued to behave in a semi-regal manner for the entirety of Henry's reign. No longer would she live in the shadows; she wanted Henry's subjects to see and recognize her for who she was: the 'noble princess' Margaret.

A telling reflection of Margaret's attitude towards her status can be seen in her jewellery collection. It seems that her lifelong fondness for clothes may have been equalled by a love of jewels. Certainly, one of the surviving inventories found in the keeping of one of her ladies, Edith Fowler, was crammed full of precious pieces. The historian Maria Hayward has shown that at the time of her death Margaret owned plate and jewels worth a staggering £4,213 4s 3½d (£2,805,820), in addition to numerous household items that were worth another fortune; at her death, the total value of her goods was believed to be an eye-watering £15,000 (£10,000,000).[45] Outward display meant everything – something that Margaret is likely to have become aware of at a young age through the example of kings and queens. She was particularly conscious of the way in which clothes and jewels could be used to create an impression of dazzling magnificence, so important for communicating to those at court and in the streets the security, stability and rank of a royal house. Margaret often employed the services of a Stamford goldsmith and in keeping with her piety and her desire to show her religiosity, many of her jewels had a religious theme – popular in the late fifteenth and early sixteenth centuries – such as the cross of gold with a crucifix, enamelled gold images that featured John the Baptist and St Jerome, a piece of the Holy Cross set in gold with pearls and precious stones, and items that included the Virgin Mary, St Katherine and St Margaret in their design.[46] In 1505, she would also receive a gift of beads that had been blessed by the Pope. Also to be found among the rich assortment of beautiful objects were sapphires and rubies set in gold, a gold chain, gold and silver buttons, pairs of beads, the image of a lady in a ship, numerous pearls, and a pomander decorated with marguerite daisies – a symbol adopted by Margaret, as it was a pun on her name – and a common design element that appeared on many of her jewels and household items.[47] In addition, there were two pieces of unicorn horn, in all likelihood representing Margaret's belief that it could be used as a cure for poison. Similarly, payments were made for rings and the setting of them – one contained a sapphire – as well as for brooches. Even her spectacles – used increasingly later in her life – were made from gold and ordered from a goldsmith, and numerous cases for them were also fashioned.[48]

Many of these costly pieces would have been used to adorn Margaret's clothes, which her inventories show were equally lavish and, according to her accounts, purchased with great regularity. Robert Hilton supplied many of her clothes, and black was evidently her favoured colour. Given that the dye for this was expensive, it was a further indication of her immense wealth. Among her wardrobe were gowns of black velvet edged with ermine, mink and sables, gowns of satin, and others that were made of crimson and tawny velvet.[49] There was 'certain apparel of cloth of gold, silks and furs', and petticoats of scarlet furred with both black and white lambs' wool.[50] Other accessories such as slippers, gloves, sleeves, bonnets and frontlets also appear, painting an image of a woman who cared greatly about her appearance. Many of these items would have been stored in coffers, and two wooden travelling chests that once belonged to Margaret are now in the possession of Westminster Abbey. One was used to store the indentures for Henry VII's building work at the abbey.

Although Margaret's surviving portraits show her favour for black, they do not reflect her passion for fine clothes and jewels. Aside from the stained glass in the church at Landbeach that depicts a more youthful Margaret, the remainder of her portraits were painted after her death and all appear in a similar style. Each was probably based upon a portrait that was painted during her lifetime, probably dating from around 1500. The one now hanging in St John's College is the most famous, and has recently been confirmed as being the first piece of work painted by the Flemish artist Maynard Wewyck. It was always believed that the portrait, in which Margaret can be seen wearing the traditional widow's garments, had been brought to the college in the late sixteenth century, but it has been proven that it actually arrived in 1534.[51] Tree-ring dating has shown that the portrait dates from prior to 1521, confirming the documentary evidence that it was commissioned on the instructions of Bishop Fisher in around 1510. It is the earliest large-scale portrait of an English woman, and also serves as evidence of her piety: Margaret can be seen kneeling at prayer, her hands raised and her prayer book open before her.[52] There are other portayals of Margaret, such as a miniature that may have been completed by Lucas Horenbout, a full-length portrait in Christ's College, another in Hever Castle and one in the National Portrait Gallery. These are all in the same style as the St John's portrait, and none of them reflect the richness of her character. They are in part responsible for obscuring the far more colourful and characterful evidence of a woman who was certainly pious but who saw few contradictions between religion and revelry – who took her religious observances seriously, but was able to combine them with her ability to have a good time.

Margaret's image of greatness was enhanced by her behaviour, for Fisher recalled that 'in favour, in words, in gesture, in every demeanour of herself so great nobleness did appear, that what she spake or did it marvellously became her'.[53] Furthermore, for all this wealth and luxury, Margaret was in no way profligate. We are fortunate enough to have access to a relatively complete set of her surviving accounts between 1489 and 1509. In among the payments for materials such as silk for costly garments, purchases of rose water, lavender for washing her clothes, offerings on religious days, rewards to the King and Queen's minstrels and a Scottish fool, and payment for the mending of a clock, there is a fascinating constant.[54] Throughout the hundreds of pages that her account books span, one can rarely be found where her carefully scrawled signature does not appear at bottom – this was a woman who was in full control of her money and knew where it was going down to the last penny. In an interesting link, her son would do exactly the same. By this stage of her life, Margaret could well afford even these extravagances – indeed, later on it appears as if Margaret was so rich that she struggled to know what to do with all her money and she never fell into debt. But for all this, she kept a vigilant eye on the incomings and outgoings of her coffers. We see a woman who wanted to know how her money was being spent, and who wanted to be in control of her assets. In many respects this is unsurprising, for Margaret had always taken a keen interest in the administration and running of her estates. Her need to keep track of her money, though, may have become particularly pressing given that during the reign of Richard III all of her assets – and thus control – had been handed over to her husband Stanley, leaving Margaret helpless.

This determination to manage her own affairs bears great resemblances to the behaviour she displayed when keeping lists (or remembrances, as she referred to them) of those who served her daughter-in-law and Katherine of Aragon. It seems to indicate more than a desire to be kept abreast of affairs, showing rather a woman who liked to be in full control over all aspects not only of her own life, now that she was able to, but also of those close to her.

This interest in her finances seems to have been one of the factors that has led to Margaret being unfairly misrepresented as more serious and dour than she in fact was. In this, she is not alone. It has been well established that Henry VII was not the miser he was once portrayed as, for his court was often full of revelry and merriment in which Margaret frequently partook. Indeed, Margaret, while having bequeathed to her son her penny-counting ways, appears to have passed on many of her more extravagant habits and hobbies as well. Having said that, she could also be acquisitive, and was capable of ruthless behaviour when it came to obtaining what she believed to be rightfully hers.

In December 1487 the royal family celebrated Christmas at Greenwich. It was a joyous occasion for which much of the nobility were present, and during which 'there were many and divers plays'.[55] Margaret herself was fond of such revels, and on occasion rewarded the King's players for their efforts. Another time, she gave a reward to a child who played a song for her during a visit to Boston in Lincolnshire, and a payment can be found among her accounts to some Spaniards who 'danced the Morris'. She loved to be entertained, and had a fool named Skip who wore high-heeled shoes. Several payments for Skip's clothes and shoes appear in Margaret's accounts, as well as for washing them. It seems that – possibly as a result of his death – Skip was later replaced by a fool named Reginald. On one occasion, payment was made for conveying 'Reginald my Lady's idiot' from Hatfield to Richmond, presumably in order to entertain his mistress. Margaret was also fond of other kinds of entertainment: in December 1497, for example, the King paid 'my lady the King's mother's poet' 66s 8d (£2,200), while in 1506 a reward was given to Prince Henry's players for performing for the family at New

Year.[56] The identity of the poet is unknown, but Margaret was certainly responsible for the patronage of John Skelton, who later served as tutor to her grandson Prince Henry. Henry VII also enjoyed gambling and tennis, and, like his mother, was exceptionally fond of jewels. Between 1492 and 1507 he spent an exorbitant sum – more than £110,000 (£73,700,750) – on a variety of pieces.[57] Often they came from France, such as in 1499 when Henry outlaid £2,000 (£1,340,000).[58] Neither was this a rare occurrence; similar payments appear at regular intervals. He often used the services of a Parisian jeweller named Jacques, although he also employed London goldsmiths such as Bartholomew Rede and Thomas Exmew.[59] Both he and Margaret are also known to have ordered items from John Arnold, another London goldsmith. Henry enjoyed clothes and other finery, and his kingship gave him the opportunity to indulge in all of the pleasures that he had hitherto been denied by reason of his exile and near penury.

On Christmas Eve the King went to mass dressed magnificently in 'a rich gown of purple velvet furred with sables'.[60] The following day – Christmas Day – he sat down to dinner in his Great Chamber next to the Long Gallery, but he did not dine with his family. Instead, Margaret joined the Queen and her ladies as they enjoyed dinner in the Queen's Chamber. There was a buoyant atmosphere, and the court remained at Greenwich to celebrate New Year. Since at least the fourteenth century it had been traditional for gifts to be exchanged on New Year's Day as opposed to Christmas Day, and Margaret's accounts are littered with references to such gifts, or more frequently rewards to the servants of those who had brought her gifts. In the 1470s, for example, she had ordered gifts for the ladies in her household from a London goldsmith, and following her son's accession she regularly rewarded his servants for delivering his gift to her each year. That evening 'there was a goodly disguising', but in the traditional manner the celebrations did not come to an end until twelfth night.[61] It was then that the King and Queen went in procession to evensong. Both wearing their crowns and arrayed in beautiful clothes, they were joined by Margaret who 'had on a rich coronall'.[62] She often wore her coronet on public ceremonial occasions such as this, doubtless as a way of enhancing her majesty and to communicate her power. Nobody could fail to miss that she came 'in like mantle and surcoat as the Queen, with a rich coronall on her head, and walking aside the Queen's half train'.[63] Such was the demeanour of the woman who behaved as though she were an uncrowned queen.

CHAPTER 18

Too Much for My Hand

A T EASTER 1488, Margaret and her husband joined the court at Windsor. Her surviving accounts show that she always made the traditional offerings that were expected at this time of year, as well as providing Maundy money. The court remained at Windsor to celebrate St George's Day, which was to be an occasion of the utmost significance for Margaret: she became an honorary Lady of the Garter, and would be the last woman in England to be so until 1901.[1] The Order of the Garter had been founded by Margaret's ancestor, Edward III, in 1348, and was (and remains) the highest order of chivalry in England. Margaret was not the first woman to be so honoured, for her daughter-in-law Elizabeth of York had also been appointed by her father in 1477, following in a long line of royal and noble ladies.[2] Margaret was, nevertheless, the only woman to be appointed by Henry VII, which served to underline their special relationship further. As she attended matins with the Queen, both women wore identical garter gowns; an 'old scarlet gown with garters' was found among her possessions after her death.[3] They were treated with equal deference, and throughout the course of the celebration they were always seen together: riding to evensong in a sumptuous chair covered with costly cloth of gold, followed by twenty-one ladies and gentlewomen, attending great feasts. This was also reflected in a song that was sung on the occasion:

> O knightly order, clothed in robes with Garter:
> The Queen's grace and thy mother, in the same.[4]

Margaret was keen to be seen as an important part of the dynasty that Henry and Elizabeth were creating. This can also be seen in her later inclusion in a window portraying the royal family that was commissioned for the Church of the Friars Observant in Greenwich in 1503. In the image of 'Lady Margaret the King's Mother', she was depicted wearing 'robes like a princess, coronel on head and rod of gold in her hand'.[5] Sadly, neither the window nor the church survive.

Henry VII's subjects evidently recognized that Margaret's position within the royal family was greater than that of the majority of previous king's mothers, and indeed seem to have treated her with similar deference as to the Queen. It was expected that a queen ought to be charitable, and Elizabeth of York's surviving accounts show many payments given in reward both to the poor and to those that had brought her gifts. In September 1502, for example, Elizabeth rewarded a woman who had brought her some apples, while on another occasion she did the same in recognition of a present of birds.[6] In a similar manner to the Queen, Margaret made numerous payments in reward to those that had brought her gifts, such as 'a woman that brought my lady's grace flowers' at Northampton, and, at another time, a woman who gave her a present of strawberries.[7] As her surviving accounts show, Margaret was able to use her wealth and position to do much good to those who were less fortunate, and – as will soon become clear – she did precisely that.

At Whitsuntide, Margaret and her husband had rejoined the court at Windsor. It was a summer filled with merriment, in which the King 'hunted and sported him merrily', activities that Margaret had once taken great pleasure in.[8] She remained with the court for most of the remainder of the year, celebrating All Hallows at Windsor before returning to Westminster, and going on from there to the Palace of Sheen for Christmas. Likewise, when the court travelled to Hertford for the Easter of 1489, Margaret joined them.[9] By this time, she would have been aware that her daughter-in-law was to bear another child. The royal family seemed set to blossom.

On All Hallows Eve, the Queen took to her carefully prepared chamber at Westminster, 'greatly accompanied with ladies and gentlewomen', at the head of which was Margaret, who was to play a leading role in the ceremony surrounding the birth of her second grandchild.[10] The Queen's chamber had been sumptuously decorated with cloth of blue arras decorated with golden fleurs-de-lys, and a magnificent bed as well as a pallet. As was the custom, the birth of Elizabeth's child was to be an exclusively female process, and Elizabeth Wydeville had also arrived to support her daughter.

At nine o'clock in the evening of 28 November, Margaret was overjoyed when the Queen was safely delivered of a princess. There was an added reason to be joyful, for the baby was to be 'named Margaret after my Lady the King's Mother'.[11] Margaret would grow to be extremely fond of her first-born granddaughter and namesake, and on this occasion there was no question as to who would play the role of godmother. The christening took place the day after the baby's birth, and was an unsurprisingly lavish affair. According to the *Heralds' Memoir*, Westminster was 'prepared as of old time been accustomed for kings children'.[12] Lady Berkeley carried the infant princess from the Queen's Chamber, while the Queen's sister, Princess Anne, bore the chrism. Before her came Margaret's half-brother, John Welles, carrying 'a rich salt of gold garnished with precious stones'.[13] When the party arrived at the porch of Westminster, which was 'royally beseen, and had a rich ceiling of embroidery work', they were greeted by John Alcock, Bishop of Ely.[14] It was he who was to conduct the ceremony. Joining 'the high and excellent princess my lady the King's Mother' at the font in the role of godmother was the Duchess of Norfolk, while the Princess's godfather was Margaret's friend John Morton, Archbishop of Canterbury.[15] Once the ceremony was complete, John Welles presented Margaret's christening gift to her granddaughter and goddaughter on her behalf: 'a chest of silver and gilt full of gold'.[16]

Princess Margaret's christening had not been the only celebration to be staged that day, for Margaret's grandson was also enjoying a moment in the limelight. On 21 November, three-year-old Prince Arthur arrived in London from Farnham. Though Margaret was fond of him, she had seen little of him during his early years, and neither was she to be a part of the ceremony that necessitated his visit. On the same day as his sister's christening in another part of Westminster, having first been made a Knight of the Bath, Arthur was created Prince of Wales and Earl of Chester, following in the footsteps of heirs apparent since 1301.[17] During the ceremony, Stanley and the Earl of Arundel had carried the cape and coronal.

In light of their new addition and Arthur's ennoblement, Margaret and her family had extra cause for celebration as the court began the Christmas festivities at Westminster, but 'that season there were the measles so strong, and in especial amongst the ladies and the gentlewomen, that some died of that sickness'.[18] Soon afterwards, the court removed to Greenwich in order to celebrate Christmas Day and New Year. Perhaps as a result of the sickness, there were no disguisings and few plays that season, but there was 'an abbot of misrule that made much sport and did right well his office'.[19] On New Year's Day, the King rewarded his officers of arms, as did the Queen and Margaret. The sickness did not affect their spirits, for the royal family was flourishing.

ON 11 SEPTEMBER 1490, Henry VII and his Council gathered at Woking. They had come to meet the ambassadors of the Emperor Maximilian in order to sign a treaty. By its terms, the two countries would unite against France – indeed, with financial support from Margaret to the tune of a thousand marks (£300,000), in October 1492 Henry briefly set sail across the Channel, although he soon came to terms with Charles VIII.[20] At the same time, the Treaty of Medina del Campo, which had been signed the previous March by the joint Spanish sovereigns Ferdinand of Aragon and Isabella of Castile, was ratified. The treaty not only sued for peace between England and Spain, but arranged for the marriage of Prince Arthur with the youngest of the Spanish Infantas, Katherine.[21] This topic would dominate English politics for the next decade, and would be shaped by events that threatened the security of Margaret's whole family.

MARGARET'S DAUGHTER-IN-LAW, ELIZABETH of York, proved to be a fertile bride, and by the autumn of 1490 she was pregnant once more. The following summer her mother, Elizabeth Wydeville, made a brief appearance from Bermondsey in order to attend the birth, and Margaret was naturally also present. On 28 June 1491, the Queen gave birth to a prince at Greenwich. He was named Henry after his father, and though, as usual, Margaret recorded his arrival, she did so with none of the meticulous detail with which she had recorded Prince Arthur's – just the date, rather than the time, in Henry's case.[22] Neither was it just the baby's grandmother who omitted the details, for none of the contemporary chroniclers made more than a passing reference to his birth – a clear sign of Henry's status as the spare, rather than the heir. Even so, when the baby Prince was christened at the Church of the Friars Observant in Greenwich, it was with all of the pomp that would have been expected, the ceremony being performed by Bishop Fox.[23] The infant Henry joined his elder sister Margaret in the nursery; unlike Arthur, these royal children were to be raised in the Thames-side palaces rather than in the Surrey countryside. The nursery was established primarily at Eltham, which provided convenient access for their parents – and grandmother – to visit them. Eltham was one of only six royal palaces large enough to accommodate and feed the entire Tudor court.[24] The swans that glided across the moat wore enamelled badges displaying the Beaufort portcullis around their necks. Eltham was a former favourite of both Henry VI and Edward IV, who had built the splendid Great Hall in the 1470s. It was one of the largest in medieval England, boasting an impressive oak hammerbeam roof that can still be seen, and was to be the scene of the visit of the humanist scholar Desiderius Erasmus in 1499, when he came with Thomas More to see the royal children.[25]

By the end of 1491 the Queen was pregnant once more, but her confinement was marred by sadness when news arrived that her mother had died on 8 June 1492 at Bermondsey, at the age of about fifty-five. A recently discovered letter in the National Archives, dating from 1511 and written by the Venetian ambassador, claimed that the late queen had died of the plague.[26] This is the only near contemporary source to make such a claim, but on 10 April Elizabeth Wydeville had made her will, suggesting that her health was fragile. In this, her straitened circumstances became clear: pointedly omitting any reference to the King or his mother, she claimed that 'I have no worldly goods to do the Queen's Grace, my dearest daughter, a pleasure with, neither to reward any of my children, according to my heart and mind, I beseech Almighty God to bless her Grace.'[27] She asked to be laid to rest simply besides her royal husband at Windsor. It is impossible to envisage what Margaret's feelings may have been about the death of the woman whose court she had once attended – with whom she had once plotted – and who she now shared a family with. She did not attend the late queen's funeral, although her half-brother, John Welles, was present – almost certainly as a representative on behalf of his wife Cecily, who was also absent. Less than a month after Elizabeth Wydeville's death, on 2 July the Queen gave birth to a daughter at Sheen. Princess Elizabeth joined Margaret and Henry in the royal nursery.

The following year, it was decided that Prince Arthur – like his late uncle, Edward V, before him – should take up residence at Ludlow Castle in order to continue his education, and be schooled in the art of government. Arthur was a serious and studious boy; unsurprisingly, André, who also tutored him, praised his understanding of literature and grammar and flatteringly described him as 'that noblest and most liberally educated prince of Wales'.[28] He was an heir to be proud of, and the King had invested all of his hopes for the future in him. Margaret was particularly fond of her first-born grandchild, who was tall and fair, resembling his mother in looks, and on occasion she sent messages to 'my lord prince' and received them in return. In around 1495 she made him the gift of a copy of Cicero's *De Officiis* – a book on the best way to live fulfilling one's moral obligations – which was beautifully illuminated with his arms and is now in Emmanuel College, Cambridge.[29] Arthur's biographer, Sean Cunningham, has suggested that after 1493 Margaret and her husband are likely to have been regular visitors to Ludlow, though he acknowledges that this is hard to prove.[30] It is, nevertheless, plausible that Margaret would have paid a visit when travelling between London or Woking and her husband's estates in the north. Given that Arthur was very seldom at court with his family and thus saw his grandmother infrequently, such visits would have provided Margaret with a rare opportunity to spend time with her grandson. Cunningham has also underlined the influence she had in shaping Arthur's household, with her nephew Sir Richard Pole fulfilling the role of Chamberlain, to which he was appointed in 1493. Margaret was always eager to show favour to her family in whichever quarter she was able, in so doing binding them and their allegiances closer both to herself and to the royal family.

Margaret took an interest in all of her grandchildren, of whom she was extremely proud. Given that she was strongly family orientated, this is unsurprising, and her accounts provide touching glimpses into her relationships with them. On one occasion, for example, she sent gifts of brooches to the Princess Margaret and Prince Henry; on another, clothes were purchased for the two boys.[31] Similarly, her husband appears to have shared a good relationship with the royal children, for an inventory of Prince Henry's jewels shows that he was once given 'a George of gold' by his step-grandfather.[32] The royal family were very close, and Bacon remarked that Henry VII cared deeply for his children, being 'full of paternal affection, careful of their education, aspiring to their high advancement, regular to see that they should not want of any due honour and respect'.[33] Her grandchildren provided Margaret and her daughter-in-law with another shared interest, for Elizabeth was a devoted mother. As will later become apparent, there were occasions when they worked together in order to safeguard their welfare.

MUCH OF THE 1490s was occupied with other, more distressing matters. In the autumn of 1491, another pretender to the throne emerged in Cork: initially he claimed to be the Earl of Warwick, but his story changed and he was soon proclaiming himself to be Richard, Duke of York – the younger of the Princes in the Tower. In Ireland many die-hard Yorkists seized upon his close physical resemblance to the Duke, and there could be no denying that his manners, bearing and knowledge of court affairs rendered him a regal figure. Yet, like Lambert Simnel, this boy was no prince. His name was Perkin Warbeck, and he was the son of a boatman who hailed from Tournai in Flanders. In spite of his fraudulent claims, Warbeck continued to plague Henry VII for many years. This in turn is likely to have caused Henry's family a great deal of distress. It was not long before it became apparent that the Pretender had enlisted the support of the Duchess of Burgundy, at whose court he arrived in November 1492. The Duchess publicly declared that she recognized Warbeck as her long-lost nephew, a claim that is particularly interesting given that the only occasion on which she had ever met York was during her visit to England in 1480 – York was then not quite seven years old. Her grudge against Henry had not lessened with time; indeed, as André declared, 'a woman's wrath is eternal'.[34] Her support of Warbeck, though, caused a significant deal of alarm. Henry would later write to Gilbert Talbot of 'the perseverance of the same her malice, by the untrue contriving eftsoon of another feigned lad called Perkin Warbeck'.[35] In an attempt to convince other European rulers of his credibility, Warbeck himself took the time to write to Isabella of Castile conveying the story of his escape from the Tower and the murder of his elder brother, Edward V – yet he would never be drawn on the details. The Spanish queen was not taken in, although she was concerned about where this latest threat left her daughter, Katherine, who was to marry Prince Arthur. Others seemingly were duped by Warbeck's trickery, and Vergil later claimed that these included some of Henry's own courtiers. Some felt compelled to join him, being 'moved partly by resentment and partly by greed'.[36] Henry was understandably anxious about the latest threat to his throne, and Vergil declared that 'unless the deception was quickly recognised as such by all, some great upheaval would occur'.[37]

It was the appearance of the Pretender that prompted a very deliberate decision from Henry. On 27 October 1494, Margaret accompanied the King and Queen as they sailed down the Thames from Sheen to Westminster. They were soon joined by the youngest of Henry's sons, Prince Henry, who had been summoned from the nursery at Eltham. On 30 October the three-year-old Prince – who would grow to resemble his grandfather, Edward IV, in looks – was created a Knight of the Bath, just as his elder brother had once been.[38] The following day, Margaret watched with her daughter-in-law as her grandson took part in the ceremony that witnessed his creation as Duke of York. Given that the dukedom of York had once been held by the younger of the Princes in the Tower – the same identity that Perkin Warbeck claimed – Henry's creation served to highlight the belief that the real York was dead, and that Warbeck was an imposter. Following the ceremony, a procession formed, which Margaret and the Queen joined – the former wearing her coronet, and the latter her crown. In celebration of the occasion, three days of jousts were held, with Henry VII's daughter, the Princess Margaret, distributing many of the prizes. On the second day, though, the competitors wore Margaret's own livery, and it was she who distributed the prizes. When the festivities came to an end, Margaret joined the court as they moved to Greenwich to celebrate Christmas. While they enjoyed the customary revelries, however, they were on the brink of receiving news that shook Margaret to the core.

Sir William Stanley, Margaret's brother-in-law, had been well rewarded for his loyalty to her son, with one London chronicler reporting that 'this was a man of great might in his country'.[39] He had also grown wealthy in the King's service, and André believed that he 'possessed great stores of riches'.[40] None of this, it seemed, was enough for him, for on 6 January 1495 the King travelled to the Tower. Grave news had reached him concerning William Stanley: he had become involved in the Perkin Warbeck conspiracy.

When Warbeck had initially appeared, Vergil claimed that Sir Robert Clifford – a Yorkist – had been 'sent by the king as a spy into Flanders to find out whether the popular rumours about the youth were true or not and whether any of the English nobility were taking sides with him'.[41] When the King questioned Clifford upon his return, he apparently revealed a number of names, including that of Sir William Stanley. On learning of William's involvement, initially Henry refused to believe it. But having been presented with proof, Vergil reported that he 'grievously mourned that William was in the plot, since he was Chamberlain and Henry entrusted him with all his affairs'.[42] He was shocked and in a state of disbelief, but soon gave the order for William's arrest.

If Henry was shocked, so too were Margaret and her husband, who had been completely unaware of his brother's dealings. William's actions seem to have gone no further than words, and stemmed from a conversation he had had with Sir Robert Clifford. Vergil says that during the course of this, some said that William had said of Warbeck that 'if he were sure that the man was Edward's son he would never take up arms against him. Such sentiments would indicate lukewarmness towards King Henry rather than treason.'[43] His reason for becoming disenchanted with Henry has been the subject of debate. It is true that he had not been raised to the peerage in the same manner as his brother, and this may have given him reason for disgruntlement. But in other ways he was 'wealthiest of all'.[44]

In spite of William's words, initially the King seemed bent on preserving his life. Understandably he was partially concerned about alienating his stepfather, Stanley, 'of whose most zealous loyalty he was well aware'.[45] Ultimately, however, Henry became fearful of the consequences if he let William live; thus his Chamberlain was sentenced to death. On the morning of 16 February, William was taken from the Tower to nearby Tower Hill and executed. His goods were seized, and an inventory of his belongings from his seat of Holt Castle reveals the extent of his wealth.[46] Vergil, who said that William was 'proud-spirited and frankly confessed to being in some degree an offender', also acknowledged that he was 'beyond doubt a valiant soldier and had been brought low (as they say) through the very loftiness of his pride'.[47] In spite of his treason, the King paid the sum of £15 19s (£10,700) for William's burial at Syon.[48] Four years later, he was also contributing to paying off the dead man's debts.[49]

The fall of Sir William Stanley shocked his contemporaries, many of whom – perhaps Margaret among them – believed that he would be spared. His involvement with the Pretender must have been difficult for both Margaret and her husband to comprehend, but there is no evidence that either of them intervened to save his life. Stanley's family were now tainted with treason, but the death of his brother does not seem to have caused a rift with his stepson. Stanley continued to appear in Henry's accounts for the rest of his life, and André was quick to underline that the 'faithfulness, constancy, and integrity of the rest of his family shone more brightly at that time. And may their steadfast and unwavering devotion toward our king shine as an example from day to day.'[50]

The scandal surrounding Sir William Stanley's end had died down by the summer when Margaret and her husband jointly hosted a visit from the King and Queen to Lathom and Knowsley, for which visits Margaret had given orders for plate to be conveyed from London. On 1 July the royal couple had left the capital, and by 27 July they had reached Lathom after a leisurely progress. They were there in order 'to comfort [the king's] mother, whom he did always tenderly love and revere', and during their time with Margaret they seemingly enjoyed themselves; the King's accounts note a payment at Knowsley to 'the women that sang before the King and Queen'.[51] That same month, Warbeck made a weak attempt to invade, but after finding the people off the coast of Deal 'determined to resist the royal foes', he sailed to Scotland.[52] Here James IV, who even arranged for Warbeck's marriage to his cousin, Lady Katherine Gordon, enthusiastically welcomed him.[53] For the time being, Warbeck was destined to remain a thorn in Henry's side.

The year was destined to be one of loss, for on 14 September 1495 the three-year-old Princess Elizabeth, a beautiful child, died at Eltham. Her family were devastated, and it was left to Morton to arrange the funeral. The body of the little Princess was conveyed in state to Westminster Abbey, where a tomb of black marble was erected to her memory.[54] Margaret and her son were dealt a further crushing blow on 21 December when Jasper Tudor died at Thornbury Castle.[55] He had been an almost constant presence in Henry's life, and had faithfully supported Margaret throughout some of the most testing moments. Henry had given them a common purpose and brought them together to form a successful partnership, his wellbeing and security being more important to them than their own from the start. In so doing they had placed their lives in jeopardy, neither wavering in their devotion, with Jasper serving to fill the void that had been left by the death of the father that Henry had never known. His death therefore left an unfillable gap. In a final show of love and respect to his dearly beloved uncle, the King and Queen travelled to Keynsham to witness his interment in the abbey of his choice.[56] They were accompanied by many nobles, but there is no record of Margaret joining the party.[57]

By the time of the Princess Elizabeth's death in September, the Queen was already pregnant with her fifth child. The arrival of another daughter at Sheen on 18 March 1496, named Mary, probably brought some much-needed comfort and joy into the lives of the royal family. Yet in the background, the problem of Perkin Warbeck still lurked.

It was the month following Princess Mary's birth that Margaret wrote to the Earl of Ormond, the Queen's Chamberlain, from Sheen in order to 'thank you heartily that ye list so soon remember me with my gloves the which were right good save they were too much for my hand. I think the ladies in that parts be great ladies all, and according to their great estates they have great personages.' This portrays something of her sense of humour, for the 'great ladies' to whom she referred was intended as a jibe against the Duchess of Burgundy, who was clearly larger than Margaret! In February a treaty had been agreed whereby trading relations – suspended by Henry in light of the Duchess's support of Warbeck – were restored, but in so doing the Duchess was unable to continue her support of the Pretender. Nevertheless, Margaret's feelings about the woman who harboured such a vendetta against her son had evidently not thawed. By the same token, though Warbeck had been deprived of Burgundian support, the threat of invasion still loomed.

On a lighter note, the rest of Margaret's letter to Ormond conveyed much of her affection for her family as well as her relief at the Queen's recovery – presumably as a result of Princess Mary's birth:

As for news here I am sure ye shall have more cert then I can send you, blessed be God the King the Queen and all our sweet children be in good health the Queen hath been a little crased [unwell] but now she is well God be thanked. Her sickness is so good as I would but I trust hastily it shall with good grace whom I pray give you god sped in your great matters and bring you well and soon home.[58]

In the summer, Margaret joined the King and Queen on progress, where she was afforded the opportunity to tour her estates in Dorset. Travelling via Hampshire and the Isle of Wight, the royal party visited Christchurch, where the King made several offerings, and Poole.[59] At the end of July, Margaret was given the chance to view the progress of Corfe Castle, a property that her son had granted to her in 1487. In personal terms Corfe held immense importance as it was a former Beaufort property that had once been owned by her father – it may even have been where he died. Upon acquiring the castle, Margaret had immediately begun a lavish programme of rebuilding, and through her efforts Corfe once more became a resplendent palace.[60] During the course of their visit, Margaret and her son had a chance to enjoy some leisure time, and the mood was full of revelry. The King's accounts note payments to 'Dick, the fool's master', as well as money for cards and goshawks.[61] There was also an opportunity to visit Wimborne Minster, where Margaret's parents lay entombed, and here too the King made an offering.[62] The following year, he would grant Margaret a licence to found a chantry dedicated to the Annunciation of the Virgin Mary in the Minster – Margaret very likely chose this spot in order to celebrate and exhibit the success and continuation of her house.[63] The party then made their way through Wiltshire, Bath and Bristol, before arriving at Woodstock at the end of August.

THE PRESENCE OF Warbeck remained a continuing cause for alarm, but in the summer of 1497 Henry was faced with a further threat. The men of Cornwall had become fed up with the King's heightened taxes – raised in an attempt to take action against the Scots in retaliation for their support of Warbeck – and soon word arrived that the rebels were marching on London. The royal family were at Sheen when the news reached them, and they immediately sought the greater protection of London. They were plainly fearful of the threat posed by the rebels – so much so that in June 'the Queen with my lord of York' travelled to Coldharbour to join Margaret.[64] After six days, however, mother and son travelled to the greater security of the Tower upon hearing alarming reports of the rebels' advance, though it is unclear if Margaret joined them. As the rebels continued to approach the city, they met with no resistance, and it was left to the trusty Earl of Oxford to take control of the royal army. The two sides met at Blackheath on 17 June, and to Margaret's great relief Oxford succeeded in defeating the rebels – a thousand Cornishmen were killed, and a jubilant Margaret noted the success in her Book of Hours.[65]

In August the royal family moved to Woodstock, there to celebrate the betrothal of Margaret's grandson, ten-year-old Prince Arthur, to the eleven-year-old Spanish Infanta, Katherine of Aragon. It was left to the Spanish ambassador, Roderigo de Puebla, to stand in for the Infanta, and the following February the marriage was ratified. Yet it would be several years before it was solemnized. The family were still at Woodstock in September when the Venetian ambassador visited, and he was extremely impressed by what he saw. Henry received him in a small, tapestry-hung hall. As he leaned across a gilt chair covered with cloth of gold, the ambassador was struck by the King's magnificent clothes: he wore 'a violet coloured gown, lined with cloth of gold, and a collar of many jewels, and on his cap was a large diamond and a most beautiful pearl'.[66] During the course of the visit, the ambassador was also given the opportunity to meet the Queen, who was 'dressed in cloth of gold'.[67] As was her custom, Margaret stood to one side of her and Prince Arthur. The ambassador did not note his impressions of Margaret, although he did report that 'the Queen is a handsome woman'.[68]

Though the Cornish threat had been vanquished, Warbeck remained at large. By the autumn, however, James IV had become tired of his guest, and was wearier still of the drain Warbeck placed on his financial resources. He urged him to action, and Warbeck finally left Scotland for Ireland. The response he received was cold, for the formerly rebellious

Irish lords had now made peace with Henry VII. In a final attempt to win support, on 7 September Warbeck landed in Cornwall in what was to be the beginning of the second rebellion of the year originating in the county. On 17 September he laid siege to Exeter, but though he burnt two of the city gates he found little support and was soon driven off. He made it as far as Taunton before he learned that the royal army was approaching. Losing his nerve, Warbeck abandoned his supporters and fled to the New Forest, where he took sanctuary at Beaulieu Abbey. It was not long before Henry's men caught up with him, and having been 'promised pardon he thereupon put his trust in Henry's official clemency'.[69] He surrendered on 5 October, and before long had made a full confession about his true identity. Henry finally had the Pretender in his custody, and he 'returned to London in triumphal style', bringing Warbeck with him.[70] The King was 'greeted by all his subjects with the profoundest respect and affection, because with so rapid and fortunate a campaign he had disposed of a dangerous conspiracy and because he brought back with him as a captive the leader of it'.[71] Crowds gathered to catch a glimpse of the Pretender as he passed, 'for most accounted it miraculous that a man of such humble origins should have been bold enough to seek to acquire by guile so great a kingdom'.[72] Warbeck was immediately placed in the Tower, but displaying the same leniency that he had once shown to Lambert Simnel, Henry was merciful. Unlike Simnel, it soon became clear that Warbeck would not heed the mercy he had been shown.

Warbeck was not held in the Tower for long and was soon residing at court. Here he was reunited with his wife, who had been treated honourably by the King and came under the protection of the Queen. In November the Venetian ambassador reported that 'he is a well favoured young man, 23 years old, and his wife a very handsome woman; the King treats them well, but did not allow them to sleep together'.[73] In December, however, the Milanese ambassador related that 'Perkin has been made a spectacle for everybody and every day he is led through London, in order that everyone may perceive his past error. In my opinion he bears his fortune bravely.'[74] It is unclear how Margaret felt about her son's attitude towards the Pretender, but after all of the emotional trauma she had been forced to endure by his hand she is certainly likely to have been wary. Unbeknown to her, there was further anxiety around the corner.

At Christmas the royal family and the court were celebrating at Sheen. It was here that 'upon St Thomas day at night in the Christmas week about 9 of the clock, began a great fire within the King's lodging, and so continued unto 12 of the night and more'.[75] The fire ravished the palace with such 'violence whereof much and great part of the old building was burned', and much of the interiors were destroyed.[76] In what must have been an extremely frightening experience, the royal family escaped unharmed, and miraculously nobody died, 'which was to the King's singular comfort'.[77] Shortly afterwards, however, Henry paid £20 (£13,400) in reward to 'them that found the King's jewels at Sheen' – presumably among the rubble.[78] In spite of the devastation, Henry was determined to rebuild his palace, and spent a vast sum. By 1501 much of the work was complete, and it was indeed a marvel to behold, highly influenced by ideas of Burgundian architecture. The new palace was renamed Richmond, in honour of the King's previous earldom and the title that his mother still bore – perhaps also in a touching reminder of Henry's father.[79] It was a splendid place indeed, boasting a library, a chapel, and a hall decorated with the statues of mighty warrior kings. There were also magnificent grounds in which the royal family could enjoy recreation, and it quickly became the King's favoured residence. Given how fraught the last few years of Henry's reign had been, it must have offered some much-needed respite.

As had become the usual pattern, Margaret remained a constant presence by her son's side in the following year of 1498. Although at the end of May she had turned fifty-five, she was journeying regularly throughout the realm, and that summer was no different. She joined the King as they travelled throughout the Thames-side palaces, and was with him and the Queen when they journeyed through East Anglia. Their tour took them to, among others, Castle Hedingham, Bury St Edmunds, Walsingham, and Norwich, where they arrived in August. By 7 September they had reached Margaret's Northamptonshire residence, Collyweston. The main topic of conversation there is likely to have been Prince Arthur's marriage to Katherine of Aragon, for which plans were well underway. As usual, Margaret was determined to have her say.

The Right Noble Puissant and Excellent Princess

IN JULY 1498 the Spanish ambassador de Puebla relayed to his sovereigns the eager involvement of Margaret and the Queen in the plans for the arrival of Katherine of Aragon. This included their desire that Katherine should speak French with her sister-in-law, Margaret of Austria, in order 'to be able to converse in it when she comes to England'. This would be a necessity, he explained, because neither Margaret nor her daughter-in-law understood Latin, 'and much less, Spanish'.[1] But it was not just the language barrier that Margaret was concerned about. De Puebla also expressed the women's wish that 'the Princess of Wales should accustom herself to drink wine. The water of England is not drinkable, and even if it were, the climate would not allow the drinking of it.'[2] Margaret and the Queen were clearly eager for Katherine to be prepared for what lay ahead of her. Once the arrangements had been concluded, Elizabeth wrote to Queen Isabella, assuring her of their good wishes towards her daughter. In the letter, Elizabeth warmly conveyed that she was keen to do all that she could to accommodate her future daughter-in-law, who 'we think of and esteem as our own daughter'.[3] There is no record of Margaret writing in a similar manner, though she is likely to have shared the Queen's sentiments towards the newest member of their family. In the same way as she had for her daughter-in-law, no doubt in an indication of her interest, she later had a list of Katherine's attendants drawn up.[4] This may also, perhaps, reveal a desire to be kept well informed – and in control – of court management and of the way in which the Princess's household was organized. Always fond of detail, Margaret invariably seems to have been eager to know as much as possible about the lives of those close to her and her family.

At this time the King and Margaret were probably pondering the problem of Warbeck, who had remained a thorn in Henry's side. Disregarding the leniency with which he had been treated, on 9 June he had escaped from Westminster. Though he began making his way towards the Charterhouse at Sheen, it was not long before the King's men caught up with him. There is some indication that Henry's servants deliberately encouraged his escape in order to provide the King with an excuse to move against him, and indeed it seems to have been all too easy for Perkin to slip past his guards.[5] Given that Henry was embroiled in negotiations for the marriage of Prince Arthur and Katherine of Aragon, this is certainly plausible. The Spanish sovereigns were always eager for news of him, for they viewed his presence in England as an obstacle to their daughter's marriage – they did not want to send Katherine into a realm where her father-in-law might be toppled by a pretender, and Perkin's presence was becoming an embarrassment. This time, his treatment was to be less gentle. De Puebla reported that Warbeck spent two days in the pillory, and he was subsequently 'secured in such a manner, and in such a prison, that, with the help of God, he will never be able to play such a trick again'.[6] Imprisoned in a windowless cell in the Tower where 'he sees neither sun nor moon', those who saw him soon afterwards were shocked by the change in him – de Puebla reported that his appearance had altered so much that it was his belief that 'his life will be very short'.[7] For the time being though, Henry remained intent on sparing Warbeck's life.

FEBRUARY 1499 WAS mingled with sorrow and joy. On 9 February, John Welles, 'the king's uncle', died.[8] He had joined his nephew in exile during the uncertain days of Richard III's reign and offered him his support at Bosworth, and had patently been close to his half-sister, Margaret; in his will he left instructions that he was to be buried 'as the King and Queen, and the Lady Margaret Countess of Richmond and Derby', as well as his own wife

Cecily, should choose.[9] It is unknown from where the impetus came, though in all probability it was either Margaret or Henry, but he was interred in the old Lady Chapel in Westminster Abbey. Almost two weeks later, on 21 February, Elizabeth of York gave birth to a son at Greenwich. The Spanish ambassador, Don Pedro de Ayala, revealed that 'there had been much fear that the life of the Queen would be in danger, but the delivery, contrary to expectation, has been easy'.[10] This child was one for whom Margaret had a special affection, and she duly rewarded the Queen's midwife in thanks for his safe delivery. Named Edmund after Henry's father, the infant was also given Margaret's father's title of Duke of Somerset. Once more Margaret was called upon to fulfil the role of godmother when the christening, which was, naturally, 'very splendid', took place. Verily, as the Spanish ambassador observed, 'the festivities [were] such as though an heir to the Crown had been born'.[11] As he had done for the births of all of his children, Henry gave orders that the font from Canterbury was to be borrowed for the occasion.[12] In her usual manner, Margaret took the responsibility of being a godparent seriously. She outlaid £100 (£67,000) on a christening gift for the little boy, and took a great interest in him. Prince Edmund joined his brother and sisters at Eltham, where Erasmus remembered seeing the infant in his nurse's arms during his visit later that year.

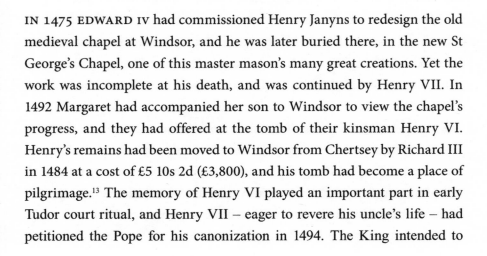

IN 1475 EDWARD IV had commissioned Henry Janyns to redesign the old medieval chapel at Windsor, and he was later buried there, in the new St George's Chapel, one of this master mason's many great creations. Yet the work was incomplete at his death, and was continued by Henry VII. In 1492 Margaret had accompanied her son to Windsor to view the chapel's progress, and they had offered at the tomb of their kinsman Henry VI. Henry's remains had been moved to Windsor from Chertsey by Richard III in 1484 at a cost of £5 10s 2d (£3,800), and his tomb had become a place of pilgrimage.[13] The memory of Henry VI played an important part in early Tudor court ritual, and Henry VII – eager to revere his uncle's life – had petitioned the Pope for his canonization in 1494. The King intended to build a magnificent tomb for himself within the chapel and a shrine to Henry VI. It was with this in mind that Margaret followed suit, contributing money to the chapel and planning her own memorial there. On 1 March 1497, the King granted his mother a licence to 'found a chantry for four chaplains, with power to increase the number' in St George's Chapel, 'to be called the chantry of the Blessed Jesus and St Mary the Virgin'.[14] On 18 July, Margaret's former chaplain Christopher Urswick, now the Dean of Windsor, granted consent for the chantry.[15] The following year, however, everything changed when it became known that Henry VI had actually harboured a desire to be buried in Westminster Abbey. Thus Henry VII agreed that his uncle's remains should be moved there, where he planned to build a shrine behind the main altar.[16] His plans went further, for he also decided to build a magnificent new Lady Chapel in the abbey. The King's attempts to have his uncle canonized never materialized, however, nor were his remains ever moved from Windsor – it transpired to be a long and complicated process that eventually ground to a halt following Henry VIII's separation from the Church of Rome. Predictably, when her son's intentions became known, Margaret's plans changed. On 28 April 1499, she asked for her chantry request at Windsor to be cancelled: from now on, her efforts, too, would be centred on Westminster.[17]

Following the demolition of the old one, on 24 January 1503 the foundation stone of the new Lady Chapel at Westminster was laid. By this time Henry had decided that he too would be buried in the new chapel of his creation, and had probably appointed Henry Janyns to oversee some of the work. Though it was incomplete at the time of Henry's death, the result when it was finished in 1512 was a spectacular, fan-vaulted chapel containing statues of saints in wall niches, the red rose of Lancaster, the Beaufort portcullis, the Welsh dragon, the Richmond greyhound, and the daisy or marguerite that Margaret adopted as one of her symbols. It was a dramatic and breath-taking expression of both Henry's magnificence, and that of his dynasty. In 1506, Margaret confirmed an earlier agreement she had made, whereby two priests were to offer up prayers for

Margaret and the king her son during their lives and thereafter for their souls and also for the souls of her late husband Edmund, Earl of Richmond father of the king, her parents John duke of Somerset and Margaret his wife and all her other progenitors and ancestors, her late husbands Thomas, Earl of Derby and Henry, Lord Stafford, Elizabeth late queen of England late wife to the king and their issue deceased and all the souls that Margaret will have prayed for and all Christian souls.[18]

Ensuring that the souls of those with whom she had spent her life were well cared for was important to her; particularly at Westminster, where she and her son intended to be laid to rest.

Margaret's personal piety was evident, but she also very publicly displayed it – in so doing, it became an integral part of her identity. Her patronage extended to other religious foundations, not all of which were in England; on one occasion she gave money to St John's Hospital in Rome. Closer to home, Syon was the first Bridgettine monastery in England, and there is ample evidence for Margaret's involvement there.[19] Located in Isleworth on the outskirts of London, the monastery had been founded by Henry V in 1415. The patronage of her grandmother Margaret Holland, who had also purchased several expensive books for the monastery, very likely triggered Margaret's interest. Margaret's accounts show a steady stream of payments for boat hire to convey her to and from Syon, where she often came to visit her goddaughter, Margaret Windsor, and Margaret Pole, who had moved to the monastery following the death of her husband in 1504.[20] Not only did Margaret give Lady Pole and Margaret Windsor money while at Syon, but she also made various other payments there, including several offerings to St Bridget.[21] Syon lay a very short distance from Richmond, and the Charterhouse at Sheen was another institution that earned both Margaret's and her son's interest. In her will she bequeathed money to both monasteries.

In addition to the chantry chapels of her foundation, Margaret also paid for work to the church at Sampford Peverell in 1498, which formed a part of her Devon estates. Here she added the south aisle and porch, and the Old Rectory had been built for her use. Members of her family, such as her half-sister, Margaret St John, also founded chantries. By 1492 'the King's aunt' was Abbess of Shaftesbury, and on 2 March she was granted a licence to found a perpetual chantry there that would offer prayers for the King, Queen, Margaret, and the souls of their mother and Oliver St John.[22] Likewise, in 1489 Thomas Rotherham had been licensed to establish a chantry in York Minster to pray for the King, Queen, Prince Arthur, Margaret and her parents.

Bishop Fisher remarked that Margaret was 'to God and to the church full obedient and tractable searching his honour and pleasure', and this can be seen in both her accounts – which are full of offerings and other payments reflecting her religiosity – and her religious foundations.[23] Her other religious activities were also vast, and included the regular distribution of alms – at Westminster she even established an almshouse for thirteen poor women, and almshouses were also in place at her own properties. The one at Collyweston was sophisticated enough to have running water. Her charity went further; as Fisher explains:

> poor folks to ye number of 12 she daily and nightly kept in her house, giving them lodging, meat and drink and clothing, visiting them as often as she conveniently might. And in their sickness visiting them and comforting them, and ministering unto them with her own hands. And when it pleased God to call one of them out of this wretched world she would be present to see them depart and to learn to die.[24]

She often engaged personally

> her hands in giving alms unto the poor and needy, and dressing them also when they were sick and ministering unto them meat and drink. These merciful and liberal hands to endure the most painful cramps so grievously vexing her and compelling her to cry.[25]

The pain from which Margaret was suffering was probably arthritis. Charity was an expected part of fifteenth-century life, but it is apparent that Margaret's contribution was both heartfelt and went above and beyond the call of duty. Her accounts contain numerous examples of money she gave for the relief of the poor, and she often purchased clothes for their benefit. On one occasion, materials were bought in order to make a gown for a poor woman, while at another time a bill was settled for 'hose bought for poor folk'. But it was not only the poor whom Margaret was eager to help; she once also provided money for a priest who was in prison, though further details of this are unknown. She plainly had a genuine sense of moral obligation to use her wealth to the advantage of those less fortunate, and Fisher was therefore right to say that 'merciful also and piteous she was unto such as was grieved and wrongfully troubled and to them that were in poverty or sickness or any other misery'.[26]

Margaret's wealth and position provided her with the opportunity to extend her patronage in other quarters. She had always cherished a fondness for books, and her chapel contained numerous fine mass books, which were all beautifully bound.[27] As Fisher said, 'she had divers books in French wherewith she would occupy herself when she was weary of prayer', as well as translating them.[28] Books were an interest that she shared with her son, so she was doubtless gratified when Henry appointed the first royal librarian: Quintin Poulet, who hailed from Lille.[29] She made regular payments for books, but with her position she also perceived a greater opportunity to bestow her own patronage.[30]

In 1472, William Caxton had established his own printing press in Westminster, and had been fortunate enough to enjoy the patronage of Margaret of York, Duchess of Burgundy, Edward IV and Elizabeth Wydeville among others.[31] Shortly after Henry VII's accession, Margaret, too, threw her patronage behind the printer, and by way of thanks he dedicated two books to her – he would also dedicate one to her eldest grandson, Prince Arthur.[32] Her backing had a huge effect on Caxton's business and immediately brought him to the notice of those at court, including the King. In a further sign of her warm relationship with her daughter-in-law, Margaret and Elizabeth – who also patronized the printer – jointly commissioned Caxton for a copy of *The Fifteen O's*, reputedly written by St Bridget of Sweden, to whom Margaret had a special devotion – presumably for her widespread acts of charity – and who was founder of the Bridgettine order.[33] As the title suggests, all fifteen of the prayers of which the book was composed began with 'O Blessed Jesu'. In 1483, Margaret had also purchased a copy of the French romance *Blanchardyn and Eglantine* from the printer, and much has been made of the parallels between the story of the couple it portrays and that of Henry VII and Elizabeth of York in the perilous days of Richard III's reign.[34] Margaret was discernibly fond of the book, for in 1489 Caxton related that it was through her 'good grace, and her commandment' that he had been ordered to 'reduce and translate it unto our maternal and English tongue'. In his dedication, though, he mixed up Margaret's title with that of her mother, referring to her as 'the right noble puissant and excellent princess, my redoubted lady, my lady Margaret Duchess of Somerset'. Though Caxton himself described the romance as 'honest and joyful to all virtuous young noble gentlemen and women', the subject matter shows that not all of the books enjoyed by Margaret were of a serious nature.[35]

Caxton was not the only printer fortunate enough to have Margaret's support. In 1494, at her request, Wynkyn de Worde printed Walter Hilton's *Scala Perfectionis* or *The Ladder of Perfection*. It came complete with a glowing dedication:

> *This heavenly book more precious than gold*
> *Was late direct with great humility*
> *For godly pleasure. Thereon to behold*
> *Unto the right noble Margaret as ye see*
> *The king's mother of excellent bounty*
> *Henry the seventh that Jesus him preserve*
> *This mighty princess hath commanded me*
> *To emprint this book her grace for to deserve.*[36]

The book was a religious work of mystic theology that described the soul's journey of contemplation, and provided spiritual exercises that were centred around the soul. It is likely to have been this interest in cleansing one's soul of sin that attracted Margaret to it, thereby demonstrating that she took an interest in reading about religion as well as practising it. She was in the happy position of being able to choose texts that appealed to her, and, given that she purchased a further copy in 1507, *The Ladder* evidently did so. She was also happy to distribute it, and, together with her daughter-in-law, she gave a copy to Lady Mary Roos, one of the Queen's ladies.[37] Both women had taken the time to personalize the gift, adding inscriptions, of which Margaret's read: 'Mistress Roos, I trust in your prayers, the which I pray you I may be partner of. Margaret R, the King's Mother.'

Margaret was the chosen dedicatee of ten books, five of which came from Wynkyn de Worde. Authors often selected their dedicatee with a mind to acquiring support from a wealthy patron, and this is likely to have been the thinking behind a dedication that Margaret received from Inghelbert Hague in Rouen (whom she had never met). Dedications were sometimes also an acknowledgement of a dedicatee's intellect or interest, or a token of thanks for support already given. Two came from another fortunate recipient of her patronage, Richard Pynson.[38] Pynson's name first appeared in relation to Margaret in the early 1500s, and it was doubtless through her influence that he came to the attention of the King. In 1503 the first payments to Pynson appear in Henry VII's accounts, and it was clear that he was a regular customer.[39] But it was from Margaret that the highest orders stemmed. In 1505 she paid Pynson for a hundred books that were delivered to Syon on her orders.[40] The following year, a further fifty were bought from him, which were of her own translation.[41] On another occasion, she rewarded a monk of the Charterhouse for books that he had given to her.[42]

Literature was an important part of Margaret's life, and would remain so until her final days. Though she regularly purchased books, unfortunately the subject matter is frequently unrecorded. She is, however, known to have owned a copy of Geoffrey Chaucer's *The Canterbury Tales*, as well as of

Froissart's *Chronicles*, among other texts. By the time of her death she had amassed an impressive library, and took great pleasure in its many pages.

Several of Margaret's books survive, including the beautifully decorated and illuminated prayer book that she had commissioned for her husband Stanley.[43] She often used books as gifts, presenting a Book of Hours that had once belonged to her father to Lady Anne Shirley, the wife of Sir Ralph Shirley. The book, in St John's College, Cambridge, contains a personal message from Margaret to the recipient: 'my good Lady Shirley pray for me that giveth you this book, I heartily pray you. Margaret, mother to the king'.[44] It is also possible that she passed a book that had once been owned by her grandmother, Margaret Holland, to her daughter-in-law the Queen, who was likewise fond of books.[45] Another of these very personal mementoes was given to Lady Scrope.

ON 19 MAY 1499 the marriage by proxy of Prince Arthur and Katherine of Aragon was conducted at Bewdley in Worcestershire. Once again, de Puebla stood in for the Infanta; it would be more than two years before she would set foot on English soil. Arthur's marriage had dominated the political arena for more than a decade, and Henry was eager that his alliance with the most powerful sovereigns in Europe ought to be consolidated as soon as possible. The continuing presence of the Earl of Warwick and Warbeck, however – though both were esconced in the Tower – left the Spanish reluctant to send their Infanta to England. From Henry's perspective it was vital that England should ally with Spain – even if it meant bloodshed. He now perceived an opportunity to rid himself of Warbeck – and Warwick – for good.

The Earl of Warwick's existence had been a sad one; as well as him enduring years in captivity, it is possible that he suffered from some kind of disability – Vergil later claimed that he could not tell a goose from a capon. It is unlikely to have been a coincidence that the Earl's cell in the Tower lay close to that of Warbeck's that summer; within a short space of time the two young men were reportedly plotting together, although they were almost certainly set up through the auspices of a double agent, Robert Cleymound. By 3 August the King had been made aware of it, and in November both men were put on trial for their lives. They were inevitably found guilty and condemned for treason. It is possible that Margaret felt some sympathy for the young Earl over the hand that fate had dealt him, for his only real crime had been his blood. Still, while he lived, his presence as a Plantagenet heir made him a continual target for dissenters, and her concern for her family's safety would have overruled any sentiment: in order to ensure this, both Warwick and Warbeck must die. With their removal, there was no reason why plans for Katherine of Aragon's journey to England could not proceed.

On 23 November, Warbeck was 'drawn from the Tower of London to Tyburn, and there hanged and beheaded'.[46] Before he died, he once more swore that he was not the son of Edward IV, thereby confirming his true identity. His body was taken to the priory of the Austin Friars in the city for burial, and in a gruesome example to the King's subjects, his head was set upon London Bridge. His widow, Lady Katherine Gordon, remained at court, where the King continued to show her great favour and paid her servants' wages.[47] She remarried three times, dying in 1537.[48] Five days after Warbeck's demise, on 28 November, the twenty-four-year-old Earl of Warwick was executed on Tower Hill. Vergil wrote sadly that 'the entire population mourned the death of the handsome youth', and, indeed, Margaret and her son may have been regretful of what had come to pass.[49] Nevertheless, at the stroke of the axe another candidate for Henry's throne had been removed. As with many of his ancestors, Warwick's remains were interred at Bisham Abbey at the King's charge.[50]

It was not for nothing that Katherine of Aragon would later claim that her marriage was made in blood. Yet with both Warbeck and Warwick definitively dealt with, Henry was finally able to make arrangements for Prince Arthur's wedding. Ferdinand and Isabella were pleased with developments – two potential threats to their daughter's future security had been removed – and the following year the Spanish ambassador was able to report to them cheerfully that 'England has never before been so tranquil and obedient as at present'.[51] He continued, 'now that Perkin and the son of the Duke of Clarence have been executed, there does not remain "a drop of doubtful Royal blood," the only Royal blood being the true blood of the King, the Queen, and, above all, of the Prince of Wales'.[52] In the eyes of both Margaret and her son, this was all that mattered. With everything seemingly safe, there was no reason why the marriage of Margaret's eldest grandson could not go ahead.

In May 1500, the King and Queen travelled to Calais, primarily on matters of diplomacy. There is no record of Margaret accompanying them, so she had probably remained at home. The royal couple landed back in England on 16 June, and almost immediately, tragedy hit them. Three days after their arrival, their youngest son Edmund, who had reached his first birthday in February, succumbed to an unknown illness at Hatfield. His death devastated Margaret and her family, and in accordance with custom it was left to the Duke of Buckingham to assume the role of chief mourner at the youngster's funeral. The little Prince's corpse was conveyed 'honourably' to Westminster Abbey, where he was buried close to the Shrine of St Edward.[53] Three months later, on 15 September, Margaret's ally Cardinal Morton died at Knole – he was interred in Canterbury Cathedral.[54] Margaret had known him for years, and he had proved a willing ally and conspirator when she had plotted with Buckingham in 1483 to overthrow Richard III. From now on, it would be Richard Fox, Bishop of Durham – a man with whom Margaret was on excellent terms – who was foremost in the King's favour.[55] By this time, however, Margaret was spending an increasing amount of time away from court: indeed, she was establishing a court of her own elsewhere.

CHAPTER 20

My Godly Mistress, the Lady Margaret

I N 1487 HENRY VII had granted his mother a huge amount of property, which spanned counties including Devon, Hertfordshire, Westmorland and many more.[1] Among the properties were Tattershall Castle and Maxstoke Castle, where she began a programme of rebuilding.[2] But there was another property that, from 1499, became Margaret's principal residence: Collyweston, which lay around three miles south-west of Stamford.[3] Collyweston had originally been built by Sir William Porter in the early fifteenth century, and was an attractive manor house. In 1441 Ralph, Lord Cromwell, who was responsible for enlarging it, purchased the house, and following his death in 1455 it passed first to Warwick the 'Kingmaker' and then to George, Duke of Clarence. When Clarence was executed in 1478, Collyweston became Crown property. When it came into Margaret's ownership, Collyweston was gradually transformed into a palace, rendering it unrecognizable from its humble beginnings. John Leland later veritably acknowledged that the house 'for the most part is of a new building by the Lady Margaret, mother to Henry VII'.[4] Featuring prominently in the work undertaken by Margaret was glass that proudly proclaimed her Beaufort heritage.[5] She spent staggering sums on the property, in so doing ensuring that the magnificence of Collyweston – which became her primary seat in the early 1500s – inspired awe in those who visited. It was a home that was as comfortable as it was luxurious, and as the 1490s progressed Margaret would spend an increasing amount of time at her Northamptonshire residence. Here she was a queen in all but name, and mistress of her own household.

The exterior of Collyweston was built to impress, and had two splendid clock-houses. The interior was equally splendid, and boasted a Presence Chamber, a chapel, a library, magnificent apartments for Margaret and her family, and a jewel house. This fell under the keepership of Edward Bothe, who was employed to ensure that his mistress's treasures were securely kept. In an indication of Margaret's love of money, there was also a counting house.

Margaret seems to have taken a particular interest in her gardens – something she had in common with her daughter-in-law – and delighted in the planning of them with the help of William Love. Collyweston featured beautiful pleasure gardens, as well as orchards, herb gardens, fishponds and a deer park.

All of Margaret's homes were lavishly furnished, but this was particularly in evidence at Collyweston. The amount of material wealth that she acquired was staggering, as we can see from the inventories of her chapel and household plate. In a reflection of the importance that religion played not only in Margaret's life but also in that of her household, there were numerous copes (ecclesiastical vestments) in blue, crimson, purple and green, many of which were embroidered with her arms and symbols; one featured Margaret's arms with a coronal, while another contained the Beaufort portcullis and a coronal.[6] Her chapel contained numerous beautiful objects, including decorative altar cloths. One magnificent pair were made of crimson velvet embroidered with marguerites.[7] Another, made of red velvet – later given to Christ's College – was embroidered with marguerites and an image of St Margaret.[8] These were not the only beautiful items to be found in Margaret's chapel, for there were also splendid gold cups featuring a number of designs: those that contained Margaret's arms, another fashioned like a serpentine, gold salts [salt cellars] containing precious stones, plate featuring saints including St Anthony, St George, St Anne and St Margaret with a green dragon, were all among the sumptuous collection.[9] Margaret had a special devotion to many of these saints, and this is reflected in her magnificent chapel trove. In a further indication of the importance she placed upon the plate in her chapel, on one occasion a goldsmith was paid to make a container in which to hold

ABOVE: Margaret Beaufort. Margaret's surviving portraits show her wearing the attire of a widow and reflect her immense piety, which was at the very centre of her life.

ABOVE: Henry VII. The bond between Margaret and her son, forged at birth, was the most important relationship of her life.

LEFT: Beaufort Portcullis, King's College Chapel, Cambridge. The symbol of the Beaufort family was adopted by both Margaret and Henry VII.

BELOW: Prince Arthur. Margaret's eldest grandson was the heir of the Tudor dynasty, but he tragically died in 1502 at the age of fifteen.

ABOVE: Katherine of Aragon. The Spanish Princess was married to Margaret's grandson, Arthur, in 1501. Katherine later became the wife of Margaret's younger grandson, Henry.

RIGHT: John Fisher, Bishop of Rochester. Fisher joined Margaret's household in 1494 and the two became close friends. It is from Fisher that many of the details of Margaret's life are gleaned.

ABOVE LEFT: Statue of Margaret, St John's College, Cambridge. Margaret's statue can be seen in the courtyard of St John's College in a tangible reminder of its foundress.

ABOVE RIGHT: St John's College, Cambridge. Margaret's second college was not established until 1511, two years after her death.

RIGHT: The gatehouse of Christ's College, Cambridge. The college of Margaret's foundation forms part of her lasting legacy, and numerous payments for the building of it can be found in her accounts.

LEFT: The Lady Chapel, Westminster Abbey. Begun on Henry VII's orders, the chapel was described as 'the wonder of the world' by the sixteenth-century traveller, John Leland.

BELOW: Tomb of Henry VII and Elizabeth of York, Westminster Abbey. The centrepiece of Henry VII's Lady Chapel is the magnificent tomb that commemorates the founders of the Tudor dynasty: Margaret's son and daughter-in-law.

LEFT: Henry VIII. Margaret's younger surviving grandson became the sole male heir of the Tudor dynasty following the death of his brother, Arthur. Margaret acted as unofficial regent on Henry's behalf during the first few weeks of his accession.

RIGHT: Margaret's tomb, Westminster Abbey. A masterpiece of Renaissance sculpture, Margaret's lifelike tomb was created by the Florentine sculptor, Pietro Torrigiano.

holy water – evidently Margaret believed that something sumptuous was required to store something so sacred.[10]

Many of the objects Margaret owned not only provide details of her homes and belongings, but also offer crucial information into different aspects of her personality as well as her magnificence as the King's mother. Her chapel plate was one such example, but her domestic plate also showed signs of this. Margaret's pride in her role can be seen by her adoption of Henry VII's arms on items such as gilt pots, while other pieces emphasized her own origins – carving knives, for example, decorated with marguerites and portcullises. Objects such as gilt spoons were reflective of Margaret's piety, being partially shaped like strawberries – believed to be the fruit of righteousness and sometimes symbolic of the fruitfulness of the Virgin Mary.[11]

Thanks largely to Margaret's accounts, we know a fair deal about those who made up her household, all of whom wore the blue and silver livery of the Beaufort family, which featured the portcullis from the family crest. Between two and four hundred people (the latter figure comes from Henry Parker and is almost certainly an exaggeration) were employed at Collyweston – a huge number, particularly when one considers that Margaret's household at Woking in the 1460s had been made up of around fifty people, and had been considerably smaller in the brief interlude between Stafford's death and her marriage to Stanley. There were clearly enough to attend to her every need. Reginald Bray was, of course, a trusted and integral member of the household, while Hugh Oldham, appointed as her receiver in 1492, was responsible for overseeing all of her estates in the West Country. Margaret thought highly of him, and in 1501 he became her receiver-general.[12] Roger Ormeston was her Chamberlain until his death in 1504, when the role was taken over by Margaret's nephew, John St John. Her secretary was Henry Hornby, who was also the dean of her chapel, and there were several cofferers (treasurers), including Miles Worsley. There were three gentlewomen: Edith Fowler, Elizabeth Massey and Alice Parker, while Elizabeth Collins was a chamberer who would later serve Katherine of Aragon.[13] She was remembered after Margaret's death with a financial reward of 26s 8d (£900).

There can be no doubt that Margaret was a woman who inspired great loyalty, and whose kindness and generosity improved the lives of many. All of those who knew her were genuinely fond of her, and she was beloved by her household, who were well treated and had the utmost respect for their mistress. Fisher remarked that 'full courtesy answer she would make to all that came unto her', going so far as to state that 'of marvellous gentleness she was unto all folks, but specially unto her own, whom she trusted and loved right tenderly. Unkind she would not be unto no creature, or forgetful of any kindness or service done to her before.'[14] Her household was run 'with marvellous diligence and wisdom', and in her usual desire to observe etiquette, she ordered 'reasonable statutes and ordinances for them, which by her officers she commanded to be read four times a year. And oftentimes by herself she would so lovingly courage every of them to do well.'[15] Fisher painted a flattering picture, but so too did Henry Parker.[16] Though written later, his account reveals a great deal of what life in Margaret's household was like. Referring to her as 'my godly mistress the Lady Margaret', Parker was highly complimentary.[17] He explained that 'I was ever one by her special commandment, and bout her person, either in that room to be her carver, or her cup-bearer.'[18] He both admired and had a good relationship with her, and she in turn appears to have been fond of him. It is from Parker that we get a glimpse of Margaret in her everyday life, for he painted a vivid picture of the regularities and habits of her household. Much of this was dominated by her religious observances:

> *her grace was every morning in the chapel betwixt six and seven of the clock, and daily said matins of the day with one of her chaplains. And that said from seven til it was eleven of the clock, as soon as one priest had said mass in her sight another began. One time in a day she was confessed, then going to her dinner how honourably she was served I think few kings better, her condition always at the beginning of her dinner was to be joyous, and to hear those tales that were honest to make her merry. The midst of her dinner either her amner or I, read some virtuous tale unto her of the life of Christ, or such like, the latter*

end of her dinner again she was disposed to talk with the bishop or with
her chancellor which sat at her board end of some godly matter.[19]

Parker's account was similar to that given by Fisher. The latter claimed
that Margaret often rose at five o'clock each morning, and so devout
was she that following her morning prayers she heard 'with one of her
gentlewomen ye matins of our lady, which kept her to then she came
in to her closet, where then with her chaplain she said also matins of
ye day. And after that daily heard four or five masses upon her knees,
so continuing in her prayers and devotions unto ye hour of dinner.'[20] In
spite of the break for dinner – usually served at around 11 o'clock in
the morning – Margaret never indulged. Fisher was adamant that 'her
sober temperance in meats and drink was known to all them that were
conversant with her'.[21] In fact, she fasted regularly, and continued to do
so until the end of her life. Although 'for age and feebleness albeit she
were not bound yet those days by ye church were appointed she kept them
diligently and seriously, and in especial ye holy lent throughout yet she
restrained her appetite til one meal and til one fish on ye day, beside her
other peculiar fasts of devotion'.[22] Margaret took her devotion further than
this, for underneath her beautiful clothes she 'had her shirts and girdles of
hair, which when she was in health every week she failed not certain days
to wear sometime'.[23] The result was that 'her skin as I heard her say was
pierced therewith'.[24] In the same way that it began, Margaret's day would
end with prayers, for 'she failed not to resort unto her chapel', where she
prayed on her knees.[25] Later in life, however, her arthritis caused 'her
back pain and disease'.[26] Nevertheless, 'divine service which daily was
kept in her chapel with great number of priests, clerks and children to
her great charge and cost, her tongue occupied in prayer much part of
the day'.[27] Her chapel and the staff that it encompassed were a vital part
of her everyday life, and at Collyweston its importance is highlighted by
the fact that it rivalled that of the royal household in terms of its size and
the way in which it was organized.[28] The children who formed a part of
Margaret's chapel staff were an active part of life at Collyweston, and

were given an education at Margaret's expense.[29] They sat at desks in a chamber in the palace from where they were taught grammar, and there are frequent references to them in Margaret's accounts.[30] On one occasion, for example, they were rewarded for singing two songs for her pleasure.

The structure at Collyweston was only marginally smaller than that of the royal court – with Margaret, rather than the King or Queen – at the top. Here she was the sole mistress, and it was she who dictated how life there was run. Hers was the deciding voice when it came to organizing the important festivities of the year, which were frequently celebrated according to her status with great pomp. Christmas, for example, was often joyous, and Parker described one such occasion:

> *In Christmas time she kept so honourable a house, that upon one new year's day I being her sewer of the age of fifteen years, had five and twenty knights following me of whom mine own father was one, and sitting at her table the Earl of Derby her husband, the Viscount Welles, the old Lord Hastings, the Bishop of Lincoln, and by her person under her cloth of estate the Lady Cecily King Edward's daughter your aunt.*[31]

Clearly, then, Margaret often had noble company at this time of year, and doubtless played the role of hostess to perfection, as she had always done. This occasion was not a one-off, for at Christmas 1505 Margaret had engaged an abbot of misrule to oversee the celebrations, which in a reflection of her own pleasure included morris dancers and players.[32] Neither was her hospitality restricted to members of her family and the nobility who deigned to visit and enjoy her hospitality. For,

> *no poor man was denied at that said feast of Christmas if he were of any honesty, but that he might come to the buttery, or to the cellar to drink at his pleasure, her liberality was such that there came no man of honour or worship to her as there came many of the greatest of the realm, but that they were well rewarded.*[33]

It is clear that Collyweston offered an impressive backdrop for Margaret to hold sway over her household, as well as providing a luxurious setting for the visits of friends, family and nobles. None could fail to admire the lavish interiors and furnishings, or complain of the generous hospitality that was offered. But there was more to Margaret's midlands palace than that.

Behind Collyweston's impressive façade, it had another role to play. It was here that Margaret set up her administrative headquarters as she began serving as the King's unofficial lieutenant in the midlands, with her authority stretching into the north too. Thus she was in control of a large portion of the country. For this reason, not everything at Collyweston was built for domestic pleasure, and when Margaret was arranging her structural improvements she included among the buildings a counting house and even a jail. At her own charge, in order to assist her she 'provided men learned for the same purpose evenly and indifferently to hear all causes, and administer right and justice to every party'.[34] Thus, with the support of her own council, Margaret was authorized to settle disputes and administer justice on the King's behalf; in so doing, she 'broke new ground', for never before had a woman been entrusted with such a role.[35] She heard numerous depositions, including one against John Stokesley, who was accused of several offences including the baptism of a cat, and another concerning slanders made about her son's ancestry emanating from a Colchester tavern.[36] Others begged for her intervention, such as Isabel Elmes, who wrote to 'the right excellent princess and her good lady's grace the king's mother' to ask for her help in settling a property dispute.[37] Margaret's involvement in all of these cases shows the level of power and influence she was wielding in her son's name from the comfort of her own home, and none recognized this better than Margaret. More significantly, such a prominent role was completely unprecedented and therefore extraordinary; never before had a queen, let alone a queen mother, been so active in the administration of justice in the king's name. Margaret – with her son's support and approval – had carved a new post for herself within the Tudor regime.

Similarly, her letters during this period reveal another side of her character. They differ entirely in tone from those she wrote to her son, and demonstrate the approach that she took to business matters. This can be seen in a letter written to the Mayor of Coventry, headed authoritatively 'By the King's Mother'. The letter was in response to a complaint made by a burgher of the city named Owen, and Margaret commanded the Mayor 'to call afore you the parties comprised in the same complaint'. She was eager that he ought to resolve the issue 'so as no complaint be made unto us hereafter in that behalf. Endeavouring you thus to do, as ye tend the King's pleasure and ours, and the due ministration of justice.'[38]

Margaret attended to business with tenacity; she was vigilant and could even be ruthless. Indeed, as she had demonstrated when pursuing her son's title and lands when they were stripped from him, if she believed something to be right, she would pursue it with dogged conviction. And this commitment to what Margaret saw as justice appears to have characterized her role as law enforcer. Indeed, Fisher commented 'it is not unknown how studiously she procured justice to be administered by a long season so long as she was suffered'.[39] She did not shirk from taking decisive action, and though Fisher claimed that Margaret 'was not vengeful, or cruel, but ready anon to forget and to forgive injuries done unto her', she was also eager to ensure that justice was done.[40] With this in mind it is easy to see why the Collyweston jail was occasionally in use.

Margaret's accounts reveal that wherever she was she was extremely active. There was a continual stream of rewards given to messengers who both brought and conveyed news. When she was not with the King they were constantly in contact; on one occasion a messenger was paid for 'riding unto the king at divers times', while on another a servant rode from Collyweston to Woodstock to deliver messages.[41] Though there are few surviving examples of the letters between mother and son, those that remain convey their affection. On one occasion, for example, Henry took care to address Margaret as 'my most entirely well beloved Lady and mother'.[42] He valued his mother's opinion and was not afraid to ask her advice. In turn, Margaret did not hesitate to ask her son for favours for others when she felt it appropriate. They often spoke about matters of business, and on one occasion she asked for Henry's aid when actively seeking to hoodwink her husband Stanley:

My good king,

I have now sent a servant of mine into Kendal, to receive such annuities as be yet hanging upon the account of Sir William Wall, my lord's chaplain, whom I have clearly discharged; and if it will please your majesty's own heart, at your leisure, to send me a letter, and command me that I suffer none of my tenants be retained with no man, but that they be kept for my lord of York, your fair sweet son, for whom they be most meet, it shall be a good excuse for me to my lord and husband; and then I may well, and without displeasure, cause them all to be sworn, the which shall not after be long undone.[43]

AS THE AUTUMN of 1501 approached, anticipation about the arrival of Prince Arthur's bride began to build. In September, Arthur had turned fourteen, and having been born in December 1485, Katherine of Aragon was just under a year older. Lavish preparations for the coming wedding had begun to take shape the previous year, and the King had spent the enormous sum of £14,000 (£9,323,400) on jewels for the occasion.[44] The marriage of an heir to the throne during his father's lifetime had not occurred in England since 1361, when the Black Prince married Joan of Kent.[45] In recent years Margaret had spent much of her time at Collyweston, but there was no question of her avoiding the capital on this momentous occasion – the greatest of Henry VII's reign: Margaret was determined to play her part.

CHAPTER 21

Right Royal and Pleasantly Beseen

I N AN INDICATION of its importance, Margaret recorded Katherine of Aragon's journey to England in her Book of Hours. The Spanish Princess had set sail from the port of Corunna on 17 August, but storms had driven the ships back to Spain and they were forced to wait for better conditions. At last, on 2 October Margaret was able to note the Princess's arrival at Plymouth, where 'a large retinue of Spanish nobles' accompanied her.[1] Katherine soon began making her way towards the capital of her new land, drawing awe from the English people along the way. By 4 November she had made it as far as Dogmersfield in Hampshire, and it was here that she would meet her future husband and father-in-law for the first time. Having spent years negotiating for the Spanish Princess's hand, Henry VII was naturally eager to meet the girl who would be England's future queen. Upon his arrival, however, the King was told that Katherine 'was in her rest', but he responded that he would see the Princess even 'if she were in her bed'.[2] He was not to be disappointed, for in spite of the protests of the Spanish ambassador, when Katherine appeared, 'the most goodly words' were exchanged 'to as great joy and gladness' of all of those present.[3] Katherine's ladies and minstrels soon joined them, and 'with right goodly behaviour and manner they solaced themselves with the disports of dancing', to the great delight of all who were present.[4]

Arriving back at Richmond on 9 November, the King was reunited with his wife, to whom he 'made privy of the acts and demeanour between himself, the Prince, and the Princess, and how he liked her person and behaviour'.[5] Margaret may also have been present, but if not she would soon have learned of her son's satisfaction.

Three days later, Katherine arrived in London. In order to ensure that she received a welcome fit for a future queen, the city had spent a fortune on preparations, and the splendour of the festivities delighted those who observed them. A number of elaborate pageants were staged across the city, and among the imagery that featured were red dragons, red roses and 'a white hart with a crown of gold about his neck and a chain of golden links coming from the crown'.[6] No contemporary was left in any doubt of the wealth and prestige of Henry VII's dynasty, in what has been described as 'a masterpiece of ingenuity'.[7] The royal family had also gathered to witness the pageants – albeit in secret. In Cheapside, the King and Prince Arthur, who were joined by Oxford, Stanley and others, watched from one chamber, while in another Margaret accompanied the Queen with her two granddaughters and 'many other ladies of the land' to watch the entertainment.[8] Meanwhile, her youngest grandson Prince Henry had joined Katherine as she rode through the city 'upon a great mule richly trapped after the manner of Spain'.[9] She was gorgeously bedecked in 'rich apparel on her body after the manner of her country', with her fair auburn hair hanging about her shoulders, topped by a hat.[10] The crowds cheered endlessly as she passed.

Following Katherine's joyous entry into London, she was taken to meet the King and Queen at Baynard's Castle. This was the first occasion on which Elizabeth met her future daughter-in-law, and Katherine took great pleasure in the 'goodly visiting and sight of the Queen' and the King.[11] She in turn was welcomed into the folds of her new family 'with pleasure and goodly communication, dancing, and disports'.[12] Margaret's name is not mentioned, so it is unclear whether she met Katherine at this time. If she did not, then she would not have long to wait.

The magnificent Old St Paul's Cathedral towards the east of the city had been chosen as the setting for Arthur and Katherine's wedding on 14 November. In preparation for the royal nuptials, the cathedral had been sumptuously decked out with 'plates, jewels, and relics of wonderful riches and preciousness'.[13] No expense had been spared for the celebrations of this momentous occasion that signalled the cementing of a powerful alliance between England and Spain.

Margaret watched the nuptials privately. Arthur and Katherine were to be the centre of attention, and as Katherine arrived at the cathedral, her white satin train borne by the Queen's sister Cecily, 'after her followed a hundred ladies and gentlewomen', all sumptuously dressed.[14] A London chronicler recorded that 'wonderful it was to behold the riches of garments and chains of gold, that that day were worn' by the lords who attended the wedding.[15] Arthur was magnificently adorned in white satin, and the young couple were married by Henry Deane, Archbishop of Canterbury, 'where was present in secret manner the King, the Queen, my Lady the King's Mother', all of whom 'stood secretly in a closet'.[16] The royal minstrels 'struck up and made such melodies and mirth as they could, the which was comfortable and joyful to hear'.[17] For Henry VII and Margaret the marriage was the culmination of all their hopes. So happy was she at this moment that Fisher later recalled that she had wept with joy 'at the great triumph'.[18]

As Katherine and Arthur were put to bed that evening, there followed one of the most controversial wedding nights in English history. According to later depositions, the following morning it was Margaret's nephew, Maurice St John – a member of the Prince's household – who asked his master how he had fared, to which Arthur replied that he had that night been in the midst of Spain. By contrast, Katherine would later swear that her marriage had never been consummated. But that was all in the future, and in November 1501 the mood was nothing other than celebratory.

On a personal level, Margaret's feelings about her grandson's bride are unclear, though it is wholly possible that she felt the same warmth and enthusiasm towards Katherine as her son did – she would later take care to bequeath her a magnificent girdle and a gold cup that was bettered only by those she left to her grandson, Henry. Several members of Margaret's household would later transfer their service to Katherine's household, including Margaret's nephew John St John. Likewise, people to whom Margaret had shown favour were also held in high regard by Katherine, notably Lady Margaret Pole. Margaret would also undoubtedly have been impressed by Katherine's education, which gave them a shared interest: the Spanish Princess was skilled at both music and dancing, and would later earn praise from Erasmus for her scholarly abilities. Margaret had certainly shown a great interest in Katherine, demonstrated in her earlier requests – coupled with those of Elizabeth of York – to ensure that the Spanish Princess was adequately prepared for her arrival in her new land. Such concern was typical of Margaret, and there is every reason to believe that she was as eager as the rest of her family to make the Princess feel welcome. She also recognized Katherine's prestigious connections and the benefits that this brought to her own family, and would have seen her as the means through which the next generation of the Tudor dynasty would stem. It would have been to Katherine whom all of England – including Margaret – looked for the arrival of a male heir, in the same manner as they had once done to Elizabeth of York. Elizabeth had amply succeeded in fulfilling this role, and Margaret would have been both hopeful and expectant that Katherine would do the same.

Arthur and Katherine's wedding celebrations were set to continue for several days, and Margaret had decided that she should take up the baton. Coldharbour was to be the setting for the next stage of the revelries, and Margaret had employed William Bolton to carry out improvements in preparation. She was pleased with the new ovens, the glazing, the painting of the stairs and the improvements to the gardens. A coppersmith by the name of William Horn had been paid for making two dozen portcullis badges – how they were used is unclear, but Margaret was evidently eager to take the opportunity to proclaim her Beaufort origins to the Spanish Princess. She had even given orders at this time for the 'making and writing of a play'.[19] Additionally, many costly materials had been purchased, doubtless in an attempt to show Coldharbour at its best. The day after the wedding, 'the reverent and most worshipful my Lady the King's Mother' hosted a dinner 'at her lodging within the City of London called the Coldharbour, for whom that place was right royal and pleasantly beseen and addressed, enhanged with rich cloth of Arras, and in the hall a goodly cupboard made and erect with great plentieth of plate, both silver and gilt'.[20] Margaret had ordered her cooks to prepare a sumptuous feast, and those in attendance were served with 'divers wines abundant and plenteous'.[21] Numerous entertainments had also been arranged, including music from the Queen's minstrels and those of the Earl of Northumberland, the Prince's trumpeters, as well as a juggler, named Matthew, who was in the employ of the Earl of Oxford. Katherine could not fail to have been impressed with her host's hospitality. But that was only the beginning, and that same evening the party left Coldharbour and travelled the short distance to Derby House, where Margaret's husband hosted a supper. Here, they celebrated with 'right worshipful cheer and parleyance as my Lady the King's Mother did unto them at their dinner'.[22] Margaret had played her part to perfection.

Other celebrations ensued, including a mass at St Paul's for which Margaret was plausibly present – her husband certainly was. An elaborate joust was staged at Westminster, at which Margaret joined the Queen, Katherine, and her granddaughters, 'with many other ladies and gentlewomen of honour'.[23] There was a great feast at Westminster Hall, which was 'furnished and filled with as goodly and rich treasure of plate as ever could lightly be seen'.[24] This was followed by 'a good disguising', which Margaret doubtless enjoyed.[25] It was her youngest grandson, Prince Henry, who stole the show, for while dancing with his sister Margaret, 'perceiving himself to be encumbered with his clothes, suddenly cast off his gown and danced in his jacket' with his sister.[26] This was so joyous that 'it was to the King and Queen right great and singular pleasure', and Margaret – always eager to embrace such merriment – probably felt the same warmth.[27]

When the festivities finally ceased, the serious business of Arthur's marriage began. Princess Katherine was afforded no time to get to know her new family, for in December the newlyweds bade farewell. Leaving London behind they travelled more than a hundred and fifty miles to Shropshire, there to take up residence at Ludlow Castle. Arriving in mid-December during a bitter winter, it was here that Arthur and Katherine set up court and prepared to celebrate Christmas.

AS NEW YEAR passed and 1502 dawned, Margaret had much with which to occupy her time. Though the marital prospects of her eldest grandson were now settled, Henry VII immediately turned his attention to his eldest daughter. In January, twelve-year-old Princess Margaret was betrothed to James IV of Scotland, the ceremony taking place in the Queen's chamber at Richmond. Talks for the marriage had been staged over the course of several years, and in 1498 Henry had expressed his concerns that his daughter was 'so delicate and weak that she must be married much later than other young ladies'.[28] It seems that the Princess was, like her grandmother, a slow developer. In echoes of her own experience, Margaret had doubtless influenced him, for he continued, 'the Queen and my mother are very much against this marriage. They say if the marriage were concluded we should be obliged to send the Princess directly to Scotland, in which case they fear the King of Scots would not wait.'[29] In their concern for the Princess's welfare, Margaret had combined forces with the Queen, and Henry had evidently paid them heed. They were probably also aware that James IV, although 'as handsome in complexion and shape as a man can be', was a notorious womanizer with a string of mistresses and bastards.[30] But at the beginning of 1502, Princess Margaret was three years older, and though her grandmother is not listed among those who attended the betrothal, the level of ceremony would surely have gratified her. The celebrations lasted several days, and immediately the young Queen of Scots was treated with an increased level of ceremony. Her parents, and probably Margaret too, took a great deal of care in preparing the youngster for her new role, and though she was not to leave for Scotland immediately, costly new garments for her wedding trousseau were ordered. In 1503, Henry would outlay the exorbitant sum of £16,000 (£10,655,300) for jewels 'for the Queen of Scots as for the King's own use'.[31]

Margaret's absence from her granddaughter's betrothal ceremony can be easily explained, for at this time she had business of her own. Fisher later claimed that Margaret 'most hated' avarice, yet she was never afraid to pursue what she believed to be rightfully hers.[32] At the beginning of 1502, following in her son's footsteps, Margaret made her own visit to Calais.[33] This was rather remarkable given that she was fifty-seven – old by contemporary standards – and the journey cannot have been comfortable. Nevertheless, she had a very important matter of business to attend to, chiefly pursuing a debt that had been owed to her family since before her birth and which she was determined to settle.[34] The debt had been inherited by the French King, Louis XII, and with her strong sense of obligation Margaret was determined to obtain what was owed.[35] It was probably on 14 January 1499 that Margaret wrote to her son in a tone of optimism about the affair:

My own sweet and most dear King and all my wordly joy, in as humble manner as I can think I recommend me to your Grace, and most heartily beseech our lord to bless you; and my good heart where that you say that the French King hath at this time given me courteous answer and written letters of favour to his court of Parliament for the treve expedition of my matter which so long hath hanged, the which I well know he doth especially for your sake.[36]

She continued by expressing her thanks to Morton, who had evidently been of assistance, as well as assuring Henry that if she were successful in obtaining the debt, it would be his. In a final demonstration of her maternal affection, she ended her letter with a blessing: 'Our Lord give you as long good life, health, and joy, as your most noble heart can desire, with as hearty blessings as our Lord hath given me power to give you. At Collyweston, the 14th day of January, by your faithful true bedwoman, and humble mother, Margaret R.'[37] By 1502, however, the issue continued to drag on. That Margaret was prepared to travel to France in an attempt to settle the matter personally is a testament to how seriously she took it, but the debt, despite Margaret's best efforts, was never fully repaid during her lifetime. In 1504 she formally handed it over to her son, for which, in his own words, 'in my most hearty and humble wise I thank you'.[38]

MARGARET WAS BACK in England when the royal family were struck with a devastating tragedy. In April, news reached London that an attack of a fearful sickness had descended on Ludlow, with which the Princess of

Wales may have been infected. Katherine would recover from her illness, but for her groom it was to prove fatal. Arthur's health appears to have been fragile for some time, and though it has been suggested that he was infected with the sweating sickness, it is more probable that he had contracted a form of consumption (tuberculosis).[39] On 2 April – less than five months after his marriage – Margaret recorded the death of her beloved grandson in her Book of Hours.[40] There is no record of whether she was with the court at Greenwich when a messenger arrived bearing letters from Sir Richard Pole, the Prince's Chamberlain. It was left to the King's chaplain to deliver the crushing news that Henry's 'dearest son was departed to God'.[41]

The effect was devastating. Though the King and Queen attempted to comfort each other, their grief was profound. They now had just one son on whom the future of their dynasty lay. In spite of her heartbreak, the Queen tried to remind her husband that 'my Lady his mother had never no more children but him only, and that God by His Grace had ever preserved him and brought him where that he was'.[42] She assured him that they still had a 'fair, goodly and towardly young Prince and two fair Princesses, and over that, God is where He was, and we both young enough'.[43] Though Margaret's reaction to Arthur's death is not recorded, the behaviour of his parents allows us to surmise some of the grief she felt. Arthur was not the first of his siblings to succumb to death, but he was the one upon whom the greatest emphasis had been placed. At Ludlow the Prince's body had lain in state in his chamber, 'under a table covered with rich cloth of gold, having a rich cross over him', but on the King's orders the funeral cortège then made its way to Worcester.[44] Among those in attendance were Arthur's faithful servants, Sir Richard Pole and Maurice St John, who had begun his career as a member of Henry VII's bodyguard. The heartbroken King paid £666 16d (£444,000) for the Prince's burial in Worcester Cathedral, where his tomb can still be seen.[45] His widow, meanwhile, returned to London.

Henry VII was painfully aware that only one life now stood between the future succession of his family and disaster. Within weeks of Arthur's death the Queen was pregnant. As Margaret grieved for her grandson, it remained to be seen whether the arrival of her unborn grandchild could help to heal the wounds that Arthur's death had inflicted. Suddenly, the Tudor dynasty whose future had looked so bright in September 1486, now hung by a thread.

CHAPTER 22

In Everything Like to the Queen

A S THE QUEEN'S pregnancy progressed, it became clear that her health was delicate. She had not borne a child for three years since Edmund in 1499, and Margaret may therefore have been concerned when Elizabeth began a progress that took her far from home. One of her stops took her to Raglan Castle, where Margaret's son had spent some of his childhood and where her host was Margaret's cousin, Sir Charles Somerset.[1] She returned to London in time for Christmas, which the court spent at Richmond. At New Year, Elizabeth rewarded Margaret's servant Richard Bygot for conveying her mother-in-law's gift – perhaps in an indication of Elizabeth's affection and gratitude towards her mother-in-law, the reward he received was larger than that of any other servant.[2] Towards the end of January 1503, Elizabeth prepared for her confinement.[3]

The Queen took to her chamber in the Royal Apartments at the Tower. With her favourite midwife Alice Massy in attendance, it was here that on 2 February, Candlemas Day, she gave birth prematurely. Her child was not the hoped-for son who would have strengthened the male continuance of her dynasty, but a daughter, named Katherine. Furthermore, it quickly became clear that all was not well, as the Queen's health began to decline at an alarming rate. Puerperal fever may have set in, but iron-deficiency anaemia has also been suggested.[4] Whatever the cause, on 11 February – her thirty-seventh birthday – Elizabeth of York died.[5] Seven days later, on 18 February, baby Katherine followed her mother to the grave. She was buried in Westminster Abbey. It was a tragic outcome and the culmination of a terrible two years for Margaret's family. Her three surviving young grandchildren were motherless, with only their grieving father and grandmother to turn to for comfort. Margaret was now the closest female relative the royal children had. It was on the orders of 'the right high, mighty and excellent Princess Margaret, Countess of Richmond' that a set of ordinances for the court mourning of ladies was drawn up, almost certainly as a result of the Queen's death.[6] These stipulated precisely the apparel that all rank of women were expected to wear following a death; interestingly, the king's mother was 'to wear in everything like to the queen', which partially consisted of an elaborate mantle and train.[7]

On 23 February the Queen was given a stately funeral at Westminster Abbey, the ceremony being performed by Richard FitzJames, Bishop of London. No expense had been spared, and Elizabeth's funeral effigy was bedecked in the full regalia of a queen of England.[8] She was laid to rest in the abbey, where a splendid memorial would later be erected to her memory, although neither Margaret nor her son would live to see it. In spite of his grief, Henry VII considered remarrying, with his widowed daughter-in-law Katherine of Aragon and Joanna of Naples – the niece of Ferdinand of Aragon – put forward as candidates. Yet neither of these materialized, and Henry remained a widower for the rest of his life, leaving Margaret as the leading lady in the land. She continued to advise him in political matters, and was deferred to for her wisdom. Her influence had not gone unnoticed among her contemporaries and foreign ambassadors, and she was believed to wield power comparable to that of many of the men in the King's inner circle. This belief may indeed be credible, for given the constancy with which Margaret was sending messengers to her son and received them in return, it is difficult to believe that they would not have consulted one another about matters of business and affairs of state – even if only on occasion.

Following the death of the Queen, Margaret seems to have assumed a greater degree of responsibility for the care of her grandchildren, although there is no evidence that she played a role in their education.[9] She was certainly eager to ensure that a high level of ceremony was employed for the departure of her granddaughter the Queen of Scots in the summer, and extra plate had been brought from Coldharbour for the occasion. On 27 June, Henry VII and his daughter left Richmond and London behind. It would transpire to be a forty-one-day progress for the young Queen as she journeyed north to meet her new husband, James IV. The first stop on their travels was to 'a place of the right high and mighty Princess my Lady his Mother', with Margaret noting carefully in her Book of Hours that on 5 July 'King Henry the VIIth and the Queen of Scots his daughter, with a great multitude of lords and other noble persons, came to Collyweston unto my lady his mother'.[10] This was intended to be a huge progress – one of the most important of Henry's reign. According to the *Great Chronicle of London*, when the King and his daughter arrived at Collyweston, having been escorted by John St John, 'they were joyously received'.[11] The importance Margaret placed on the visit can be seen in the preparations and building work that she had ordered, which included the glazing of the windows, new chimneys, lead on the roof, and borrowing hangings from Fox, now Bishop of Winchester.[12] It was the need to ensure that it provided a fitting setting for the visit that, as Jones asserted, 'marked the transformation of Collyweston into a palace'.[13] In her usual style, Margaret was the perfect hostess.

The royal visit to Collyweston was full of the splendours and entertainments that would have been expected, but it was over all too soon. Having 'tarried a certain season after their pleasure, the which season expired', it was time for the young Queen of Scots to leave her family.[14] Margaret's granddaughter, who was 'richly dressed', bade a tender farewell to her father and grandmother.[15] As she rode out of Collyweston 'with an honourable company of lords and ladies' that had been appointed by her father, the young Queen proceeded to make her stately journey towards her new land.[16] She was formally married to James IV on 8 August in the chapel at the Palace of Holyroodhouse. Margaret would never see her granddaughter again, but her accounts show that, particularly in the months following the Princess's departure, her grandmother was eager to keep in touch. In September she arranged for messages to be sent to Queen Margaret, and in November she rewarded a servant who had brought messages from Scotland in return.[17] Likewise, she would have been delighted when the Queen of Scots gave birth to her first child and Margaret's first great-grandchild – a son named James – on 21 February

1507. Tragically, the boy died the following February, by which time his mother was once again pregnant.[18]

Margaret had formerly expressed her disapproval and concern at her granddaughter being married too young, but as the Queen of Scots was approaching her fourteenth birthday – generally considered to be a more acceptable age for consummation – there is no evidence that she was unhappy at the King's decision to send his daughter north at this time. While Margaret had claimed for herself a role of great independence, separate from her husband and subject only to her own authority, she still recognized the advantages of marriage for those who were not in her position and took a proactive role in arranging matches for her family and friends. Given her influence and proximity to the King, having some kind of connection with Margaret was believed to be advantageous by many of her contemporaries.[19] She was therefore granted the wardship of many noble children, and saw to it that these children were all raised well and often married well.[20] Just days after her granddaughter's departure from Collyweston, on 16 July Margaret hosted the wedding of her niece, Elizabeth St John. The King was evidently also fond of Elizabeth, for it was he who paid for the festivities. Yet there is no doubt that it was Margaret who was the instigator, assuredly in an attempt to ensure the future security of another member of her family. Her groom was Gerald Fitzgerald, the heir of the Earl of Kildare, who had been raised 'in his youth and tender age' at the King's court.[21] By contrast, Elizabeth had been raised in Margaret's household along with her sister Eleanor, which would have been viewed as a significant honour by their parents.

Not all marriages met with Henry's approval. It was probably in 1502 that Margaret's widowed sister-in-law, Cecily Welles, took another husband. His name was Thomas Kyme, a man of far inferior standing to his wife, and hailing from Lincolnshire. It seems to have been a genuine love match, but one for which Cecily had failed to gain the King's consent. When he discovered it, he was so incensed that he banned Cecily from court. Margaret had always been fond of Cecily – it is even possible that Cecily had joined her household following the death of first husband.[22]

Given Kyme's origins as a Lincolnshire man – very much home territory to Margaret – it is possible that she also knew him. It was to Margaret that Cecily now turned, seeking shelter at Collyweston. Henry Parker later said of his mistress that 'I could not sufficiently laud nor commend her high virtues and her honour', and in her characteristic generosity she did not hesitate to take Cecily in.[23] She also proved herself to be a useful ally to the disgraced princess, and intervened with the King on her behalf. The result was that some of Cecily's lands were restored to her in 1504, but she lived out the rest of her days in obscurity.[24] She and Margaret remained close, and in 1503 Margaret made Cecily a gift of 'a fine image' on a parchment.[25] A room was also later reserved for her use at Margaret's borrowed palace of Croydon.

WITHIN A SHORT space of time, by the end of 1503 Margaret's family had become considerably smaller: with her eldest granddaughter gone, she now had just one grandson and one granddaughter left to occupy her time. Though she remained in contact with them, Margaret's appearances in London and at court were becoming far less frequent.[26] Instead, much of her time was spent at Collyweston, but although she was approaching old age her energy seemed boundless. She continued to work tirelessly on her son's behalf, and she displayed no signs of slowing down. She was nevertheless left greatly saddened when, on 5 August, her trusted servant Reginald Bray died. Bray had been one of the most continuous and loyal figures in Margaret's life for the past four decades: she had first met him during her marriage to Henry Stafford, and he had offered her years of faithful and devoted service, risking his life during the reign of Richard III while in her service. Bray had been more than a faithful servant, for he had become a dear friend whom Margaret had relied upon. His death signified a further broken link with Margaret's past, and came amid a painful period of loss in her life. Though Bray had been married, he did not leave behind any children. At his own request he was buried at St George's Chapel, Windsor, in whose construction he had assisted.[27] This explains why his arms can be seen scattered at various points on the chapel's roof; in his lifetime he had contributed significant sums towards the building of the chapel, which is surely his greatest legacy.

The opening years of the 1500s were a time of great upheaval for Margaret, much of it unwelcome. On 29 July 1504, her husband Stanley died. Margaret was not with him when he breathed his last for they had spent much of the past decade living apart, though at New Year they had exchanged gifts in the same manner as they had always done.[28] Nevertheless, she is likely to have been saddened by the death of the man with whom she had shared a successful working partnership for the past thirty years. Though their marriage had not been based on love, it had been mutually advantageous and friendly. When the news of Stanley's death reached Collyweston, Margaret and her household assumed full mourning. In his will – of which his sons were the executors – he left instructions that 'my Lady my wife shall peaceably enjoy all the lordships, manors, etc, assigned for her jointure'.[29] He left Margaret no personal bequests, but he left none either to any of his other family members, which may indicate that the writing of the will was undertaken in haste. However, he was also aware that Margaret's personal wealth meant that she lacked for nothing, and that she was able to provide herself with anything she needed. Notwithstanding this, he did leave his stepson the King a gold cup, entreating him to be good to his family and ensure that his final wishes were carried out, for 'I have been a true servant'.[30] Stanley left instructions that he was to be buried in the church of his ancestors at Burscough near Lathom. It was where 'the bodies of my father, mother, and other of my ancestors lay buried, having provided a tomb to be there placed, with the personages of myself and both my wives'.[31] Despite his hopes, Margaret never joined him there.

There was no question of Margaret remarrying – it was neither desirable nor necessary – and instead she chose to renew her vow of chastity, promising Bishop Fisher 'with full purpose and good deliberation for the weal of my sinful soul with all my heart promise from henceforth the chastity of my body, that is never to use my body having actual knowledge of man after the common usage in matrimony'.[32] As a result of Stanley's death, Margaret's landed income was boosted by £3,000 (£2,000,000) a year, and it would not be long before she put the extra money to good use.

FOLLOWING THE DEATH of Prince Arthur in 1502, his widow Katherine of Aragon had remained in England. Her parents had been vehemently opposed to Henry VII's brief consideration of marrying her himself, with Queen Isabella describing the notion as 'a very evil thing'.[33] Instead, plans were put in place for her marriage to Margaret's youngest grandson – the King's only surviving male heir – Prince Henry. On 23 June 1503, a formal marriage treaty had been drawn up and was ratified by Katherine's parents. As the Prince was just short of his eleventh birthday at this time, plans for the wedding were put on hold, and in early 1504 Henry was formally created Prince of Wales. But everything changed following the death of Katherine's mother on 26 November 1504. Katherine was rendered significantly less valuable in the marriage stakes thanks to the complications in the Spanish succession, which meant that her father was now King of Aragon only, and Henry VII therefore dithered over what to do with her. She took up residence at Durham House on the Strand, but at the instigation of the King, on 27 June 1505 Prince Henry repudiated their betrothal in front of Bishop Fox and others. Katherine had no idea, and within months the King stopped paying her pitiful allowance. This forced her to return to the court at Richmond, but her circumstances remained dire: she was unable to pay her servants, and even resorted to pawning some of her jewels and plate in order to buy food. It was a far cry from the welcome she had been afforded in 1501.

Margaret's feelings about her son's cruel treatment of Katherine are unknown, and her accounts offer little insight into her relationship with the Spanish Princess. She had once taken as great an interest in her arrival as had the King, but following Prince Arthur's death it seems unlikely that she had much to do with Katherine. The language barrier between the two women presented a major problem, rendering communication extremely difficult, but even so, if contemporary reports of Margaret's kind nature are to be believed, it would have been natural for her to have felt some sympathy for Katherine's plight. At this time, however, Margaret's mind was very much occupied with her own affairs, for she was busy embarking upon an enterprise of the utmost importance: her legacy.

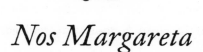

CHAPTER 23

Nos Margareta

T HE 'LADY MARGARET mother to Henry VII founded and endowed a grammar school in Wimborne', complete with a schoolmaster, John Leland later observed.[1] It was only natural that the town in which her parents lay entombed would hold great appeal to Margaret, but scholarship had also long been a passion of hers. Yet it was one in which, by reason of the circumstances of her life, she had been unable to fully indulge. By reason of the death of Elizabeth of York and the departure of Margaret, Queen of Scots, the demands of her family had lessened, ensuring that Margaret had an opportunity to pursue her interest. Women were not permitted to attend university, but Margaret was nevertheless part of a circle that had strong links with both Oxford and Cambridge. One of these had been Reginald Bray, who had been appointed Steward of the University of Oxford in 1496. Thanks to her friendship with another, though, Margaret's attentions were directed elsewhere. For the rest of her life she would be a dedicated patron.

In 1494 the court was at Greenwich when Margaret first met John Fisher, the man who would become one of her greatest friends, and from whom many of the details of her life are sourced. Having been born in around 1469, Fisher was more than twenty years Margaret's junior, and hailed from Beverley in Yorkshire. Though he was the son of a merchant, in 1484 he had been fortunate enough to earn a place at Cambridge, where his mother had supported him.[2] Fisher was exceptionally intelligent and excelled at university, where he completed not only a degree but also a Master's. Following his graduation, he took orders to become a priest, and returned to the north, where he took up a post as the Vicar of Northallerton. It was not long, though, before he returned to his university city, for in 1494 he was offered a position as Senior Proctor of Cambridge. It was at this time that he came to the notice of the King's Mother, for

> *at length his name grew so famous, that, passing the bonds of the university, it spread over all the realm, in so much as the noble and virtuous lady, Margaret, Countess of Richmond and Derby, mother to the wise and sage prince King Henry the VIIth, hearing of his great virtue and learning, ceased not till she had procured him out of the university to her service.*[3]

So impressed was she with Fisher that Margaret determined that he ought to join her household, and after just a few years in his role he became her chaplain and confessor. More importantly, though, the two immediately struck up a lifelong friendship and Margaret seems to have put in a good word with her son on Fisher's behalf; the result was that he was created Bishop of Rochester in 1504. What was more, Fisher's position in Margaret's household ensured that he was perfectly placed to encourage his mistress in regards to her educational patronage.

Margaret was by no means the first high-ranking lady to take an interest in this quarter, for the precedent had long since been set. In 1341, for example, Robert de Eglesfield had founded Queen's College, Oxford, in honour of Margaret's ancestress, Queen Philippa.[4] Similarly, six years later, Marie de St Pol, the widowed Countess of Pembroke, had been granted a licence to found Pembroke College, Cambridge.[5] Margaret's family also had strong links to Cambridge. Her kinsman, Henry VI, had been responsible for the patronage of many educational institutes, founding Eton College close to Windsor Castle in 1440, King's College, Cambridge, and All Souls College, Oxford. He had also taken an interest in God's House, another Cambridge foundation that had been begun by a priest named William Byngham in 1439. Henry had been passionate about his scholarly pursuits, and it was an interest that was shared by his wife, Queen Margaret. It was she who had founded Queen's College, Cambridge, in 1448, and had sent her Chamberlain, Sir John Wenlock, to lay the foundation stone on her behalf.[6] Though Margaret herself was just a small child at this time, she is likely to have admired the examples set by the King and Queen. Elizabeth Wydeville had also shown an interest in Queen's, and it was refounded under her patronage in 1465. In turn, Anne Neville became the college's patron, though Elizabeth of York did not follow suit. Margaret had visited Cambridge before, and in September 1489 refreshments, including a roast buck and pike, had been prepared for her.[7] On 1 and 2 September 1498, she had accompanied the King and Queen during their visit to the city, but it would be some years until she began to pursue her own projects. At the end of 1504, she had been granted a licence to 'found a perpetual chantry of one preacher of God's Word, to be called the chantry in honour of the name of Jesus and of the Annunciation of St Mary the Virgin, in the University of Cambridge'.[8] But Margaret had greater plans for educational patronage, although the precedent had already been set. She was eager not only to emulate the example of those before her, but to surpass it. She succeeded, in so doing earning herself a reputation as a great benefactress and philanthropist whose legacy continues to educate scholars today.

Margaret had originally planned to split her patronage between Oxford and Cambridge, and on 1 March 1497 the King had granted her a licence to 'found a perpetual lectureship of sacred theology' in both universities.[9] Both were to be called 'the lectureship of Margaret, mother of King Henry VII'.[10] In grateful thanks, Oxford had written to express their gratitude: 'Those most respected kings, prelates, and generals, and men of almost every rank of society have been solicitous for our welfare and the progress of education; but it has remained for one princess, of rank most exalted and of character divine, to do that which none have done before.'[11]

Although, with Fisher's encouragement, Margaret's energies were very much directed towards Cambridge, she nevertheless maintained a good relationship with Oxford, and helped them when she was able. Three of her letters to the university survive – two of which were written from Buckden in the summer of 1500 – and her goodwill is evident. Given its proximity to Collyweston, however, Cambridge suited Margaret, and her representatives were also regular visitors to the city. Following the death of Elizabeth of York, Margaret's patronage began with Queen's College, but she also took an interest in Jesus College, which had been founded by Bishop John Alcock, the former tutor of Edward V, in 1496. In May 1503 she gave £26 towards the building work.[12] This was not enough for Margaret, and it was not long before she turned her attentions towards creating her own foundations. With Fisher's encouragement, Margaret cast her eye on God's House, which had been founded in 1439 by William Byngham but which was greatly impoverished. Henry VI had also shown an interest in God's House, and this unquestionably appealed to Margaret. She intended to expand it and renamed it Christ's College, the licence being granted on 1 May 1505.[13] Although it was fully established at the time of her death, the building work at Christ's would not be completed until later. In 1508, however, Pope Julius II issued a bull confirming its foundation. It still survives in the National Archives, beautifully decorated with Margaret's arms, the arms of England and the Tudor rose in pen and ink.[14]

Modern visitors to Christ's are left in no doubt as to who was responsible for its foundation, for Margaret's coat of arms displaying the mythical yales – adopted by Margaret after 1485 – and the Beaufort portcullis proudly adorn the gatehouse underneath a statue of the college's patroness. Much evidence of Margaret's involvement at Christ's can still be seen, including the window on the north wall of the chapel and the Beaufort arms and motto, *Souvent me Souvient* (I often remember) above the entrance to the master's lodge. The glass, probably dating from 1510, shows her wearing a coronet and kneeling at a desk in front of a Book of Hours. Her symbols are stamped all over the college, and when, from 1505, she began to visit the city on a regular basis, a suite of four rooms for her use was reserved there. These can still be seen, beautifully decorated with the badges of both the Beauforts and the Tudors. One of the rooms contained an oratory that overlooked the chapel, where Margaret could pray in private. She would later bequeath the college 'the Beaufort Cup', which still survives – a beautiful silver-gilt cup dating from 1507, exquisitely engraved with roses and marguerites, portcullises and fleurs-de-lys, proudly displaying Margaret's heritage.[15]

Neither was this the only piece she left to the college, for much of her plate and many of her books were also bequeathed. Payments for the building of the college, overseen by James Morice, clerk of the works at Collyweston, are littered throughout her accounts, testimony to her personal interest in the project. On one occasion she even paid for 'the making of a seal for Christ's College'.[16] In order to support her new foundation, on 14 July 1507 the King granted Margaret the abbey of St Mary de Pratis in Norfolk, with a licence enabling her to pass it over to the Master of Christ's, 'first begun by Henry VI and by her increased, finished and established'.[17]

For both the city of Cambridge and the university, Margaret's patronage was of crucial importance and boosted public awareness. She seems to have been a fairly regular visitor, and was always warmly received. In July 1507, she rewarded 'a poor woman that brought my lady's grace a cake' during the course of her visit to Christ's, and two years earlier when she had arrived in the city, she was greeted with almost royal ceremony.[18] The bells of the city churches were rung out in celebration, and Margaret was eager to show that the Tudors were avid supporters of the city's educational foundations. The following year, the King visited, joined by his mother, and through Fisher's persuasions he donated money towards the completion of King's College Chapel – the chest in which it was sent can still be seen in the chapel today. Henry's interest did not, though, reach the same heights as that of Margaret's, and neither would the work be complete at the time of his death. Notwithstanding this, it is full of the symbols of the Tudor dynasty.

Margaret was eager that as many people as possible ought to be given access to her foundation, but she also expected her scholars to work hard. It was with this in mind that a series of statutes were put in place in order to ensure the smooth running and good order of the college. On 3 October 1506, Margaret's statutes were delivered on her behalf to the Master of Christ's. The statutes still survive, written on vellum and including Margaret's arms, her badges of the marguerite, rose and portcullis, and the opening words, *Nos Margareta* (We Margaret), were written in Margaret's own hand.[19] The statutes included stipulations concerning punishments and rewards for those who excelled, and from these we are able to glean further insights into what was important to Margaret. For example, she stated that 'There are three things which we desire all the Fellows of this College to care for above all things, namely, the worship of God, the increase of the faith, and probity of morals.'[20] When visiting Christ's on one occasion, Margaret peered out of a window, where she saw the dean punishing one of his students. Leaning out of the window, Margaret exclaimed: '*Lente, lente!*' (Gently, gently!). Another point that she clearly specified was that the souls of her son and grandchildren ought to be prayed for, as well as her own, both during and after life. Prayers were also to be said for the souls of Edmund Tudor, 'my husband and father of the King my Son', her parents, Elizabeth of York, Henry VI, his wife and son, William Byngham, and John Broklee, another significant benefactor.[21]

Margaret treated her patronage with the utmost seriousness, and intended to extend it as far as possible. Fisher would later record that she 'builded a college royal to ye honour of ye name of Christ Jesus, and left to her executors another to be built to maintain his faith and doctrine'.[22] In truth, in 1508 it was Fisher who had informed Margaret of the poor state of the Hospital of St John the Evangelist in Cambridge. She in turn intended to transform the hospital into a college that would be able to support fifty scholars, but this was no easy feat. In order to refound a religious house as another institution, the permission of the Bishop of Ely was necessary. Given that the Bishop was Margaret's stepson, James Stanley, this did not appear to present too great a problem, and he readily agreed. However, thanks to a series of delays, the matter would not be settled in Margaret's lifetime, and it was only after her death that St John's College was founded in 1511 – pushed through by Fisher, who retained the utmost admiration for Margaret, as we have seen, extolling her many virtues and remaining loyal to her memory. The college later attracted the interest of Katherine of Aragon, who had perhaps been inspired by her grandmother-in-law. As at Christ's, symbols of Margaret's patronage can be seen all over St John's. Her consideration and enthusiasm for her foundations is an accurate reflection of her personal interest in education, but she took this to a greater level and several steps further than any of her female predecessors, aided by her wealth, position and the contacts that these brought her. Her passion and energy for her foundations can be seen throughout her accounts, as can her generous nature. Margaret's determination to create a lasting legacy for herself as a patroness of learning was built into the very fabric of Cambridge – in the bricks and mortar of Christ's and St John's – so successfully that it is still remembered in both colleges today.

AFTER 1505 MARGARET began to spend less time at Collyweston, and more at Hatfield and Croydon, which lay closer to London.[23] She even borrowed the former Yorkist stronghold of Fotheringhay Castle for a brief spell. None of these properties was owned by her: the red-brick palace at Hatfield had been built by Morton in 1480 and was to become the home of the bishops of Ely – Margaret's stepson, James Stanley, later owned it upon his appointment in 1506, while Croydon, built between 1443 and 1452, was a residence of the Archbishops of Canterbury. Here, Morton had also made various improvements, and much of his work is still in evidence. Following his death, it became the property of William Warham. Clearly, though, Margaret felt at home in properties that were owned by churchmen. During Margaret's residency – as at Hatfield – she took care to ensure that it was filled with all of her luxurious home comforts, and she paid for various improvements. For example, she arranged glazing and plumbing work at Croydon, while at Hatfield items featuring her portcullis were scattered throughout the house, along with cloths of estate made of purple velvet, black velvet and cloth of gold. There was also a sumptuous crimson satin bed embroidered with gold portcullises, and another of white damask.[24] Many of the pieces from her beautiful tapestry collection were displayed here, depicting scenes from the Bible and mythology. Items found in the closet next to her bedchamber included powder boxes and a purse with cramp rings used for the relief of ailments, two pairs of gold spectacles, an image of the Salutation of our Lady, a pair of Spanish gloves and an indenture containing the details of Margaret's jointure from Stanley.[25] As was the case in all of her residences, life was conducted on a luxurious scale, and copious amounts of food and wine were ordered for consumption at Hatfield. It would not be long before Margaret's skills as a hostess were called upon once more, and in a most important capacity.

In January 1506, Philip of Castile and his wife Juana – sister of Katherine of Aragon – were sailing to Spain in order to take possession of the Castilian throne when they were caught in a storm.[26] They were shipwrecked off the Dorset coast, and had no choice but to depend upon the hospitality of Henry VII. Henry's accounts note a reward given to a man that 'brought the King word of the landing of strangers in the West Country', and when he heard of Philip's arrival, Henry immediately gave orders for a lavish welcome to be prepared for his guests.[27] Underneath it all, however, he saw an opportunity. In her usual desire to be kept abreast of affairs, Margaret had a report prepared describing Philip's reception, which still survives among her papers.[28]

Philip began making his way towards Windsor, where the King rode to meet him a mile outside of the town. As the party travelled towards the castle, Henry had ensured that there was a due level of ceremony, and Margaret's step-grandson the Earl of Derby – who had succeeded her late husband to the title – carried the sword of state before the King. Henry's guest was then treated to an opulent display of hospitality, and the entertainments included a dance performed by Princess Mary and the court ladies. But the King was determined to turn the unexpected visit to his advantage. In July 1501, Edmund de la Pole, Earl of Suffolk – brother of the Earl of Lincoln who had been killed at Stoke in 1487 – had gone into voluntary exile with his younger brother, Richard.[29] The brothers had travelled to Flanders, where Suffolk had hoped to enlist the support of the Emperor Maximilian in order to make a bid for the throne. He had received some support, including from Sir James Tyrell and the King's own brother-in-law, William Courtenay. Tyrell had been executed on 6 May 1502, while Courtenay and Suffolk's youngest brother, William, had been thrown into the Tower.[30] But Suffolk and his brother had remained at large, for Henry had been unable to reach them. By 1506, however, Suffolk was the guest of Philip of Castile, and with the King now effectively his prisoner, Henry seized on his opportunity. On 9 February the two monarchs signed a treaty, under the terms of which Philip agreed to extradite Suffolk and his brother back to England. He was also created a Knight of the Garter, for which the King paid a London goldsmith for providing an elaborate collar.[31] The following day, Philip's wife Juana, who had travelled separately from her husband and at a slower pace, reached Windsor. Soon though, the party travelled to Richmond to provide Henry with an opportunity to dazzle his guests with his splendid new palace. Determined that his mother ought not to be left out, he issued orders for Margaret to arrange a sumptuous entertainment for them at Croydon.[32]

In her usual consummate manner, Margaret prepared to play her role. In April she summoned her ten-year-old granddaughter Princess Mary – already growing into a beauty – to join her, her servants conveying the Princess from Richmond. When the royal party – which included her grandson Prince Henry – arrived, Margaret had prepared a lavish feast. The entertainment, though, was actually provided by Philip's entourage. A performance by his musicians ensued, perhaps in the magnificent Great Hall that had been installed in around 1452. There was also time for Margaret to present her grandson with a generous gift of a new horse, which had been dressed with a magnificent new saddle made of cloth of gold. What Margaret's impressions of Philip and Juana were can only be imagined, but Katherine of Aragon would no doubt have appreciated the opportunity to be reunited with her sister. In a deliberate ploy to prevent her from complaining to Juana about her treatment, however, there was little time for this. Likewise, the visit of her sister and brother-in-law placed her future in jeopardy, for Philip discussed the possibility of several marriages with Henry. One of these was between Prince Henry and Philip's daughter, Eleanor, while another was suggested with Princess Mary and Philip's son, Charles.[33] This was probably an arrangement of which Margaret heartily approved, for marriage to the leading European dynasties provided an effective way of strengthening and securing the future of her own family.

Soon after their visit to Croydon, Philip and Juana sailed for Spain on 16 April. Philip had been true to his word, Suffolk having arrived back on English soil the previous month – an occasion Margaret noted in her Book of Hours. He was immediately taken to the Tower, where – as with Simnel, Warbeck and Warwick before him – Henry intended to treat him with relative leniency. He was not executed, but would remain locked up for the rest of Henry's reign. Unfortunately for Suffolk, Margaret's grandson felt differently, and in 1513 the Earl met his end on the executioner's block.[34] His younger brother Richard, meanwhile, remained at large, and was killed at the Battle of Pavia in 1525.[35] William de la Pole remained in the Tower until his death in 1539.

IN THE LATER years of Henry's reign, as he grew older, he exhibited an increasing desire for privacy and began to seclude himself in his apartments as far as was possible. He had also become very suspicious, and with good cause given that he had spent the entirety of his reign deflecting the threat posed by rival contenders to the throne. Both he and Margaret employed spies to ensure they would get to hear of any subversive plots and be able to deal with them swiftly. The death of both Prince Arthur and Elizabeth of York in swift succession had served to highlight the fragility of the royal family, and Margaret was just as eager to secure the Tudor dynasty as Henry was. This was even more pertinent given that Henry's health was becoming progressively fragile.

At New Year 1507, Margaret had become aware that her son's health was in decline; it had in fact been failing for some time. As early as 1504, Henry had complained to Margaret of problems with his eyesight, but early in 1507 he became so unwell that it was feared he would not live. For six days he was so sick with quinsy that he was unable to eat or drink. Margaret's role as a mother was always her foremost priority, and she immediately moved to Richmond to nurse him. She began ordering medical supplies, and took charge of paying the King's servants – she even went as far as purchasing black materials in preparation for mourning. So she was greatly relieved, although perhaps somewhat surprised, when he rallied. By the autumn, indeed, so good was his recovery, Henry had resumed the pastimes of which he was so fond, including hunting. One who was not so fortunate was Margaret's former sister-in-law, Cecily, who died on 24 August.[36] Margaret had long been fond of Cecily, whom she had known since the latter had been a child and supported through the storm caused by Cecily's marriage to Thomas Kyme. So saddened was Margaret by her death that, determined to ensure that her memory was honoured according to her rank, she contributed towards the costs of Cecily's funeral.

Henry VII's recovery was only temporary, for by now he was suffering from what was probably consumption. In 1508 he fell sick once more, and by now the emphasis was firmly on the next generation: in particular, Margaret's grandson Prince Henry was emerging as the shining star of the Tudor court. In June 1507, the Prince reached his sixteenth birthday, and that month Margaret watched proudly as he participated in his first joust. It had been she who had ordered his first saddle and harness to mark the occasion, and she was doubtless delighted – although anxious – to see him taking such pleasure in a sport about which he was passionate.[37] The following year she would also send him a gift after he had been 'running at the ring'.[38] Prince Henry brought a young and vibrant energy to the court of his ailing father, and was extremely popular. With the future of his dynasty hinging on the life of just one son, however, the King kept his son on a tight lead and in close proximity. This inevitably led to friction between father and stifled teenage son, who yearned to break free. He would not have long to wait.

By Christmas 1508, more marriage negotiations appeared to be moving towards a happy conclusion. Though Philip of Castile had died in the autumn of 1506 – months after his visit to England – negotiations for the marriage of his heir, Charles, to Princess Mary had continued.[39] On 17 December the marriage by proxy was staged: from now on Mary was to be addressed as the Princess of Castile.

In February 1509, the King once more lapsed into illness. He had been staying at Hanworth, but preparations were put in place for him to return to Richmond as swiftly as possible. He quickly grew worse, and word was sent to his mother at Coldharbour.[40] Margaret, in spite of the fact that she herself was in fragile health, once again rushed to be by his side. She hurried to Richmond, arranging for her belongings – which included her favourite bed, to follow her – and anxiously prepared to nurse Henry once more. But she may have been aware that the end was approaching, for the King was suffering from tuberculosis. The realization that her son was going to die before she did must have been hard to bear. There had been just thirteen years between them, but all of his life she had striven to protect him, supporting him in adversity and revelling later in his glory. She had missed out on most of his childhood and adolescence; now, for the second time, he was about to be taken from her – this time permanently. In a sermon preached after his death, Fisher wrote of the piety that Henry had displayed in his final days. Margaret, who would almost certainly have witnessed this first-hand, would have been proud and probably overwhelmed with emotion. As Fisher recalls, at one point in the sermon 'all that stood about him scarcely might contain them from tears and weeping'.

On 21 April, the King heard mass for the last time. Later that day, he slipped from life into death at the age of fifty-two. Margaret was left utterly devastated.

CHAPTER 24

A Woman Most Outstanding

B Y THE END of March, Henry had known that he was dying. While he was still able, the ailing King dictated his final will, and it was a characteristically detailed document. Unsurprisingly, Henry requested that he be laid to rest in the spectacular new Lady Chapel that he was creating in Westminster Abbey. He wanted to be buried among his relatives, and made particular reference to his royal grandmother, Katherine of Valois, who lay close to the Lady Chapel with Henry V. He left thorough instructions for the creation of his tomb, which he was to share with his deceased wife, Elizabeth of York. It was intended to be a celebration of the Tudor dynasty that they had created together, but it was not begun until 1512. When it came to overseeing his wishes, true to form there was one person who Henry could be sure would fulfil all of his requests to the best of her ability. At the top of the King's list of executors was 'our dearest and most entirely beloved mother Margaret Countess of Richmond', who was to be assisted by the Archbishop of York, the Bishop of Winchester, John Fisher, and many others.[1] For the last time, Henry put his trust in Margaret by relying on her to honour his memory even after his death. It was a task that Margaret – as with everything relating to her son – would do her utmost to fulfil.

Henry VII's achievements, though often overlooked, ought not to be underestimated. Through his marriage to Elizabeth of York, he had largely succeeded in uniting a country that was torn and divided by war and faction. Together they had created a new dynasty, and England was starting to prosper. The royal coffers were full, and at his death the Venetian envoy reported that Henry had 'accumulated more gold than that possessed by all the other Christian kings'.[2] All of this passed into the hands of his heir – Margaret's grandson – who succeeded his father as Henry VIII. In order to organize matters and ensure his smooth succession, the late King's death was initially kept a secret. But there was little to fear. Henry VIII would become the most famous monarch of the Tudor dynasty, and he was from the start exceptionally popular. Vergil wrote that 'everybody loved him', and in appearance he was very like his grandfather Edward IV, being both tall and comely.[3] A Venetian envoy concurred, declaring that the new King was 'liberal and handsome', as opposed to his father, whom he described as being 'a most miserly man but of great genius'.[4] This was, of course, not quite true, but there was no denying the heartfelt enthusiasm expressed for young Henry.

At the time of his accession, Henry VIII was just a couple of months short of his eighteenth birthday. Though many would have considered him old enough to reign by himself, he was legally still a minor: he would have to wait a few short weeks more. It was therefore left to his formidable grandmother Margaret to take up the reins of government and act as regent on Henry's behalf. This was never an official post, but nevertheless Margaret was determined to ensure that her grandson's accession was as smooth as possible: she need not have worried. In spite of her sex, Margaret had earned the utmost respect and admiration of those who had served on her son's Council and at court. Everyone was aware of her abilities and of Henry's VII's implacable faith in her, and for a brief time she held sway over her grandson's realm: for the first time, Margaret was officially recognized in her role of uncrowned queen.

In the aftermath of her son's death, as her body continued to weaken, Margaret knew that she would not be around to support her grandson for long. Her foremost concern was therefore to ensure that men whom he could trust, and who would act in the best interests of England and her family, surrounded him. Unsurprisingly, most of these were men whom Margaret and her son had relied upon, and included John Fisher, her illegitimate cousin Charles Somerset (formerly Beaufort and now also Baron Herbert), and Richard Fox, Bishop of Winchester. Margaret was careful to confirm that these men knew what was expected of them. Another of the Council's first acts was to order the arrest of the King's hated tax collectors, Richard Empson and Edmund Dudley. Their methods had been harsh, and Henry's subjects had loathed them as a result. Margaret may have actively encouraged their arrest, for Dudley had once crossed her in a deal over property.[5] They were executed on 17 August 1510.

Much of Margaret's time, however, was spent in arranging her son's funeral: the bill, settled in July, amounted to an exorbitant £8,474 4s 6d (£5,640,000). The late King's executors signed the warrants, at the head of which was Margaret, who, in her usual style, signed herself Margaret R. It was recorded that the King's embalmed body was brought 'out of the privy chamber to the great chamber and rested there three days, on each day three masses and dirges being sung by a mitred prelate; then carried to the hall for three days with like services; then to the chapel for three days'.[6] Among the expenses were hangings of black cloth, many of which were allotted for the use of the King's servants. Included amid the recipients of these hangings were Margaret's ladies, among them Lady Jane Guildford. Jane had grown up in Margaret's own household with her brother Nicholas Vaux, and not only served Elizabeth of York, but had also been appointed governess to Margaret's granddaughters.[7] Margaret's chamberer, 'Perrot the French woman' – Perrot Doryn – was also incorporated.[8] Money was set aside for alms and livery provided for the mourners. The funeral procession was elaborate. The late King's coffin was moved from Richmond to St Paul's, where Bishop Fisher preached a mass and a sermon on 10 May; 'which sermon was printed at the special request of the right excellent princess Margaret, mother unto the said noble prince'.[9] The following day, the coffin was removed to Westminster, where the funeral service and burial were to take place. There, the King's household broke their staves of office and cast them into the grave, before departing for 'a great and sumptuous feast'.[10]

Though the contract for Henry's tomb was not signed until 26 October 1512, the result following its completion in 1518 was, as he had anticipated, magnificent. A splendid black marble tomb-chest adorned with the bronze-gilt effigies of Henry and Elizabeth of York dominates the Lady Chapel, surrounded by a brass screen.[11] A fitting monument to the first king and queen of the new dynasty.

AT THE BEGINNING of May, Margaret travelled by water from Richmond to the Tower, where her grandson was in residence. She was delighted when, on 19 May, he granted his grandmother her former palace of Woking, which is likely to have been at her own request.[12] As she returned to the home she had loved so dearly though, it would be for the last time.

Within a matter of weeks after his accession, the young King had resolved to wed, declaring his intention to marry his brother Arthur's widow, Katherine of Aragon – five years his senior. There is no reason to believe that Henry's decision met with anything other than Margaret's approval. Whether she had any influence in her grandson's choice is unclear, but the decision was certainly popular. Henry would later claim that his father, on his deathbed, had ordered him to marry Katherine. For the Spanish Princess, it brought all of the uncertainty of the last few years to a welcome end. In stark contrast to the celebrations that had marked Katherine's marriage to Arthur, the wedding was to be a small and private affair. On 11 June, Henry and Katherine were married at Greenwich, and preparations were put in place for their joint coronation. It is unclear whether Margaret was present to witness her grandson take his marriage vows – she had been at Greenwich three days earlier, so it is possible – but she was certainly there to see what came next, much of which had been arranged at her command.

On 24 June the crowds were out in force to celebrate the coronation of Henry VIII and Katherine of Aragon. It was a magnificent affair for which huge sums had been outlaid, and the people of London cheered rapturously as the royal couple passed through the streets of the city. The royal couple were bedecked in the costly materials that Margaret's son and daughter-in-law had worn when they celebrated their marriage years earlier, and Margaret had also outlaid a substantial sum on new garments.[13] Tawny velvet, satin and silk were to be worn by her and her ladies for the occasion, as well as black bonnets, which had been bought especially.[14] In spite of her magnificent new clothes, Margaret – as she had done on previous occasions – once again watched the coronation celebrations in private. Joined by her granddaughter Princess Mary, she paid for the use of a house in Cheapside to watch as the royal couple processed from the Tower to Westminster.[15] By the same token, she privately observed the ceremony in Westminster Abbey, which was conducted by William Warham, Archbishop of Canterbury. Though she 'had full great joy' at her grandson's triumph, Fisher notes, not unsurprisingly given what we know of Margaret's character, that 'she let not to say that some adversity would follow'.[16] Henry's coronation was the third that Margaret had attended in the last three decades, and she had lived through the reigns of five monarchs prior to her grandson's accession. The usual celebrations and revelries ensued, and for several days afterwards there were 'tournaments and many sorts of games'.[17] Though Margaret partook in the traditional coronation banquet in Westminster Hall, she no longer had the energy for such entertainments; indeed, the coronation turned out to be the last occasion on which she would ever see her grandson.

In May, Margaret had reached her sixty-sixth birthday, and her health was extremely fragile. Fisher explained that she was fearful that, had she lived longer,

Her body daily should have waxen more unwieldy, her sight should have been darked, and her hearing should have dulled more and more, her legs should have failed her by and by. And all the other parts of her body waxed more crased every day, which things should have been matter to her of great discomfort.[18]

Margaret's poor health had probably been exacerbated by the death of her beloved son, but Vergil's claim that 'while all were revelling in joy and light-heartedness' she was 'seized by a sudden illness' is untrue.[19] The reality is that she had been ailing for some time. It may have been some form of food poisoning or similar that worsened Margaret's condition, for when recollecting the end of his mistress, Henry Parker claimed that during the recent coronation banquet she 'took her infirmity, with eating of a cygnet', which immediately made her incredibly sick.[20] Following her grandson's coronation, she retired to the abbot's house within Westminster Abbey.[21] Aware that she faced imminent death, the location was almost certainly a deliberate choice, reflecting both her desire to be buried close to her son, and her own connection with the abbey. She had striven for control in all aspects of her life; why should death be any different?

On 28 June, Henry VIII reached his eighteenth birthday and, with it, his majority. But it was clear that Margaret would not live to see him reign. In the same way that she had organized her life, so too had she long been prepared for her death. Fisher recalls that there were many present to witness how with 'her heart and soul she raised her body to make answer thereunto' as her end approached.[22] Margaret's great-nephew Reginald Pole – son of Lady Margaret Pole – would later claim that, as death drew close, Margaret was fearful for her grandson. She was, he said, worried that Henry would turn away from God, a comment that Pole probably made in light of subsequent events. In truth, Margaret had done all that she could in order to safeguard her grandson's future and his realm. Realizing that death was swiftly approaching, on 29 June she summoned

her ghostly father, being shriven and receiving the blessed sacrament of the alter, the bishop said mass before her, and as he lift up the precious host this worthy Lady expired, and so as she had honoured the blessed sacrament, even so the last thing that ever she saw as I do think was God.[23]

If Margaret really died as the bishop lifted the host, it was an appropriate end for the woman who had set so much store by her faith. As a result, Henry Parker believed that she 'is now joyful in that celestial court of heaven, where she shall be in eternal felicity for ever'.[24]

The reaction of Margaret's three surviving grandchildren to her death is unrecorded, but coming in such close proximity to that of their father it is likely to have hit them hard. Certainly, for others who had known her, it came as a great tragedy, and she was deeply mourned. Those in her household regretted that they *should forego so gentle a mistress, so tender a lady then wept they marvellously, wept her ladies and kinswomen to whom she was full kind, wept her poor gentlewomen whom she had loved so tenderly before, wept her chamberers to whom she was full dear, wept her chaplains and priests, wept her other true and faithful servants.*[25]

Fisher, in the sermon preached shortly after her death, went as far as to claim that

All England for her death had cause of weeping. The poor creatures that were wont to receive her alms, to whom she was always piteous and merciful. The students of both the universities to whom she was as a mother. All the learned men of England to whom she was a very patroness. All the virtuous and devout persons to whom she was as a loving sister, all ye good religious men and women whom she so often was wont to visit and comfort. All good priests and clerks to whom she was a true defenderess. All the noble men and women to whom she was a mirror and example of honour.[26]

Similarly, Vergil praised Margaret as being 'a woman most outstanding both in her pious love of God and charity to all men, and whose countless virtues each one of us may find it easier to admire than to analyse'.[27]

Margaret had been a wealthy woman, and typically had taken great care when it came to composing her will. She had worked on it over the course of many years, and among the executors, Margaret had appointed John St John, the son of her half-brother who had served as her Chamberlain since 1504. Bishop Fox was also included, as were former members of her household. But it was John Fisher, Margaret's trusted friend and chaplain, who had been tasked with the role of chief executor. He took the responsibility seriously, and would go to a great deal of trouble to ensure that Margaret's final wishes were met.

Fascinatingly, throughout her will she refers to herself as 'Princess': a final statement to the world about how she saw herself and how she wished to be remembered. She may not have worn a crown, but Margaret would ensure that she was remembered as royalty.

Unsurprisingly, Margaret's first thoughts were for the welfare of her soul. She also took great care to ensure that detailed instructions were left in regards to her wishes for her Cambridge foundations: 'the said Princess willed, that all her plate, jewels, vestments, altar cloths, books, hangings, and other necessaries belonging to her chapel in the time of her decease, and not otherwise bequeathed, should be divided between her said colleges of Christ and St John'. It was the responsibility of Edward Bothe, her master of the jewel house, to ensure that these goods were handed over to Dr Thomson, the Master of Christ's. The pieces bequeathed were rich indeed, and included crucifixes, a gold chalice, candlesticks, altar cloths, and mass books.[28] Other religious foundations were also left various items, including Wimborne Minster, Syon, the Charterhouse at Sheen, and the parish church at Collyweston.[29] Interestingly, Fisher, Henry Hornby and Lord Mountjoy purchased items such as carpets, pieces of tapestry and cloths of estate from Margaret's former collection, which were carefully noted in her inventories.[30] Additionally, Fisher had also been left various other pieces of plate by his former friend.

All of Margaret's bequests serve as testimony both to her generosity and to her staggering wealth. Even at her end she had been thinking of others, and she left instructions that on the day of her death alms to the sum of £133 6s 8d (£88,800) were to be distributed to the poor.[31] Her family were also to receive generous bequests, chiefly of jewels. The highest value of goods was naturally left to her grandson, the King, and included several gold cups, as well as books from her treasured library. Katherine of Aragon, Margaret, Queen of Scots and Princess Mary were also included, the latter of whom was bequeathed a gold cup garnished with precious stones and pearls decorated with white harts, on the horns of which were a long sapphire.[32] Neither were Margaret's friends and servants forgotten; many were left personal bequests that served perhaps to highlight the relationship that they had once shared with this extraordinary woman.

On 3 July, Margaret's body was moved from the abbot's house into

Westminster Abbey, where it lay in state within the abbey refectory until it could be buried. She had left detailed instructions in her will for her funeral, which was conducted with all of the pomp and ceremony that she had planned; black satin was provided for covering her coffin, and the total cost of the funeral came to £1,021 (£680,000).[33] Fisher composed and read the 'mourning remembrance' for 'the noble princess Margaret, Countess of Richmond and Derby, mother unto King Henry VII, granddame to our sovereign lord that now is, upon whose soul almighty God have mercy', extolling the manner in which Margaret had met her death and comparing her to a scriptural Martha.[34] Fittingly, it was published by Wynkyn de Worde, whom Margaret had patronized for the greater part of his career.

Margaret had left instructions for her burial in the magnificent Lady Chapel within Westminster Abbey, 'which is now begun by the said our most dear son'. On 23 November 1511, more than two years after her death, the contract for her tomb was signed. It was to be created by the Florentine sculptor Pietro Torrigiano, whose work would have an instrumental effect on Renaissance tombs and who was later responsible for the tomb of Henry VII and Elizabeth of York.[35] The commission was carried out with painstaking detail, as can be seen in the surviving accounts. In 1513 the Flemish painter Maynard Wewyck was paid 'for making the picture and image of the said lady', and many other payments were made besides.[36] Though it would take many years to complete the work, the result was stupendous: Margaret's intricately sculpted face was almost certainly modelled on a death mask, her features appearing unmistakeably lifelike. Many arms are displayed on the tomb in an indication of those with whom Margaret wished to be associated: Edmund Tudor and Thomas Stanley, Henry VII and Elizabeth of York along with the Royal Arms, Henry VIII and Katherine of Aragon, and Margaret's parents; there was also a shield – now lost – probably depicting the arms of her grandparents. On 27 December 1511, a payment of 20s (£650) was made to Erasmus for 'the epitaph about my lady's tomb', which was composed in Latin.[37] The Bilbao iron grill that surrounds her tomb was provided by St John's College, Cambridge, in grateful thanks to their patroness, and was completed in 1529 by the English smith Cornelius

Symondson. It was once beautifully painted, and featured coats of arms and other decoration that was personal to Margaret. Today, the tomb of the uncrowned queen is one of the masterpieces of Westminster Abbey and one of the most splendid examples of a Renaissance monument. It is a memorial that Margaret would have been proud of.

Margaret's legacy was enduring and worthy of celebration. She had used her wealth and her position to help improve the lives of others, her values being wrought in the stones of the Cambridge colleges that she founded and supported. In this vein she had worked to subsidize and patronize scholars, religious foundations and authors, in so doing often affording them opportunities that they may not have found elsewhere. She had been well loved and was well mourned by those who knew her: the poor to whom she had given alms and sustenance, the children of her chapel whose education she had paid for, her household who had served her devotedly, and her family whose interests she had always placed before her own. It had been hard won indeed.

Margaret had not only survived all of the obstacles that life had thrown at her and that could well have left her broken – she had thrived. The intelligent, generous and conscientious young woman who had grown in Bletsoe's tranquil security had never lost those personable qualities despite the numerous blows. She had instead used them to adapt to the unpredictable political climate in which she found herself, setting aside matters of ego and family loyalty that had felled many of her kin. She had learned quickly the need to be flexible where necessary, and had emerged as a woman of extraordinary determination and self-possession, capable of raising her son to be a King. Early life had taught her the perils of being a pawn, and she had worked hard to exercise control wherever she could. Setting aside matters of the heart, she chose husbands based on the advantages they could offer her and the protection they could provide, rather than on the basis of any sense of romance or attraction.

Having always found strength in her faith – likely instilled in her during the earliest days of her youth – it must have seemed as though God had truly blessed Margaret and her family, who had always been her primary consideration. She left behind her a dynasty that would be the most talked of in British history, whose foundations she had striven to instil, risking her life in the process. Yet Margaret, it would appear, never felt truly secure, being wracked throughout her life by anxiety, which in turn appears to have lent her boundless energy in pursuing security and stability for herself and her family. That energy was always tied to her deep love for her son, her 'dear heart', and the true love of her life. It is little wonder, therefore, that when Henry met his end, Margaret too – long plagued by ill health – drifted into death. But for all her worry and tragedy, she had succeeded in what she had set out to do, and so, as Bishop Fisher said upon her death: 'therefore we put aside all weeping and tears, and be not sad and heavy as men without hope. But rather we be glad and joyous.'[38]

The Tudor Legacy

AT THE TIME of Margaret's death, the world in which she had lived began to change rapidly. Many of these changes came at the instigation of her beloved grandson Henry VIII, and would have profound consequences for Margaret's family and many of those to whom she had been close. Not all would have been welcome to Margaret.

The accession of Henry VIII signified the beginning of a lively period at court, where entertainment and revelry revolved around the dazzling couple. In February 1510, Queen Katherine gave birth to a stillborn girl, but just months later – less than a year after Margaret's death – the Queen became pregnant once more. The realm erupted into celebrations when a son was born on New Year's Day 1511, immediately christened Henry in honour of his father. The Tudor dynasty begun by Margaret's son seemed set to continue. But such confidence would be short-lived. For the infant Prince Henry died just a month after his birth, and became one of five infants born to the royal couple who would not survive, leaving the future of the dynasty uncertain. The sole survivor of Henry and Katherine's marriage was a girl, Mary, born in 1516.

In Scotland, meanwhile, the life of Margaret's eldest granddaughter and namesake was destined to be turbulent. In 1513 the country found itself at war with England, and having led his army south to invade, Margaret's husband James IV was slain on 9 September at the Battle of Flodden, his forces defeated by her brother's army. Katherine of Aragon, who was acting as regent while her husband was in France, gave orders that the Scottish King's bloodied coat was to be sent to Henry VIII as a war trophy, and even contemplated sending the dead King's body. With his father's death, Margaret's one-year-old great-grandson succeeded to the Scottish throne as James V, leaving his mother at the head of a regency for as long as she remained a widow.[1] Yet Queen Margaret's life quickly spiralled out of control. The following year, she remarried on 6 August, taking as her second husband Archibald Douglas, Earl of Angus. This marriage not only alienated the Scottish nobles, but also ensured that Margaret lost her position as regent. Fleeing across the English border, in October 1515 she gave birth to a daughter at Harbottle Castle in Northumberland. The infant was called Margaret, and was raised largely at her uncle Henry VIII's court, where the fallen queen travelled to soon after recovering from her daughter's birth.

When Queen Margaret arrived in London, she was reunited not only with her brother, but with her younger sister Mary too. Mary's earlier betrothal to Charles of Castile had been dissolved in 1513, when Henry VIII believed that he had found a better match for his sister. Thus it was that on 9 October 1514, Mary was married to Louis XII of France. The marriage was hugely unappealing to the English Princess, who at eighteen was described as 'a nymph from heaven' with a lively and passionate nature. Her groom, by contrast, was 'a gouty old man' of fifty-two.[2] But it was not a match she would have to endure for long, for after just three months of marriage Louis died on 15 January 1515. It was probably in the middle of the following month that Mary took her future into her own hands. Eager to avoid another husband being thrust upon her, she was secretly married to Charles Brandon, Duke of Suffolk – a close friend and jousting companion of her brother. When the news was broken to Henry VIII, he was furious, but eventually, having agreed to pay a large fine, the couple were welcomed back to England in May. Mary was now Duchess of Suffolk, and spent much of her time at her brother's court.

Having spent more than a year in England, Queen Margaret was allowed in 1517 – after a reconciliation had been achieved with her son's regent, the Duke of Albany – to return to Scotland.[3] Over the next few years, however, matters ran far from smoothly, and in 1527 she was divorced from her husband and married for a third time the following year. Her groom was

Henry Stewart, Lord Methven, but in time Margaret tired of him and sought a further divorce. Although on this occasion her wishes were not granted, she set a precedent that her brother would seek to follow. By 1526 long-standing cracks in Henry VIII's marriage were magnified when the King fell in love. The object of his desire was Anne Boleyn, the daughter of an English knight and one of Katherine's ladies. The following year it became apparent that Henry's marriage was damaged beyond repair. Claiming that his lack of a legitimate son was God's judgement that his union with Katherine was unlawful, he began proceedings to have his marriage annulled on the basis that Katherine's marriage to his brother Arthur had been consummated. His intention was to marry Anne Boleyn instead, by whom he felt confident he could sire sons. Yet it was to be no simple process, and the events of the following six years would not only split the King's – and therefore Margaret's – own family, they would also divide the country. In so doing, the entire course of the monarchy changed permanently.

Henry VIII's desire to be rid of Katherine of Aragon, combined with the Pope's refusal to comply with Henry's demands, sparked the English Reformation, as Henry separated from the Catholic Church, instead declaring himself Head of the English Church. His actions were too much for many of his subjects – including some of Margaret's friends – to stomach. Margaret herself would have been undeniably horrified. So too would she have been appalled by the Dissolution of the Monasteries – many of which she had helped to support and were close to her heart.

In May 1533, Henry's Archbishop of Canterbury, Thomas Cranmer, declared his marriage to Katherine of Aragon to be null and void. Henry had already married Anne Boleyn, who was also pregnant with what her husband confidently believed to be a son. Margaret's youngest granddaughter, Mary, Duchess of Suffolk, made no secret of her sympathy for the plight of her sister-in-law. She was reported to have used 'opprobrious language' about Anne Boleyn, but this does not seem to have caused a permanent rift in her relationship with her brother. Notwithstanding this, her support for Katherine was destined to be tragically short-lived, for Mary's health was fragile. In June 1533, she died at Westhorpe Hall in East Anglia at the age of thirty-seven. She left behind two daughters, Frances and Eleanor, the former of whom became mother to the ill-fated Grey sisters.[4] They would later endure their own bitter tragedy at the hands of Margaret's great-granddaughters, the future Tudor queens Mary and Elizabeth. After a brief thirteen-day reign, Lady Jane Grey met a bloody end on the executioner's block on 12 February 1554, while her two younger sisters were victims of Elizabeth's wrath when they dared to marry without her consent – both were forced to endure imprisonment. Others were unfortunate enough to feel Henry's wrath when they refused to bend their conscience to his will. Margaret's good friend Bishop Fisher was one of those who refused to bow to the King's new authority as Head of the English Church. Having endured a harsh confinement in the Tower, Fisher was beheaded on Tower Hill on 22 June 1535. He was canonized in 1935.

Until her end, Katherine of Aragon refused to accept Archbishop Cranmer's judgement on her marriage, and having been banished from court she lived out the rest of her days in a series of uncomfortable houses. She died on 7 January 1536 at the age of fifty-one. Meanwhile, fate was about to deal Anne Boleyn a cruel hand. Despite Henry's hopes, she failed to provide him with a son, and of four possible pregnancies just one daughter survived. She was named Elizabeth. By the spring of 1536, Henry had tired of Anne, and having been accused of trumped-up charges of adultery and incest with her own brother, she met her end at the hand of an expert French swordsman on 19 May at the Tower.

It was not until 12 October 1537 that Henry was at last provided with a legitimate male heir. But it came at a price, for the experience cost his third wife, Jane Seymour, her life. He married three more times, but produced no further children. As with his father before him, the future of his dynasty rested on the life of a sole male heir.

Henry's dynasty, though, was better secured than that of James V, son of Margaret, Queen of Scots. James's first marriage to Madeleine of Valois had produced no children, and though he sired two sons by his second wife, Marie de Guise, tragically both died within a day of one another in April 1541.[5] His mother would not live to see the birth of his sole surviving heir, for on 18 October 1541 Queen Margaret died at Methven Castle in Perthshire.[6] On 8 December the following year, Marie de Guise gave birth to a daughter, Mary. Six days later, her father died, leaving the infant Queen of Scots born in the midst of decades of strife between England and Scotland. Things would not be fully settled until 1603.

On 28 January 1547, Henry VIII died, the latter part of his reign by no means mirroring the glory of the first. His nine-year-old son, Edward, succeeded him. Though a minor, Edward was a zealous Protestant, and continued the religious changes started by his father. But there was no time to ensure that their foundations were truly secure. When Edward died unmarried and childless at the age of fifteen in 1553, a brief power struggle saw Lady Jane Grey – appointed the King's Protestant successor – eventually lose her head for treason at the hands of another of Margaret's great-granddaughters, Mary I. The sole surviving child of Henry VIII's union with Katherine of Aragon, Mary – like her great-grandmother Margaret before her – was exceptionally pious. She immediately took steps to restore England to Catholicism, but her desire to produce a Catholic heir to succeed her did not bear fruit – her marriage to Philip of Spain was childless and unhappy. She died unpopular and alone on 17 November 1558.

Succeeded by her half-sister Elizabeth, it was through this daughter of Anne Boleyn that Margaret's dynasty arguably reached its zenith, somewhat fittingly, under the leadership of a woman. Elizabeth would die childless, for like Margaret before her she had decided that her fate would not be dictated by powerful men – she would be mistress of her own destiny. A royal *femme sole*, she in many ways emulated the earlier example of her great-grandmother, choosing in her case to do so without the support of a husband. It is Elizabeth who is remembered by history as one of the Tudor dynasty's most celebrated monarchs, often revered as 'the Virgin Queen'.

Elizabeth's death in March 1603 brought the Tudor dynasty – begun by Margaret's son in 1485 – to an end. But Margaret's family continued to reign, for the man who succeeded to the English throne was Margaret's great-great-great-grandson: James VI of Scotland and I of England.[7] For the first time, the two kingdoms were united, and they remain so to this day:

as a result, Margaret's bloodline endures likewise. Every English monarch since Henry VIII – meaning every British monarch since 1603, including Queen Elizabeth II – has been able to trace their descent from Margaret, as could her grandson, James V, across the border in Scotland.[8] It is a fitting and enduring legacy for the woman who had striven so hard to achieve a crown for her family.

So too is the elegy written in Margaret's memory by John Skelton on 16 August 1516:

> *Inspire my elegy, ye sacred nine,*
> *For pious Marg'ret mix your tears with mine.*
> *Within this pile a King's fam'd mother lies;*
> *Henry, who in yon stately edifice*
> *In splendour lives with many a noble peer,*
> *'Tis his grand parent lies inhumed here.*
> *Queen Tanaquil's exalted mind and birth,*
> *(Whom Livy's pen extolls 'bove all on earth)*
> *Fall short of Marg'rets; ev'n Penelope*
> *Was less renowned for chastity, than she;*
> *Prudent as Abigail, King David's wife;*
> *As Hester bold, in hazarding her life*
> *To plead her people's cause; resembling three*
> *The noblest Princesses in history.*
> *Reader, I pray, whoe'er thou art, thy tears*
> *For such a Princess offer, and thy prayers.*
> *Grief forbids more; To write I listless try,*
> *Since our great benefactress here doth lie,*
> *And all regard is lost for probity.*
> *For now to sing of death it scarce avails;*
> *Even death itself to startle sinners fails.*
> *D'you ask, what modern honour means? 'Tis this,*
> *Instead of virtue, 'tis lasciviousness.*
> *The virtuous die, it's true, but they shall rise*

Again to praise, and Charon's power despise.
Men now live, as they lift; nothing can dart,
Or make the least impression on their heart;
No sepulchres of Dukes, no monuments
Of Kings or Senators, no precedents
Of past or frequent funerals, have the power
T'affright the present age from sinning more.
To write what none will ever regard 'tis vain,
As Juvenal avers; so I'll refrain.
He that defaces, spoils, or takes away
This script, may Satan snatch him as his prey
Forthwith, and on him all his rage display.
Thou great illustrious ruler of the sky,
Who made the world and reigned eternally;
Gracious admit this Princess to thy throne,
Renowned for several virtues, like thy own.[9]

Following in Margaret's Footsteps – Places to Visit

Many of the homes that Margaret Beaufort once enjoyed and the palaces she frequented are sadly lost to us. However, some of the places – or fragments of them – in which the most momentous events of her life were staged are still extant, providing tangible glimpses into Margaret's world.

Lamphey Palace, Pembrokeshire

The home where Margaret spent most of her brief marriage to Edmund Tudor is now a romantic ruin. Nevertheless, it is still possible to stand in the roofless Great Hall and admire the impressive architecture. Similarly, the footprint of much of the palace survives, including the inner gatehouse and some of the domestic quarters.

Pembroke Castle, Pembrokeshire

The mighty stronghold where Margaret gave birth in the winter of 1457 is now a ruin, although much of the structure of the castle still remains. The Henry VII Tower survives, and until recently it has traditionally been cited as the place where Henry Tudor was born. This is, though, unlikely to be true.

Maxstoke Castle, Warwickshire

The castle that probably hosted Margaret's third marriage survives, and is now a privately owned home. Richard III deliberately slighted Maxstoke in 1484 in the aftermath of the Buckingham Rebellion, and Henry VII later granted it to Margaret. She undertook a programme of rebuilding at the castle, some of which can still be seen. It is occasionally open to the public.

Raglan Castle, Monmouthshire

Margaret herself did not live at Raglan, but her son Henry Tudor did when he became the ward of Sir William Herbert in 1462. Here he lived in comfort, for Herbert invested a vast sum on improvements to Raglan. Margaret and her husband Henry Stafford spent a week at Raglan when they visited Henry in 1467, and could not have failed to be impressed with the castle they saw. Raglan is now an impressive ruin, entered via a great gatehouse. It is still possible to get a flavour of the grandeur in which Henry Tudor lived, for much of the medieval fabric of the castle remains.

Woking Palace, Surrey

Most of Margaret's one-time-favourite home has now vanished, but it is still possible to gauge a sense of some of the tranquillity that so attracted her to Woking. A fourteenth-century barrel vault still stands, as does a small amount of a Tudor brick building that may have been a tennis court. The site has been subject to many excavations in recent years, which have uncovered some interesting finds. These include floor tiles and a beautiful hatpin.

Cambridge

The most tangible evidence of Margaret's presence in Cambridge comes in the form of the two colleges of her foundation: Christ's and St John's. Her symbols and rooms at Christ's have been discussed, and similar badges can be found scattered across St John's. Margaret's statue also adorns the main college gatehouse, while the archives house many of her papers. Margaret's full-length portrait by Maynard Wewyck can also be seen.

Westminster Abbey, London

Margaret's final resting place is still a place of worship as well as a major tourist attraction. Her splendid tomb lies in the south aisle of the Lady Chapel of her son's creation, as does the spectacular double monument of Henry

VII and Elizabeth of York. Likewise, the tombs of several of Margaret's ancestors and descendants can still be seen, including those of Elizabeth I and Mary, Queen of Scots. The magnificent Queen's Gallery contains many objects relating to Margaret, such as one of her travelling chests and the beautiful prayer book that she commissioned for Lord Stanley.

ABBREVIATIONS

Add MS   Additional Manuscript

BL   British Library

CCR   *Calendar of Close Rolls*

CPR   *Calendar of the Patent Rolls Preserved in the Public Record Office, 1476–1509*, 3 vols (London, 1901–16)

CSPS   *Calendar of State Papers, Spain*, G.A. Bergenroth *et al.* (ed.), 13 vols (London, 1862–1954)

CSPV   *Calendar of State Papers, Venice*, R. Brown *et al.* (ed.), 38 vols (London, 1864–1947)

L & P   *Letters and Papers, Foreign and Domestic, of the Reign of Henry VIII, 1509–1547*, J. Brewer *et al.* (ed.), 21 vols (London, 1862–1932)

SJLM   St John's College Archives, University of Cambridge

TNA   The National Archives

WAM   Westminister Abbey Muniments

Notes on Sources

1   Alice was the granddaughter of Margaret's half-brother, John St John. She was also a beneficiary of Margaret's will. One of Alice and Parker's daughters, Jane, married Anne Boleyn's brother, George, Viscount Rochford. Jane was executed in February 1542 alongside Katherine Howard for aiding and abetting the Queen's adulterous behaviour.

2   J. Fisher, 'Mornynge Remembraunce had at the moneth mynde of the Noble Prynces Margarete Countesse of Rychemonde and Darbye', available via Early English Books Online, p. 3.

3   N. Pronay and J. Cox (eds), *The Crowland Chronicle Continuations: 1459–1486* (London, 1986); See also H.T. Riley (ed.), *Ingulph's Chronicle of the History of Croyland* (London, 1854).

4   D. Mancini, *De Occupatione Regni Anglie per Riccardum Tercium*, trans. and ed. as *The Usurpation of Richard III*, C.A.J. Armstrong (2nd edition, Oxford, 1969).

5   D. Hay (ed.), *The Anglica Historia of Polydore Vergil* (London, 1950); H. Ellis (ed.), *Three Books of Polydore Vergil's English History* (London, 1844).

6   B. André, *The Life of Henry VII*, trans. D. Hobbins (New York, 2011).

Introduction

1   J.R. Lander, 'The Crown and the Aristocracy in England, 1450–1509', *Albion*, 8:3 (1976), p. 213.

2   N. Williams, *The Life and Times of Henry VII* (London, 1973), p. 110.

3   In 1965 Margaret formed the subject of Betty King's novel *The Lady Margaret*, which focused on the relationship between Margaret and her second husband, Edmund Tudor. It was portrayed as a great love story that resulted in the birth of Henry Tudor. *The King's Mother* followed this in 1969, which continued Margaret's story after Edmund's death. In the 1972 BBC series *The Shadow of the Tower*, Marigold Sharman played the role of Margaret. The series was extremely well received and showcased Margaret's relationship with her son. She was also portrayed as ambitious, and even ruthless when it came to the safety of her son and family. For example, in the penultimate episode Margaret can be seen urging her son to execute the Earl of Warwick in order to secure his own safety. Though it is possible that she did so, there is no contemporary evidence to support this.

4   S. Gristwood, *Blood Sisters* (London, 2012), p. 6.

Chapter 1: Noble Blood

1   In 1327 Bletsoe's then owner, John de Patishull, had received a licence to crenellate the house. The medieval Bletsoe Castle no longer survives, and instead a Grade II listed building now stands on the site it once occupied. Following the death of Margaret's mother,

it came into the hands of John St John, Margaret's half-brother. It passed through several generations of the St John family.

2 See M.K. Jones and M.G. Underwood, *The King's Mother: Lady Margaret Beaufort, Countess of Richmond and Derby* (Cambridge, 1992), p. 32, for the history of the book.

3 Fisher, 'Mornynge Remembraunce', p. 2.

4 The eldest of Edward III and Philippa's sons was Edward, the Black Prince. When Edward predeceased his father on 8 June 1376, his son, Richard, became the King's heir. The births of Lionel, Duke of Clarence, John of Gaunt, Edmund, Duke of York, and Thomas, Duke of Gloucester, followed that of the Black Prince. Additionally, four surviving daughters were born of the marriage.

5 Blanche was the younger daughter of Henry, first Duke of Lancaster and Isabel de Beaumont. She was married to Gaunt on 19 May 1359 at Reading Abbey. The couple also had two other sons, who died in infancy.

6 Blanche died on 12 September 1368 at Tutbury Castle, possibly as a result of the Black Death that raged through Europe in the mid-fourteenth century. Gaunt was heartbroken, and it was not until 21 September 1371 – three years after Blanche's death – that he remarried Constance. Constance's mother was María de Padilla, a Castilian noblewoman who had been Pedro's mistress before she became his wife.

7 The couple still managed to produce two children, of which one, a daughter named Catherine, survived infancy.

8 Alison Weir confirms that it is uncertain when the affair began, but it was certainly taking place by late spring 1372. A. Weir, *Katherine Swynford: The Story of John of Gaunt and his Scandalous Duchess* (London, 2007), p. 103. Katherine was the daughter of Sir Paon de Roët, although the identity of her mother is uncertain. Paon was a faithful servant of Queen Philippa, into whose household his daughter Katherine seems to have been placed at an early age. See Weir, *Katherine Swynford*, pp. 2–6.

9 Philippa became Queen of Portugal through her marriage to João I in 1387, and Elizabeth was later Duchess of Exeter.

10 Weir highlighted that every English monarch since 1461 is descended from Katherine, as well as no fewer than five American presidents. Weir, *Katherine Swynford*, p. 2.

11 Beaufort had been lost to the French in 1369. See Weir, *Katherine Swynford*, p. 111.

12 Constance was buried at great expense in the Church of St Mary in Leicester, where Blanche's father also lay entombed. Mary de Bohun, first wife of Gaunt's son Henry, who died within a few months of Constance, was also buried there. The church no longer survives. After an unsuccessful military campaign, Gaunt had also renounced his claim to the Castilian throne on condition that his daughter, Catherine, be married to the Trastámaran heir, Henry. In 1390 the couple became king and queen of Castile, and thus Gaunt's hopes for the throne were finally realized, albeit in a different form than he had originally anticipated. Catherine's marriage to Henry III produced three surviving children, including John II, King of Castile. Among John's children from his second marriage were Isabella, mother of Queen Katherine of Aragon.

13 Parliament Rolls of Medieval England, Richard II: January 1397.

14 Henry became a Cardinal and one of the most powerful men in England, Joan became Countess of Westmorland and produced a number of children who became involved in Margaret's story, while Thomas was a distinguished military commander.

15 H. Ellis (ed.), *Original Letters Illustrative of English History*, I (London, 1824–46), p. 164.

16 Gaunt was laid to rest beside his first wife, Blanche, in Old St Paul's Cathedral. Katherine Swynford outlived him, dying on 10 May 1403. She was buried in Lincoln Cathedral, where her tomb and that of her daughter, Joan, still survive.

17 Contemporary chroniclers provided conflicting reports as to the manner in which Richard

met his death: some suggested that he was deliberately starved to death, others that he refused all food, and some that he died by different means altogether. He was buried first at Kings Langley, but in 1413 his remains were moved to the tomb he had commissioned for himself in Westminster Abbey.

18 Margaret was the daughter of Thomas Holland, Earl of Kent, who was in turn the son of Richard II's mother, Princess Joan of Kent, from her first marriage.

19 CPR 1405–8, p. 284.

20 The hospital had been founded in 1147 by Queen Matilda, consort of King Stephen. Other medieval queens had also shown an interest in it, notably Philippa of Hainault.

21 John had previously been buried in the Trinity Chapel within the cathedral, as was Margaret Holland's second husband, Thomas, Duke of Clarence. However, following Margaret's death on 31 December 1439 at Bermondsey Abbey, a magnificent tomb was erected in St Michael's Chapel in memory of the two men, with Margaret lying between them.

22 The eldest daughter, Joan Beaufort, married James I of Scotland on 12 February 1424. When her husband was murdered in 1437, Joan attempted to assert her authority in the name of her son, James II. She was unsuccessful. The youngest Beaufort daughter, Margaret, married the Earl of Devon.

23 Henry Beaufort died during the siege of Rouen.

24 CPR 1436–41, p. 515.

25 Riley (ed.), *Ingulph's Chronicle*, p. 389.

26 Like his father, Thomas was buried in Canterbury Cathedral.

27 The Château de Vincennes still survives, as does the donjon in which Henry V died.

28 L. Kingsford (ed.), *Chronicles of London* (Oxford, 1905), p. 74.

29 Riley (ed.), *Ingulph's Chronicle*, p. 391.

30 Ibid, p. 398; CPR 1436–41, p. 515.

31 CPR 1436–41, p. 515.

32 Jones and Underwood, *King's Mother*, p. 27.

33 The identity of Tacyn's mother is unknown.

34 Fisher, 'Mornynge Remembraunce', p. 2.

35 Tombs of members of the Stourton family can still be seen in the church at Mere, Wiltshire.

36 Oliver St John was the heir of John St John by his wife, Isabel Paveley.

37 M.K. Jones, 'The Beaufort Family and the War in France, 1421–1450', unpublished PhD thesis (University of Bristol, 1982), p. 9.

38 TNA, C 1/24/230.

39 Jones stated that his position as the heir of the first Earl, and his closeness in blood to the Crown, made him a natural choice. See M. Jones, 'John Beaufort, Duke of Somerset and the French expedition of 1443', in R.A. Griffiths (ed.), *Patronage, the Crown and the Provinces* (Gloucester, 1981), p. 80.

40 Riley (ed.), *Ingulph's Chronicle*, p. 399.

41 N.H. Nicholas (ed.), *Proceedings and Ordinances of the Privy Council of England*, V (London, 1834–7), p. 252.

42 Ibid.

43 J. Benet, 'Chronicle for the years 1400–1462', ed. G.L. and M.A. Harriss, *Camden Miscellany*, XXIV, Camden Society, 4th series, 9 (1972), p. 21.

44 Riley (ed.), *Ingulph's Chronicle*, p. 399.

45 Somerset returned either to Corfe Castle, the main family home, or to Kingston Lacy. The ruins of Corfe can still be seen, the castle having been largely destroyed during the English Civil War. It was here that Edward the Martyr was murdered in 978. Kingston Lacy became a part of the royal Duchy of Lancaster in the fourteenth century and was visited by John of Gaunt. There is still a house at Kingston Lacy, now the property of the National Trust, but

it is the product of a later age.

46 Riley (ed.), *Ingulph's Chronicle*, p. 399.

47 See J.S. Davies (ed.), *An English Chronicle of the Reigns of Richard II, Henry IV, Henry V, and Henry VI* (London, 1856), p. 60.

48 The royal peculiar was abolished in 1846.

49 The Tudor traveller John Leland would later declare that Somerset 'lieth buried in a goodly tomb with his wife in the south side of the prebestry'.

50 I am indebted to Alison Weir for bringing this to my attention and for sending me some beautiful images of the likeness. See Fen Edge Archaeology Group website, www.feag. co.uk.

51 See TNA, E 135/3/21.

52 CPR 1441–46, p. 283.

Chapter 2: Of Singular Wisdom

1 S. Bentley, *Excerpta Historica or Illustrations of English history* (London, 1831), p. 4.

2 Fisher, 'Mornynge Remembraunce', p. 2.

3 Ibid.

4 Suffolk had been injured during the siege of Harfleur in 1415, while his father had died of dysentery. Just weeks later, Suffolk's brother – their father's heir – was killed at the Battle of Agincourt. In 1429 Suffolk was captured during the siege of Orléans, but he was ransomed the following year.

5 Chaucer had been married to Katherine Swynford's sister, Philippa, making their daughter a relative of Margaret's. At the time of her marriage to Suffolk, Alice had already been widowed twice. She had been married at the age of eleven to Sir John Philip, who died in 1415 while campaigning in France with Henry V. She later married Thomas Montacute, Earl of Salisbury. Neither of these marriages produced any children. Alice's magnificent tomb can still be seen in the church at Ewelme, Oxfordshire.

6 Fisher, 'Mornynge Remembraunce', p. 2.

7 CPR 1446–52, p. 1. Letters Patent dating from 16 September 1446 refer to the fact that Suffolk 'bought of late the keeping of Anne'. Anne was also the niece of Eleanor Beauchamp, the wife of Margaret Beaufort's uncle, Edmund.

8 Jones and Underwood, *King's Mother*, p. 38.

9 CPR 1441–6, p. 283.

10 Suffolk's great-grandfather was a wool merchant who had lent Edward III money. He rose in prominence and was knighted in 1339. Richard II later created his son Earl of Suffolk in 1385.

11 Ellis (ed.), *Three Books*, p. 156.

12 Ibid.

13 M.R. James (trans.), *Henry the Sixth: A Reprint of John Blacman's Memoir* (Cambridge, 1919), p. 27.

14 Ibid.

15 H. Maurer, *Margaret of Anjou: Queenship and Power in Late Medieval England* (Woodbridge, 2003), p. 77.

16 Blacman, *Memoir*, p. 29.

17 Margaret's mother was Isabella, the daughter of Charles, Duke of Lorraine.

18 A.R. Myers, 'The Household of Queen Margaret of Anjou, 1452–3', *Bulletin of the John Rylands Library*, 40:1 (1958), p. 86.

19 Henry VIII dissolved Titchfield Abbey, and although it was transformed into a grand Tudor

mansion by Thomas Wriothesley, it is now in ruins. Both Richard II and Henry V visited.

20 CSP Milan, I (26).
21 Images of Margaret survive in two contemporary manuscripts, a medal and a prayer roll.
22 T. Rymer (ed.), *Rymer's Foedera*, XI (London, 1739–45), p. 76. This ring later passed into the ownership of Henry VIII, where it is recorded in his 1530 inventory.
23 See Myers, 'Household of Queen Margaret', p. 87.
24 Blacman, *Memoir*, p. 29.
25 Gristwood, *Blood Sisters*, p. 12.
26 TNA, E 101/409/14, TNA, E 101/409/17, TNA, E 101/410/2, TNA, E 101/410/8, TNA, E 101/410/11.
27 Cardinal Beaufort died at Wolvesey Castle on 11 April, and was buried in Winchester Cathedral, where his tomb can be seen.
28 Eleanor was the widow of Thomas, Lord Roos. Amongst Eleanor and Somerset's children were Elizabeth, born the same year as Margaret Beaufort. Other children included the third and fourth dukes of Somerset.
29 Following Edmund's death, it was to Maxey Castle and the household of Margaret's mother that his widow fled. She would later marry one of Margaret Beauchamp's own servants, Walter Rokesley.
30 Tacyn married Reginald Grey, seventh Baron Grey of Wilton. The family resided in Bletchley in Buckinghamshire, where the tomb of Tacyn's father-in-law, Richard Grey, can still be seen in St Mary's Church. She died in 1494.
31 SJLM/1/1/2/1, f. 19; Jones and Underwood, *King's Mother*, p. 31. James I visited Bletsoe on several occasions as the guest of Lord St John. Domvile reported that on one such visit when James was hunting nearby, he asked to see the embroidery, hearing that his ancestress had created it. See Lady M. Domvile, *The King's Mother: Memoir of Margaret Beaufort, Countess of Richmond and Derby* (London, 1899), p. 8.
32 Fisher, 'Mornynge Remembraunce', p. 2.
33 Ibid.
34 WAM 5472, f. 33. On Margaret's orders, William Bailey was sent to return the books to the Duchess.
35 G. Ballard, *Memoirs of Several Ladies of Great Britain* (London, 1775), p. 13.
36 See Jones and Underwood, *King's Mother*, p. 184.
37 Fisher, 'Mornynge Remembraunce', p. 2.
38 C.A. Halsted, *Life of Margaret Beaufort, Countess of Richmond and Derby* (London, 1839), p. 18. The Duchess's lifestyle can be inferred from an epitaph that once adorned the tomb of Ralph Lannoy in Bletsoe Church, in which he was styled 'Cofferer and Keeper of the Wardrobe to the most noble Margaret, Duchess of Somerset'. Jones and Underwood have also drawn attention to the fact that the Duchess had a swan farmer by the name of David Philip, giving a further indication as to her lifestyle.
39 Calendar of Papal Registers, X, p. 245.
40 William Thorpe had built Maxey Castle in the 1370s.
41 The precise identity of John Neville has been difficult to pinpoint owing to the fact that there were several of that name during this period, but it is probable that he was a son of Ralph Neville, Earl of Westmorland, and his second wife Joan Beaufort – daughter of John of Gaunt and Katherine Swynford. He would therefore have been a cousin of Margaret's father.
42 Calendar of Papal Registers, IX, p. 579.
43 Ibid.
44 CPR 1446–52, p. 44.
45 Lord Welles was later buried beside Joan Waterton in St Oswald's Church, Methley.

His eldest daughter, Cecily Welles, married Sir Robert Willoughby and produced a son, Christopher Willoughby, Baron Willoughby de Eresby.

46 Riley (ed.), *Ingulph's Chronicle*, p. 400.
47 Parliament Rolls of Medieval England, Henry VI: November 1449.
48 Ibid.
49 Ibid.
50 Ibid.
51 Ibid.
52 J. Fenn (ed.), *The Paston Letters*, I (London, 1787), p. 39.
53 N. Davis (ed.), *The Paston Letters* (Oxford, 2008), p. 28.
54 Ibid.
55 There is no memorial to Suffolk, although the splendid tomb of his son John and his wife Elizabeth Plantagenet lies in the church.
56 Calendar of Papal Registers, X, pp. 471–4.
57 Ibid.
58 Ibid.
59 D. Seward, *A Brief History of the Wars of the Roses: The Bloody Rivalry for the Throne of England* (London, 1995), p. 7.

Chapter 3: A Marvellous Thing

1 D. Starkey (ed.), *The Inventory of King Henry VIII: The Transcript*, trans. P. Ward (London, 1998), p. 238. A portrait of Henry V is also listed.
2 TNA, E 36/84; Blacman, *Memoir*, p. 36.
3 Blacman, *Memoir*, p. 36.
4 Ibid.
5 Fisher 'Mornynge Remembraunce', p. 2.
6 Ibid.
7 Ibid.
8 Ibid.
9 Ibid.
10 Ibid.
11 Ibid.
12 Parliament Rolls of Medieval England, Henry VI: October 1427.
13 Ibid.
14 Ellis (ed.), *Three Books*, p. 62.
15 Dating from 1385, the tomb that Gronw Fychan ap Tudur shares with his wife, Myfanwy, survives in St Gredifael's Church, Penmynydd. It originally stood in Llanfaes Friary, but was moved to St Gredifael's following the Dissolution of the Monasteries. The church also contains a window displaying the symbols of the Tudor family. The Welsh inscription translates as 'Unity is like a rose on a river bank, and like a House of Steel on the top of a mountain'. Part of the original fifteenth-century glass was destroyed by vandals in 2007, but has since been restored.
16 Hay (ed.), *Anglica Historia*, p. 5.
17 A.H. Thomas and I.D. Thornley (eds), *The Great Chronicle of London* (London, 1983), p. 173. A further son known as either Edward or Owen was also born, who later became a monk. In 1502 Henry VII's accounts record money for his burial. TNA, E 101/415/3, f. 98v. Vergil also referred to a daughter, although she is not mentioned in other contemporary sources.

18 Katherine of Valois was laid to rest in Westminster Abbey, near her husband Henry V. However, her tomb was destroyed in 1509 to make way for the Lady Chapel, and she remained unburied until 1878. During that time many visitors saw her corpse, including Samuel Pepys, who recorded his experience in his diary. Part of her funeral effigy can be seen in the abbey.

19 Blacman, *Memoir*, p. 30. The abbey is now in ruins but had many important links to Margaret's family. Elizabeth Chaucer became a nun at Barking in 1381 – she was a niece of Katherine Swynford, her parents being the poet Geoffrey and Katherine's sister, Philippa.

20 Rymer (ed.), *Rymers Foedera*, X, pp. 817–34.

21 Blacman, *Memoir*, p. 31.

22 Ibid.

23 Newgate had been built in 1188 but was rebuilt many times before it was finally demolished in 1904. Notable prisoners over the centuries included Ben Jonson, Daniel Defoe and William 'Captain' Kidd.

24 J.G. Nichols (ed.), *Chronicle of the Grey Friars of London*, Camden Society (London, 1851), p. 17.

25 Parliament Rolls of Medieval England, Henry VI: March 1453.

26 Ibid.

27 CPR 1452–61, p. 78.

28 TNA, E 404/69/145.

29 Clarendon is now a ruin, and lies in the grounds of Clarendon Park.

30 Benet, 'Chronicle', p. 35.

31 Kingsford (ed.), *Chronicles of London*, p. 163.

32 Somerset was also the Prince's godfather, as was the Archbishop of Canterbury, while the Duchess of Buckingham was his godmother.

33 A. Weir, *Lancaster and York: The Wars of the Roses* (London, 1995), p. 187.

34 R.A. Griffiths and R.S. Thomas (eds), *The Making of the Tudor Dynasty* (Gloucester, 1985), p. 41.

35 Fenn (ed.), *Paston Letters*, I, p. 81. His secretary was also sent to the shrine of St Edward the Confessor at Westminster Abbey to offer on his master's behalf.

36 Ibid, p. 83.

37 The order for his release was dated 5 February 1455 from Westminster. CCR 1454–61, p. 9.

38 The Parliamentarians largely destroyed Sandal Castle following a siege during the English Civil War in 1645. It now lies in ruins.

39 CSP Milan, I (23).

40 Ibid.

41 Benet, 'Chronicle', p. 38.

42 Ellis (ed.), *Three Books*, p. 96.

43 J. Gairdner (ed.), *Gregory's Chronicle, or the Historical Collections of a Citizen of London in the Fifteenth Century*, Camden Society (London, 1876), p. 198.

44 CSP Milan, I (23).

45 The abbey is the modern day St Albans Cathedral.

46 Gairdner (ed.), *Gregory's Chronicle*, p. 198.

47 CSP Milan, I (23).

Chapter 4: At War Together in Wales

1 This child was the future Henry V, born on 16 September 1386.

2 Jones and Underwood, *King's Mother*, p. 95.

3 SJLM/3/2/1.
4 In the seventeenth century, Oliver Cromwell's army desecrated St David's Cathedral, and in so doing caused damage to Edmund's tomb. It was not until 1873 that Thomas Waller restored the brass, which was originally created on the orders of Henry VII.
5 Parliament Rolls of Medieval England, Henry VI: July 1455.
6 CSP Milan, I (23).
7 Griffiths and Thomas, *Making of the Tudor Dynasty*, p. 43.
8   Parliament Rolls of Medieval England, Henry VI: July 1455.
9 Fenn (ed.), *Paston Letters*, I, p. 137.
10 Some parts of the ruins of Carmarthen Castle can still be seen, most substantially the gatehouse.
11 Although Caldicot Castle is a ruin, having been largely destroyed by the Parliamentarians in the seventeenth century, significant parts survive.

Chapter 5: My Good and Gracious Prince, King and Only-Beloved Son

1 The inscription on the tomb is as follows: 'Under this marble stone here enclosed resteth the bones of the noble Lord, Edmund Earl of Richmond, father and brother to kings; the which departed out of this world in the year of our Lord God, 1456, the third day of the month of November; on whose soul Almighty Jesu have mercy. Amen.'
2 N.H. Nichols (ed.), *Testamenta Vetusta*, I (London, 1826), p. 431.
3 André, *Life of Henry VII*, p. 10.
4 The keep still survives, although, like the rest of Pembroke Castle, it is now a ruin.
5 At least one person, John Whithorn, was incarcerated in the dungeon and starved to death over a land dispute in the fourteenth century.
6 The oriel window has not survived, although it is possible to see where it once was.
7 Although in the fifteenth century the new year did not officially begin until March, for the purposes of clarity and ease of use I have deemed it to start on 1 January in keeping with the Julian calendar.
8 André, *Life of Henry VII*, p. 10.
9 Westminster Abbey MS 39. Viscount Dillon presented the prayer book in 1923.
10 The Henry VII Tower still survives, and today contains a wax tableau depicting the scene of Henry Tudor's birth.
11 Williams, *Life and Times of Henry VII*, p. 12.
12 André, *Life of Henry VII*, p. 6.
13 Ibid., pp. 8–9.
14 Cited in C.H. Cooper, *The Lady Margaret: A Memoir of Margaret, Countess of Richmond and Derby*, ed. J.E.B. Mayor (Cambridge, 1874), p. 67.
15 I am extremely grateful to Suzanne Schuld, an experienced nurse, and her medical colleagues, for taking the time to share their thoughts on this matter. Similarly, to my mother, Sylvia Howard, a midwife with over thirty years' experience.
16 M. Jones, in P. Gregory, D. Baldwin and M. Jones, *The Women of the Cousins' War* (London, 2011), pp. 256–7.
17 André, *Life of Henry VII*, p. 11.

Chapter 6: Lady Stafford

1 Buckingham's royal blood stemmed from his mother, Anne of Gloucester, who was the daughter of Edward III's youngest son, Thomas of Woodstock. Buckingham's father, Edmund Stafford, was killed fighting for Henry IV at the Battle of Shrewsbury in 1403.

2 Anne, Duchess of Buckingham, and York's wife, Cecily Neville, were sisters.

3 E. Norton, *Margaret Beaufort: Mother of the Tudor Dynasty* (Stroud, 2010), p. 49.

4 CPR 1485–94, p. 95. Joan's husband, Philip, was described as the King's servant and was also rewarded. Husband and wife may have been members of Jasper Tudor's household.

5 Henry Stafford is believed to have been born in around 1425, but his precise date of birth is unknown.

6 Margaret was the fourth of Edmund Beaufort's surviving daughters. When her husband Humphrey died in 1458, Margaret later remarried Sir Richard Dayrell. Together they had a daughter, also named Margaret. The younger Margaret married James Tuchet, Baron Audley, who was later executed by Henry VII for his involvement in the Cornish Rebellion of 1497.

7 Anne was the daughter of Ralph Neville and Joan Beaufort.

8 See Jones and Underwood, *King's Mother*, pp. 143–4.

9 WAM 6660.

10 Jones and Underwood, *King's Mother*, pp. 143–4.

11 WAM 5472, f. 45.

12 Ralph Griffiths as referenced in Jones and Underwood, *King's Mother*, p. 41.

13 Norton, *Margaret Beaufort*, p. 53.

14 CPR 1452–61, p. 433.

15 E. Venables, 'Bourne: its Abbey and Castle', *Associated Architectural Societies, Reports and Papers*, 20 (1889), p. 5.

16 André, *Life of Henry VII*, p. 10.

17 Jones and Underwood, *King's Mother*, p. 40.

18 CPR 1452–61, p. 545.

19 Eccleshall Castle was largely destroyed during the English Civil War, but was rebuilt at the end of the seventeenth century. It is now a private residence.

20 CSP Milan, I (38).

21 Pronay and Cox (eds), *Crowland Chronicle*, p. 111.

22 Mary had been married to James II of Scotland, who died on 3 August 1460 following the explosion of a piece of artillery during the siege of Roxburgh Castle. Mary acted as regent on behalf of the couple's son, James III, until 1463.

23 Pronay and Cox (eds), *Crowland Chronicle*, p. 111.

24 Weir, *Lancaster and York*, p. 252.

25 CSP Milan, I (54).

Chapter 7: Like a Fugitive

1 He was buried in the Grey Friars in Hereford, which no longer stands.

2 Gairdner (ed.), *Gregory's Chronicle*, p. 211.

3 Ibid. Leanda De Lisle has suggested that the mad woman could actually be the mother of Owen's illegitimate son, David. See L. De Lisle, *Tudor: The Family Story* (London, 2013), p. 25.

4 CSP Milan, I (71).

5 CSP Milan, I (91).

6   Weir, *Lancaster and York*, p. 284.

7   Riley (ed.), *Ingulph's Chronicle*, p. 426.

8   CSP Milan, I (79).

9   Gairdner (ed.), *Gregory's Chronicle*, p. 215.

10 CSP Milan, I (69).

11 P. Commynes, *Memoirs: The Reign of Louis XI 1461–83*, trans. M. Jones (London, 1972), p. 188.

12 T. More, *The History of King Richard III: A Reading Edition*, ed. G.M. Logan (Indiana, 2005), p. 5; Riley (ed.), *Ingulph's Chronicle*, p. 424.

13 Ellis (ed.), *Three Books*, p. 172.

14 More, *King Richard*, p. 5.

15 CPR 1461–67, p. 12. John married Constance Green, who was the daughter of Sir Henry Green. Little is known of their marriage, but they sired a son, Edward.

16 M. Jones and M. Underwood, 'Lady Margaret Beaufort', *History Today*, 35 (1985), p. 24.

17 CPR 1461–7, p. 30.

18 Ibid., p. 99.

19 Ibid., p. 100.

20 Henry Windsor to John Paston, cited in K. Dockray, *Edward IV: A Source Book* (Stroud, 1999), p. 28.

21 Weir, *Lancaster and York*, p. 308.

22 Parliament Rolls of Medieval England, Edward IV: November 1461.

23 Margaret, Countess of Shrewsbury, is another notable example.

24 Parliament Rolls of Medieval England, Edward IV: November 1461.

25 CPR 1461–7, p. 114.

26 Raglan Castle is now a spectacular ruin.

27 The outcome of Formigny was a French victory, during which many of the English were taken prisoner.

28 Anne was born in around 1430, and had three other siblings. Her family's lands were largely in Herefordshire.

29 They would sire at least ten children, many of whom made prestigious marriages. Herbert also had several illegitimate children, from one of whom the line of the current earls of Pembroke are descended; William would marry Mary Wydeville, sister of Queen Elizabeth Wydeville, and later Richard III's illegitimate daughter, Katherine. He also served in the household of Richard's son, Prince Edward. Walter was wed to Anne Stafford, the daughter of Henry Stafford's nephew, Henry, Duke of Buckingham.

30 Nichols (ed.), *Testamenta Vetusta*, I, p. 305.

31 Commynes, *Memoirs*, p. 354.

32 CPR 1485–94, p. 332.

33 André, *Life of Henry VII*, p. 11.

34 Ibid., p. 10.

35 Ibid., pp. 10–11.

36 CPR 1461–7, pp. 212–13.

37 In the seventeenth century, Sir George Buck would claim that the title of Richmond was conferred upon Clarence because the King 'was in great mislike of the young Earl of Richmond, Henry Tudor', but there is no evidence to confirm this. See G. Buck, *The History of King Richard III*, ed. A.N. Kincaid (Gloucester, 1982), p. 18.

38 Griffiths and Thomas, *Making of the Tudor Dynasty*, p. 61.

39 C. Ross, *Edward IV* (London, 1975), p. 65.

40 Jones and Underwood, *King's Mother*, p. 45.

41 C.L. Scofield, 'Henry, Duke of Somerset, and Edward IV', *English Historical Review*,

21:82 (1906), p. 300.

42 Ibid., pp. 301–2.

43 Somerset was buried in Hexham Abbey, which, though dissolved in 1537, still stands.

44 Commynes, *Memoirs*, p. 188.

45 Among them were Arthur Plantagenet, and Grace, who later attended Elizabeth Wydeville's funeral.

46 Ross, *Edward IV*, p. 84.

47 Bona's sister, Charlotte, was Louis's second wife. They were both daughters of Louis, Duke of Savoy, and his Cyprian wife, Anne.

48 Mancini, *Usurpation*, p. 61.

49 The name Wydeville is variously spelt and commonly appears as Woodville.

50 Jacquetta was the daughter of the Count of St Pol, and had been married to Bedford in 1433. She had married Richard Wydeville in secret in early 1437.

51 Mancini, *Usurpation*, p. 61. This former husband was Sir John Grey, who had been killed fighting for Margaret's own house of Lancaster at the Second Battle of St Albans in 1461.

52 Ibid.

53 Ibid.

54 Ibid.

55 J.O. Halliwell (ed.), *A Chronicle of the First Thirteen Years of the Reign of King Edward the Fourth, by John Warkworth* (London, 1839), pp. 3–4; cited in Dockray, *Edward IV*, p. 47.

56 Mancini, *Usurpation*, pp. 61–3.

57 Halliwell (ed.), *Warkworth's Chronicle*, pp. 3–4.

58 CSP Milan, I (138).

59 Blacman, *Memoir*, p. 43.

60 Ibid., p. 41.

Chapter 8: A Long Gown for My Lord

1 The fishponds can still be seen today.

2 SJLM/4/2/2; TNA, PROB 11/7/2.

3 R. Poulton and G. Pattison, *Woking Palace* (Woking, 2017), p. 1.

4 P. Arnold and R. Savage, *Woking Palace: Henry VIII's Royal Palace* (Woking, 2011), p. 7.

5 Ibid., p. 20.

6 Gilpyn remained at Woking until his death in 1500. He was buried in St Peter's Church, although the plate that once adorned his tomb no longer survives.

7 See WAM 5472, f. 5r for example.

8 Bray was born in around 1440, the son of a surgeon from Worcester; see WAM 5472 and WAM 5479 for numerous receipts and expenses kept by Bray; WAM 32377 for Bray's later receipts and charges on Margaret's lands.

9 Katherine later joined the household of Elizabeth of York. She died in 1508 and was buried with her husband in St George's Chapel, Windsor.

10 WAM 5472, f. 45r.

11 Ibid., f. 43r.

12 SJLM/1/1/3/2, f. 107.

13 WAM 5472, f. 40r–v.

14 Ibid., ff. 5r–6r.

15 WAM 12185, f. 104. Mortlake Palace was owned by the Archbishops of Canterbury, and was visited by monarchs frequently in the medieval period. It no longer survives.

16 Henry Bourchier was created Earl of Essex soon after Towton. His heir, William, married

Anne Wydeville. John Bourchier also served as Constable of Windsor Castle.

17 Walter Blount came from a family of Derbyshire origin. As a result of his first marriage to Helena Byron, Blount had six children. He was made a Knight of the Garter in 1472, and his stall plate can be seen in St George's Chapel, Windsor. He also stood as godfather to Elizabeth of York.

18 WAM 5472, f. 5r. The Mitre was a famous London inn, mentioned in Samuel Pepys' diary.

19 Ibid. This was John Arundel, who had become Bishop of Chichester in 1459. He died in 1477 and was buried in Chichester Cathedral. Other entries in Stafford's accounts show that they were both rowed to Lambeth on one occasion, while on another Margaret was conveyed to Westminster. WAM 5472, f. 5v.

20 Jones and Underwood, *King's Mother*, p. 141.

21 Ibid., pp. 157–8.

22 Prior to the move, the Duchess's servants are known to have visited Woking.

23 At this time Elizabeth was the widow of William, Baron Zouche, who had died in 1462. Before the end of 1471, Elizabeth had remarried, taking as her second husband John Scrope, Baron Scrope of Bolton.

24 WAM 12181, f. 52.

25 The ruins of Crowland Abbey can still be visited.

26 Fisher, 'Mornynge Remembraunce', p. 7.

27 WAM 6658.

28 WAM 12185, f. 39.

29 CSP Milan, I (162).

30 The ruins of Denbigh Castle are still extant; Gairdner (ed.), *Gregory's Chronicle*, p. 237.

31 Ibid.

32 Jones and Underwood, *King's Mother*, p. 48.

33 Ibid., p. 140.

34 WAM 12186, f. 42; Jones and Underwood, *King's Mother*, p. 47.

35 Commynes, *Memoirs*, p. 188.

36 In his will Pembroke requested that he be buried in Abergavenny, but he was instead interred in Tintern Abbey. He also reminded his wife to 'take the said order that ye promised me as ye had in my life, my heart and love'. TNA, PROB 11/5/430.

Chapter 9: Divine Prophecy

1 WAM 5472, f. 43r.

2 Ibid., f. 41v.

3 Queen Elizabeth's father, Earl Rivers, and her younger brother, Sir John Wydeville, had gone to ground after hearing of the Yorkist defeat at Edgecote, but Warwick's men caught up with them at Chepstow. There was to be no mercy, and on 12 August both men were executed at Kenilworth Castle.

4 H. Owen and J.B. Blakeway, *A History of Shrewsbury*, I (London, 1825), p. 248.

5 Corbet's wife was Elizabeth Devereux, daughter of Sir Walter Devereux, Anne Herbert's brother.

6 Walter was loyal to the house of York, and – in spite of his sister's connection to Henry Tudor – fought for Richard III at the Battle of Bosworth in 1485. He was killed during the battle, and was attainted soon after. The ruins of Weobley Castle can still be visited. Following Henry VII's accession it became the property of Sir Rhys ap Thomas, who spent heavily on improvements.

7 WAM 5472, f. 44v.

8 Ibid., f. 43v.

9 Ibid., ff. 46r–47v. See also M. Hicks, *False, Fleeting, Perjur'd Clarence: George, Duke of Clarence, 1449–78* (Gloucester, 1980), p. 45.

10 See M.K. Jones, 'Richard III and Lady Margaret Beaufort: A Re-assessment', in P.W. Hammond (ed.), *Richard III: Loyalty, Lordship and Law* (London, 1986), p. 34.

11 Having fought for Edward at Hexham, John was already a recipient of his favour. In 1472 he was made a Knight of the Garter.

12 Richard Welles had been married first to Joan, a niece of Thomas, Earl of Salisbury, which explains their inclusion in the Salisbury Roll. He later married Margery Ingelby.

13 Parliament Rolls of Medieval England, Edward IV: June 1467.

14 CPR 1461–7, p. 357.

15 The private feud was with Sir Thomas Burgh, during the course of which Burgh's house was destroyed.

16 Norton, *Margaret Beaufort*, p. 88.

17 WAM 12184, f. 48r.

18 CPR 1467–77, p. 294.

19 As the party approached Calais, Lord Wenlock, who was in command, had received orders to refuse them entry. Commynes reported, 'instead of welcoming him they fired several cannon shots at him'. Their ship was therefore forced to remain out of port, and before long the Duchess of Clarence went into labour. The birth was riddled with complications, and though the Duchess survived, her baby son did not. Commynes, *Memoirs*, p. 182.

20 CSP Milan, I (189).

21 CSP Milan, I (196).

22 Hastings was unswervingly loyal to Edward IV, but he was also married to Warwick's sister, Katherine.

23 CSP Milan, I (197).

24 Ibid.

25 More, *King Richard*, p. 76.

26 Commynes, *Memoirs*, p. 187.

27 Ibid., p. 189.

28 André, *Life of Henry VII*, p. 11.

29 Ibid.

30 Ibid.

31 Ibid., p. 12.

32 WAM 12183, f. 19r–v; Tunstall had remained with Henry VI during his exile in Scotland, and had been attainted in 1461.

33 André later recalled that Henry VI had counselled his nephew to flee abroad 'so that he might escape the fierce hand of the enemy', but André's chronology had probably become confused with a later point. See André, *Life of Henry VII*, p. 12.

34 Expenses incurred throughout this short trip included firewood for Henry's chamber at Maidenhead, new horseshoes and horses. Four were needed for Margaret to complete the last leg of the journey.

35 Following his accession to the throne, there are a number of references to the playing of cards in Henry's accounts. In 1494, for example, 40 shillings were outlaid for the King's losses at Windsor. See BL, Add MS 7099, f. 14.

36 Griffiths and Thomas surmise – almost certainly correctly – that this is likely to have been the last occasion on which Margaret saw Henry before he fled abroad in 1471. See *Making of the Tudor Dynasty*, p. 69.

37 WAM 12183, f. 25r.

38 Hicks, *Clarence*, pp. 84–5.

Chapter 10: Heaven Protects him who has No Burial Urn

1 Commynes, *Memoirs*, p. 195.
2 Ibid.
3 WAM 12189, f. 58r.
4 Commynes, *Memoirs*, p. 194.
5 H. Ellis (ed.), *Original Letters Illustrative of English History*, I (London, 1825), pp. 140–1.
6 Kingsford (ed.), *Chronicles of London*, p. 183.
7 Thomas and Thornley (eds), *Great Chronicle of London*, p. 213. On 21 April 1471, Edward IV granted Lady Scrope a pardon on account of her Lancastrian sympathies. This was doubtless in grateful thanks for her services to his wife. CPR 1467–77, p. 258.
8 Halliwell (ed.), *Warkworth's Chronicle*, p. 16.
9 Commynes, *Memoirs*, p. 195.
10 Pronay and Cox (eds), *Crowland Chronicle*, p. 125.
11 Kingsford (ed.), *Chronicles of London*, p. 184.
12 CSP Milan, I (213); both men were later taken to Bisham Priory for burial.
13 Pronay and Cox (eds), *Crowland Chronicle*, p. 127.
14 Ibid.
15 Ibid.
16 Today the sacristy door in Tewkesbury Abbey is covered with the plates of armour from slaughtered Lancastrians.
17 There are numerous accounts of the Prince's death, the *Arrival of King Edward IV* claiming that Edward was 'fleeing to the town wards, and slain, in the field'. Commynes also stated that he was killed on the battlefield, while a later source wrote that 'there was slain in the field, Prince Edward, which cried for succour to his brother-in-law the Duke of Clarence'. By contrast, the *Great Chronicle of London* claimed that Edward was captured and taken before Edward IV. There, the fallen Prince, making a remark that was 'contrary his pleasure, the king smote him on the face with the back of his gauntlet', and he was killed soon after by one of the King's servants.
18 The Beaufort brothers were both ceremonially reinterred in Tewkesbury in December 1488.
19 Weir, *Lancaster and York*, p. 408.
20 Commynes, *Memoirs*, p. 196.
21 Kingsford (ed.), *Chronicles of London*, pp. 184–5.
22 She was buried in Angers Cathedral, although there is no monument.
23 Ellis (ed.), *Three Books*, p. 156.
24 André, *Life of Henry VII*, p. 19.
25 More, *King Richard*, p. 12.
26 Dockray (ed.), *Three Chronicles*, p. 38.
27 Pronay and Cox (eds), *Crowland Chronicle*, p. 131.
28 Halliwell (ed.), *Warkworth's Chronicle*, p. 21.
29 Weir, *Lancaster and York*, p. 409.
30 Ellis (ed.), *Three Books*, p. 154.
31 André, *Life of Henry VII*, p. 12.
32 Ibid.
33 Ibid., p. 13.
34 Ibid.
35 Ibid.
36 Ibid., p. 14.
37 Ellis (ed.), *Three Books*, p. 155.

38 André, *Life of Henry VII*, p. 14.
39 Ibid. Francis was the son of Richard of Brittany and Margaret of Orléans. Richard was the youngest son of Duke John IV of Brittany, and though both his elder brothers succeeded their father, neither had a living male heir at the time of their deaths. Thus, in 1458, Francis succeeded his uncle.
40 Ellis (ed.), *Three Books*, p. 155.
41 Ibid.
42 TNA, PROB 11/7/2.
43 Ibid.
44 Ibid.
45 No monument survives, but in the church today there are two altar tombs, one of which may have belonged to Stafford's parents.

Chapter 11: Grace and Favour of the King's Highness

1 Le Ryall once stood on the site now occupied by the College of Arms; Jones and Underwood, *King's Mother*, p. 144. These three ladies were Elizabeth Johnson, Jane Atkins and Elizabeth Denman.
2 Joan was the daughter of Sir Robert Goushill. Henry IV had knighted Robert for his bravery following the Battle of Shrewsbury in 1403. The tomb he shares with his wife, Elizabeth Fitzalan, can be seen in St Michael's Church in Hoveringham, Nottinghamshire.
3 The wedding took place in 1451 at Middleham Castle. The marriage was successful in personal terms, producing eleven children, although eight of these died young. The three that survived were all sons: George, Edward and James. George was well favoured by both Edward IV and Henry VII; Edward was a soldier who played a prominent role at the Battle of Flodden; James became Bishop of Ely.
4 This was Joan Strange, whose mother, Jacquetta Wydeville, was the Queen's sister.
5 Jones and Underwood, *King's Mother*, p. 40; Westminster Abbey MS 39. This object is the only surviving artefact relating to Margaret and one of her husbands.
6 Jones and Underwood suggest that this may have been Knowsley, one of Stanley's main residences near Liverpool. They also clarify that the marriage took place between the creation of Margaret's first will on 2 June, and the arrangement of the marriage settlement, which was staged on 12 June. See *King's Mother*, p. 59; Knowsley still stands, but is the product of the eighteenth century.
7 J. Lewis, 'Lathom House: The Northern Court', *Journal of the British Archaeological Association*, 152:1 (1999), p. 150. A fireback from Knowsley emblazoned with Margaret's arms still survives. See J. Hoult, *The Vill, Manor and Township of Knowsley* (Liverpool, 1930), p. 32.
8 Cited in Lewis, 'Lathom House', p. 150.
9 Derby House was destroyed during the Great Fire of London.
10 See C. Skidmore, *Bosworth: The Birth of the Tudors* (London, 2013), p. 98.
11 In around October 1472, the two had been taken to Suscinio, a chateau at Sarzeau that was used as a summer palace by the dukes of Brittany. After about a year, they were moved to Nantes. Following their separation, Jasper was taken to Josselin, which still stands, as does Largoët.
12 Griffiths and Thomas, *Making of the Tudor Dynasty*, p. 90.
13 Commynes, *Memoirs*, p. 354.
14 Ibid., p. 237.
15 Ibid., p. 353.

16 André, *Life of Henry VII*, p. 20.

17 Ibid.

18 TNA, E 36/207; A.R. Myers, 'The Household of Queen Elizabeth Woodville, 1466–7', *Bulletin of the John Rylands Library,* 50 (1967–8), pp. 207–15.

19 Princess Mary was fourteen when she died in 1482. The two who died in infancy were Margaret, who was born and died in 1472, and George. He was born in 1477 and died in 1479.

20 L. Toulin Smith (ed.), *John Leland's Itinerary in England and Wales in or about the years 1535–43*, I (London, 1964), p. 5. One piece of stonework and a mound are all that survive of Fotheringhay Castle, which is best known as the place in which Mary, Queen of Scots, was executed in 1587. Anne was the first of Edward's siblings to be both at Fotheringhay, as were Margaret and Richard.

21 Ibid., p. 4.

22 Riley (ed.), *Ingulph's Chronicle*, p. 475.

23 Though the princesses are unnamed, they are likely to have been the two eldest, Elizabeth and Mary.

24 A.F. Sutton, L. Visser-Fuchs and P.W. Hammond (eds), *The Reburial of Richard, Duke of York, 21–30 July 1476* (London, 1996).

25 Riley (ed.), *Ingulph's Chronicle*, p. 475.

26 The York tombs were destroyed during the Reformation, but new ones were created around the altar on the orders of Elizabeth I.

27 Ellis (ed.), *Three Books*, p. 205.

28 Griffiths and Thomas, *Making of the Tudor Dynasty*, p. 83.

29 Mancini, *Usurpation*, p. 63.

30 Anne had been living in Clarence's household, and Croyland reported that the Duke had gone as far as to have her disguised as a kitchen maid in order to keep her from Gloucester. See Pronay and Cox (eds), *Crowland Chronicle*, p. 133; the Countess of Warwick had taken sanctuary at Beaulieu when she learned of the death of her husband at Barnet, and thus, although she was still alive, Clarence had taken control of all of her lands – her daughters' inheritance.

31 Isabel's child, Richard, died within months of his birth. Isabel was buried in Tewkesbury Abbey.

32 The suggestion to marry Mary had come from Clarence's sister, Margaret of Burgundy, who was her stepmother. Mary later married Maximilian, future Holy Roman Emperor. She was tragically killed at the age of twenty-five when she was thrown from a horse and broke her back; Mancini, *Usurpation*, p. 63.

33 Mancini, *Usurpation*, p. 63.

34 BL, Stowe MS 1047, f. 204v.

35 Duffy pointed out that there is no record of the Duchess's burial at Wimborne, and that in the nineteenth century it was claimed that she was buried in the church at Lydiard Tregoze. It was Margaret who was responsible for the commissioning of her parents' tomb at Wimborne, so there is no reason to believe that her mother was not interred there alongside her father. See M. Duffy, *Royal Tombs of Medieval England* (Stroud, 2011), p. 233.

36 Cited in Jones and Underwood, *King's Mother*, p. 60.

37 SJLM/4/4/2.

38 WAM 32378.

39 Pronay and Cox (eds), *Crowland Chronicle*, p. 149.

40 Margaret was the daughter of Mary of Burgundy, the lady whose hand the Duke of Clarence had previously coveted.

41 Mancini, *Usurpation*, p. 59; Riley (ed.), *Ingulph's Chronicle*, p. 483.

42 More, *King Richard*, p. 5.
43 Mancini, *Usurpation*, p. 59.

Chapter 12: A Boar with his Tusks

1   Ellis (ed.), *Three Books*, p. 172.
2   Pronay and Cox (eds), *Crowland Chronicle*, p. 155.
3   More, *King Richard*, p. 5.
4   Stanley laid siege to the border town of Berwick and succeeded in taking it.
5   Edward became known as Edward of Middleham, but his birthdate has been much disputed. Various dates between the end of 1473 and 1476 have been suggested.
6   More, *King Richard*, pp. 9-10.
7   Most notably, Richard's skeleton revealed that he suffered from severe scoliosis.
8   Mancini, *Usurpation*, p. 63.
9   Ibid., p. 71.
10 Ibid.
11 Ibid.
12 Ibid, p. 73.
13 Pronay and Cox (eds), *Crowland Chronicle*, p. 155.
14 Ibid., p. 75.
15 Mancini, *Usurpation*, p. 75
16 Buckingham and Katherine had two sons and two daughters. The eldest son, Edward, became the third Duke of Buckingham but was executed in 1521, while the second son, Henry, became Earl of Wiltshire and died in 1523. Elizabeth married the Earl of Sussex, and Anne married the Earl of Huntingdon.
17 Described by More as 'a right honourable man', Rivers had been supervising his nephew's education at Ludlow. More, *King Richard*, p. 18.
18 Pronay and Cox (eds), *Crowland Chronicle*, p. 157.
19 Ibid., p. 79.
20 Ibid., p. 81.
21 Ibid., p. 157.
22 K. Dockray, *Richard III: A Source Book* (Stroud, 1997), pp. 55–6.
23 Mancini, *Usurpation*, p. 91.
24 More, *King Richard*, p. 56.
25 Ibid., p. 57.
26 Ibid.
27 Hastings was buried in the chantry chapel that he himself had founded, which still survives. There is no effigy.
28 Mancini, *Usurpation*, p. 91.
29 More, *King Richard*, p. 57.
30 Ibid.
31 Ibid., p. 58.
32 Ellis (ed.), *Three Books*, p. 181.
33 Ibid., p. 182.
34 Mancini, *Usurpation*, p. 89.
35 More, *King Richard*, p. 39.
36 Mancini, *Usurpation*, p. 89.
37 Ibid.
38 Kingsford (ed.), *Chronicles of London*, p. 190.

39 More, *King Richard*, p. 48.

40 Thomas and Thornley (eds), *Great Chronicle of London*, p. 234.

41 Mancini, *Usurpation*, p. 93.

42 Ibid.

43 More, *King Richard*, pp. 48-9.

44 Pronay and Cox (eds), *Crowland Chronicle*, p. 159.

45 Ellis (ed.), *Three Books*, p. 183.

46 Today this passage, from *Wisdom of Solomon* 4:3, forms a part of what most Protestants term the Apocrypha, which is not included in the standard Bible. In 1483 it was, though, considered to be a part of the Latin Bible, and it was also included in the King James Bible. It is accepted in the list of Deuterocanonical books by the Roman Catholic Church.

47 More, *King Richard*, p. 77.

48 Eleanor Butler was the daughter of John Talbot, Earl of Shrewsbury. She was married to Thomas Butler, and died in 1468.

49 Edward, Earl of Warwick, had been born in February 1475 at Warwick Castle. Mancini says that Gloucester had summoned the ten-year-old boy to London, and 'commanded that the lad should be kept in confinement in the household of his wife'. See *Usurpation*, p. 89.

50 Ibid., p. 97.

51 Ellis (ed.), *Three Books*, p. 167.

52 More, *King Richard*, p. 13.

53 F. Bacon, *The History of the Reign of King Henry VII*, ed. Vickers, B. (Cambridge, 1998), p. 64. The Tudor chronicler Edward Hall also claimed that Margaret sought an alliance with Richard on her son's behalf. See H. Ellis (ed.), *Hall's Chronicle* (London, 1809), pp. 388–9.

54 Kingsford (ed.), *Chronicles of London*, p. 191.

55 A.F. Sutton and P.W. Hammond (eds), *The Coronation of Richard III: The Extant Documents* (Gloucester, 1983), p. 169. Other ladies included the Duchesses of Suffolk and Norfolk, and the Countesses of Surrey and Nottingham.

56 Ibid., p. 276.

57 Mancini, *Usurpation*, p. 101.

58 Sutton and Hammond (eds), *Coronation of Richard III*, p. 169.

59 Ibid., pp. 294–7.

Chapter 13: The Head of that Conspiracy

1 Mancini, *Usurpation*, p. 93.

2 J. Stow, *The Annales or Generall Chronicle of England* (London, 1615), p. 460.

3 Ibid.

4 More, *King Richard*, p. 98; Brackenbury had been appointed to this post on 17 July.

5 Ibid.

6 Pronay and Cox (eds), *Crowland Chronicle*, p. 161.

7 Tyrell's father had been executed in 1462 for his part in an alleged plot to kill Edward IV. He nevertheless remained a Yorkist, and was knighted at the Battle of Tewkesbury.

8 More, *King Richard*, p. 99.

9 Ibid.

10 A. Weir, *Elizabeth of York: The First Tudor Queen* (London, 2013), p. 99.

11 More, *King Richard*, p. 100.

12 Ibid.

13 Ibid. The skeletons of two children were discovered in the White Tower by workmen in 1674, and were widely believed to be those of the Princes. They were buried with full

honours in Westminster Abbey. More wrote that, at a later date, a priest of Sir Robert Brackenbury's 'took up the bodies again and secretly interred them'. Ibid., p.101

14 Ibid., p. 100.

15 He was executed on 6 May 1502 for aiding a Yorkist claimant to the throne, Edmund de la Pole, Duke of Suffolk.

16 See A. Weir, *The Princes in the Tower* (London, 1992).

17 Thomas and Thornley (eds), *Great Chronicle of London*, pp. 236–7.

18 André, *Life of Henry VII*, pp. 8, 20.

19 Nichols (ed.), *Chronicle of the Grey Friars*, p. 23; Commynes, *Memoirs*, p. 354.

20 Buck, *History of King Richard III*, p. 163.

21 Croyland describes them as having 'a specially appointed guard'. See Pronay and Cox (eds), *Crowland Chronicle*, p. 163.

22 Kingsford (ed.), *Chronicles of London*, p. 191.

23 The ruins of Brecknock can still be seen, but most of the castle was pulled down during the English Civil War.

24 More, *King Richard*, p. 105.

25 Ellis (ed.), *Three Books*, p. 194. See also Weir, *Princes in the Tower*, p. 148.

26 Weir, *Princes in the Tower*, p. 148

27 More, *King Richard*, p. 105.

28 Ellis (ed.), *Three Books*, p. 195.

29 Buck, *History of King Richard III*, pp. 63–4.

30 Commynes, *Memoirs*, p. 354.

31 Edward, Earl of Warwick, the son of the attainted Duke of Clarence, was a popular candidate. Likewise, John de la Pole, Earl of Lincoln, was the son of Richard III's sister, Elizabeth.

32 Ellis (ed.), *Three Books*, p. 195.

33 Ibid.

34 Ibid., p. 196.

35 Ibid.

36 Ibid., p. 189.

37 Ibid., p. 196.

38 Ibid. Thomas Ramney was later executed on Richard III's orders.

39 The Stanley family had supported Urswick through his education at Cambridge, and it is likely to have been through them that he met Margaret, whose household he joined in 1482. He would enjoy both her patronage and that of her son for the rest of his life. He died in 1522, and a drawing of the brass that once adorned his tomb in Hackney Church still survives.

40 Ellis (ed.), *Three Books*, p. 197.

41 Ibid.

42 André, *Life of Henry VII*, p. 20.

43 Pronay and Cox (eds), *Crowland Chronicle*, p. 163.

44 Jones and Underwood, *King's Mother*, p. 64.

45 Ellis (ed.), *Three Books*, p. 195.

46 Ibid., p. 204.

47 S.B. Chrimes, *Henry VII* (London, 1972), p. 21.

48 Commynes, *Memoirs*, p. 354.

49 Pronay and Cox (eds), *Crowland Chronicle*, p. 163.

50 Ellis (ed.), *Three Books*, p. 198.

51 A. Raine (ed.), *York Civic Records*, I, Yorkshire Archaeological Society (1939–41), pp. 83–4.

52 Kingsford (ed.), *Chronicles of London*, p. 191.
53 See P. Kibre, 'Lewis of Caerleon, Doctor of Medicine, Astronomer, and Mathematician (d. 1494?)', *University of Chicago Press on behalf of The History of Science Society*, 43 (1952), p. 102.

Chapter 14: Mother of the King's Great Rebel and Traitor

1   Welles had fled England in August when his property – Maxey – was seized; Richard succeeded to the title of Earl Rivers following the execution of his brother in 1483; Lionel was Bishop of Salisbury but died in around 1484; Edward had been appointed Admiral of the Fleet in the aftermath of Edward IV's death.
2   CPR 1476–85, p. 411.
3   Ellis (ed.), *Three Books*, p. 203.
4   Buck, *History of King Richard the Third*, p. 30.
5   Ellis (ed.), *Three Books*, p. 204.
6   Parliament Rolls of Medieval England, Richard III: January 1484.
7   Ibid.
8   Ibid.
9   Ibid.
10 Ellis (ed.), *Three Books*, p. 204.
11 BL, Add MS 12060, f. 22v.
12 Pronay and Cox (eds), *Crowland Chronicle*, p. 171; Ellis (ed.), *Three Books*, p. 210.
13 Ellis (ed.), *Original Letters*, I, p. 149.
14 Ellis (ed.), *Three Books*, p. 210.
15 Precisely when Elizabeth Wydeville left sanctuary is unknown, as are her whereabouts.
16 Ellis (ed.), *Three Books*, p. 210.
17 Ibid., p. 205.
18 Ibid.
19 Pronay and Cox (eds), *Crowland Chronicle*, p. 171. It was long thought that Edward was buried in the church at Sheriff Hutton, but the tomb once assumed to belong to him is now believed to represent another. His place of burial therefore remains uncertain, and the church at Middleham has also been suggested.
20 Ibid.
21 Richard did, however, have two illegitimate children: John of Gloucester and a daughter named Katherine.
22 M. Jones, '"For My Lord of Richmond, a *pourpoint* … and a palfrey": Brief remarks on the financial evidence for Henry Tudor's exile in Brittany 1471–1484', in L. Visser-Fuchs (ed.), *The Ricardian*, XIII (2002), p. 283.
23 Griffiths and Thomas, *Making of the Tudor Dynasty*, p. 117.
24 Ellis (ed.), *Three Books*, p. 205.
25 Ibid.
26 Ibid., p. 206.
27 In 1498 Charles died and was succeeded by his cousin, Louis XII. Louis married Margaret's granddaughter, Princess Mary, in 1514. He died three months later.
28 Anne would rule as regent until 1491, sharing power with her husband, Peter of Bourbon; Ellis (ed.), *Three Books*, p. 206.
29 Ibid.
30 Ibid., p. 207.
31 André, *Life of Henry VII*, p. 21.

32 Ellis (ed.), *Three Books*, p. 208.

33 J.O. Halliwell (ed.), *Letters of the Kings of England*, I (London, 1848), pp. 161–2.

34 Pronay and Cox (eds), *Crowland Chronicle*, p. 175.

35 Ibid.

36 Henry had not forgotten that his former guardian, William Herbert, had wished to marry him to his daughter, Maud. At some time in the 1470s, however, Maud had married Henry Percy, fourth Earl of Northumberland. At this time, she did have younger unmarried sisters, although Katherine, Anne, Isabel and Margaret all later wed.

37 Ibid.

38 See Weir, *Elizabeth of York*, pp. 121–42.

39 Pronay and Cox (eds), *Crowland Chronicle*, p. 175.

40 Ibid.

41 Anne was twenty-eight at the time of her death. In spite of the rumours, she almost certainly died of natural causes.

42 Pronay and Cox (eds), *Crowland Chronicle*, p. 175. No tomb was ever raised to her memory, but she was buried on the southern side of the High Altar.

43 Ibid.

44 Ibid.

45 J.O. Halliwell (ed.), *The Most Pleasant Song of Lady Bessy* (London, 1847), p. 2.

46 Ellis (ed.), *Three Books*, p. 212.

47 A.F. Pollard (ed.), *Reign of Henry VII from Contemporary Sources*, I (London, 1913), p. 4.

48 Ellis (ed.), *Three Books*, p. 209.

49 Oxford came from a strong Lancastrian background, and though Edward IV had initially treated him well, Oxford had repaid him by becoming embroiled in Lancastrian plots. In September 1473 he had taken control of St Michael's Mount in Cornwall, but he was forced to surrender the following February. He was imprisoned in Hammes Castle, and attainted in 1475.

50 Ellis (ed.), *Three Books*, p. 208.

51 André, *Life of Henry VII*, p. 22.

52 Commynes, *Memoirs*, p. 397.

53 Ibid.

54 Pronay and Cox (eds), *Crowland Chronicle*, p. 177.

55 Ibid.

Chapter 15: The Priceless Crown

1 Ellis (ed.), *Three Books*, p. 216.

2 Pronay and Cox (eds), *Crowland Chronicle*, p. 179.

3 Incidentally, Corbet was also the stepson of Stanley's brother, William. Corbet had been the result of his father's marriage to Elizabeth Hopton. Elizabeth was William Stanley's second wife, and they had wedded some time around 1471. The couple had a daughter, Jane.

4 David Owen had been born at Pembroke Castle in 1459, so it is plausible that Henry may have spent some time with him in the earliest days of his childhood.

5 Pronay and Cox (eds), *Crowland Chronicle*, p. 179.

6 Ibid.

7 Riley (ed.), *Ingulph's Chronicle*, p. 501.

8 Pronay and Cox (eds), *Crowland Chronicle*, p. 179.

9 Ibid. Savage continued in his support of Henry, but though he survived Bosworth, he was killed during the siege of Boulogne in 1492.

10 Ibid.

11 Gilbert Talbot was a younger son of the second Earl of Shrewsbury, who had been slain at the Battle of Northampton.

12 Ellis (ed.), *Three Books*, p. 218.

13 Hay (ed.), *Anglica Historia*, p. 75.

14 Ellis (ed.), *Three Books*, p. 218.

15 Ibid.

16 William Shakespeare, *Richard III*, Act V, Scene 3.

17 Robert Ferrers, second Earl of Derby, built the abbey in 1148. It only housed a small community, but was dissolved in 1538. Parts of it still survive; BL, Add MS 59899, f. 32r; TNA, E 36/215, f. 133. Thomas Penn pointed out that, in 1503, Henry paid for a stained-glass window depicting St Armel, the King's favourite Breton saint. This was in grateful thanks for his victory. See T. Penn, *Winter King: The Dawn of Tudor England* (London, 2011), p. 148.

18 Ellis (ed.), *Three Books*, p. 221.

19 Nichols (ed.), *Chronicle of the Grey Friars*, p. 24.

20 Pronay and Cox (eds), *Crowland Chronicle*, p. 179.

21 BL, Add MS 12060, f. 20r. Bygot had previously served Queen Anne Neville.

22 Pronay and Cox (eds), *Crowland Chronicle*, p. 179.

23 Ibid.

24 Ellis (ed.), *Three Books*, p. 221.

25 Pronay and Cox (eds), *Crowland Chronicle*, p. 181.

26 BL, Add MS 12060, f. 20r.

27 Pronay and Cox (eds), *Crowland Chronicle*, p. 181.

28 Ibid.

29 BL, Add MS 12060, f. 20r.

30 Pronay and Cox (eds), *Crowland Chronicle*, p. 181.

31 Ibid.

32 Ibid.

33 Cited in Dockray, *Richard III*, p. 123.

34 Ellis (ed.), *Three Books*, p. 224.

35 William was the father of Charles Brandon, Duke of Suffolk, later a close confidant of Margaret's grandson, Henry VIII. He also married Margaret's granddaughter, Princess Mary, following her marriage to Louis XII. Their granddaughters were the ill-fated Grey sisters.

36 Ellis (ed.), *Three Books*, p. 224.

37 Cited in Dockray, *Richard III*, p. 123.

38 Pronay and Cox (eds), *Crowland Chronicle*, p. 183.

39 Richard was also the last King of England to be killed in battle.

40 Ellis (ed.), *Three Books*, p. 226.

41 Pronay and Cox (eds), *Crowland Chronicle*, pp. 181–3.

42 André, *Life of Henry VII*, p. 8.

43 Ibid.

44 Commynes, *Memoirs*, p. 355.

45 Pronay and Cox (eds), *Crowland Chronicle*, p. 183.

46 Ibid.

47 Ellis (ed.), *Three Books*, p. 226.

48 Ibid. Richard's remains were discovered in September 2012 following excavations at the

site of the Greyfriars church in Leicester. In March 2015 they were reinterred at Leicester Cathedral.

49 BL, Add MS 7099, f. 30.
50 BL, Royal MS 2 A XVIII, f. 31v.
51 The Book of Hours is now in Lambeth Palace Library, MS 474. Richard also added his birthdate, 2 October, to the book.
52 Ibid.

Chapter 16: My Lady the King's Mother

1   BL, Royal 2 A XVIII, f. 32.
2   The Coronation Chair had been made for Edward I, and has been used at the coronation of every monarch since 1308. It is still on display in Westminster Abbey.
3   Fisher, 'Mornynge Remembraunce', p. 6.
4   Ibid.
5   André, *Life of Henry VII*, p. 31.
6   Hay (ed.), *Anglica Historia*, pp. 145–6.
7   CSPS, I, p. 123.
8   Cited in Cooper, *Lady Margaret*, p. 210.
9   She died on 25 June 1486.
10 André, *Life of Henry VII*, p. 33.
11 Bacon, *Reign of Henry the Seventh*, p. 32.
12 Ibid.
13 John Holland's brother, Thomas Holland, was the father of Margaret's grandmother, Margaret Holland.
14 Coldharbour once stood to the east of Cannon Street Station, but was destroyed during the Great Fire of London. An office block at 89 Upper Thames Street now stands on the site it once occupied.
15 See C.L. Kingsford, 'On Some London Houses of the Early Tudor Period', *Archaeologica*, 71 (1920–1), p. 26.
16 Ibid., p. 24.
17 TNA, E 404/79; Margaret had been born on 14 August 1473 at Farleigh Hungerford Castle in Somerset.
18 CPR 1485–94, p. 113; SJLM/9/1/1; Buckingham's chamber had a new door fitted. He was executed on charges of high treason on 17 May 1521 by Margaret's grandson, Henry VIII; Henry was created Earl of Wiltshire in 1510.
19 BL, Add MS 12060, f. 22v.
20 Fisher, 'Mornynge Remembraunce', p. 2.
21 TNA, E 40/3989.
22 His mother was Joan Hill. Somerset married Elizabeth, the daughter of William Herbert by Mary Wydeville; Jones and Underwood suggest that Somerset's change of name may have been in order for Henry VII to present himself as the true Beaufort heir. See *King's Mother*, p. 72.
23 Kibre, 'Lewis of Caerleon', pp. 102–3.
24 CPR 1485–94, p. 15. This grant took place on 23 September 1485.
25 Ibid., p. 67.
26 Ibid., p. 55.
27 Ibid., pp. 61, 45.
28 Parliament Rolls of Medieval England, Henry VII: November 1485, Part 1.

29 On 13 December he was also given the office of chief justice of South Wales. See CPR 1485–94, p. 47.

30 Ibid.

31 Parliament Rolls of Medieval England, Henry VII: November 1485, Part 1.

32 Ibid.

33 Ibid.

34 Ibid.

35 From 1464 Cecily had also begun styling herself 'queen by rights' in her letters. This was undoubtedly as a result of her husband's earlier claims.

36 See also S. Fisher, "'Margaret R": Lady Margaret Beaufort's self-fashioning and female ambition', in C. Fleiner and E. Woodacre (eds), *Virtuous or Villainess? The Image of the Royal Mother from the Early Medieval to the Early Modern Era* (Basingstoke, 2016).

37 Lewis, 'Lathom', p. 161.

38 Fisher, 'Mornynge Remembraunce', p. 3.

39 Parliament Rolls of Medieval England, Henry VII: November 1485, Part 1.

40 André, *Life of Henry VII*, p. 35.

41 BL, Royal 2 A XVIII, f. 28.

42 Stow, *Annales*, p. 472.

43 André, *Life of Henry VII*, p. 34.

44 TNA, E 36/210, f. 30, for an offering made at the tomb of Henry VI.

45 Ibid., f. 58.

46 CPR 1485–94, p. 128.

47 J.T. Rosenthal, *The Purchase of Paradise: The Social Function of Aristocratic Benevolence, 1307–1485* (London, 1972), p. 31.

48 CSPS, I, p. 178.

49 Ibid., p. 164.

50 SJLM/9/2/1.

51 Halliwell (ed.), *Letters of the Kings*, I, p. 181.

52 Hay (ed.), *Anglica Historia*, p. 7.

53 CSPS, I, p. 163.

54 Bacon, *Reign of Henry the Seventh*, p. 206.

55 M. Underwood, 'The Pope, the Queen and the King's Mother', in B. Thompson (ed.), *The Reign of Henry VII*, V (Stamford, 1995), p. 73.

56 Bacon, *Reign of Henry the Seventh*, p. 207.

57 Ibid., p. 42.

58 BL, Add MS 7099, f. 4; TNA, E 101/414/6, f. 73v; TNA, E 101/415/3, f. 72v.

59 E. Cavell (ed.), *The Heralds' Memoir 1486–1490: Court Ceremony, Royal Progress and Rebellion* (Donington, 2009), p. 98.

60 Cecily Neville lived in quiet retirement following Henry VII's accession. She died on 31 May 1495 at Berkhamsted Castle. In her will, Cecily bequeathed Margaret 'a portuos with claspes of gold covered with blacke cloth of golde'.

61 Fisher, 'Mornynge Remembraunce', p. 2.

62 R. Olson, 'Margaret Beaufort, Royal Tapestries, and Confinement at the Tudor Court', *Textile History*, 48 (2017), p. 237; J. Leland, *Antiquarii de Rebus Britannicis Collectanea*, ed. T. Hearne, IV (London, 1612), pp. 179–80.

63 BL, Add MS 4712, ff. 3–22.

64 Leland, *Collectanea*, IV, pp. 179–80.

65 BL, Royal 2 A XVIII, f. 32.

66 Bacon, *Reign of Henry the Seventh*, p. 44.

67 André, *Life of Henry VII*, p. 36.

68 Leland, *Collectanea*, IV, p. 2; André, *Life of Henry VII*, p. 37.
69 Leland, *Collectanea*, IV, p. 205.
70 Ibid., p. 206.
71 Ibid., p. 207.

Chapter 17: Preservation of Your Most Noble and Royal Estate

1 Parliament Rolls of Medieval England, Henry VII: November 1485, Part 1.
2 Cavell (ed.), *Heralds' Memoir*, p. 117; Parliament Rolls, Henry VII: November 1487. The name has been much disputed, and it is improbable that 'Lambert Simnel' was his real name. Simnel was described as being ten years old.
3 Hay (ed.), *Anglica Historia*, p. 13.
4 It has been suggested that Lincoln's appointment to this post may have signified Richard regarded Lincoln as his heir.
5 Hay (ed.), *Anglica Historia*, p. 19.
6 That same year there was talk of arranging a marriage for Elizabeth with James III of Scotland, who had been widowed following the death of his wife, Margaret of Denmark, in 1486. The plans came to nothing as a consequence of James's death in 1488; Neville, *Henry VII*, p. 60.
7 Cavell (ed.), *Heralds' Memoir*, p. 109.
8 Margaret had been born at Fotheringhay Castle on 3 May 1446. On 3 July 1468 she was married to Charles the Bold of Burgundy at Damme in modern-day Belgium. They would have no children, and Charles died in 1477. Margaret never remarried.
9 Hay (ed.), *Anglica Historia*, p. 17.
10 Ellis (ed.), *Original Letters*, I, pp. 19–20.
11 Halliwell (ed.), *Letters of the Kings*, I, p. 171.
12 Ibid.
13 Fisher, 'Mornynge Remembraunce', p. 6.
14 Cavell (ed.), *Heralds' Memoir*, pp. 110–11.
15 Ibid., p. 110.
16 Hay (ed.), *Anglica Historia*, p. 25; Cavell (ed.), *Heralds' Memoir*, p. 118. The heralds' account states that Lovell was 'put to flight'; p. 118.
17 Vergil claimed that Simnel was still alive in 1534. Richard Symonds was imprisoned for life, and only evaded execution because he was a priest.
18 BL, Royal 2 A XVIII, f. 30.
19 Cavell (ed.), *Heralds' Memoir*, p. 128.
20 Their union was seemingly very happy, but though two daughters, Elizabeth and Anne, were born to the couple, neither survived.
21 Richard's father was Sir Geoffrey Pole. Margaret Pole's biographer, Hazel Pierce, stated that Geoffrey was a councillor of Jasper Tudor's, so he may also have had some hand in the marriage. See *Margaret Pole, Countess of Salisbury 1473–1541: Loyalty, Lineage and Leadership* (Cardiff, 2003), p. 15.
22 Jones and Underwood, *King's Mother*, p. 82.
23 Anne's wedding took place on 4 February 1495 at Westminster Abbey. Sadly, the only child born of the marriage died in 1508, and Anne herself died on 22 November 1511. Her husband later became the third Duke of Norfolk and uncle to Anne Boleyn and Katherine Howard. See TNA, E 327/191 for their marriage contract; On one occasion, Margaret's accounts note a payment to Katherine, although the reason is not stipulated.
24 Elizabeth of York's Privy Purse Expenses show that she continued to support Bridget. She

probably died in 1517.

25 TNA, E 101/425/19, ff. 1–10.
26 Cavell (ed.), *Heralds' Memoir*, p. 129.
27 Leland, *Collectanea*, IV, p. 218.
28 Ibid., p. 219.
29 Cavell (ed.), *Heralds' Memoir*, p. 131.
30 Ibid., pp. 131–2.
31 Sir David Owen appears to have died in around 1535. He was buried in St Mary's Church in Easebourne, West Sussex, where his tomb effigy can be seen.
32 Cavell (ed.), *Heralds' Memoir*, pp. 134–5.
33 Leland, *Collectanea*, IV, p. 223.
34 Cavell (ed.), *Heralds' Memoir*, p. 136.
35 Leland, *Collectanea*, IV, p. 224.
36 Cavell (ed.), *Heralds' Memoir*, p. 140.
37 Ibid., p. 141.
38 Leland, *Collectanea*, IV, p. 226.
39 Ibid., p. 227.
40 Cavell (ed.), *Heralds' Memoir*, p. 143.
41 Leland, *Collectanea*, IV, p. 227.
42 Ibid., p. 228.
43 Anne was the only surviving child of John Mowbray, Duke of Norfolk, and his wife Elizabeth Talbot. When her father died in 1476, she became a wealthy heiress, but she died at the age of eight in 1481. She was initially buried in Westminster Abbey, but her coffin was later moved to the Minoresses convent in Aldgate. It was discovered in 1964 and reburied in Westminster Abbey the following year.
44 Cavell (ed.), *Heralds' Memoir*, p. 145.
45 M. Hayward, *Dress at the Court of King Henry VIII* (Leeds, 2007), p. 84.
46 SJLM/2/3/3/4, ff. 1–3.
47 Ibid.
48 SJLM/1/1/3, f. 9.
49 SJLM/2/3/3/1, ff. 1, 3
50 SJLM/2/1/2, f. 3. SJLM/2/1/2, ff. 3–10.
51 See St John's College website, https://www.joh.cam.ac.uk/painting-mother-king-henry-vii-revealed-oldest-large-scale-portrait-english-woman.
52 Ibid.
53 Fisher, 'Mornynge Remembraunce', p. 2.
54 SJLM/1, 3 series.
55 Leland, *Collectanea*, IV, p. 235.
56 TNA, E 101/414/16, f. 7r; TNA, E 36/214, 13r.
57 A. Okerlund, *Elizabeth of York* (New York, 2009), p. 139.
58 BL, Add MS 7099, f. 65.
59 Ibid., f. 21; TNA, E 101/414/16, f. 9v.
60 Leland, *Collectanea*, IV, p. 234.
61 Cavell (ed.), *Heralds' Memoir*, p. 153.
62 Leland, *Collectanea*, IV, p. 235.
63 Ibid., p. 236.

Chapter 18: Too Much for My Hand

1 The next woman to be invested with this prestigious order was Queen Alexandra, consort of Edward VII.

2 Other ladies who had been appointed included Edward III's wife Queen Philippa, Constance of Castile, Katherine Swynford, Margaret of Anjou and Elizabeth Wydeville.

3 SJLM/2/3/3/2, f. 3.

4 Leland, *Collectanea*, IV, p. 242.

5 BL, Egerton MS 2341.

6 TNA, E 36/210, ff. 54, 58.

7 SJLM/1/1/2/1, f. 50; SJLM/1/1/5/1, f. 14v. Other payments given in reward include to someone who brought Margaret a dish of apples.

8 Leland, *Collectanea*, IV, p. 243.

9 Hertford was a Norman castle that had been granted to Elizabeth of York in 1487. Elizabeth I was later fond of it, and it is now used as a venue for weddings and private events.

10 Cavell (ed.), *Heralds' Memoir*, p. 174.

11 Leland, *Collectanea*, IV, p. 254.

12 Cavell (ed.), *Heralds' Memoir*, p. 180.

13 Ibid.

14 Ibid., p. 181. Alcock had once been the tutor of Edward V. He had been arrested by Richard III, but was later restored to the Council. He was appointed Bishop of Ely in 1486.

15 Ibid.

16 Ibid., p. 182.

17 This tradition is generally considered to have begun when Edward I invested his heir, Edward, with the title of Prince of Wales. Since the late fourteenth century, the title of Earl of Chester has only been granted alongside that of Prince of Wales.

18 Leland, *Collectanea*, IV, p. 254.

19 Cavell (ed.), *Heralds' Memoir*, p. 183.

20 Jones and Underwood emphasized that Margaret was the only person to donate grain to the expedition. See *King's Mother*, p. 81.

21 Katherine had three elder sisters, Isabella, Juana and Maria. She also had a brother, Juan, who died at the age of eighteen.

22 BL, Royal 2 A XVIII, f. 30.

23 L & P, IV (5791).

24 S. Lawson (ed.), *Eltham Palace* (London, 2011), p. 3. Eltham had been acquired by Edward II in 1305 and was given to his queen, Isabella of France.

25 An account of the visit is given in F.M. Nichols (ed. and trans.), *The Epistles of Erasmus*, II (London, 1904), p. 201.

26 See www.theguardian.com/books/2019/apr/25/white-queen-died-of-plague-claims-letter-found-in-national-archives.

27 TNA, PROB 11/9/207, f. 74.

28 André, *Life of Henry VII*, p. 4.

29 R. Hutchinson, *Young Henry: The Rise of Henry VIII* (London, 2011), p. 37.

30 S. Cunningham, *Prince Arthur: The King Who Never Was* (Stroud, 2016), p. 71.

31 SJLM/1/1/2/1, f. 25.

32 F. Palgrave, *The Antient Kalendars and Inventories of the Treasury of His Majesty's Exchequer*, I (London, 1836), p. 395.

33 Bacon, *Reign of Henry the Seventh*, p. 207.

34 André, *Life of Henry VII*, p. 60.

35 Pollard (ed.), *Reign of Henry VII*, I, p. 94.

36 Hay (ed.), *Anglica Historia*, p. 67.
37 Ibid.
38 On 8 May 1491 Arthur had been created a Knight of the Garter, and Henry's creation followed in May 1495.
39 Kingsford (ed.), *Chronicles of London*, p. 204.
40 André, *Life of Henry VII*, p. 64.
41 Hay (ed.), *Anglica Historia*, p. 75.
42 Ibid.
43 Ibid.
44 André, *Life of Henry VII*, p. 64.
45 Hay (ed.), *Anglica Historia*, p. 75.
46 TNA, E 154/2/5.
47 Hay (ed.), *Anglica Historia*, pp. 75, 77.
48 BL, Add MS 7099, f. 23. A payment of £10 is also listed to William at the time of his execution, possibly for the purpose of tipping his executioner.
49 TNA, E 101/414/16, f. 58v.
50 André, *Life of Henry VII*, p. 65.
51 BL, Add MS 7099, f. 29. At the beginning of September, Henry had returned to visit his mother at Collyweston.
52 André, *Life of Henry VII*, p. 62.
53 Katherine Gordon was the daughter of George Gordon, second Earl of Huntly. She had probably been born in around 1474.
54 An effigy once adorned the tomb but has since disappeared. The Latin inscription still survives, part of which reads 'Attrapos, the most severe messenger of Death, snatched her away but may she have eternal life in Heaven'.
55 Thornbury Castle is now a hotel.
56 Jasper left detailed instructions in his will for the construction of a tomb, though it no longer survives. See Nichols (ed.), *Testamenta Vetusta*, I, p. 430. His entrails were buried in the church at Thornbury.
57 Upon Jasper's death, the mighty Pembroke Castle – the scene of Margaret's confinement almost forty years earlier – became Crown property, although neither Margaret nor her son would ever visit it again.
58 TNA, SC 1/51/189. The letter is dated from Sheen on 25 April.
59 TNA, E 101/414/6, f. 39r.
60 BL, Add MS 29976, ff. 65–80.
61 Ibid., f. 40r.
62 Ibid., f. 41r.
63 TNA, E 135/3/21.
64 Pollard (ed.), *Reign of Henry VII*, I, p. 147.
65 BL, Royal 2 A XVIII, f. 30.
66 Pollard (ed.), *Reign of Henry VII*, p. 161.
67 Ibid., p. 162.
68 Ibid.
69 Hay (ed.), *Anglica Historia*, p. 111.
70 Ibid.
71 Ibid.
72 Ibid.
73 CSPV, I (760).
74 CSP Milan, I (550).
75 Kingsford (ed.), *Chronicles of London*, p. 222.

76 Ibid.
77 Ibid.
78 BL, Add MS 7099, f. 44.
79 Today, the gateway is the only part of Henry's magnificent palace that survives; it features his arms.

Chapter 19: The Right Noble Puissant and Excellent Princess

1 CSPS, I, p. 156.
2 Ibid.
3 Pollard (ed.), *Reign of Henry VII*, I, p. 188.
4 SJLM/9/2/1.
5 See A. Wroe, *Perkin: A Story of Deception* (London, 2003), pp. 455–7.
6 CSPS, I, p. 156.
7 Ibid, p. 190.
8 CPR 1485–94, p. 236.
9 Nichols (ed.), *Testamenta Vetusta*, I, p. 437.
10 CSPS, I, p. 205.
11 Ibid.
12 TNA, E 101/414/16, f. 54r.
13 W.H. St John Hope, *Windsor Castle: An Architectural History* (London, 1913), p. 241.
14 CPR 1494–1509, p. 79.
15 SGC, XV.58.C.13.
16 J. Wilkinson, *Henry VII's Lady Chapel in Westminster Abbey* (London, 2007), p. 4.
17 CPR 1494–1509, p. 79. Margaret's cousin Charles Somerset and his wife later chose to be buried in St George's Chapel, and their tomb can be seen in what is now called the Beaufort Chantry.
18 CCR 1500–9, pp. 290–1.
19 N. Beckett, 'Henry VII and Sheen Charterhouse', in Thompson (ed.), *The Reign of Henry VII*, p. 117.
20 See S. Powell, 'Margaret Pole and Syon Abbey', *Historical Research*, 78 (2005), pp. 563–7. Henry VII had lent Lady Pole money for the burial of her husband. See BL, Add MS 21480, f. 113v. Margaret Windsor was the daughter of Thomas Windsor, the constable of Windsor Castle.
21 SJLM/1/1/3/2, ff. 153, 157 for examples.
22 CPR 1485–94, p. 369.
23 Fisher, 'Mornynge Remembraunce', p. 2.
24 Ibid., p. 4.
25 Ibid., p. 5.
26 Ibid., p. 2.
27 SJLM/2/3/2/1, f. 20v. Most of these books were bequeathed to Christ's College, Cambridge.
28 Fisher, 'Mornynge Remembraunce', p. 3.
29 J. Backhouse, 'Founders of the Royal Library: Edward IV and Henry VII as collectors of illuminated manuscripts', in D. Williams (ed.), *England in the Fifteenth Century* (Woodbridge, 1987), p. 32.
30 See SJLM/1/1/2/1, f. 57r for example.
31 Although he was English, Caxton had first established himself in Bruges before returning to London.
32 *Eneydos* was dedicated to Prince Arthur.

33 See J. Laynesmith, *The Last Medieval Queens* (Oxford, 2004), p. 212.
34 See Jones and Underwood, *King's Mother*, p. 182.
35 L. Kellner (ed.), *Blanchardin and Eglantine* (London, 1890).
36 G. Sitwell (ed.), *The Scale of Perfection* (London, 1953).
37 Jones and Underwood, *King's Mother*, p. 183. Mary Roos' first husband, Hugh Denys, was Henry VII's Groom of the Stole. She later served Katherine of Aragon.
38 V. Schutte, 'Royal Tudor Women as Patrons and Curators', *Early Modern Women*, 9:1 (2014), p. 81.
39 In 1508, for example, twelve books were ordered from Pynson. TNA, E36/214, f. 138v.
40 SJLM/1/1/3/2, f. 27.
41 Ibid., f. 142. Jones and Underwood have pointed out that these were probably copies of the *Mirror of Gold for the Sinful Soul*. See *King's Mother*, p. 183.
42 SJLM/1/1/3/3, f. 18.
43 Westminster Abbey MS 39.
44 St John's College, MS N.24, f. 12v.
45 See Backhouse, 'Illuminated Manuscripts', pp. 184–5.
46 Nichols (ed.), *Chronicle of the Grey Friars*, p. 26.
47 See TNA, E 101/415/3, f. 66v for example.
48 Katherine's husbands were James Strangways, Sir Matthew Cradock and Christopher Ashton. It is Ashton who Katherine is buried with in Fyfield, Berkshire. The effigies of the couple were destroyed by fire.
49 Hay (ed.), *Anglica Historia*, p. 119.
50 TNA, E 101/415/3, f. 6r.
51 CSPS, I, p. 213.
52 Ibid.
53 Pollard (ed.), *Reign of Henry VII*, I, p. 216.
54 In 1480 Thomas Bourchier, who had completed substantial building work at Knole, gave the property to the See of Canterbury. From then, Archbishops of Canterbury, including Morton, whom Henry VII is known to have visited there, occupied it. Today Knole is cared for by the National Trust.
55 Fox hailed from Grantham, and was of humble origin.

Chapter 20: My Godly Mistress, the Lady Margaret

1 The grant is dated 22 March. See CPR 1485–94, pp. 154–5.
2 Tattershall is a moated, red-brick tower. Henry VIII and Charles Brandon, Duke of Suffolk, later owned it, among others. Much of the castle was destroyed during the English Civil War.
3 Collyweston was largely pulled down in the eighteenth century. Both Henry VIII and Elizabeth I visited it. Excavations are currently underway in an attempt to discover more about the palace.
4 Toulin Smith (ed.), *Itinerary*, I, p. 22.
5 Jones and Underwood pointed out that a local craftsman accidentally depicted the Beaufort yale as an antelope. Another craftsmen had to be paid to rectify this mistake. See *King's Mother*, p. 84.
6 SJLM/2/3/2/1, f. 10.
7 Ibid., f. 11.
8 Ibid., f. 16.
9 Ibid., ff. 10–38.

10 On one occasion the goldsmith of Stamford was also paid for making 'the pyx of the sacrament'.
11 SJLM/2/1/2–3, f. 18.
12 As a result of Margaret's influence, Oldham later became Bishop of Exeter.
13 In the Ante-Chapel of Christ's College, Cambridge, the monumental brass of Edith and her husband Thomas can still be seen. It is the only medieval brass to a husband and wife that can be found in any College Chapel in Oxford or Cambridge.
14 Fisher, 'Mornynge Remembraunce', p. 2.
15 Ibid., p. 3.
16 Likewise, Margaret's treasurer William Bedell later credited Margaret for 'all that I have'. See E. Norton, *The Lives of Tudor Women* (London, 2016), p. 98.
17 BL, Add MS 12060, f. 9.
18 Ibid., f. 20v.
19 Ibid., f. 21r.
20 Fisher, 'Mornynge Remembraunce', p. 3.
21 Ibid.
22 Ibid. Nevertheless, she had once received permission from the Pope to eat 'eggs, cheese, butter and other milk-meats' during Lent.
23 Ibid.
24 Ibid.
25 Ibid.
26 Ibid.
27 Ibid., p. 5.
28 F. Kisby, 'A Mirror of Monarchy: Music and Musicians in the Household Chapel of the Lady Margaret Beaufort, Mother of Henry VII', *Early Music History*, 16 (1997), p. 204. On one occasion, Margaret's accounts note the payment of a pair of organs bought for her chapel from London.
29 F. Kisby, 'Officers & Office-Holding at the English Court: A Study of the Chapel Royal, 1485–1547', *Royal Musical Association Research Chronicle*, 32 (1999), p. 24.
30 In 1506 grammar books were purchased for their use.
31 BL, Add MS 12060, f. 21v.
32 SJLM/1/1/3, f. 47.
33 BL, Add MS 12060, f.21v.
34 Fisher, 'Mornynge Remembraunce', p. 4.
35 Jones and Underwood, *King's Mother*, p. 89.
36 M. Jones, 'Beaufort, Margaret', *Oxford Dictionary of National Biography*, Online edition 2004; Jones and Underwood, *King's Mother*, p. 87.
37 TNA, REQ 2/4/246.
38 Bentley (ed.), *Excerpta*, pp. 167–8.
39 Fisher, 'Mornynge Remembraunce', p. 4.
40 Ibid., p. 2.
41 SJLM/1/1/3/3, f. 76; SJLM/1/1/3/1, f. 34.
42 Halliwell (ed.), *Letters of Kings*, p. 180.
43 Cited in Cooper, *Lady Margaret*, pp. 66–7.
44 TNA, E 101/415/3, f. 51r.
45 M.L. Beer, 'Practices and Performances of Queenship: Catherine of Aragon and Margaret Tudor, 1503–1533', unpublished PhD thesis (University of Illinois, 2014), p. 20.

Chapter 21: Right Royal and Pleasantly Beseen

1   BL, Royal 2 A XVIII, f. 32; Hays (ed.), *Anglica Historia*, p. 123.
2   G. Kipling (ed.), *The Receyt of the Ladie Kateryne* (Oxford, 1990), p. 7.
3   Ibid.
4   Ibid., p. 8.
5   Ibid., p. 9.
6   Ibid., p. 26.
7   S. Anglo, 'The London Pageants for the Reception of Katharine of Aragon: November 1501', *Journal of the Warburg and Courtauld Institutes*, 26 (1963), p. 88.
8   Kipling (ed.), *Receyt of the Ladie Kateryne*, p. 31.
9   Ibid., p. 32.
10 Ibid.
11 Ibid., p. 37.
12 Ibid., p. 38.
13 Ibid., p. 39.
14 Kingsford (ed.), *Chronicles of London*, p. 249.
15 Ibid.
16 Ibid., p. 248.
17 Kipling (ed.), *Receyt of the Ladie Kateryne*, pp. 43–4.
18 Fisher, 'Mornynge Remembraunce', p. 6.
19 SJLM/1/1/4/1.
20 Kipling (ed.), *Receyt of the Ladie Kateryne*, pp. 47–8.
21 Ibid., p. 48.
22 Ibid.
23 Ibid., p. 53.
24 Ibid., p. 55.
25 Ibid.
26 Ibid., p. 58.
27 Ibid.
28 CSPS, I, p. 176.
29 Ibid.
30 Ibid., p. 169.
31 BL, Add MS 59899, f. 27r.
32 Fisher, 'Mornynge Remembraunce', p. 2.
33 This visit has often been dated to 1501, but as Jones has shown, there is good evidence to suggest that it took place in 1502. See M. Jones, 'Henry VII, Lady Margaret Beaufort and the Orléans ransom', in R.A. Griffiths and J. Sherborne (eds), *Kings and Nobles in the Later Middle Ages* (Gloucester, 1986).
34 Following the death of Thomas, Duke of Clarence, in 1421, Margaret's grandmother Margaret Holland had inherited the custody of a valuable French prisoner, John, Count of Angoulême, who was primarily housed at Maxey Castle. He and six others had been given to the English as hostages in order to guarantee payment from his brother, Louis, Duke of Orléans, which he had promised in 1412 in order to ensure that the English left Gascony. Though a relatively small amount had been paid off, the balance was by no means settled at Margaret Holland's death. Thus Margaret's father had inherited the debt, which he gave Angoulême the opportunity to pay off. A new agreement was drawn up with Orléans, and though much of the debt remained outstanding, Angoulême was returned to Cherbourg in March 1444. When Somerset died, Margaret's mother tried her best to pursue the debt, enlisting the help of her husband Lord Welles. Yet the payments began to fall further into arrears, and were inherited by Margaret upon her mother's death.

35 As the son of the Duke of Orléans, Louis inherited the debt.
36 Ellis (ed.), *Original Letters*, pp. 46–7.
37 Ibid., pp. 47–8.
38 Ellis (ed.), *Original Letters*, pp. 44–5. Henry chose not to press the debt, but his son, Henry VIII, felt differently. It would not be settled until after both Margaret and her son were dead.
39 See Weir, *Elizabeth of York*, pp. 371–4.
40 BL, Royal 2 A XVIII, f. 29.
41 Kipling (ed.), *Receyt of the Ladie Kateryne*, p. 80.
42 Ibid., p. 81.
43 Ibid.
44 Ibid., p. 82.
45 TNA, E 101/415/3, f. 98v.

Chapter 22: In Everything Like to the Queen

 1 Somerset inherited the castle in right of his wife, Elizabeth Herbert. Elizabeth was the daughter of William Herbert, Earl of Huntingdon, the heir of Henry VII's former guardian.
 2 TNA, E 36/210, f. 85.
 3 Alison Weir has pointed out that at the end of the month the Queen's accounts show that she visited Coldharbour, but Margaret was not present. That she visited, however, is further evidence of their close relationship. See *Elizabeth of York*, p. 402.
 4 Ibid., pp. 403–4.
 5 Margaret noted the Queen's death in her Book of Hours. BL, Royal 2 A XVIII, f. 28.
 6 BL, Add MS 45133, f. 141v.
 7 Ibid.
 8 Part of the effigy still survives in the abbey today.
 9 Elizabeth of York had probably supervised their earliest lessons, and the resemblance that Henry VIII's handwriting bore to that of his mother has been noted. See D. Starkey, *Henry: Virtuous Prince* (London, 2008), p. 119.
10 Leland, *Collectanea*, IV, p. 265; BL, Royal 2 A XVIII, f. 31.
11 Thomas and Thornley (eds), *Great Chronicle of London*, p. 323.
12 SJLM/1/1/3/1, f. 117.
13 M. Jones, 'Collyweston – An early Tudor palace', in Williams (ed.), *England in the Fifteenth Century*, p. 129.
14 Ibid.
15 Leland, *Collectanea*, IV, p. 267.
16 Ibid., p. 324.
17 SJLM/1/1/3/1, ff. 117, 122, 183.
18 James died on 27 February 1508. Margaret's second child, Arthur, was born on 20 October 1509, but died on 14 July 1510.
19 B.J. Harris, 'Women and Politics in Early Tudor England', *Historical Journal*, 33 (1990), p. 264.
20 It was probably at her instigation that, in around 1500, a match had been arranged between Margaret's niece, Eleanor St John, and Henry Grey, the son and heir of the Marquess of Dorset. Eleanor was the daughter of Margaret's half-brother, Oliver St John, and his wife Elizabeth Scrope. Eleanor died childless, and Henry Grey became second Marquess of Dorset and grandfather to the ill-fated Lady Jane Grey. Margaret may also have had a hand in arranging the marriage of the Queen's first cousin, Anne St Leger, to George Manners.
21 CCR 1500–9, p. 89; in December, Margaret's accounts noted a reward to a servant of

Kildare's who brought her a gift. SJLM/1/1/3/1, f. 122. The newlyweds would eventually move to Ireland.

22 In 1499 Cecily was granted a dispensation to worship in Margaret's household, which is suggestive of the fact that the two women were spending time together regularly. See Jones and Underwood, *King's Mother*, p. 162.

23 BL, Add MS 12060, f. 22v.

24 Parliament Rolls of Medieval England, Henry VII: January 1504.

25 SJLM/1/1/3/1, f. 113.

26 Ibid., f. 122, notes a payment to a servant of Princess Mary.

27 Nichols (ed.), *Testamenta Vetusta*, I, p. 446.

28 SJLM/1/1/3/1, f. 128. Stanley is referenced at various points throughout Margaret's accounts. On one occasion, for example, she rewarded his minstrels, while on another she paid the goldsmith of Stamford for repairing candlesticks from Stanley's chapel.

29 Nichols (ed.), *Testamenta Vetusta*, II, p. 460.

30 Ibid., p. 459.

31 Ibid., p. 458; Stanley's son and heir, George, Lord Strange, had died just months earlier in December 1503 – having reportedly been poisoned following a banquet at Derby House. In consequence, Stanley's eldest grandson succeeded him.

32 Cooper, *Lady Margaret*, pp. 97–8.

33 CSPS, I, p. 295.

Chapter 23: *Nos Margareta*

1 Toulmin Smith (ed.), *Itinerary*, I, p. 257.

2 Fisher's father died in his youth, and though his mother remarried and sired further children, she remained devoted to John and his brother.

3 R. Bayne (ed.), *The Life of Fisher MS. Harleian 6382* (London, 1921), pp. 9–10.

4 The architecture has long since changed, and includes buildings designed by Nicholas Hawksmoor and Sir Christopher Wren.

5 Marie was the wife of Aymer de Valence, the half-brother of Henry III, whose tomb can still be seen in Westminster Abbey. Marie's licence to found Pembroke was granted on Christmas Eve, 1347. It was originally known as The Hall of Valence Mary.

6 J. Twigg, *A History of Queens' College, Cambridge 1448–1986* (Woodbridge, 1987), p. 1.

7 Cooper, *Lady Margaret*, pp. 46–7.

8 CPR 1494–1509, p. 371.

9 Ibid., p. 79. These are the modern Lady Margaret Professorships. See Jones and Underwood, *King's Mother*, p. 205. Lady Margaret Hall, Oxford, still commemorates her.

10 CPR 1494–1509, p. 79.

11 H. Anstey (ed.), *Epistolae Academicae Oxon*, II (Oxford, 1898), p. 614.

12 M.G. Underwood, 'The Lady Margaret and Her Cambridge Connections', *Sixteenth Century Journal*, 13 (1982), p. 69.

13 CPR 1494–1509, p. 415.

14 TNA, E 36/281.

15 T. Schroder, 'A Royal Tudor Rock-Crystal and Silver-Gilt Vase', *Burlington Magazine*, 137 (1995), p. 363.

16 SJLM/1/1/3/3, f. 8.

17 CPR 1494–1509, p. 543.

18 SJLM/1/1/3/3, f. 27.

19 See H. Rackham, *Early Statutes of Christ's College, Cambridge* (Cambridge, 1927), p. iv.

20 Ibid., p. 87.
21 Ibid., p. 89.
22 Fisher, 'Mornynge Remembraunce', p. 7.
23 Hatfield later served as a royal palace before Robert Cecil acquired it in 1607. He tore down much of the old palace and transformed it into what is now Hatfield House. Croydon Palace now forms part of an independent girls' school.
24 SJLM/2/3/1/3, ff. 24, 9.
25 SJLM/2/3/1/4, ff. 1–4.
26 Philip was the son of Maximilian and Mary of Burgundy. He married Juana on 20 October 1496, and following the death of her mother, Isabella of Castile, she became queen. However, her father Ferdinand contested this, necessitating the couple's journey to Spain.
27 TNA, E 36/214, f. 16r.
28 SJLM/9/2/2.
29 Edmund succeeded his father to the dukedom of Suffolk in 1492. As he did not have the financial means to support his title, he instead became known as the Earl of Suffolk.
30 Courtenay was attainted and remained in the Tower for the rest of Henry VII's reign. He was pardoned by Henry VIII and participated in his coronation. William de la Pole died some time between October and November 1539.
31 TNA, E 36/214, f. 19r.
32 Ibid., f. 23r.
33 Eleanor instead married first Manuel I of Portugal, and in 1530, Francis I, King of France. Charles married Isabella of Portugal.
34 Suffolk had been exempted from Henry VIII's general pardon in 1509, and was executed on 30 April 1513 on Tower Hill.
35 In 1525 Richard had joined the King of France's army at Pavia. He was buried in the church there following his death in the battle.
36 There is some debate as to where Cecily's resting place is. Quarr Abbey on the Isle of Wight is a possibility. The old abbey was dissolved during the reign of Henry VIII.
37 Jones and Underwood, *King's Mother*, p. 79.
38 SJLM/1/1/3, f. 93.
39 Philip died suddenly on 25 September of natural causes, although whispers of poison abounded. He was laid to rest in the Royal Chapel of Granada, where his wife and her parents are also entombed.
40 Margaret had continued to make payments for the upkeep of Coldharbour in recent years, including for a broken chimney, a bar of iron 'for my lady's closet', and 'a great new key made for the great door' standing next to the front gate. SJLM/1/2/3.

Chapter 24: A Woman Most Outstanding

1 T. Astle (ed.), *The Will of Henry VII* (London, 1775), p. 42.
2 L & P, I (17).
3 Hay (ed.), *Anglica Historia*, p. 151.
4 L & P, I (17).
5 Gristwood, *Blood Sisters*, p. 330.
6 L & P, I (4).
7 Weir, *Elizabeth of York*, p. 451. Jane and Nicholas's parents were William Vaux and Katherine Peniston. William had been killed fighting at the Battle of Tewkesbury, while his wife had served first Margaret of Anjou, and later Elizabeth of York. Jane married Sir Richard Guildford, and some time following his death in 1506 she married Sir Anthony

Poyntz.

8 Cooper, *Lady Margaret*, p. 135. Jones and Underwood suggest that Perrot may first have been employed to help with Margaret's command of the French language or else Katherine of Aragon's. See *King's Mother*, p. 164. In her will, Margaret left Perrot an annuity 'if she tarry within this realm'.

9 J.E.B. Mayor (ed.), *The English Works of John Fisher* (London, 1876), p. 268.

10 L & P, I (4).

11 Henry VII had left money in his will for the completion of the Lady Chapel and his tomb. The eventual cost of the tomb totalled over £9 million in modern money; the vault would be opened in 1625 for the burial of James I.

12 L & P, I (34).

13 TNA, LC 9/50; L & P, I (82).

14 SJLM/1/1/5, f. 14r. See also Hayward, *Dress*, p. 44.

15 SJLM/1/1/5, f. 17r.

16 Fisher, 'Mornynge Remembraunce', p. 6.

17 Hay (ed.), *Anglica Historia*, p. 151.

18 Fisher, 'Mornynge Remembraunce', p. 6.

19 Hay (ed.), *Anglica Historia*, p. 151.

20 BL, Add MS 12060, f. 24r.

21 Two rooms of the abbot's house (Cheyneygates) still survive, and are often used for corporate events.

22 Fisher, 'Mornynge Remembraunce', p. 7.

23 BL, Add MS 12060, f. 24r.

24 Ibid.

25 Fisher, 'Mornynge Remembraunce', p. 5.

26 Ibid.

27 Hay (ed.), *Anglica Historia*, p. 151.

28 St John's College Quatercentenary publication, *Collegium Divi Johannis Evangelistae, 1511–1911* (Cambridge, 1911), pp. 118–20.

29 Ibid., p. 121.

30 SJLM/2/3/5, ff. 1–10.

31 Cooper, *Lady Margaret*, p. 117.

32 SJLM/2/3/2/1, f. 30.

33 Hayward, *Dress*, p. 65.

34 Fisher, 'Mornynge Remembraunce', p. 1.

35 Torrigiano was born in 1472. Though he had completed other commissions, Margaret's is likely to have been the first tomb of his creation.

36 R.F. Scott, 'On the Contracts for the Tomb of the Lady Margaret Beaufort, Countess of Richmond and Derby, Mother of King Henry VII, and Foundress of the Colleges of Christ and St John in Cambridge', *Archaeologica*, 66 (1915), p. 370.

37 Ibid.

38 Fisher, 'Mornynge Remembraunce', p.7.

Epilogue

1 James V had been born on 10 April 1512 at Linlithgow Palace. He was the only one of James IV and Margaret Tudor's six children to survive infancy.

2 L & P, I (3151).

3 John Stewart, second Duke of Albany, was a blood relative to James V, his grandfather

having been James II of Scotland. Though Albany had been born and raised in France, he became regent of Scotland in July 1515. He was ousted from his position in 1524, and died in France in 1536.

4   Mary's two sons, both named Henry, predeceased her.

5   The eldest of James's sons, also named James, was born on 22 May 1540. The younger, Robert, was born on 12 April 1541. Tragically, he died eight days after his birth on 20 April at Falkland Palace. The following day, his elder brother died at St Andrews.

6   Following her death, Margaret was buried in the Charterhouse at Perth. Unfortunately, this was destroyed in 1559 during the course of the Reformation.

7   James VI was the only son of Mary, Queen of Scots, as a result of her second marriage to Henry Stuart, Lord Darnley. Darnley was the son of Margaret Douglas, Queen Margaret's daughter by Archibald Douglas.

8   Margaret is also distantly related to the dukes of Beaufort, who are descended from her cousin, Charles Somerset. The title of duke of Beaufort was bestowed upon Henry Somerset, third Marquess of Worcester, by Charles II in 1682.

9   Cited in Ballard, *Memoirs*, pp. 26–7. Originally composed in Latin, the elegy was intended to hang next to Margaret's tomb.

Manuscript Sources

British Library

Additional Manuscripts   4712, 7099, 12060, 21480, 29976, 35814, 45133, 59899, 88965
Egerton Manuscripts   2341
Royal Manuscripts   2 A XVIII
Seals   C VIII 84
Sloane Manuscripts   403
Stowe Manuscripts   1047

Lambeth Palace Library

MS 474   Book of Hours

National Archives

Chancery

C1   Early Chancery Proceedings
C47   Miscellanea
C139   Inquisitions Post Mortem, Series I, Henry VI
C140   Inquisitions Post Mortem, Series I, Edward IV

Court of Wards and Liveries

WARD 2   Deeds and Evidence

Duchy of Lancaster

DL 29   Accounts of Auditors, Receivers, Feodaries and Ministers
DL 41   Miscellanea

Exchequer

E 36   Treasury of Receipt, Miscellaneous Books
E 40   Treasury of Receipt: Ancient Deeds, Series A
E 101   King's Remembrancer, Various Accounts
E 135   Miscellaneous Ecclesiastical Documents
E 154   King's Remembrancer and Treasury of Receipt, Inventories of Goods and Chattels
E 327   Augmentation Office: Ancient Deeds, Series BX
E 404   Warrants for Issue

Lord Chamberlain's Department

LC 9   Accounts and Miscellanea

Prerogative Court of Canterbury

PROB 11   Registered Copy Wills

Court of Requests

REQ   Pleadings

Special Collections

SC   Ancient Petitions

St George's Chapel, Windsor

SJC XV.58.C.13   Consent for Lady Margaret to found a Chantry in the Chapel, 1497

St John's College, Cambridge

SJLM/1   Accounts of Lady Margaret Beaufort
SJLM/2   Inventories
SJLM/3   Wills and Bequests
SJLM/4   The Inheritance of Lady Margaret Beaufort
SJLM/7   Executors of Lady Margaret Beaufort
SJLM/9   Extended Family, Heirs and Assigns
St John's College, MS N.24   Prayer Book

Westminster Abbey Muniments

Westminster Abbey MS 39   Prayer Book commissioned by Lady Margaret Beaufort for Sir Thomas Stanley
WAM 12181–90   Household Accounts of Sir Henry Stafford at Bourne and Woking, 1466–71
WAM 22830   Bill of Prests by Lady Margaret's Cofferer, 1493–4
WAM 5472   Miscellaneous Receipts and Expenses of Sir Reginald Bray, 1468–9
WAM 5479   Miscellaneous Receipts of Sir Reginald Bray, 1469–72
WAM 32348   Account of Lands of Edward Stafford, 1495–6
WAM 32377   Account of Sir Reginald Bray for Receipts and Charges on Lady Margaret's Lands
WAM 32378   Draft of a Pardon from Edward IV to Henry Tudor
WAM 32407   Miscellaneous Receipts and Expenses of Sir Reginald Bray, 1473–4
WAM 6658   Admission of Lady Margaret, Henry Stafford and Henry Tudor to Confraternity of the Order of the Holy Trinity, Knaresborough, 1465
WAM 6660   Admission of Henry Stafford and Lady Margaret to Confraternity of Burton Lazars, 1466

Printed Primary Sources

Allen, P.S. and H.M. (eds), *Letters of Richard Fox 1486–1527* (Oxford, 1929).

André, B., *The Life of Henry VII*, trans. Hobbins, D. (New York, 2011).

Anstey, H. (ed.), *Epistolae Academicae Oxon*, II (Oxford, 1898).

Astle, T. (ed.), *The Will of Henry VII* (London, 1775).

Bayne, R. (ed.), *The Life of Fisher MS. Harleian 6382* (London, 1921).

Benet, J., 'Chronicle for the years 1400–1462', ed. Harriss, G.L. and M.A., *Camden Miscellany*, XXIV, Camden Society, 4th series, 9 (1972).

Bentley, S. (ed.), *Excerpta Historica or illustrations of English history* (London, 1831).

Bergenroth, G.A. (ed.), *Calendar of State Papers, Spain, Volume 1, 1485–1509* (London, 1862).

Bliss, W.H. (ed.), *Calendar of Papal Registers relating to Great Britain and Ireland* (London, 1893).

Brewer, J.S. (ed.), *Letters and Papers, Foreign and Domestic, of the Reign of Henry VIII, 1509–47*, 21 vols and addenda (London, 1862–1932).

Brown, R. (ed.), *Calendar of State Papers, Venice, Volume 1, 1202–1509* (London, 1864).

Calendar of Ancient Deeds in the Public Record Office, I (London, 1890).

Calendar of Close Rolls: Edward IV, Henry VII (www.british-history.ac.uk).

Calendar of Patent Rolls: Henry VII: 1485–1509, 2 vols (HMSO, London, 1914–16).

Campbell, W. (ed.), *Materials for a History of the Reign of Henry VII*, 2 vols (London, 1873).

Cavell, E. (ed.), *The Heralds' Memoir 1486–1490: Court Ceremony, Royal Progress and Rebellion* (Donington, 2009).

Caxton, W., *The Game and Playe of the Chesse*, ed. Adams, J. (Kalamazoo, 2009).

Commynes, P., *Memoirs: The Reign of Louis XI 1461–83*, trans. Jones, M. (London, 1972).

Crawford, A. (ed.), *Letters of the Queens of England 1100–1547* (Stroud, 1994).

Crawford, A. (ed.), *Letters of Medieval Women* (Stroud, 2002).

Dalton, J.N. (ed.), *The Manuscripts of St George's Chapel, Windsor Castle* (Windsor, 1957).

Davies, J.S. (ed.), *An English Chronicle of the Reigns of Richard II, Henry IV, Henry V, and Henry VI* (London, 1856).

Davis, N. (ed.), *The Paston Letters* (Oxford, 2008).

Dockray, K. (ed.), *Three Chronicles of the Reign of Edward IV* (Gloucester, 1988).

Dockray, K., *Richard III: A Source Book* (Stroud, 1997).

Dockray, K. (ed.), *Edward IV: A Source Book* (Stroud, 1999).

Ellis, H. (ed.), *Hall's Chronicle* (London, 1809).

Ellis, H. (ed.), *Original Letters Illustrative of English History*, 3 vols (London, 1825).

Ellis, H. (ed.), *Three Books of Polydore Vergil's English History* (London, 1844).

Fenn, J. (ed.), *The Paston Letters*, 5 vols (London, 1787–1823).

Fisher, J., 'Mornynge Remembraunce had at the moneth mynde of the Noble Prynces Margarete Countesse of Rychemonde and Darbye', available via Early English Books Online.

Gairdner, J. (ed.), *Letters and Papers Illustrative of the Reigns of Richard III and Henry VII*, 2 vols (London, 1861–3).

Gairdner, J. (ed.), *Gregory's Chronicle, or the Historical Collections of a Citizen of London in the Fifteenth Century*, Camden Society (London, 1876).

Given-Wilson, C., Brand, P., Phillips, S., Ormrod, M., Martin, G., Curry, A. and Horrox, R. (eds), *Parliament Rolls of Medieval England* (Woodbridge, 2005).

Gough Nichols, J. and Bruce, J. (eds), *Wills from Doctors' Commons: A Selection from the Wills of Eminent Persons Proved in the Prerogative Court of Canterbury, 1495–1695* (London, 1863).

Hall, E., *Chronicle*, ed. Whibley, C. (London, 1809).

Halliwell, J.O. (ed.), *A Chronicle of the First Thirteen Years of the Reign of King Edward the Fourth, by John Warkworth* (London, 1839).

Halliwell, J.O. (ed.), *The Most Pleasant Song of Lady Bessy* (London, 1847).

Halliwell, J.O. (ed.), *Letters of the Kings of England*, 2 vols (London, 1848).

Hanham, A., *John Benet's Chronicle, 1399–1462* (Basingstoke, 2016).

Hay, D. (ed.), *The Anglica Historia of Polydore Vergil* (London, 1950).

Hayward, M. (ed.), *The Great Wardrobe Accounts of Henry VII and Henry VIII* (Woodbridge, 2012).

Heseltine, G.C. (ed.), *The Shepherd's Calendar* (London, 1930).

Hinds, A.B. (ed.), *Calendar of State Papers, Milan, Volume 1, 1385–1618* (London, 1912).

Hymers, J. (ed.), *The Funeral Sermon of Margaret, Countess of Richmond and Derby* (Cambridge, 1840).

Ingrams, J.K. (ed.), *De Imitatione Christi* (London, 1893).

James, M.R. (trans.), *Henry the Sixth: A Reprint of John Blacman's Memoir* (Cambridge, 1919).

Kellner, L. (ed.), *Blanchardin and Eglantine* (London, 1890).

Kingsford, C.L. (ed.), *Chronicles of London* (Oxford, 1905).

Kingsford, C.L. (ed.), *English Historical Literature in the Fifteenth Century* (Oxford, 1913).

Kipling, G. (ed.), *The Receyt of the Ladie Kateryne* (Oxford, 1990).

Legg, L.G.W., *English Coronation Records* (London, 1901).

Leland, J., *Antiquarii de Rebus Britannicis Collectanea*, ed. Hearne, T., 6 vols (London, 1774).

Mancini, D., *De Occupatione Regni Anglie per Riccardum Tercium*, trans. and ed. as *The Usurpation of Richard III*, Armstrong, C.A.J. (2nd edition, Oxford, 1969).

Mayor, J.E.B. (ed.), *Early Statutes of St John's College, Cambridge* (London, 1859).

Mayor, J.E.B. (ed.), *The English Works of John Fisher* (London, 1876).

The Mirroure of Golde for the Synfull Soule (London, 1522).

More, T., *The History of King Richard III*, ed. Logan, G.M. (Indiana, 2005).

Myers, A.R. (ed.), *The Household of Edward IV: The Black Book and the Ordinance of 1478* (Manchester, 1959).

Nichols, F.M. (ed. and trans.), *The Epistles of Erasmus*, 2 vols (London, 1904).

Nichols, J. (ed.), *A Collection of all the Wills, now known to be extant, of the Kings and Queens of England* (London, 1780).

Nichols, J. (ed.), Society of Antiquaries, *A Collection of ordinances and regulations for the government of the royal household, made in divers reigns: from King Edward III to King William and Queen Mary, also receipts in ancient cookery* (London, 1790).

Nichols, J.G. (ed.), *The Chronicle of Calais* (London, 1846).

Nichols, J.G. (ed.), *Chronicle of the Grey Friars of London*, Camden Society (London, 1851).

Nichols, J.G. (ed.), *Inventories of the wardrobe, plate, chapel stuff, etc. of Henry Fitzroy, Duke of Richmond, and of the wardrobe stuff at Baynard's Castle of Katherine, Princess Dowager* (London, 1855).

Nichols, N.H. (ed.), *Testamenta Vetusta*, 2 vols (London, 1826).

Nicolas, N.H. (ed.), *Privy Purse Expenses of Elizabeth of York* (London, 1830).

Nicolas, N.H. (ed.), *Proceedings and Ordinances of the Privy Council of England*, 7 vols (London, 1834–7).

Palgrave, F., *The Antient Kalendars and Inventories of the Treasury of His Majesty's Exchequer*, I (London, 1836).

Pollard, A.F. (ed.), *Reign of Henry VII from Contemporary Sources*, 3 vols (London, 1913–14).

Pronay, N. and Cox, J. (eds), *The Crowland Chronicle Continuations: 1459–1486* (London, 1986).

Raine, A. (ed.), *York Civic Records*, 2 vols, Yorkshire Archaeological Society (1939–41).

Riley, H.T. (ed.), *Ingulph's Chronicle of the History of Croyland* (London, 1854).

Rymer, T. (ed.), *Rymer's Foedera*, 16 vols (London, 1739–45).

Sandford, F., *A Genealogical history of the kings and queens of England, and monarchs of Great Britain, &c. from the conquest, anno 1066, to the year 1677* (London, 1677).

Searle, W.G. (ed.), *The Narrative of the Marriage of Richard, Duke of York with Anne of Norfolk, 1477* (Cambridge, 1867).

Searle, W.G. (ed.), *The Chronicle of John Stone, Monk of Christ Church 1415–1471* (Cambridge, 1902).

Shakespeare, W., *Henry VI, Part Three*, ed. Martin, R. (Oxford, 2001).

Shakespeare, W., *Henry VI, Part Two*, ed. Warren, R. (Oxford, 2002).

Shakespeare, W., *Henry VI, Part One*, ed., Taylor, M. (Oxford, 2003).

Shakespeare, W., *Richard III*, ed Taylor, M. (London, 2015).

Sitwell, G. (ed.), *The Scale of Perfection* (London, 1953).

Smith, G. (ed.), *The Coronation of Elizabeth Wydeville* (London, 1935).

Starkey, D. (ed.), *The Inventory of King Henry VIII*, trans. Ward, P. (London, 1998).

Stow, J., *The Annales or Generall Chronicle of England* (London, 1615).

Strachey, J. *et al.* (eds), *Rotuli Parliamentorum*, 6 vols (London, 1767–77).

Sutton, A.F. and Hammond, P.W. (eds), *The Coronation of Richard III: The Extant Documents* (Gloucester, 1983).

Sutton, A.F., Visser-Fuchs, L. and Hammond, P.W. (eds), *The Reburial of Richard, Duke of York, 21–30 July 1476* (London, 1996).

Thomas, A.H. and Thornley, I.D. (eds), *The Great Chronicle of London* (London, 1983).

Toulmin Smith, L. (ed.), *John Leland's Itinerary in England and Wales in or about the years 1535–43*, 5 vols (London, 1964).

Ullmann, W. (ed.), *Liber Regie Capelle* (London, 1961).

Wickham Legg, L.G. (ed.), *English Coronation Records* (Oxford, 1901).

Williams, C.H. (ed.), *English Historical Documents*, V (1485–1558) (London, 1967).

Wriothesley, C., *A Chronicle of England during the reigns of the Tudors from 1485 to 1559*, ed. Hamilton, W.D., I (London, 1875).

Secondary Sources

Alcock, N.W., 'Maxstoke Castle, Warwickshire', *Archaeological Journal*, 135 (1978).

Amin, N., *Tudor Wales* (Stroud, 2014).

Amin, N., *The House of Beaufort: The Bastard Line that Captured the Crown* (Stroud, 2017).

Anglo, S., 'The Foundation of the Tudor Dynasty: The Coronation and Marriage of Henry VII', *Guildhall Miscellany*, II (1960), pp. 3–11.

Anglo, S., 'The London Pageants for the Reception of Katharine of Aragon: November 1501', *Journal of the Warburg and Courtauld Institutes*, 26 (1963), pp. 53–89.

Anglo, S., *The Great Tournament Roll of Westminster: Historical Introduction* (Oxford, 1968).

Anglo, S., *Spectacle Pageantry, and Early Tudor Policy* (Oxford, 1969).

Anglo, S., 'Ill of the Dead: The Posthumous Reputation of Henry VII', *Renaissance Studies*, 1 (1987), pp. 27–47.

Anglo, S., *Images of Tudor Kingship* (London, 1992).

Archbold, W.A.J., 'Sir William Stanley and Perkin Warbeck', *English Historical Review*, 14 (1899), pp. 529–34.

Archer, I.W., 'City and Court Connected: The Material Dimensions of Royal Ceremonial, ca. 1480–1625', *Huntingdon Library Quarterly*, 71 (2008), pp. 157–79.

Armitage Smith, S., *John of Gaunt* (London, 1904).

Arnold, P. and Savage, R., *Woking Palace: Henry VIII's Royal Palace* (Woking, 2011).

Arthurson, I., *The Perkin Warbeck Conspiracy 1491–1499* (Stroud, 1994).

Ashdown-Hill, J., *The Last Days of Richard III* (Stroud, 2010).

Axon, W.E., 'The Lady Margaret as a Lover of Literature', *The Library*, 8 (1907), pp. 34–41.

Bacon, F., *The History of the Reign of King Henry VII*, ed. Vickers, B. (Cambridge, 1998).

Bagley, J.J., *Margaret of Anjou* (London, 1948).

Bagley, J.J., *The Earls of Derby 1485–1985* (London, 1985).

Bak, J.M. (ed.), *Coronations: Medieval and Early Modern Monarchic Ritual* (Oxford, 1990).

Baldwin, D., *Elizabeth Woodville: Mother of the Princes in the Tower* (Stroud, 2002).

Baldwin, D., *Richard III* (Stroud, 2012).

Ballard, G., *Memoirs of Several Ladies of Great Britain* (London, 1775).

Barron, C.M., 'The "Golden Age" of Women in Medieval London', *Reading Medieval Studies*, 15 (1989).

Beaumont James, T., *The Palaces of Medieval England 1050–1550: Royalty, Nobility, the Episcopate and their Residences from Edward the Confessor to Henry VIII* (London, 1990).

Becker, L.M., *Death and the Early Modern Englishwoman* (Aldershot, 2003).

Beer, M.L., 'Practices and Performances of Queenship: Catherine of Aragon and Margaret Tudor, 1503–1533', unpublished PhD thesis (University of Illinois, 2014).

Bennett, H.S., *English Books and Readers 1475 to 1557* (Cambridge, 1969).

Bennett, M., *The Battle of Bosworth* (Gloucester, 1985).

Bennett, M., *Lambert Simnel and the Battle of Stoke* (Gloucester, 1987).

Bennett, M.J., 'Henry VII and the Northern Rising of 1489', *English Historical Review*, 105 (1990), pp. 34–59.

Blaauw, W.H., 'On the Effigy of Sir David Owen in Easeborne Church, near Midhurst', *Sussex Archaeological Collections*, 7 (1854), pp. 22–43.

Blair, C., 'A Drawing of an English Medieval Royal Gold Cup', *Burlington Magazine*, 121 (1979), pp. 370, 372–3.

Bolland, C. and Cooper, T., *The Real Tudors: Kings and Queens Rediscovered* (London, 2014).

Borman, T., *The Private Lives of the Tudors* (London, 2016).

Borman, T., *Henry VIII and the Men Who Made Him* (London, 2018).

Bramley, P., *A Companion and Guide to the Wars of the Roses* (Stroud, 2007).

Bromley, J., 'The Heraldry of Ormskirk Church', *The Historic Society of Lancashire and Cheshire*, 58 (1906), pp. 64–90.

Brooke, C.N.L., *The Medieval Idea of Marriage* (Oxford, 1989).

Buck, Sir G., *The History of King Richard III*, ed. Kincaid, A.N. (Gloucester, 1982).

Burton, E., *The Pageant of Early Tudor England* (New York, 1976).

Campbell, L., *Renaissance Portraits: European Portrait-Painting in the 14th, 15th and 16th Centuries* (New Haven and London, 1990).

Campbell, M., *Medieval Jewellery in Europe 1100–1500* (London, 2009).

Carlson, D.R., 'The Latin Writings of John Skelton', *Studies in Philology*, 88 (1991), pp. 1–125.

Carson, A., *Richard III: The Maligned King* (Stroud, 2008).

Castor, H., *The King, the Crown, and the Duchy of Lancaster: Public Authority and Private Power, 1399–1461* (Oxford, 2000).

Castor, H., *Blood and Roses: The Paston Family and the Wars of the Roses* (London, 2004).

Castor, H., *She Wolves: The Women Who Ruled England Before Elizabeth* (London, 2010).

Cecil, Lord D., *Hatfield House* (Stockbridge, 1973).

Cherry, J., *The Middleham Jewel and Ring* (York, 1994).

Cherry, J., 'Healing Through Faith: the Continuation of Medieval Attitudes to Jewellery into the Renaissance', *Renaissance Studies*, 15 (2001), pp. 154–71.

Chrimes, S.B., *Henry VII* (London, 1972).

Clark, J.W., *Endowments of the University of Cambridge* (Cambridge, 1904).

Clarke, P.D., 'English Royal Marriages and the Papal Penitentiary in the Fifteenth Century', *English Historical Review*, 120 (2005), pp. 1014–29.

Cobban, A.B., *The Medieval Universities: Their Development and Organization* (London, 1975).

Cocke, T., '"The Repository of Our English Kings": The Henry VII Chapel as Royal Mausoleum', *Architectural History*, 44 (2001), pp. 212–20.

Cokayne, G.E., *The Complete Peerage of England, Scotland, Ireland, Great Britain and the United Kingdom*, ed. Gibbs, W. *et al.*, 12 vols (London, 1910–59).

Colvin, H.M., Ransome, D.R. and Summerson, J. (eds), *The History of the King's Works*, 6 vols (London, 1963–82).

Conway, A., *Henry VII's Relations with Scotland and Ireland 1485–98* (Cambridge, 1932).

Collinson, P., Rex, R. and Stanton, G., *Lady Margaret Beaufort and her Professors of Divinity at Cambridge 1502 to 1649* (Cambridge, 2003).

Cooper, C.H., *The Lady Margaret: A Memoir of Margaret, Countess of Richmond and Derby*, ed. Mayor, J.E.B. (Cambridge, 1874).

Coulstock, P.H., *The Collegiate Church of Wimborne Minster* (Woodbridge, 1993).

Coward, B., *The Stanleys, Lords Stanley and Earls of Derby 1385–1672: The Origins, Wealth and Power of a Landowning Family* (Manchester, 1983).

Crawford, A., 'The Queen's Council in the Middle Ages', *English Historical Review*, 116 (2001), pp. 1193–211.

Cressy, D., *Birth, Marriage and Death: Ritual, Religion and the Life-Cycle in Tudor and Stuart England* (Oxford, 1997).

Cunningham, S., *Prince Arthur: The Tudor King Who Never Was* (Stroud, 2016).

Davies, C.S.L., 'Bishop John Morton, the Holy See, and the Accession of Henry VII', *English Historical Review*, 102 (1987), pp. 2–30.

Davies, C.S.L., 'Tudor: What's in a Name?' *History*, 97 (2012), pp. 24–42.

De Lisle, L., *Tudor: The Family Story* (London, 2013).

Dean, K., *The World of Richard III* (Stroud, 2015).

Delman, R.M., 'Gendered Viewing, Childbirth and Female Authority in the Residence of Alice Chaucer, Duchess of Suffolk, at Ewelme, Oxfordshire', *Journal of Medieval History* (2019).

Demers, P., '"God may open more than man maye vnderstande": Lady Margaret Beaufort's Translation of the De "Imitatione Christi"', *Renaissance and Reformation*, 35 (2012), pp. 45–61.

Dickinson, J.C., *The Shrine of Our Lady of Walsingham* (Cambridge, 1956).

Dodson, A., *The Royal Tombs of Great Britain: An Illustrated History* (London, 2004).

Domvile, Lady M., *The King's Mother: Memoir of Margaret Beaufort, Countess of Richmond and Derby* (London, 1899).

Drimmer, S., 'Beyond Private Matter: A Prayer Roll for Queen Margaret of Anjou', *Gesta*, 53 (2014), pp. 95–120.

Duffy, E., *Marking the Hours: English People and their Prayers, 1240–1570* (Yale, 2006).

Duffy, M., *Royal Tombs of Medieval England* (Stroud, 2011).

Eales, J., *Women in Early Modern England, 1500–1700* (London, 1998).

Earle, P., *The Life and Times of Henry V* (London, 1972).

Edwards, A.S.G., 'Northern Magnates and their Books', *Textual Cultures*, 7 (2012), pp. 176–86.

Elton, G.R., *The Tudor Revolution in Government: Administrative Changes in the Reign of Henry VIII* (Cambridge, 1953).

Emery, A., *Greater Medieval Houses of England and Wales, 1300–1500: Volume 3, Southern England* (London, 2006).

Erlanger, P., *Margaret of Anjou* (London, 1970).

Evans, J., *A History of Jewellery 1100–1870* (New York, 1953).

Evans, J., *Magical Jewels of the Middle Ages and the Renaissance* (New York, 1976).

Fahy, C., 'The Marriage of Edward IV and Elizabeth Woodville: A New Italian Source', *English Historical Review*, 76 (1961), pp. 660–72.

Fen Edge Archaeology Group Website, www.feag.co.uk.

Fetherston-Dilke, M.C., *Maxstoke Castle* (Bidford-on-Avon, 2008).

Fisher, S., '"Margaret R": Lady Margaret Beaufort's self-fashioning and female ambition', in Fleiner, C. and Woodacre, E. (eds), *Virtuous or Villainess? The Image of the Royal Mother from the Early Medieval to the Early Modern Era* (Basingstoke, 2016).

Foister, S., 'Paintings and Other Works of Art in Sixteenth-Century English Inventories', *Burlington Magazine*, 123 (1981), pp. 273–82.

Fraser, A., *The Six Wives of Henry VIII* (London, 1992).

Galvin, C. and Lindley, P., 'Pietro Torrigiano's Portrait Bust of King Henry VII', *Burlington Magazine*, 130 (1988), pp. 892–902.

Gill, L., 'William Caxton and the Rebellion of 1483', *English Historical Review*, 112 (1997), pp. 105–18.

Gillespie, V., 'Syon and the English Market for Continental Printed Books: The Incunable Phase', *Religion and Literature*, 37 (2005), pp. 27–49.

Girouard, M., *Life in the English Country House* (Harmondsworth, 1980).

Given-Wilson, C., 'The court and household of Edward III, 1360–1377', unpublished PhD thesis, University of St Andrews, 1976.

Given-Wilson, C. and Curteis, A. (eds), *The Royal Bastards of Medieval England* (London, 1984).

Goodwin-Austen, R.A.C., 'Woking Manor', *Surrey Archaeological Collections*, 7 (1874).

Gray, A. and Brittain, F., *A History of Jesus College Cambridge* (London, 1979).

Green, R.F., 'Historical Notes of a London Citizen, 1483–1488', *English Historical Review*, 96 (1981), pp. 585–90.

Gregory, P., Baldwin, D. and Jones, M., *The Women of the Cousins' War* (London, 2011).

Griffiths, R.A., *The Reign of Henry VI* (London, 1981).

Griffiths, R.A., 'Henry Tudor: The Training of a King', *Huntingdon Library Quarterly*, 49 (1986), pp. 197–218.

Griffiths, R.A. and Thomas, R.S. (eds), *The Making of the Tudor Dynasty* (Gloucester, 1985).

Gristwood, S., *Blood Sisters: The Hidden Lives of the Women Behind the Wars of the Roses* (London, 2012).

The *Guardian*, www.theguardian.com/books/2019/apr/25/white-queen-died-of-plague-claims-letter-found-in-national-archives.

Gunn, S., 'Henry VII in Context: Problems and Possibilities', *History*, 92 (2007), pp. 301–17.

Gunn, S., *Henry VII's New Men and the Making of Tudor England* (Oxford, 2016).

Gunn, S. and Monckton, L. (eds), *Arthur Tudor, Prince of Wales: Life, Death and Commemoration* (Woodbridge, 2009), pp. 20–30.

Gunn, S.J., 'The Courtiers of Henry VII', *English Historical Review*, 108 (1993), pp. 23–49.

Haggard, D.J., 'The ruins of Old Woking Palace', *Surrey Archaeological Society Collections*, 55 (1958).

Halsted, C.A., *Life of Margaret Beaufort, Countess of Richmond and Derby* (London, 1839).

Hampton, W.E., *Memorials of the Wars of the Roses* (Gloucester, 1979).

Hanham, A., *Richard III and his Early Historians 1483–1535* (Oxford, 1975).

Harper, S.P., 'London and the Crown in the Reign of Henry VII', unpublished PhD thesis (University of London, 2015).

Harris, B.J., 'Power and Personal Relations: Elite Mothers and Sons in Yorkist and Early Tudor England', *Signs*, 15 (1990), pp. 606–32.

Harris, B.J., 'Women and Politics in Early Tudor England', *Historical Journal*, 33 (1990), pp. 259–81.

Harris, B.J., 'A New Look at the Reformation: Aristocratic Women and Nunneries, 1450–1540', *Journal of British Studies*, 32 (1993), pp. 89–113.

Harris, B.J., 'The View from My Lady's Chamber: New Perspectives on the Early Tudor Monarchy', *Huntingdon Library Quarterly*, 60 (1997), pp. 215–47.

Harris, B.J., *English Aristocratic Women 1450–1550* (Oxford, 2002).

Harris, B.J., 'The Fabric of Piety: Aristocratic Women and Care of the Dead, 1450–1550', *Journal of British Studies*, 48 (2009), pp. 308–35.

Hart-Davis, A., *What the Tudors and Stuarts Did for Us* (London, 1996).

Harvey, A. and Mortimer, R. (eds), *The Funeral Effigies of Westminster Abbey* (Woodbridge, 1994).

Harvey, B., *Westminster Abbey and its Estates in the Middle Ages* (Oxford, 1977).

Hayward, M., *Dress at the Court of King Henry VIII* (Leeds, 2007).

Heinze, R.W. *The Proclamations of the Tudor Kings* (Cambridge, 1976).

Hepburn, F., *Portraits of the Later Plantagenets* (Woodbridge, 1986).

Hepburn, F., 'The Portraiture of Lady Margaret Beaufort', *Antiquaries Journal*, 72 (1992), pp. 118–40.

Hicks, M., *Richard III* (Stroud, 1991).

Hicks, M., 'Crowland's World: A Westminster View of the Yorkist Age', *History*, 90 (2005), pp. 172–90.

Hicks, M., *Anne Neville: Queen to Richard III* (Stroud, 2007).

Hicks, M.A., *False, Fleeting, Perjur'd Clarence: George, Duke of Clarence, 1449–78* (Gloucester, 1980).

Hicks, M.A., 'The Piety of Margaret Lady Hungerford', *Journal of Ecclesiastical History*, 38 (1987), pp. 19–38.

Hilton, L., *Queens Consort: England's Medieval Queens* (London, 2008).

Hochstetler Meyer, B., 'The First Tomb of Henry VII of England', *Art Bulletin*, 58 (1976), pp. 358–67.

Hogrefe, P., 'Legal Rights of Tudor Women and the Circumvention by Men and Women', *Sixteenth Century Journal*, 3 (1972), pp. 97–105.

Hooker, J.R., 'Some Cautionary Notes on Henry VII's Household and Chamber "System"', *Speculum*, 33 (1958), pp. 69–75.

Horrox, R., *Richard III: A Study of Service* (Cambridge, 1989).

Hoult, J., *The Vill, Manor and Township of Knowsley* (Liverpool, 1930).

Howard, M., *The Early Tudor Country House: Architecture and Politics 1490–1550* (London, 1987).

Hutchinson, R., *Young Henry: The Rise of Henry VIII* (London, 2011).

Impey, E. and Parnell, G., *The Tower of London: The Official Illustrated History* (London, 2000).

James, S.E., *Women's Voices in Tudor Wills, 1485–1603: Authority, Influence and Material Culture* (Farnham, 2015).

Jansen, S.L., *The Monstrous Regiment of Women: Female Rulers in Early Modern Europe* (Basingstoke, 2002).

Jones, D., *The Hollow Crown: The Wars of the Roses and the Rise of the Tudors* (London, 2014).

Jones, M., 'John Beaufort, Duke of Somerset and the French expedition of 1443', in Griffiths, R.A. (ed.), *Patronage, the Crown and the Provinces* (Gloucester, 1981).

Jones, M., 'Henry VII, Lady Margaret Beaufort and the Orléans ransom', in Griffiths, R.A. and Sherborne, J. (eds), *Kings and Nobles in the Later Middle Ages* (Gloucester, 1986).

Jones, M., '"For My Lord of Richmond, a *pourpoint* ... and a palfrey": Brief remarks on the financial evidence for Henry Tudor's exile in Brittany 1471–1484', in Visser-Fuchs, L. (ed.), *The Ricardian*, XIII (2002), pp. 283–93.

Jones, M., 'Margaret Beaufort: Mother of the Tudors', *BBC History Magazine* (2017), pp. 50–5.

Jones, M. and Underwood, M., 'Lady Margaret Beaufort', *History Today*, 35 (1985).

Jones, M.K., 'The Beaufort Family and the War in France, 1421–1450', unpublished PhD thesis (University of Bristol, 1982).

Jones, M.K., 'Richard III and Lady Margaret Beaufort: A re-assessment', in Hammond, P.W. (ed.), *Richard III: Loyalty, Lordship and Law* (London, 1986).

Jones, M.K., 'Sir William Stanley of Holt: Politics and Family Allegiance in the late Fifteenth Century', *Welsh History Review*, 14 (1988).

Jones, M.K., 'Somerset, York and the Wars of the Roses', *English Historical Review*, 104 (1989), pp. 285–307.

Jones, M.K., *Bosworth 1485: Psychology of a Battle* (Stroud, 2002).

Jones, M.K. and Underwood, M.G., *The King's Mother: Lady Margaret Beaufort, Countess of Richmond and Derby* (Cambridge, 1992).

Kaufman, P.I., 'Polydore Vergil and the Strange Disappearance of Christopher Urswick', *Sixteenth Century Journal*, 17 (1986), pp. 69–85.

Keiser, G., 'Patronage and Piety in Fifteenth-Century England: Margaret Duchess of Clarence, Symon Wynter, and Beinecke MS. 317', *Yale University Library Gazette*, 60 (1985), pp. 32–46.

Kibre, P., 'Lewis of Caerleon, Doctor of Medicine, Astronomer, and Mathematician (d. 1494?)', *University of Chicago Press on behalf of The History of Science Society*, 43 (1952), pp. 100–108.

Kingsford, C.L., *English Historical Literature in the Fifteenth Century* (Oxford, 1913).

Kingsford, C.L., 'On Some London Houses of the Early Tudor Period', *Archaeologica*, 71 (1920–1).

Kipling, G., *The Triumph of Honour: Burgundian Origins of the Elizabethan Renaissance* (Leiden, 1977).

Kisby, F., 'The Royal Household Chapel in Early-Tudor London, 1485–1547', unpublished PhD thesis, University of London, 1996.

Kisby, F., 'A Mirror of Monarchy: Music and Musicians in the Household Chapel of the Lady Margaret Beaufort, Mother of Henry VII', *Early Music History*, 16 (1997), pp. 203–34.

Kisby, F., 'Officers and Office-Holding at the English Court: A Study of the Chapel Royal, 1485–1547', *Royal Musical Association Research Chronicle*, 32 (1999), pp. 1–61.

Lander, J.R., 'The Crown and the Aristocracy in England, 1450–1509', *Albion: A Quarterly Journal Concerned with British Studies*, 8 (1976), pp. 203–18.

Lawson, S. (ed.), *Eltham Palace* (London, 2011).

Laynesmith, J.L., *The Last Medieval Queens* (Oxford, 2004).

Laynesmith, J.L., *Cecily Duchess of York* (London, 2017).

Lee, Patricia-Ann, 'Reflections of Power: Margaret of Anjou and the Dark Side of Queenship', *Renaissance Quarterly*, 39 (1986), pp. 183–217.

Legg, P., *Winchester: History You Can See* (Stroud, 2011).

Levine, M., *Tudor Dynastic Problems, 1460–1571* (London, 1973).

Lewis, J., 'Lathom House: The Northern Court', *Journal of the British Archaeological Association*, 152 (1999), pp. 150–71.

Lewis, J.E., *London: The Autobiography* (London, 2008).

Lewis, M., *The Survival of the Princes in the Tower* (Stroud, 2017).

Leyser, H., *Medieval Women: A Social History of Women in England 450–1500* (London, 1995).

Licence, A., *Cecily Neville: Mother of Kings* (Stroud, 2014).

Licence, A., *Red Roses: Blanche of Gaunt to Margaret Beaufort* (Stroud, 2016).

Lloyd, A.H., 'Two Monumental Brasses in the Chapel of Christ's College', *Proceedings of the Cambridge Antiquarian Society*, 33 (1933).

Lloyd, A.H., *The Early History of Christ's College Cambridge* (Cambridge, 1934).

Loades, D., *Mary Rose: Tudor Princess, Queen of France, the Extraordinary Life of Henry VIII's Sister* (Stroud, 2012).

Loades, D.M., *The Tudor Court* (London, 1986).

Lodge, E., *Portraits of Illustrious Personages of Great Britain*, 4 vols (London, 1821–34).

Lowry, M.J.C., 'Caxton, St Winifred and the Lady Margaret Beaufort', *The Library*, 6 (1983), pp. 101–17.

Lucraft, J., *Katherine Swynford: The History of a Medieval Mistress* (Stroud, 2006).

Ludlow, N., *Pembroke Castle: Birthplace of the Tudor Dynasty* (Pembroke, 2001).

Lynn, E., *Tudor Fashion* (New Haven and London, 2017).

MacGibbon, D., *Elizabeth Woodville: A Life* (London, 1938).

Matthews, C.P., *The Story of the Abbey Church Bourne* (Gloucester, 1962).

Mattingly, G., *Catherine of Aragon* (London, 1942).

Maurer, H., 'Whodunit: The Suspects in the Case', *Ricardian Register*, 18 (1983), pp. 4–27.

Maurer, H.E., *Margaret of Anjou: Queenship and Power in Late Medieval England* (Woodbridge, 2003).

McFarlane, K.B., *Lancastrian Kings and Lollard Knights* (Oxford, 1972).

McFarlane, K.B., *The Nobility of Later Medieval England* (Oxford, 1973).

McIntosh, M.K., 'The Benefits and Drawbacks of *Femme Sole* Status in England, 1300–1630', *Journal of British Studies*, 44 (2005), pp. 410–38.

Mertes, K., *The English Noble Household 1250–1600: Good Governance and Politic Rule* (Oxford, 1988).

Mitchell, A., *Kingston Lacy* (Swindon, 1994).

Murray Kendall, P., *Richard the Third* (London, 1968).

Myers, A.R., 'The Household of Queen Margaret of Anjou, 1452–3', *Bulletin of the John Rylands Library*, 40 (1958), pp. 79–113.

Myers, A.R., 'The Jewels of Queen Margaret of Anjou', *Bulletin of the John Rylands Library*, 42 (1959), pp. 113–31.

Myers, A.R., 'The Household of Queen Elizabeth Woodville, 1466–7', *Bulletin of the John Rylands Library*, 50 (1967–8), pp. 207–15.

Norton, E., *Margaret Beaufort: Mother of the Tudor Dynasty* (Stroud, 2010).

Norton, E., *The Lives of Tudor Women* (London, 2016).

Oliver, C., *A Guide to the Minster Church of St Cuthburga* (Christchurch, 2016).

Olson, R., 'Margaret Beaufort, Royal Tapestries, and Confinement at the Tudor Court', *Textile History*, 48 (2017), pp. 233–47.

Okerlund, A., *Elizabeth: England's Slandered Queen* (Stroud, 2009).

Okerlund, A., *Elizabeth of York* (New York, 2009).

Orme, N., *English Schools in the Middle Ages* (London, 1973).

Ormrod, W.M., 'The Royal Nursery: A Household for the Younger Children of Edward III', *English Historical Review*, 120 (2005), pp. 398–415.

Owen, H. and Blakeway, J.B., *A History of Shrewsbury*, 2 vols (London, 1825).

Painter, G.D., *William Caxton* (London, 1976).

Penn, T., *Winter King: The Dawn of Tudor England* (London, 2011).

Perry, M., *Sisters to the King: The Tumultuous Lives of Henry VIII's Sisters – Margaret of Scotland and Mary of France* (London, 1998).

Pierce, H., *Margaret Pole, Countess of Salisbury 1473–1541: Loyalty, Lineage and Leadership* (Cardiff, 2003).

Plomer, H., *Wynkyn de Worde and his Contemporaries* (London, 1925).

Pollard, A.J., *The Wars of the Roses* (Basingstoke, 1988).

Pollard, A.J., *The Worlds of Richard III* (Stroud, 2001).

Poulton, R. and Pattison, G., *Woking Palace* (Woking, 2017).

Powell, S., 'Lady Margaret Beaufort and her Books', *The Library*, 3 (1998), pp. 197–240.

Powell, S., 'Margaret Pole and Syon Abbey', *Historical Research*, 78 (2005), pp. 563–7.

Powell, S., *The Birgittines of Syon Abbey: Preaching and Print* (Turnhout, 2017).

Rackham, H., *Early Statutes of Christ's College, Cambridge* (Cambridge, 1927).

Rackham, H. (ed.), *Christ's College in Former Days* (Cambridge, 1939).

Rawcliffe, C., *The Staffords, Earls of Stafford and Dukes of Buckingham 1394–1521* (Cambridge, 1978).

Reid, R.R., *The King's Council in the North* (London, 1921).

Reynolds, A., *In Fine Style: The Art of Tudor and Stuart Fashion* (London, 2013).

Rickert, M., 'The So-Called Beaufort Hours and York Psalter', *Burlington Magazine*, 104 (1962), pp. 238–46.

Roberts, S.E., *Jasper: The Tudor Kingmaker* (Croydon, 2015).

Robinson, J.M., *Windsor Castle: The Official Illustrated History* (London, 2011).

Rosenthal, J.T., *The Purchase of Paradise: The Social Function of Aristocratic Benevolence, 1307–1485* (London, 1972).

Rosenthal, J.T., *Nobles and the Noble Life 1295–1500* (London, 1976).

Ross, C. (ed.), *Patronage, Pedigree and Power in Later Medieval England* (Gloucester, 1979).

Ross, C.D., *Edward IV* (London, 1975).

Ross, J., *Henry VI: A Good, Simple and Innocent Man* (London, 2016).

Routh, E.M.G., *A Memoir of Lady Margaret Beaufort, Countess of Richmond and Derby, Mother of Henry VII* (Oxford, 1924).

Sadlack, E.A., *The French Queen's Letters: Mary Tudor Brandon and the Politics of Marriage in Sixteenth-Century Europe* (New York, 2011).

Saul, N., *The Three Richards: Richard I, Richard II and Richard III* (London, 2005).

Scarisbrick, D., *Tudor and Jacobean Jewellery* (London, 1995).

Scarisbrick, D., *Rings: Jewelry of Power, Love and Loyalty* (London, 2007).

Schroder, T., 'A Royal Tudor Rock-Crystal and Silver-Gilt Vase', *Burlington Magazine*, 137 (1995), pp. 356–66.

Schutte, V., 'Royal Tudor Women as Patrons and Curators', *Early Modern Women*, 9 (2014), pp. 79–88.

Scofield, C.L., 'Henry, Duke of Somerset, and Edward IV', *English Historical Review*, 21 (1906), pp. 300–302.

Scofield, C.L., *The Life and Reign of Edward the Fourth*, 2 vols (London, 1923).

Scott, R.F., 'On the Contracts for the Tomb of the Lady Margaret Beaufort, Countess of Richmond and Derby, Mother of King Henry VII, and Foundress of the Colleges of Christ and St John in Cambridge', *Archaeologica*, 66 (1915).

Seward, D., *A Brief History of the Hundred Years War* (London, 1978).

Seward, D., *A Brief History of the Wars of the Roses: The Bloody Rivalry for the Throne of England* (London, 1995).

Seward, D., *The Last White Rose: The Secret Wars of the Tudors* (London, 2010).

Shoesmith, R. and Johnson, A. (eds), *Ludlow Castle: Its History and Buildings* (Almeley,

2006).

Sicca, C.M. and Waldman, L.A. (eds), *The Anglo-Florentine Renaissance: Art for the Early Tudors* (New Haven and London, 2012).

Simon, L., *Of Virtue Rare: Margaret Beaufort, Matriarch of the House of Tudor* (Boston, 1982).

Sinclair, A. (ed.), *The Beauchamp Pageant* (Donington, 2003).

Skidmore, C., *Bosworth: The Birth of the Tudors* (London, 2013).

Skidmore, C., *Richard III: Brother, Protector, King* (London, 2017).

St John Hope, W.H., *Windsor Castle: An Architectural History* (London, 1913).

St John's College Quatercentenary publication, *Collegium Divi Johannis Evangelistae, 1511–1911* (Cambridge, 1911).

St John's College website, https://www.joh.cam.ac.uk/painting-mother-king-henry-vii-revealed-oldest-large-scale-portrait-english-woman.

Stanley, A.P., *Historical Memorials of Westminster Abbey* (London, 1868).

Starkey, D. (ed.), *Rivals in Power: Lives and Letters of the Great Tudor Dynasties* (London, 1990).

Starkey, D., 'Intimacy and innovation: the rise of the Privy Chamber, 1485–1547', in Starkey, D., Morgan, D.A.L., Murphy, J., Wright, P., Cuddy, N. and Sharpe, K., *The English Court: From the Wars of the Roses to the Civil War* (London and New York, 1987), pp. 71–118.

Starkey, D., *Six Wives: The Queens of Henry VIII* (London, 2004).

Starkey, D., *Henry: Virtuous Prince* (London, 2008).

Struthers, J., *Royal Palaces of Britain* (London, 2004).

Sutton, A. and Visser-Fuchs, L., 'A *"Most Benevolent Queen"*: Queen Elizabeth Woodville's Reputation, Her Piety and Her Books', *The Ricardian*, 10 (1995), pp. 214–45.

Sutton, A.F. and Visser-Fuchs, L., *Richard III's Books* (Stroud, 1997).

Swanson, R.N., *Church and Society in Late Medieval England* (Oxford, 1989).

Tallis, N.L., 'All the Queen's Jewels, 1445–1548', unpublished PhD thesis (University of Winchester, 2019).

Thomas, D.H., *The Herberts of Raglan and the Battle of Edgecote 1469* (Enfield, 1994).

Thompson, B. (ed.), *The Reign of Henry VII*, V (Stamford, 1995).

Thornton, T., 'Lancastrian Rule and the Resources of the Prince of Wales, 1456–61', *Journal of Medieval History*, 42:3 (2016), pp. 382–404.

Thurley, S., *The Royal Palaces of Tudor England: Architecture and Court Life 1460–1547* (New Haven and London, 1993).

Trapp, J.B., 'Christopher Urswick and his Books: the Reading of Henry VII's Almoner', *Renaissance Studies*, 1 (1987), pp. 48–70.

Tremlett, G., *Catherine of Aragon: Henry's Spanish Queen* (London, 2010).

Tremlett, G., *Isabella of Castile: Europe's First Great Queen* (London, 2017).

Tuck, A., *Richard II and the English Nobility* (London, 1973).

Twigg, J., *A History of Queens' College, Cambridge 1448–1986* (Woodbridge, 1987).

Underwood, M.G., 'The Lady Margaret and her Cambridge connections', *Sixteenth Century Journal*, 13 (1982), pp. 67–82.

Underwood, M.G., 'Politics and Piety in the Household of Lady Margaret Beaufort', *Journal of Ecclesiastical History*, 38 (1987), pp. 39–52.

Venables, E., 'Bourne: its Abbey and Castle', *Associated Architectural Societies, Reports and Papers*, 20 (1889).

Visser-Fuchs, L., 'The Casualty List of the Battle of Barnet', *The Ricardian*, 8 (1988).

Ward, J.C., *English Noblewomen in the Later Middle Ages* (London, 1992).

Warnicke, R.M., 'The Lady Margaret Beaufort, Countess of Richmond (d. 1509) as seen by John Fisher and by Lord Morley', *Moreana*, 19 (1982).

Warnicke, R.M., 'The Lady Margaret, Countess of Richmond; a Noblewoman of Independent

Wealth and Status', *Fifteenth Century Studies*, 9 (1984).

Warnicke, R.M., 'Sir Ralph Bigod: a Loyal Servant to King Richard III', *The Ricardian*, 6 (1984).

Warnicke, R.M., *Elizabeth of York and Her Six Daughters-in-Law: Fashioning Tudor Queenship, 1485–1547* (Basingstoke, 2017).

Warrior, J., *A Guide to King's College Chapel Cambridge* (Cambridge, 1994).

Weightman, C., *Margaret of York: The Diabolical Duchess* (Stroud, 2009).

Weir, A., *Britain's Royal Families: The Complete Genealogy* (London, 1989).

Weir, A., *The Princes in the Tower* (London, 1992).

Weir, A., *Lancaster and York: The Wars of the Roses* (London, 1995).

Weir, A., *Henry VIII: King and Court* (London, 2001).

Weir, A., *Katherine Swynford: The Story of John of Gaunt and his Scandalous Duchess* (London, 2007).

Weir, A., *Elizabeth of York: The First Tudor Queen* (London, 2013).

Weir, A., 'A Tudor of Rare Talent', *BBC History Magazine* (2013).

Westlake, H.F., *Westminster Abbey* (London, 1923).

Wilkinson, J., *Henry VII's Lady Chapel in Westminster Abbey* (London, 2007).

Williams, D. (ed.), *England in the Fifteenth Century* (Woodbridge, 1987).

Williams, D.M. (ed.), *Raglan Castle* (Cardiff, 1998).

Williams, N., *The Life and Times of Henry VII* (London, 1973).

Wolffe, B.P., *Henry VI* (London, 1981).

Woodman, F., *The Architectural History of Canterbury Cathedral* (London, 1981).

Wroe, A., *Perkin: A Story of Deception* (London, 2003).

ACKNOWLEDGEMENTS

Uncrowned Queen has taken me on an incredible journey: it has challenged me, frustrated me, shocked me, inspired me, but most of all it has given me the opportunity to work with and meet some amazing people – many have had a greater impact than they will realize. This is my chance to thank them. The book is dedicated to my grandparents, but I would like to share that dedication with someone else. My superb – now former – editor (and forever friend!), Fiona Slater, has been as enthralled by Margaret as I have, and has stuck by me and inspired me throughout my writing career to date. I cannot thank her enough for all of her commitment both to me and to my books: *Uncrowned Queen* is for you too, Fiona, with heartfelt thanks.

I would like to express my sincerest gratitude to everyone at Michael O'Mara Books for their continued championship of me. Especial thanks to Louise Dixon for all of her dedication in ensuring that the book made it across the finish line, and to Nick Fawcett for pulling the text into such good shape. Likewise, Claire Potter, my editor at Basic Books, has been instrumental in the construction of the book, and has been incredibly supportive. Huge thanks are also due to Alara Delfosse and Saskia Angenent for all of their hard work on my behalf.

Thanks to the team at Watson Little, but most particularly my agent, Donald Winchester. Thank you so much for all of your support, and for patiently listening when panic set in! Your calm words of reassurance made the world of difference.

I'm very grateful to Jean Follett from the Friends of Woking Palace for taking the time to show me around the remains of Margaret's former home, and to Chris Close of Collyweston Historical Society for updating me on the archaeological evidence uncovered at the site of Margaret's splendid palace.

Thanks to Christine Reynolds of the Westminster Abbey Muniments, and to the patient staff at the British Library and the National Archives. Also to Tracy Deakin and her assistants at the St John's College archives, who were incredibly helpful during my visits.

Alison Weir was kind enough to draw my attention to the jumbled glass portraying Margaret in the church at Landbeach and sent me several photographs. I'd also like to thank her for her unwavering support, and for the many conversations we've shared about Margaret. Likewise to Tracy Borman and Sarah Gristwood, who have both been incredibly generous with their time, enthusiasm and encouragement. Julian Humphrys was a star for reading an early draft of the book and sending me useful pointers, and thanks to John Cooper for his thorough feedback. I have also been fortunate enough to draw on the expertise of Michael Jones, whose knowledge of Margaret is second to none. Thank you for inspiring me. Thanks are also due to Elizabeth Norton, Kate Williams and Joanne Paul.

Particular thanks go to my wonderful mother, Sylvia, for taking the time to share her extensive medical knowledge with me – you are the most amazing woman I know, and I'm privileged to call you my mother. I am also indebted to Suzanne Schuld for listening to my medical theories and for going to great lengths to help me obtain answers – thank you to you and your colleagues.

My friends are all superstars, but especial thanks go to Chris Warwick for his endless championing of me. Also to Keita Weston, Kerrie Britten, Amelia Douchet and Donna Kelly for all of your warmth, loyalty and love. I'd also like to thank your beautiful girls: Ava, Manon and Amelia respectively, who are wonderful friends to my stepdaughter Olivia, and who I have been proud to watch growing into such lovely young ladies.

As always, my family are the ones who have been forced to put up with me (and Margaret) for the last two years, and no words can express my gratitude. Our newest addition, Nell, has brought some much needed sunshine into our lives, and my two lovely stepchildren, Charlie and Olivia, have been the best. Particular thanks to my Dad, who has driven me across the country in pursuit of Margaret, read drafts of the book and given me endless support. Finally, my amazing fiancé Matt, I can say nothing other than you rock my world! To everyone that has been a part of my journey, my sincerest thanks.

INDEX

349